403-13

rites
of
passage

**A Memoir of the
Sixties in Seattle**

rites
of
passage

**A Memoir of
the Sixties in Seattle**

Walt Crowley

University of Washington Press
Seattle and London

Library of Congress Cataloging-in-Publication Data
Crowley, Walt.
    Rites of Passage : a memoir of the sixties in Seattle / Walt Crowley.
    p.   cm.
    Includes bibliographical references and index.
    ISBN 0-295-97492-3 (alk. paper)
    1. Popular culture--Washington (State)--Seattle--History--20th
century. 2. Seattle (Wash.)--Social life and customs. 3. Crowley, Walt.
4. Seattle (Wash.)--Biography. 5. United States--History--1961--1969.
I. Title.
F899.S45C76 1995
979.7'772--dc20

                                                          95-38660
                                                              CIP

The paper used in this publication meets the minimum requirements of
American National Standard for Information Sciences—Permanence of
Paper for Printed Library Materials, ANSI Z39.48-1984.

For Marie

And the Memory of
George Arthur
John Cunnick
Ed Devine
David "Doc" Eskanazie
Darrell Bob Houston
Stan Iverson
Andy Shiga
and
Susan Stern

Contents

Preface:
When Were the
Sixties?

The Revolution was an eschatological certainty, a given, a future already unfolding . . .

—Todd Gitlin

A few years ago, Hilda Bryant invited me to lecture her journalism class at Seattle University on the "underground press." My claim to expertise on this subject was based on three years writing, drawing, and agitating at the *Helix*, Seattle's underground newspaper from 1967 to 1970, and other activities as part of "the movement."

Staring out from the lectern at thirty or so bright young faces for whom the Seventies were ancient history, I quickly realized that this assignment was not as easy as it first seemed. I also felt faintly ridiculous, a living fossil reanimated à la *Jurassic Park* to illustrate an extinct form of life.

My audience listened wide-eyed to tales of psychedelic drugs, beins, bizarre newspapers, demonstrations, riots, wars, and dreams of political and cultural revolution. Their questions cut to the chase: Why did we do those things? Where did we get our ideas from? What the hell were we thinking of?!

My reply was that it made sense at the time. Explaining *why* it made sense at the time is the goal of this book.

Rites of Passage is part memoir and part history. It is propelled chiefly by the evolution of my own thinking and participation in the New Left and the underground press, and it therefore focuses on events which I witnessed or felt deeply. At the same time, this book attempts to describe the context in which I and my comrades operated. Foremost, I have tried to evoke how it felt to be young, idealistic, and more than a little foolish during the period. The Sixties truly were my "rites of passage" from childhood to some semblance of adulthood.

This book is subtitled "A Memoir of the Sixties in Seattle," rather than vice versa, because I and many of my contemporaries lived first in a generational zeitgeist—"the movement" and later "the revolution"—and second in any particular locality. Events, abetted by television, music, and other media—united us in a powerful if ultimately illusory collective gestalt outside history or geography.

My approach to this story leads to obvious idiosyncrasies. Although the underground press gave me a good vantage point during the Sixties, I was hardly omniscient. This book is concerned mostly with developments in politics and media because that's what I was most concerned with in the Sixties. Activities which were less conspicuous in my life at that time, particularly the music scene and early stages of the environmental and women's rights movements, receive less detailed treatment than they deserve. Similarly, for every person or incident cited in this account, another hundred could make rightful claim to inclusion.

At the same time, this book is not merely reminiscence. I learned almost immediately that the old joke is true: if you can remember the Sixties, you weren't there. Conversely, if you were there, you can't remember it, at least not straight. Many of my most cherished "memories" had to be reclassified as hallucinations before this book was done.

So I conducted extensive research into the period, including rereading every edition of *Helix*, the old *Seattle Magazine* (1964–70), and the *Seattle Post-Intelligencer*, as well as most of the *Seattle Times*, and virtually every major book of or about the period (please see the bibliography). This work yielded a 250-page chronology of international, national, local and cultural developments and incidents from 1960 through 1972, a condensed version of which closes this volume, along with an index of the *Helix* and major Seattle-area concerts.

From these sources, I tried to reconstruct a sense of the ideas and events which shaped the period and, in particular, how they impinged on life in Seattle. While this book does not pretend to be a comprehensive history of either the period or of Seattle's development during it, it should provide a serviceable overview of both to readers approaching these topics for the first time.

To readers with firsthand experience of Seattle and America a quarter of a century ago, let me acknowledge a fundamental truth: the

Sixties were plural. The "decade" embraces such profound experiences for so many on so many planes of existence and in so many areas of activity that it is impossible to speak of it in the singular. It was a period of tragedy, triumph, and transcendence for tens of millions of Americans, which means that *the* Sixties book can never be written.

In early discussions with other Sixties survivors, I confronted an unexpected question: *When* were the Sixties?

It's not hard to define "what" the Sixties were. Most can agree on the main ingredients: Vietnam and the explosion worldwide of wars for national liberation; civil rights and emergence of "black power" and other cultural-identity movements; rock and roll and the rise of a youth-directed market for culture and products in tempo with the adolescence of the Baby Boom; and drugs and a Dionysian "counterculture" devoted to preindustrial values of love, experience, and community.

(It may surprise some that I do not include the movements for women's liberation and environmental protection in the list above. It is not to disparage them or to deny the force they gained during the chronological Sixties, but they reached critical mass a little later—and the Seventies are so impoverished a decade that we should leave it some claim to fame.)

There are several dates on which one might start the Sixties clock. The technically correct date is January 1, 1961, since we count decades like fingers, from one to ten, not from ten to nine.

More than one commentator have suggested pushing that date back eleven months to the first Greensboro lunch counter sit-in on February 1, 1960. This marked the beginning of a new phase in the civil rights movement and led directly to the creation of one of the period's most important groups, the Student Non-Violent Coordinating Committee, yet SNCC's cause and style had roots going back at least as far as the 1955 Montgomery bus boycott.

An equally valid argument might turn the clock even further back to January 1, 1959, when fidel Castro drove Fulgencio Batista from Cuba in one of the first and most influential victories for a "national liberation movement." But the cause of independence from colonialism did not originate with Castro, and his own struggle dates back at least to 1953.

Many vote for the election of President John Kennedy on November 8, 1960, or his inauguration on January 20, 1961, or, more somberly, his death on November 22, 1963. The former dates did engender great hope and optimism, and Kennedy's assassination was the first shot in the fusillade of political violence which helped to define the decade.

Some argue for the Gulf of Tonkin incident and passage of the eponymous resolution in August 1964 as signaling a new phase in the war in Vietnam, but we were already being sucked into the swamp years earlier. And choosing this date leaves us with a decade nearly half finished before it "begins."

These are political coordinates, of course, and while this is chiefly a political book, the legitimacy of other coordinates must be acknowledged.

Foremost, there was the music. My friend Joe Vinikow, a music historian, argues that the Sixties began with the Beatles, and particularly their first American tour in February 1964. He believes this began to heal the ache from Kennedy's assassination, and no less than Jerry Garcia, of the Grateful Dead, agrees that "suddenly, it was a good flash."

The therapeutic aspects of the Beatles notwithstanding, clearly they brought an entirely new synthesis to the former American monopoly on rock and roll. But what of their predecessors on these shores, particularly Elvis Presley and Buddy Holly, who made a "black" music "white" and accessible even in Liverpool? And we should not forget the folk revival led by Joan Baez, Bob Dylan, and a host of singers who gave fresh voice to ancient lyrics of anguish and struggle and led a restless audience in new songs of alienation and rebellion.

Then there is literature. The poetry of the Beats became the mantras of the Hippies, yet most of the work was written in the fifties by men already graying in the Sixties. We should also not forget science, particularly the great race into orbit and to the moon, launched literally with Sputnik on October 4, 1957.

The baby boom may seem a unique Sixties phenomenon, but most members of the boom were born before 1957 and tempered by the culture of the fifties before reaching the magic decade. Similarly, the Sixties did not invent sex. The period's famous "sexual revolution" was more of a coincidence, thanks to the pill and penicillin. Contrary to conservative rhetoric, people were loving freely long before the Sixties made it relatively (and temporarily) safe.

Dating the end of the Sixties is equally difficult. As Abbie Hoffman commented, the Sixties "were such a good decade, they stole two extra years." Perhaps even more. Many pinpoint the Kent State massacre of May 4, 1970, as the beginning of the end, but the largest demonstration against the war in Vietnam still lay a year in the future. A strong argument can be made for the presidential campaign of 1972, which closed one chapter with Senator McGovern's defeat and opened another with the Watergate burglaries.

The war in Vietnam offers at least two possible dates: completion of the American withdrawal in 1973, and the fall of Saigon in 1975, but accepting this would seem to deny the Seventies ownership of its own events and identity. In terms of music, art, culture, and social change there is no defined border between the decades. One could argue that the Sixties did not come to closure until one of its own moved into the White House, but the relentless harassment of Bill Clinton, House Speaker Newt Gingrich's sneering condemnation of "counterculture McGoverniks," and reaction to Robert McNamara's belated mea culpa on Vietnam suggest that the old generational battles are still being fought thirty years later.

The problem is that history does not come bundled up in neat decennial packages. Trying to impose arbitrary chronological brackets on any continuum of events is about as practical as wrapping soup in a newspaper: the contents spill out of both ends and spread everywhere.

It is easier to identify the middle of the Sixties: the May 1968 campus uprisings. This was the moment when "the revolution" became real for all sides, but there were as many personal revolutions as there were people in the Sixties.

The Sixties hit American culture like an atomic bomb. For each of us who was there, the consequences were different. Some were standing at the point of impact, some further away. Some were exposed, some shielded. Some were killed, some maimed, some merely wounded, and some emerged without a scratch.

Tens of millions of us were there when the Sixties struck. They

happened to each of us at our appointed moment, a personal Hiroshima that seared the clock in our souls. We each know the time it hit.
That is when the Sixties were.

Many people made this book possible, beginning with my wife, Marie McCaffrey, who worked tirelessly in her profession as a graphic designer to give me the chance to concentrate on what seemed like endless research, writing, and rewriting. Her faith in this project sustained me more than once when I might have given it up as hopeless, and her design skills created these pages.

Second, I want acknowledge the support and encouragement of the University of Washington Press. The confidence of its director Don Ellegood and associate director Pat Soden brought this book into being. Editors Julidta Tarver, Marilyn Trueblood, and Lane Morgan, editorial assistant Toni Reineke, and academic readers Stephanie Coontz and David Olsen made it much better than it might otherwise have been. Photographs generously provided by Alan Lande, Paul Dorpat, Michael Mates, and Robin Reid gave visual force to my pale descriptions.

My research was greatly aided by the Washington Center for the Book and its director, Nancy Pearl, who extended to me the use of the wonderful C.K. Poe Fratt Writer's Room in the Seattle Public Library. I was also aided immeasurably by City Librarian Liz Stroup, and the staffs of both the Seattle Public Library and the University of Washington's Pacific Northwest Collection.

Thanks are also due the *Seattle Weekly*, *Eastside Week*, and new *Seattle* magazine, for permitting me to work out some of the material for this book in their pages.

Finally, I want to thank my friends who endured my obsession with the Sixties when they should have just poured a beer over my head.

—Walt Crowley
August 1995

rites
of
passage

**A Memoir of the
Sixties in Seattle**

Chapter 1:
Growing Up
Subversive

In truth, there is no
theory which is not a fragment,
and a carefully prepared
fragment, of an autobiography.
—Paul Valery

I first saw Seattle from the windows of the Great Northern's Empire
Builder early one November morning in 1961. Three days out
from Chicago, the train delivered my mother and me to King
Street Station, where my father waited to take us to our new home.
My eyes filled with tears, but not of joy.

A long, twisting route had brought me to that moment. I was
born fourteen years earlier in a middle class suburb of Detroit. No
one knew it then, least of all me, but I was one drop in a swelling wave
of more than 3.8 million births in 1947. That year was the leading
edge of the "baby boom." This was not some postwar spurt of pent-
up passion but the first of a series of demographic tsunamis which
would not crest until 1957 or abate until 1964, when annual births
finally dropped below 4 million. In all, 75 million Americans were
born between 1946 and 1964. Nearly 50 million of us hit our teens
and early twenties between 1960 and 1972 and were old enough to
participate as leaders or followers in shaping the Sixties.

Huge as the baby boom was in absolute numbers, it loomed even
larger in relative terms. The boom followed upon the fertility bust of
the Depression and war years and thus overwhelmed the generation
of its parents, teachers, professors, and other social guardians. As
Landon Jones documents in *Great Expectations,* his history of the baby
boom, nobody was prepared for my generation, and society never got
ahead of the wave.

But the magnitude of the baby boom cannot alone explain the
unprecedented character of its impact on politics, popular culture,

art, and social values. This golden cohort was not merely the largest in history, it was also the richest, healthiest, and best educated, and it was born and reared in the world's most powerful nation flush with confidence, idealism, and not a little arrogance. The adolescence of the baby boom also coincided with a profound transformation of economic organization from capital industry to mass consumerism, dramatic technological innovation, and also great dread. We were shaped by both unprecedented affluence and anxiety, the first children raised with televised mass marketing and the prospect of nuclear mass destruction.

The boom did not erupt from the large families typically raised by farmers and the urban poor to provide a domestic work force and hedge against infant mortality. Most children of the boom were raised with one or two siblings in "nuclear" families. I, however, was raised an only child; my experience and understanding of the Sixties are conditioned by this basic natal fact, and diverge early from the lives of others raised in larger families. Beyond this, my upbringing was not exactly average, which deserves a little explanation. My father was a scientist, inventor, and militant atheist. My mother was a feisty British war bride raised in the working class row houses of Hartlepool, Sheffield, and Hull. Both were independent, energetic, and confident citizens eager to build a new world up from the ruins of World War II. Neither of my parents was active politically, but our house resounded with discussions of current events and solutions to the world's problems. The coffee table was piled high with magazines—news, science, and science fiction—which provided my first reading.

My parents instilled in me a fierce individualism, a passion for justice, a faith in rationalism, and a historical optimism which refuses to surrender to objective reality. I acquired a firm set of ethical and political coordinates, with technocratic progressivism supplying the vertical axis and a compassionate humanism supplying the horizontal. I grew up a "liberal" without ever having to ask why, for a thinking, caring person could be nothing else.

Beyond the obvious influence of my parents, my political outlook owed much to television, as did that of most of my contemporaries. Conservatives like to argue that we were shaped by a "liberal media." They have a point, but the wrong one. There is no doubt that television shaped the political consciousness of my generation. The content of news broadcasts—footage from far-off wars in Korea and the Middle East, the Army-McCarthy hearings, scenes of federal troops guarding Negro children during the integration of Little Rock's Central High School, and interviews with Allen Ginsberg and other beatniks—each in its way undermined faith in the established order and created an appetite for something new and better. If breakfast cereals could improve themselves every other week, why couldn't the world?

Fidel Castro's triumphant entry into Havana in January 1959 marked the real beginning of the Sixties. His victory against a ruthless dictator and impossible odds inspired young people above and below the Rio Grande, and the apparent heavy-handedness of the U.S. government muted any shock when Castro declared his socialism and affiliated the island with the Soviet Union after the Bay of Pigs invasion. We had given him no other choice, many felt. Beyond this, Castro's vigor and relative youth, and even more conspicuously that of Che Guevara, made these revolutionaries the first political heroes of the television age.

Their beards didn't hurt, either, for they entwined in a kind of spiritual link with those other hirsute revolutionaries, the Beats. The prose and poetry of Allen Ginsberg, Jack Kerouac, William Burroughs, Gregory Corso, Gary Snyder, and the rest of this fraternity of the lost expressed the confusion, disgust, and rage spawned by modern consumer society among its young, as well as their appetite for new spiritual verities and an aching hunger for wholeness.

Beyond the news, "liberal bias" was reinforced by the content of numerous television dramas. Programs such as "Perry Mason," "Have Gun—Will Travel," "Peter Gunn," and "The Defenders" were rarely explicitly political, but each routinely pitted strong individuals against unjust authority, mass prejudice, or conniving economic interests. All their heroes (not just Richard Boone) were latter-day Paladins, fighting against the system for truth, justice, and the American way. Meanwhile, the movies provided corporeal messiahs for the new restlessness such as Marlon Brando and, most definitively, James Dean.

Skepticism toward authority comes naturally to kids. For my generation it was reinforced by the acid wit of *Mad Magazine,* the existential zaniness of Ernie Kovaks, and the gentler but no less subversive humor of Steve Allen, Sid Caesar, and later Bob and Shelley Berman. Each transmitted an inside joke to eager youngsters: despite what your parents and teachers say, the world is crazy!

Science fiction, too, was a fundamentally seditious force. Its basic message was that this world was dwarfed by forces and possibilities beyond mundane reality. The great sci-fi writers of the 1950s and early 1960s—Asimov, Clarke, Pohl, van Vogt, Anderson, Simak, Heinlein, et al.—and the best movies of the era (*Forbidden Planet* and George Pal's oeuvre) introduced young minds to ecology, cultural relativity, dystopia, the law of unintended consequences, and the ambiguities of progress which would later find political expression in a broad skepticism toward "modern" life. By 1959, Rod Serling was leading weekly tours of "The Twilight Zone," of which virtually every Boomer is a naturalized citizen.

And if you did not read or watch science fiction, you lived it. The great, overarching fact of life was that it could end at any moment in a blinding flash of nuclear energy. Beginning with Sputnik on October 4, 1957, the sky became littered with satellites and intercontinental ballistic missiles, any one of which might come crashing down on your house in the first act of the last war. Awareness of this awful contingency was reinforced daily with civil defense drills, news reports, movies, and TV shows. It even invaded your childhood dreams: the eerie light, the atomic torus rising silently on its stem, the panic that you couldn't find your parents amid the rubble, the knowledge that you were already dead even as you lived.

Finally, there was the music. Jazz and folk set the new mood to music, but neither could compete with "rock and roll," a phrase coined in 1951 by Cleveland d.j. Alan "Moondog" Freed to package black rhythm and blues for white audiences. Elvis Presley advanced the cause with his first television appearances in 1956, and Dick Clark institutionalized it when his Philadelphia-based "American Bandstand" went national via ABC in 1957, while Top-40 radio stations took over the AM dial.

Rock and roll's alchemy of participatory energy, visceral rhythm, and romantic melancholy provided instant relief for existential angst and an insatiable thirst for more. It also opened a back door between the inner cities and outer suburbs through which more than music would later pass, and it reinforced the identification of many young whites with the blacks they watched on TV battling police dogs, fire hoses, and white-hooded bigots.

Ed Sullivan censored Elvis' swiveling hips (on his second appearance, by the way), and religious and cultural conservatives organized record-burning rallies to protest the "negrofication" of American music. But the damage was done: future rebels without a cause found a new beat and not even Ricky Nelson proved immune.

Such were the thoughts, sights, and sounds which made me and most other members of my generation "liberal" by 1960. How else could we have possibly turned out?

The specific circumstances of my life reinforced such influences and planted the seeds for future radicalism. Three incidents serve to illustrate my own development.

In 1953, we moved from the Detroit area to Flint, the grubby General Motors company town later made famous by Michael Moore's documentary, *Roger and Me.* My clearest memory of my sixth year was my first and only nanny, a large black woman named Elizabeth. She was funny, loving, and vibrant and a completely new experience for me. Earlier in Detroit, I had seen "colored people" (the polite term in those days), but I had not had any personal contact with a black human being.

I had also never had any contact with racial prejudice before. I can still vividly recall a trip to the grocery store with Elizabeth during which white people stopped and glared at us because we were holding hands. She released her grip and warned me not take her hand until we were out of the store. It was a mystery to me, but even at my young age I could feel the hate and fear generated by this innocent gesture of affection.

"Nigger" was a word that never crossed the lips of either my mother or father, and they were quick to scold anyone who used such an epithet, even in suburban Washington, D.C., where we first encountered the "Colored Only" signs of legal segregation. My parents cheered the 1954 Supreme Court ruling mandating integrated education, but the separation of the races was so great in those days that I never attended school with more than a few token Negroes in even the most progressive cities.

I had a history of good relations with my teachers until I entered the fourth grade back in suburban Detroit. My teacher (we'll call her Mrs. Smith) was a fundamentalist Southern Baptist who inserted religion into virtually every subject. Michigan, like most states of the time, erected a very low wall between state and religion in public education. In Mrs. Smith's class it was more like a chalk line, which she erased with enthusiasm.

Each school day began with the Pledge of Allegiance, followed by the recital of the Lord's Prayer, followed by Mrs. Smith's reading of a passage from the Bible, followed by a silent prayer. This was not the end of our religious instruction, however. Whenever an opportunity presented itself, Mrs. Smith would insinuate the "fourth R" or her political views into our lessons.

When the infamous Sen. Joseph McCarthy finally succumbed to a debauched liver and dementia in 1956, Mrs. Smith had us all bow our heads in homage while she intoned a heartfelt eulogy to a "great American." When Adlai Stevenson challenged Dwight Eisenhower in that year's presidential election it was made clear that "good Americans" supported "the General." When we began to study rudimentary science and I proudly displayed my drawings of dinosaurs and space ships, she informed me that such things were blasphemies and tools of the devil.

My final clash with Mrs. Smith came in the last minutes of one school day when she decided to take a religious census of her class. In descending order, the attending Baptists, Methodists, Presbyterians, other miscellaneous Protestants, Catholics, and, finally, Jews were asked to raise their hands. At the end, Mrs. Smith locked onto me like a heathen-seeking missile. "Walter, why didn't you raise your hand?"

Innocently, I replied, "We don't believe in god." Mrs. Smith swelled with righteous fervor and explained in no uncertain terms to both me and the class that I, my father, and my mother were doomed to roast in the fires of hell for time everlasting, and it would serve us right. I was saved from the eternal flames by the school bell, and fled home in tears to break the terrible news to my parents. Mother didn't take it well. She plopped me into the Olds and tore back to the school where she gave Mrs. Smith a taste of own brand of fire and brimstone and then demanded an audience with the principal. He was of a more liberal bent, and directed Mrs. Smith to put a lid on her evangelism. She and I stewed under it for the rest of the term. (Remember this story the next time somebody claims that prayer in the public schools is harmless.)

In the summer of 1958, I traveled with my mother to England and then to Brussels for the World's Fair. There, beneath the looming, tubular mass of the Atomium, the great struggle between East and West was waged in architecture and exhibitry. The East won hands down. The Soviet Union's pavilion was a massive glass barn. The exhibits on the main floor consisted entirely of heavy machinery, tractors, and models of giant nuclear plants and factories. Spacecraft, real and proposed, soared overhead. The huge hall was bracketed by two heroic statues: a muscular laborer held a hammer aloft and an equally powerful peasant woman brandished a giant sickle. When viewed from the mezzanine, their tools overlapped to form the icon of Communism.

In stark contrast, the U.S. pavilion was an ornate, filigreed donut, filled with exhibits that looked as if they had been lifted from a photo spread in *Vogue*—pretty but vacuous, and utterly irrelevant to the needs and aspirations of the Third World visitors attending the Fair. The pavilion had one redeeming feature: a basement soda fountain serving Coca Cola and real American hot dogs. It was mobbed. Thus the U.S. won the stomachs of the world, while the Soviets captured their hearts and minds. Not an inaccurate harbinger of events to come. For an impressionable eleven-year-old American, the Soviet appeal was breathtaking: I had seen the future, and it was really neat.

My parents were not overtly political, but they did more than just speculate about a better future. They worked to create it. My father in particular dedicated his life to inventions which he hoped would help transform the world. Although he was trained as a chemist, my father's passion was aeronautical engineering. He became a missile engineer at Chrysler and worked with Wernher von Braun's team in creating the Redstone and Jupiter rockets for the Army. At home, he tinkered with designs for various flying machines. After a couple of crashes in a home-built autogiro, Father found a new mission in life: flight without height. His answer was the "air cushion vehicle," better known today by its British name "hovercraft." His pursuit of development capital took us from Michigan to the Washington, D.C., area, then to Connecticut.

Soon after we settled into a new house on a wooded half-acre in Ridgefield, Connecticut, Boeing recruited my father with a promise that he would direct a major development project for air cushion vehicles. I was informed in October 1961 that we were moving to a place called Seattle. I looked it up in the atlas and found it uncomfortably close to Alaska and distant from anywhere else.

Father flew out west to scout a house for us. My mother was averse to a transcontinental plane flight, so we traveled first class to Seattle by train courtesy of the Boeing Airplane Company. I had no idea what awaited us at the other end of the line. Late in the trip, we encountered a passenger in the dome car who was returning to Seattle. He asked where we would be living. My mother replied that Father had found a house in Lake City. He said this was good because I wouldn't "have to go to school with niggers."

My heart sank.

Chapter 2:
Troublemakers

In a city, as in a world, it
takes all kinds.

—Murray Morgan

I f the clay of my personality was still damp at age fourteen, the same could be said of Seattle when I arrived virtually on the city's 110th birthday. I like to think that we grew up together; certainly we both changed during the next ten years.

I was singularly underwhelmed by the city. Having lived much of my life close to three of the nation's largest cities, I found Seattle puny, provincial, and puritanical. I would learn only much later about the richness of its past and the titanic struggles for wealth, labor, and reform which shaped the city's destiny. Stories of old strikes and scandals had no place in the classroom, least of all at Jane Addams Junior High School. Neither, from what I could tell, did education.

I had left Ridgefield High School, consistently rated one of the nation's best, to enter what was regarded as one of the worst in an undistinguished system. It wasn't really a school at all but an asylum for victims of juvenile dementia and hormonal hysteria. On my first day, I walked into the lunch room to discover a full-scale food fight in progress. Sandwiches, cartons of milk, and assorted fruits arced overhead while prowling bullies hijacked the trays of weaker students. Shocked, I marched directly into the administration office to alert officials to this obvious collapse in social discipline. The vice principal listened to my appeal for action and then replied, "You're going to be a little troublemaker, aren't you?"

The Rev. Martin Luther King Jr. had just visited Seattle, and troublemakers were much in the news at that time. Some historians argue that the Sixties really began on February 1, 1960, when four black students refused to give up their seats until they were served at a Woolworth's lunch counter in Greensboro, North Carolina. The tactic galvanized black and white activists alike: here was something new, personal yet powerful, that individuals could do to dramatize injustice and, perhaps, shame the system into action. For young black intellectuals in particular, the "sit-in" offered an independent course of activism free of the more cautious and hierarchical approaches of the black clergy and lawyers who had brought the struggle into the Sixties chiefly via the churches and courts.

The nervousness of senior black leaders, including the Rev. King, was not unreasonable. They knew that a massive backlash could wipe out all of the progress toward integration won at such cost during the fifties. The young founders of Student Non-Violent Coordinating Committee (SNCC) recognized the dangers, too. The group was organized a few months after the "Greensboro Four" to train, support, and coordinate participants in sit-ins across the South. The work soon expanded to include community organizing and more traditional forms of activism. Two young black men rose to leadership through its ranks: Stokely Carmichael and H. Rap Brown.

SNCC did not have a monopoly on activism in the South. The new Southern Christian Leadership Conference, founded by King in 1957, was mobilizing the black churches and their congregations, the NAACP was active in the courts and legislatures, and several groups were pressing an agenda of economic justice. Prominent among these was the Congress for Racial Equality, CORE, then led by James Farmer.

A little more than a year after Greensboro, CORE upped the ante by reviving a tactic not used since 1946, the Freedom Ride, with the goal of desegregating interstate bus travel and terminals in the South. When a racist mob attacked a Freedom Bus in Alabama on May 14, 1961, burning the vehicle and beating its white and black passengers, the nation was appalled. It was only the first of many outrages to come.

The violence which greeted the Freedom Rides finally provoked the Kennedy Administration into action. Attorney General Robert Kennedy met with civil rights leaders in the summer of 1961 and urged them to shift from direct action to a longer-range strategy of voter registration. On the promise of federal assistance and protection, they agreed, and things cooled down temporarily as Andrew Young and others organized the first "citizenship classes" and voter drives.

In October 1961, the new Seattle branch of CORE led a "selective buying" campaign to compel the major downtown department stores to hire more black clerks. The campaign, which emulated similar ones in San Francisco and elsewhere, was later expanded to include "shop-ins" at area grocery stores, in which protesters would fill and then abandon their shopping carts. Similar tactics clogged up Nordstrom's during "shoe-ins." Quintard Taylor writes that Seattle yielded CORE its first employment gains for blacks and adoption of corporate "equal opportunity" policies by Nordstrom and other major retailers.

(The Seattle CORE was first led by Reginald Alleyne Jr. and then Walter Hundley, who came to Seattle in 1954 to head the leftish Church of the People in the University District. He went on to lead the Seattle Model Cities Program and to serve in the city government as director of the Seattle Office of Management and Budget and Department of Parks and Recreation. Years later I would find myself variously his employee, ally, and adversary.)

Another measure of social progress came in March 1962 when Wing Luke was elected to the Seattle City Council. He was the first nonwhite ever elected in the city, and his seat on the Council was the highest elective office yet attained by a Chinese American anywhere in the continental U.S. Luke was no mere token; he became a voice for the "other Seattle" and championed causes such as open housing and minority employment.

These signs of local activism and progress were the exception. McCarthyism, de facto segregation, a smug, pro-business press, and relative prosperity had silenced the noisier voices in Seattle following World War II. The boosters of a "Greater Seattle" preferred to repress memories of the town's more raucous and unsavory past (they might have succeeded but for authors like Murray Morgan and Bill Speidel) and projected an image of an "All-American City" soaring into the Jet Age aboard Boeing's shiny new 707s. Their greatest promotional coup was the 1962 world's fair, officially called "Century 21 Exposition"; in an ironic way, it would prove to be their undoing.

The fairgrounds were still under construction when we occupied our new home in Lake City. Soon after, Boeing confessed that there was no air cushion vehicle project and assigned my father to work on hydrofoils, a competing technology which he held in contempt. (Boeing sank millions into these quirky craft, which ride underwater wings and never made a dime.) Not long after, he finagled a transfer to the missile division, working first on the Dyna-Soar, a winged, reusable "space bomber" which is the granddaddy of the Space Shuttle, and later the silo-launched Minuteman ICBM. My mother also went to work for "The Lazy B," as most Boeing workers called their employer, as a secretary and rose to become a social assistant to president Bill Allen.

The spring of 1962 saw the opening of the world's fair. It was downright dinky compared to Brussels' sprawling exhibition, a fact I delighted in pointing out. Regardless of its deficiencies, the Seattle world's fair wrought a number of subtle but important changes. Foremost, it showcased and elevated a new kind of progressive leadership, epitomized by the late Eddie Carlson, former head of Westin Hotels and United Airlines. He practiced a sincere and effective style of inclusive politics that cut across the old class lines. His vision is suitably memorialized in the Space Needle, a modernistic lingam which, whatever its architectural merit (I happen to like it), banished the spirits of the old from the village and welcomed in the new.

The fair also salved Seattle's chronic inferiority complex as a parade of visitors marched through town: the Shah and Empress of Iran, Prince Philip of the United Kingdom, cosmonaut Gherman Titov (who scandalized the town by announcing that he had not seen god in space), astronaut John Glenn, New York Gov. Nelson Rockefeller, Vice President Lyndon Johnson, Attorney General Robert Kennedy (who would become a frequent visitor and mountain-climbing companion of Jim Whittaker), and entertainers Bob Hope, John Wayne, and Elvis Presley. Elvis had not been in Seattle since performing at Sick's Stadium in 1957, and his return to film *It Happened at the World's Fair* virtually paralyzed the city.

Highbrows used the fair to try to redeem the city's cultural reputation, which had languished since Sir Thomas Beecham, then conductor of the Seattle Symphony, condemned the town as an "aesthetic dustbin" in 1943. Current conductor Milton Katims brought Van Cliburn and Igor Stravinsky to inaugurate the new Opera House (built within the shell of the 1928 Civic Auditorium) and later staged *Aïda*.

The production was a financial disaster, but this boomeranged in the arts' favor by prompting the creation of PONCHO (Patrons of Northwest Civic, Charitable and Cultural Organizations) to expand and stabilize private funding.

The state had to bend its notorious "blue laws" to accommodate all of these outsiders in Seattle, and the flamboyant Gracie Hansen provoked blushes and titters with her Las Vegas–style Paradise International Club revue on the fair's "Gay Way." Dr. Athelstan Spilhaus, director of the U.S. Science Pavilion (now the Pacific Science Center) challenged Gracie to visit his exhibit. As reporter-historian Don Duncan relates the story, she found it "terrific, but it will never replace sex and cotton candy." She invited Spilhaus to take in her show, but there is no record that he did.

Sex and science did achieve a temporary fusion in a "Gay Way" revue called "Girls of the Galaxy," until Seattle's censors shut it down. Meanwhile, U.S. Attorney Brock Adams and the FBI led a highly public raid to shut down overt gambling at several downtown restaurants and "amusement centers." Bingo, pinballs, and other games of chance flourished in Seattle at the time, "tolerated" by officials and police under the convenient fiction that it was unclear whether or not the state constitution allowed the city to prohibit gambling.

Seattle progressives tried to exploit the civic momentum of the fair to fuel a long-sought plan for regional mass transit. The current debate over urban sprawl and pollution dated back to 1958 when attorney James Ellis and allies in the Municipal League and League of Women Voters proposed the creation of the "Municipality of Metropolitan Seattle." Metro was envisioned as a super-utility, which would be insulated from the county's notoriously corrupt and partisan politics. As originally presented to voters in March 1958, Metro would build and operate a regional water quality and sewage system, direct comprehensive planning, manage regional parks, and, most important of all, establish a regional mass transit system. Conservative voters in the suburbs defeated the plan by a narrow margin but a scaled-down Metro, limited to water quality, won approval the following fall.

At about this same time, the state began planning a new central freeway for Seattle. The Highway Department ignored Seattle's pleas for a rail transit right-of-way in the future Interstate-5, and a bold plan offered by Paul Thiry, architect of the Seattle Coliseum, to "lid" the freeway through the downtown. The state literally bulldozed its way through Seattle, destroying thousands of homes and leaving a trench that would not begin to close over for two decades.

It was clear to many that I-5 would not solve the city's growing traffic congestion and smog. Hoping to exploit the civic momentum of the fair, as well as Metro's rapid success in cleaning up the putrescent Lake Washington and the popularity of the city's new Monorail, Ellis and his allies decided to ask anew for permission for Metro to create a mass transit system. Conservatives suspected a stalking horse for a socialist dictatorship, and the AAA and other highway interests saw the system as unwelcome competition. Confused and distracted voters turned down the idea in September 1962. But Jim Ellis wasn't done yet.

Century 21 drew millions and it even made a small profit, something very rare in the world of fairs. All of these strangers in Seattle's midst challenged its provincialism and spurred a reexamination of its prudishness and prejudice. The fair opened a window, and the inshore flow refreshed the city at a moment when it might have suffocated on its own stuffiness. If you doubt this, just compare issues of *The Seattle Times* or *Post-Intelligencer* before and after 1962.

There was a moment at the fair's closing when it seemed that there would be no Century 21. Indeed, it looked as though the curtain was falling prematurely on Century 20. President Kennedy had been scheduled to officiate at the fair's closing on October 21. A few days before his visit, he begged off, claiming to be ill. The day after the fair closed, President Kennedy went on television to tell the nation that the Soviet Union had installed medium-range missiles and bombers in Cuba, and that the U.S. Navy was imposing a blockade on all shipping around the island until the weapons were removed. I remember watching the speech while talking to my girlfriend on the phone. We both figured that this was the end.

Fortunately, Soviet Premier Nikita Khrushchev blinked and the world was not canceled. No one breathed a more heartfelt sigh of relief than Lorenzo Milam, who had spent months and a small fortune cobbling together a small radio station to be called KRAB-FM.

Milam was a tall, lanky figure who seemed to shoot off like radio waves in a thousand directions at once, unimpeded by the paralyzed legs left by childhood polio. Born in 1934 in Jacksonville, Florida, Milam developed an early fascination with radio. In 1959, he acquired a transmitter with a $15,000 inheritance and applied to the FCC for an FM license anywhere one might be available. They sent him to Seattle, which, he later told *Seattle Magazine,* "sounded like a reasonably civilized place." Milam's dream was a "listener-supported" station, funded through subscriptions like an audio magazine. It was a radical approach, then being attempted in San Francisco and only two other cities.

Milam licensed a frequency, 107.7, at the farthest extreme of the FM band, a medium mostly ignored by broadcasters devoted to "Top 40" programming for teens. Milam wanted to name his station KLEE or KANT, but for its own reasons the FCC chose KRAB from his list of ten possible call-letters. Milam decided he liked it because "a crab can go in all directions. In time of danger, it can scuttle under a rock, and it is capable of delivering a vicious bite."

He recruited a team of local radio buffs including Gary Margason, Robert Garfias, and Jon Gallant; enlisted a volunteer engineer, Jeremy Lansman, from San Francisco; and leased a former doughnut shop at the corner of NE 91st and Roosevelt Way. The organization was incorporated as the Jack Straw Foundation in honor of a leader of a fourteenth-century peasant rebellion in England.

KRAB broadcast for the first time on the evening of December 13, 1962. From the beginning, KRAB offered an eclectic array of programs ranging from anarchists to Birchers, Jesuits to atheists, blue grass to raga. Early personalities included J. J. "Tiny" Freeman, Frank Krasnowsky, and Deb Das, and Milam recruited more with the promise, "Your scurrilous words are flooding the countryside, bouncing off hills and trees, ramming headlong into cows . . . filtering into that radio, into that tiny coil of heat . . . red, deep, mysterious." There was little order and no ideology to the programming, Milam freely confessed to critics from Left and Right: "My views change from day to day. I tend to agree with the individual I'm drinking beer with."

When not dialing in KRAB (or Radio Moscow) on my ancient Zenith console radio, I found a resonant voice in a syndicated television program called "Probe," which featured commentaries by Albert Burke. Former director of Graduate Studies in Conservation at Yale, Burke was hardly a leftist, but his eclectic openmindedness challenged Cold War shibboleths and exposed viewers to some of the earliest discussion of what industrial growth was doing to the planet.

By this time, I had begun classes at Ingraham High School. Although only a few years old, it was already bursting at the seams, and scores of portable classrooms filled the parking lot. Like virtually every other school system in America, Seattle didn't catch up with the Baby Boom until it was over. Almost immediately, I managed to get crosswise with the school administration. When the administration asked for volunteers to transfer to yet another new high school, Nathan Hale, for their junior year, I was first in line. I don't think Ingraham was sad to see me go.

Hale was virgin territory in the fall of 1963. Transferring juniors were the "senior" class, although we were outnumbered by a mob of freshmen. The building itself was huge, and we had it all to ourselves. I was fortunate to luck into a remarkable faculty of teachers (who, I suspect, were also "troublemakers" who had escaped or been banished from other schools) including Carol Simmons, Conner Reed, Ken Warren, and Gary Ness.

It is no reflection on these teachers' abilities to say that most of my education occurred outside the classroom. It was a heady time as American intellectuals emerged from the long hibernation under Eisenhower like hungry bears, avidly gobbling up every new idea. In the Sixties' first years, there was much to chew on.

Chapter 3:
Turning Left

*There is a spectre haunting
America—the spectre of
youth.*

—Stan Iverson

I t is difficult to describe the intellectual ferment of the early 1960s.
Every day seemed to offer up a startling new idea, discovery, or
theory. Every field was in creative turmoil—science, literature,
politics, economics, medicine—and the possibilities seemed infinite.

Among the major books to challenge conventional wisdom were
Paul Goodman's *Growing Up Absurd*, Harper Lee's *To Kill A Mocking-
bird*, Robert Heinlein's *Stranger in a Strange Land* (can you grok it?),
Anthony Burgess's *Clockwork Orange*, Joseph Heller's *Catch 22*,
Marshall McLuhan's *Gutenberg Galaxy* and *Understanding Media*, Ken
Kesey's *One Flew Over the Cuckoo's Nest*, Rachel Carson's *Silent Spring*,
Michael Harrington's *The Other America*, James Baldwin's *The Fire
Next Time*, Betty Freidan's *The Feminine Mystique*, John Kenneth
Galbraith's *The Affluent Society*, Kurt Vonnegut's *Cat's Cradle*, and Sylvia
Plath's *The Bell Jar*. Playwrights such as Edward Albee re-energized
the stage while Stanley Kubrick, Federico Fellini, Tony Richardson,
and other "new cinema" directors broke Hollywood's monopoly. Films
such as *Seven Days in May, The Manchurian Candidate*, and *Dr.
Strangelove* crystallized our paranoia and our sense of the dangerous
absurdity of modern geopolitics.

This mood created an eager audience for mega-analyses by "fu-
turist" thinkers such as Buckminster Fuller, Kenneth Boulding, Robert Theobald, and, later, Alvin Toffler and Charles Reich. In a decade
crowded with would-be prophets, Marshall McLuhan may have had
the broadest and most enduring impact. The name of this Canadian
philosopher is welded to his famous axiom, "The medium is the message," perhaps the most quoted and least understood idea of the age.

First expressed in *The Gutenberg Galaxy* and amplified in *Understanding Media: The Extensions of Man*, McLuhan's insight was that "the 'message' of any medium is the change of scale or pace or pattern that it introduces into human affairs." As the first citizens of his "global village," my generation fulfilled many of McLuhan's predictions that TV would inspire a greater activism coupled with a cultural reaction stressing pretechnocratic values of experience and community.

The period planted the seeds for a garden of new "isms"—feminism, structuralism, environmentalism—and it revived the long-frozen roots of Marxism. As McCarthyism faded, it became acceptable, even fashionable, to revisit Karl Marx. Khrushchev himself had contributed to this redux with his famous repudiation of Stalin in 1956 and his affirmation of a policy of "peaceful coexistence" with the West (notwithstanding the brutal suppression of the Hungarian revolution). This "revisionism" was condemned by Mao Tse-tung and other hardliners, but it helped to rehabilitate democratic socialist parties in Europe, particularly Willy Brandt's German Social Democrats and Harold Wilson's British Labour Party. "National liberation" movements in Africa, Latin America, and Asia also posed a new challenge to the old order as indigenous peoples struggled against the vestiges of European and even American colonialism. Most of the leaders of this new "Third World" (the phrase was Josip Tito's, I believe) were not coy about their socialist credentials and goals: Egypt's Nasser, India's Nehru, Indonesia's Sukarno, Ghana's Nkruma, the Congo's Lumumba, Kenya's Kenyatta, and, of course, Cuba's Castro. The idea of "monolithic" communism could not contain all these movements or deny the legitimacy of their popular grievances.

Another event contributed to Marx's "rehabilitation" in the early Sixties: the translation of his long-ignored *Economic Philosophical Manuscripts* of 1844. This helped to reinforce the synthesis of Marx with Existentialists, particularly in Albert Camus and Jean-Paul Sartre (though they split over Stalin), and neo-Freudians such as R. D. Laing and Erich Fromm. In many ways the young Karl Marx, with his humanism and near-poetry of alienation, was the progenitor of the New Left, just as the mature Marx, with his carbuncles and tortured calculus of surplus wage value, was the patriarch of the Old. Speaking across a century as one twenty-four-year-old addressing others of like age, this "new" Marx helped to rekindle long-stifled dreams of revolutionary change.

With all these ideas whirling about, I was desperate to find others with whom to explore the new possibilities they promised. Finding the future, particularly on the Left, proved much harder than I expected.

The Seattle area had once supported a robust Left and numerous movements for radical reform and utopian community life. Its working class was among the most militant in the nation, leading the nation's first general strike in 1919, and providing a strong base for the Industrial Workers of the World, or "Wobblies" as they were better known. Postmaster General "Big Jim" Farley acknowledged this radical tradition in the 1930s with his famous (possibly apocryphal) toast "to the 47 states and the Soviet of Washington."

This "Old Left" emerged from World War II in good shape, but the onset of the Cold War legitimized a series of purges within government, education, organized labor, and the Democratic Party. The Left proved to be its own worst enemy, however, and Seattle's contingent fractured along lines paralleling the the national scene. With the exception of a few notable hold-outs such as Harry Bridge's longshoremen, organized labor cleansed itself of anyone who questioned capitalism. Pro-business union leaders such as Seattle-based Teamsters head Dave Beck exploited the anti-Communist mood to consolidate power and silence critics of labor corruption and co-optation.

Norman Thomas' Socialist Party had long ago lost any appetite for revolutionary agitation, and Communist ranks were doubly devastated by Khrushchev's denunciation of Stalin and invasion of Hungary. Some Party members found a new hero in Mao Tse-tung and echoed his repudiation of Soviet "revisionism." Others sought a purer revolutionary theory in the ideas of Leon Trotsky, who had himself been exiled by Stalin in 1928 and was later assassinated, but most could not stomach the internal politics of the main party bearing Trotsky's torch, the Socialist Workers Party. Several of the latter formed a local Trotskyist group, the Freedom Socialist Party, in 1966, led by Frank Krasnowsky and his then-wife, Clara Fraser (who later founded Radical Women). They found a home at "Freeway Hall," beneath the new I-5 bridge, where they later tangled with their former socialist landlord named Ivar Haglund, who had grown rich shucking "Acres of Clams" for waterfront diners. Even the FSP was too constrictive for some, and they gravitated toward theoretical anarchism. Most older radicals simply gave up the struggle and either abandoned politics or entered the liberal mainstream.

Such was the state of the Left when I started frequenting the University District in search of fellow-travelers who shared my growing unease with the status quo. My own initiation to Marx came via *The Weekly People,* published by the venerable Socialist Labor Party (SLP), America's oldest—and by that time least relevant—socialist organization. I found copies of this antiquated rag in battered news boxes (they were favorite targets of fraternity goons) in the District. It was a quick leap to *The Communist Manifesto,* which knocked my socks off.

Why these dead words from a failed revolution in 1848? Why the founding philosopher of a movement I had been taught to fear and despise since kindergarten? Of course, it must be conceded that merely being forbidden emits a powerful pheromone, especially for teenagers, but Marx's appeal goes beyond that. Aristide Briand had part of the answer when he quipped that "a man who is not a socialist at twenty has no heart" (we may quibble with his self-serving conclusion, "and one who is a socialist at forty has no brains").

In America in the early Sixties, there was no one else to answer the fundamental questions which tortured young idealists. Why did so few seem to prosper in the world, and so many suffer? Why was the vast majority of humanity imprisoned by prejudice and poverty? Why even in America did most live out lives of soul-crushing monotony and exploitation?

It helped that Marx also said something that it is observably true, namely that the "political economy" is structured to benefit the wealthy and powerful at the expense of the poor and weak. But such an arrangement is not static, Marx said. A society's great classes are propelled like tectonic plates toward collision by the underlying dynamism of technological and economic change. From this friction emerges new classes, so that the seemingly stable social landscape is actually undergoing constant tension and renewal, which human beings could direct and accelerate with the proper understanding.

Conventional theorists had no comparable answers or prescriptions. Marx offered the would-be activist a stimulating intellectual challenge, an awesome responsibility, and the faith that history would vindicate his or her efforts. There was ample grist for the most Jesuitical of minds and the most romantic of souls, and it explains why Marx, so long and loudly denounced in the United States in the Fifties, became a magnet for student radicals in the Sixties.

My first brush with the "New Left" came not in the U District but on Skid Road, as today's Pioneer Square was then better known. I wandered into the Id Bookstore, which was located a few doors south of Yesler on First, and discovered a cornucopia of seditious literature: Paul Krassner's *Realist* magazine, Fidel Castro's *History Will Absolve Me*, and a little pamphlet titled "The Port Huron Statement"—the seminal manifesto of the New Left.

The call for a New Left had been voiced most urgently by C. Wright Mills, who also coined the phrase. His books *White Collar* and *The Power Elite* offered a leftist but nondoctrinaire critique of American society along class lines, and he attracted a growing following among college students. Some of these gathered in June 1962 in the Michigan resort town of Port Huron to write a manifesto for a new kind of movement. The ostensible sponsor of this gathering was the League for Industrial Democracy, a nearly moribund socialist organization founded in 1905. Alan Haber, director of LID's youth auxiliary, convinced his elders to let him try to revive campus membership under a new name, Students for a Democratic Society. Tom Hayden, then at the University of Michigan, largely wrote the final "Port Huron Statement."

The document begins, "We are people of this generation, bred in at least modest comfort, housed now in universities, looking uncomfortably to the world we inherit." The Statement strikes notes of high passion, inspired by "the permeating and victimizing fact of human degradation, symbolized by the Southern struggle against racial bigotry" and by "the enclosing fact of the Cold War, symbolized by the presence of the Bomb." It sounded a note of apocalyptic fatalism: "Our work is guided by the sense that we may be the last generation in the experiment with living," and noted this "outstanding paradox: we ourselves are imbued with urgency, yet the message of our society is that there is no viable alternative to the present."

Foremost, the Statement is a manifesto against apathy, for "feeling the press of complexity upon the emptiness of life, people are fearful of the thought that at any moment things might be thrust out of control." SDS rejected such trepidations and offered "this document of our convictions and analysis: an effort in understanding and changing the conditions of humanity in the late twentieth century, an effort rooted in the ancient, still unfulfilled conception of man attaining determining influence over his circumstances of life."

SDS blamed the liberal corporate state and its academic lackeys for banishing the discussion of human values from politics and for failing to address the fundamental issue of alienation, by dint of which, "loneliness, estrangement, isolation describe the vast distance between man and man today." SDS's remedy was "participatory democracy," a new kind of personal and public politics by which "decision-making of basic social consequence be carried on by public groupings . . . as the art of collectively creating an acceptable pattern of social relations [and] bringing people out of isolation and into community."

The most important and enduring contribution of the Port Huron Statement is its revival of a word not spoken for a long time in American political discourse—"values." The Statement declares, "Making values explicit—an initial task in establishing alternatives—is an activity that has been devalued and corrupted" by hypocrisy and double-speak on both sides of the Iron Curtain.

Here, finally, were people who echoed my own cries in the wilderness. It was a collective howl that has welled up in the hearts of young men and women throughout history, but had never before been voiced by so many at one time. Hayden and his comrades did not know it at the time (and would have been horrified by the suggestion), but they had written a manifesto for a revolution of, by, and for youth.

By the spring of 1963, "the movement" had found a melody to go with the words of protest in the revival of folk music. New singers such as Joan Baez and Peter, Paul & Mary revived the music of Woody Guthrie and a long line of balladeers of rural and urban injustice. Others, such as Bob Dylan, who had made his Greenwich Village debut the year before, began expressing the anxieties and urges of a new generation in their own lyrics.

Long-blacklisted performers such as Pete Seeger found themselves wanted again—but not on Jack Linkletter's televised "Hootenanny." This led to the show's boycott by major performers, and it folded after one season in 1963. Folk gave the movement its anthem, "We Shall Overcome," which was actually copyrighted by Guy Carawan in 1962. If he collected a royalty on just one-millionth the number of the times that song was performed in the Sixties, he must have become a very rich man.

The New Left did not arrive in Seattle until 1965, so I tried to find kindred spirits in more conventional organizations. The primary centers for any remotely creative left-wing discussion were provided, ironically, by churches: Episcopalians at St. Mark's, the black churches of the Central Area, the congregation of Friends in the University District, and the Reverend Peter Raible's University Unitarian Church.

University Unitarian's auxiliary, Liberal Religious Youth, provided me with the closest thing to a forum but it was hobbled by the liberal obsession with "balance." No speaker or viewpoint from the Left could be entertained without being carefully counterbalanced by some kook from the Right. Thus I heard a disproportionate number of speakers from the John Birch Society rebut any and all of the most mild leftist assertions. As Abbie Hoffman later observed, "I knew of no case of a left-winger being given a speaking date to balance" a conservative. The other members of LRY didn't mind as much as I; they were older and chiefly interested in sex, dope, and rock and roll.

I next sought comradeship in the local Democratic Party and found a sympathetic ear in my district chairman, Phil Mahoney. He was confined, however, by the studied indifference of higher leaders who were not about to offend U.S. Sen. Henry "Scoop" Jackson. Even the "senior" senator, Warren G. Magnuson, one of the last of the great New Deal warriors, generally deferred to his junior on matters of defense and international affairs.

Around this time, I happened to meet Senator Jackson. My father took me to a banquet of the Boeing engineers' "union" (really a company guild) which Jackson addressed. Being among friends, "the Senator from Boeing" outlined his strategy for the Cold War in candid terms. The goal, simply, was to continue to ratchet up the arms race so that the Soviet Union would waste resources on its military instead of addressing its own people's needs. It was a strategy of economic attrition which would end in bankrupting the enemy. The Red Chinese presented a slightly different problem. Their lack of a modern industrial infrastructure demanded a different approach than that toward the Soviet Union. So he closed with a fervent appeal for the construction of "dirty bombs" to irradiate the Chinese masses. I was horrified by this calm explication of geopolitical cynicism and mass murder. My father introduced me to the senator and I asked if perhaps his bankruptcy ploy might backfire and undermine the U.S. economy as well as the Soviets'. He patted me on the back and gave me a copy of his book on national defense.

So much for the Democrats. I searched for a group that might share my sympathies and first misgivings about Vietnam, kindled by TV images of Buddhist monks burning themselves alive, and found the local World Without War Council office in the U District. They were focused chiefly on the issue of nuclear testing and disarmament. It was there that I obtained my first "peace symbol" button, but beyond this, the council was essentially useless. Its "concern" over issues of war and peace never seemed to translate into any concrete positions or action. Critics have alleged that it was and remains a front for the State Department (or worse), designed to siphon off idealists into endless and meaningless debate. I can't verify this, although I briefly served on the council board in the early Eighties. I dubbed it the "World Without Change Council" and resigned when it refused to oppose U.S. policies in El Salvador and Nicaragua.

My Marxist catechism was a desultory course of study, and any good cadre would no doubt disapprove, but it was I think the best way to approach the subject. The SLP introduced me to a purer and also gentler Marxism, which fiercely denounced the Soviet Union as nothing more than a brutal form of "state capitalism." Most of the available books, other than Marx's own works and a few sympathetic interpreters, were also chiefly critical of Lenin and Marx's other self-appointed trustees. Thus, I was vaccinated from the outset against Marxism's virulent sectarianism, a protection that later allowed me to keep my head when everyone around me was losing theirs.

So I became Nathan Hale's resident Commie. One of my first acts of "civil disobedience" was to refuse to say the Pledge of Allegiance in morning "home room." This led to a trip to the office and suspension. I made my first call to the Seattle branch of the American Civil Liberties Union, and was back in school the next day. When the school administration refused my request to go hear Norman Thomas speak at the UW, I skipped school for the first and only time.

Of course it was all a game at first, but others were playing for keeps.

Chapter 4:
The End of
Camelot

*For years I have heard the
word "Wait . . ." This
"Wait" has always meant
"Never."*

—**Martin Luther King Jr.**

I n light of later events, many have forgotten that SDS and much
of the rest of the New Left began with the goal of urging the
Kennedy Administration to the Left, not overthrowing the
government. Their initial aim was to radicalize the Democratic Party
and neutralize its conservative Southern Bloc. They ultimately
succeeded, but in ways and with consequences nobody anticipated.

There was reason for guarded optimism in 1963. Kennedy concluded a treaty with Britain and the Soviet Union banning atmospheric
nuclear tests in the atmosphere (French President DeGaulle, who was
building a nuclear force independent of NATO, balked). The U.S.
and Soviet Union also established the first "hot line" (actually a telex,
not a telephone), long advocated by Sen. Henry Jackson. Kennedy
had also begun to shed his reticence in openly promoting civil rights.
In April, civil rights agitation in Birmingham, Alabama, yielded the
sharpest confrontations yet—and lasting images of blacks set upon by
Sheriff "Bull" Connor's police dogs and fire hoses.

The Birmingham campaign resulted in the arrest of M. L. King
Jr., which prompted a call of sympathy from President Kennedy to
King's wife Coretta. Kennedy was starting to take a stand, and he
dispatched troops to Birmingham on May 12. Six days later, the President finally delivered a strong, unequivocal speech on behalf of civil
rights reforms at Tennessee's Vanderbilt University.

On June 11, the spotlight shifted to the University of Alabama,
where Gov. George Wallace staged a carefully choreographed obstruc-

tion to block the enrollment of three black students. The next day, NAACP field secretary Medgar Evers was gunned down in his driveway in Jackson, Mississippi (his killer was not convicted until 1994). One week later, Kennedy submitted the first version of what would become the Omnibus Civil Rights Act of 1964.

On June 15, 1963, Seattle's nascent civil rights movement took a major new step when the Rev. Mance Jackson and other black ministers led 1,000 from Mt. Zion Baptist Church to Westlake Mall in the city's first significant civil rights march. The local movement took another step on July 1, when a brief city hall sit-in by members of the Central District Youth Club compelled a reluctant city council to empanel a Human Rights Commission with a mandate to propose an open housing ordinance within ninety days. Mayor Clinton later appointed longtime community activist Philip Hayasaka to head the commission, but the inclusion of only two black members, the Reverends Samuel McKinney and John Adams, prompted another city council sit-in in late July.

Civil rights was no longer a "Southern problem" and M. L. King Jr. saw the opportunity to reunify the movement. He began organizing the "March for Jobs and Freedom" in Washington, D.C. Nearly a quarter of a million citizens from around the nation rallied in the capital on August 28, and heard King announce from the steps of the Lincoln Memorial, "I have a dream!" Some 1,500 marched in Seattle, and on the same day the Seattle School Board voted to permit students to transfer to schools outside their neighborhoods for the first time in order to promote voluntary desegregation.

In September, Birmingham began to desegregate its schools under court order. The euphoria of that achievement found a tragic counterpoint on September 15, when racists set fire to a black church, burning four children to death within its walls.

In Seattle, the city council (with the notable exception of Wing Luke) dragged its feet in fulfilling its promise to adopt an open housing ordinance. Civil rights advocates responded with a huge rally at Garfield High School on October 20, attracting 3,000 to 5,000 participants depending on who was doing the counting. The council got the message, at least partly, and adopted a housing ordinance five days later—subject to a referendum the following March.

The apparent progress on civil rights was not matched by events in Vietnam. This distant corner of Asia had not yet registered much on the national consciousness. In fairness to Kennedy, he had inherited this nasty little war from his predecessors. Truman started it by rebuffing postwar appeals for U.S. sanction and aid from Ho Chi Minh, who had led the resistance to the Japanese. Truman might have cultivated Ho as the Tito of Asia, but instead he acceded to France's demands to reclaim Vietnam and rebuild its former empire. To add injury to insult, the French installed Japan's puppet, Bao Dai, as head of the new state. Ho left Hanoi and began organizing in the countryside.

President Eisenhower carried this policy forward, providing aid to France and Vietnam in fighting to suppress Ho's "Vietminh" guerrillas. It wasn't enough, and the Vietminh defeated the French in 1954 in a decisive battle at Dienbienphu. At this point, the interests of Red China, which had never quite trusted its Vietnamese comrades, intersected with those of the U.S., and Chou En-lai prevailed on Ho to accept a "temporary" partition of Vietnam along the 19th parallel until elections could be organized for a final reunification. Pretexts were soon found to postpone any voting permanently.

Refugees took their cue, and picked which side of the line they wanted to be on when the fighting resumed. The largest numbers, including many Catholics from the old colonial capital of Hanoi, streamed south, as Ho began setting up a socialist Democratic Republic of Vietnam. After much turmoil, the U.S. finally found its champion in Ngo Dinh Diem, a rather timid Catholic politician. The real power, it soon turned out, was exercised by his brother Ngo Dinh Nhu and his wife, the imperious Madame Nhu. Hanoi responded on December 20, 1960, by approving an initially independent National Liberation Front for South Vietnam, soon called the "Vietcong" (Vietnamese Communists).

This was the situation Kennedy inherited, but he did nothing to alter the trajectory of history. Kennedy declared early on, "Now we have a problem in making our power credible, and Vietnam is the place." His Secretary of Defense, former Ford president Robert McNamara, was eager to bring his "systems analysis" to bear on mastering a new kind of warfare, "low-intensity conflicts," without arousing the public, and the generals wanted to test new technology and techniques in the field. Vietnam was their laboratory, so American aid, equipment, and military "advisers" were steadily increased, while the technicians of counterinsurgency experimented with "strategic hamlets" and "air cavalry" units.

The results were poor, and by 1963 the South Vietnamese Army had become increasingly restive under Diem's inept command, corruption flourished, and Buddhists chafed under blatantly pro-Catholic policies. This last turmoil finally seared Vietnam into the American mind when, on June 11, 1963, a Buddhist monk named Quang Duc calmly set himself on fire on a Saigon street to protest the treatment of his coreligionists. Other monks followed suit, and Buddhists were soon in a full-scale revolt.

Just as the Vietnam war began to boil over, CBS and NBC expanded their national telecasts from fifteen minutes each evening to a full half-hour (ABC didn't follow suit until 1967), and most local newscasts also expanded. Walter Cronkite became the great national "anchor," imbuing events with a paternal gravity, while NBC's team of Chet Huntley and David Brinkley defined a fresh, sprightlier style of broadcast journalism. Television news was ready for the flood of images which events were about to supply.

I vividly recall the first pictures of Vietnamese monks immolating themselves; they devastated me, but it was difficult to find anyone who would acknowledge the growing folly of American involvement in Vietnam. Like a lot of younger proto-radicals at the time, I was a rebel without a cadre. Our only hope was that President Kennedy might fulfill the faith we put in him.

As the Buddhist rebellion spread in South Vietnam during fall 1963, the Army mutinied and on November 2, with at least tacit U.S. approval, assassinated Diem and Ngo. In his history of the war, Stanley Karnow reports that Kennedy heard the news while meeting with General Maxwell Taylor, chairman of the U.S. Joint Chiefs of Staff. Taylor says that the President "rushed from the room with a look of shock and dismay on his face." Perhaps it was a premonition.

When the Nathan Hale High School p.a. system announced on the morning of November 22 that Kennedy had been shot, the shock was twofold. Not only the life of a president but the possibility of a particular future had been snuffed out. And when it was announced that Kennedy had been assassinated by an alleged Communist, I felt my first frisson of political fear. For a few days, I imagined the worst— a great round-up of everyone left of Hubert Humphrey—but it didn't happen.

Those who spin elaborate conspiracy theories about Kennedy's death would do well to contemplate the plot that wasn't: the massive purge of the American Left that could have been launched with great public support and devastating effectiveness had those in power not quickly isolated Lee Harvey Oswald as a lone lunatic instead of a left-wing terrorist. Lyndon Johnson and J. Edgar Hoover may have had their own guilty reasons for this rare act of political magnanimity, but without the Warren Commission's broad exoneration of the Left, the embryonic movements of the Sixties would have aborted that day in Dallas.

After John Kennedy's funeral, you could almost feel the G-forces as history began to accelerate. America had crossed an invisible boundary line, leaving behind the familiar landscape of postwar certainties and hurtling blindly toward an unknown destination.

President Johnson tried to restore a sense of order and confidence, and he knew that the nation's grief was not inexhaustible. He would have to move quickly to expand on the New Deal before Republicans and Dixiecrats would openly resume the obstructionism which had frustrated Kennedy. Johnson set out to accomplish everything his predecessor had proposed, and then some. His first months were truly breathtaking, beginning with his declaration of "unconditional war on poverty in America." In outlining legislation which would later establish VISTA, the Office of Economic Opportunity (OEO), Head Start, and Model Cities, Johnson also proposed an $11 billion tax cut. It was all supposed to be funded through cuts in defense spending. He also revved up the engines to push through an omnibus Civil Rights Act in July 1964 and to pass Medicare the following year.

The national mood was brighter by February 7, when four lads from Liverpool arrived to begin their first U.S. tour. The Beatles had hit the top of the charts the previous year with "I Want to Hold Your Hand." Their appearance on the "Ed Sullivan Show" on February 9 was the first of many "British Invasions." The Rolling Stones arrived in the States for their first tour in June (they played Seattle on their return in December 1965), and the Beatles launched a second tour from San Francisco in August. On the 21st, they performed before an adoring throng in the Seattle Coliseum (they also played here on their fourth and final tour in 1966).

Britain's conquest of its former colonies was not limited to music: Mary Quant sent hemlines upwards toward waistlines with the miniskirt and Carnaby Street couturiers defined a new, vaguely Edwardian "Mod" style—epitomized by "The Avengers" John Steed and Emma Peel, who hit American TV screens in 1966—to which the working class replied with a rebellious "Rocker" mode.

Back in the States, Johnson's civil rights initiatives, including a new Voting Rights law, seemed to add heat for mounting demands rather than placate advocates. Activists seemed to ask, if this much could be done, how much more might be accomplished with a little more pressure? Seattle faced the first test of its own commitment to civil rights with a March 10 referendum on the open housing ordinance. The opposition was led in large part by Dorm Braman, a member of the city council also running for mayor on the same ballot, who framed the issue as an attack on private property rights. I was appalled when Braman presented these arguments to my current affairs class (it should be noted that in 1959, the State Supreme Court had voided a pioneering 1957 state law against housing discrimination also on the grounds of violating private property rights.) Even reliable progressives such as *Argus Magazine* bought this reasoning, and so did two-thirds of the electorate. Braman was elected and open housing was defeated, along with the "COMET" proposal to halt Seattle Transit's plan for scrapping electric trolleys. Almost unnoticed, the King County Commissioners adopted an open housing ordinance, although few minorities could afford homes in the suburbs.

Another local civil rights issue also made headlines that March, when actor Marlon Brando was arrested with Puyallup tribal leader Bob Satiacum while exercising Native American treaty rights to fish without state interference at Frank's Landing on the Nisqually River. Brando was the first of many celebrities (including Dick Gregory and

Jane Fonda) to dip nets in support of the Indian fishing rights campaign, led then by Hank Adams and Bruce Wilkie, and the issue would
not be resolved until the Boldt Decision a decade later.

The following month, a new face appeared on the city's newstands:
Seattle magazine. The publication was the pet of Stimson Bullitt, son
of KING Broadcasting founder and liberal matriarch Dorothy Bullitt.
Stim was an attorney, failed Democratic candidate for Congress (which
inspired his famous book, *To Be a Politician),* and chief executive at
KING. Many credit him and associate Ancil Payne for establishing
KING-TV's long-lived dominance of broadcast news. Stim also
launched the innovative KING Screen documentary film unit, let Irving Clark Jr. introduce audiences to a liberal version of "hot talk"
radio, and was among the first, if not the first, broadcasters to editori-
alize against the war in Vietnam.

But Stim Bullitt's secret dream was to publish a magazine in Seattle on a par with Norman Cousins' *Saturday Review.* He initiated
discussions with Peter Bunzel, a veteran of the Time-Life organization, as early as 1957. Bunzel, then associate editor of *Life,* finally
agreed in 1963, but with great skepticism about Seattle and its appetite for real journalism. Bunzel made an immediate impression on
Seattle, not all to the good. He later admitted, "I was rather stuffy, I
fear, in interviewing candidates for editorial work." Indeed, he mostly
imported talent from the East. When asked why, he is said to have
replied, "Because it is easier to teach people from New York about
Seattle than it is to teach people from Seattle how to write." Over the
magazine's six and a half years, Bunzel recruited a remarkable stable of
talent from both East and West, including writers Tom Robbins, David
Brewster, Pat Douglas, Frank Chin, Ed Leinbacher, Daniel Jack
Chasan, James Halpin, and Bruce Chapman, photographer Frank
Denman, graphic designer Terry Heckler, and marketeers Don Dudley
and Gordon Bowker, to name just a few who would go on to contrib-
ute to shaping Seattle's journalistic, cultural, and political life.

The war in Vietnam faded from view during 1964 as the generals
in Saigon consolidated their regime and Johnson and Ho Chi Minh
secretly probed each other's position to see if a settlement was possible. Meanwhile, in April, Johnson named a new commander for
American forces in Vietnam: Gen. William Westmoreland.

The war was not forgotten entirely, however. Republicans accused Johnson of disguising the real extent of U.S. involvement (which he was) and Arizona Sen. Barry Goldwater, who began campaigning for the Republican nomination for president in January, demanded a more aggressive policy to go in and win the war quickly. At the same time, on the opposite end of the political spectrum, the Progressive Labor Party (a doctrinaire but effective Maoist group which split off from the U.S. Communist Party in 1962) also saw political capital in Vietnam and staged the nation's first antiwar demonstration in New York City, on "Loyalty Day," May 2, 1964.

In so doing, PLers were far ahead of the larger but more diffuse Students for a Democratic Society. SDS was focused on aiding SNCC by building a multiracial, class-based coalition with white workers in the North. Stokely Carmichael and Tom Hayden had agreed to this project, dubbed the Economic Research and Action Project (ERAP), the previous August. It reflected both a leftward evolution of SDS's thinking and SNCC's deepening ambivalence about the value of white participation in Southern organizing.

Previous pilgrimages by white liberal students to the South had left sore feelings. Confident, educated, often wealthy and a little cocky, many of these "volunteers" intimidated their black comrades, who could not match their skills and resources—or retreat north when things got tough. Tensions rose as legions of white liberals and leftists poured south for the "Freedom Summer" of 1964.

Inevitably, there was violence. On June 21, white civil rights volunteers Michael Schwerner and Andrew Goodman and their black companion James Chaney disappeared while driving near Philadelphia, Mississippi. An FBI informant led federal agents to a shallow grave near a dam, where their mutilated bodies were found on August 4. The national outrage was compounded when the FBI quickly named twenty-one suspects, including the sheriff, whom local juries refused to convict in repeated trials.

The incident created a curious backlash among black SNCC organizers, whose comrades had been brutalized and killed for decades with scant public notice or reaction. Why did the nation rise up indignantly only when it was whites who caught the brunt of racist violence? Was this not just another manifestation of a more subtle, pervasive bigotry? SNCC workers began to regard their white comrades as latter-day carpetbaggers, and deciding that their help was both too dangerous and too disruptive, they sent them home.

During the summer, racial tensions in the North finally boiled over. Harlem exploded on July 18, followed two days later by riots in Bedford-Stuyvesant. Over the next two weeks, riots broke out in Rochester, New York; Jersey City, Patterson, and Elizabeth, New Jersey; Philadelphia; and the Chicago suburb of Dixmoor. Some activists began to use a new word to describe themselves—"black"—and coupled it with other words: liberation, nationalism, and power.

Chapter 5:
Eve of
Destruction

Employers will love this
generation. They aren't
going to press any
grievances . . . There aren't
going to be any riots.
—**Clark Kerr (1959)**

I n August 1964, President Johnson made two historic miscalculations which would shape the balance of the Sixties and undo his dreams of a "Great Society."

On August 2, the destroyer USS *Maddox* exchanged gunfire with North Vietnamese patrol boats in the Gulf of Tonkin. Two days later, the President told the American people over national TV, the *Maddox* and a second destroyer, the USS *Turner Joy,* were again attacked. This second engagement, it is now known, was a complete fabrication and the first incident greatly exaggerated. With U.S. support, South Vietnam had begun raiding the northern coast. The *Maddox* and *Turner Joy* were stationed off shore to "light up" North Vietnamese radar by simulating attacks, and thereby provide South Vietnamese ships with targets. The North Vietnamese did not know they were engaging U.S. ships, but for Johnson it was enough to prove aggression in requesting congressional authority to prosecute the war "by any means necessary." The House agreed unanimously on August 7 and only two U.S. Senators, Oregon's Wayne Morse and Alaska's Ernest Gruening, dissented. Vietnam was still so low on the national political radar that passage of the Gulf of Tonkin Resolution didn't even rate front-page coverage in many newspapers.

Johnson's second miscalculation came when the Democratic National Convention assembled in Atlantic City on August 25. Fannie Lou Hamer and others brought a rump Mississippi Freedom Democratic Party delegation to the convention and demanded to be seated instead of the official all-white delegation, elected under rules which excluded black participation. It was a crucial test for Johnson, the party, and the cause of reform. They flunked.

Johnson sought a compromise with the seating of two token MFDP delegates and appointed Sen. Hubert Humphrey, floor manager for the new Civil Rights Act and Vice President-apparent, to be his liaison with the movement. Humphrey in turn enlisted the aid of senior civil rights leaders to pressure the Mississippi activists into an accommodation. The MFDP felt betrayed, and left Atlantic City disgusted with both white and black liberals. Meanwhile, the official Mississippi delegation was seated, and then walked out.

Atlantic City embittered the youngest and most idealistic members of SNCC and the civil rights movement. For many, it slammed the door not only on the Democratic Party, but on liberals in general, on reform, on any future trust in whites, and on the goal of integration itself. Civil rights became a meaningless term, for black people were on their own, and only they could defend and advance their own interests.

In retrospect, knowing that Johnson would win two months later in an historic landslide, one wonders why he didn't support the MFDP's just demands. But Johnson did not treat his victory as a certainty and he was facing a virtual secession of Southern Democrats led by Governor George Wallace, who had racked up impressive votes in the midwestern and northern primaries. Further, Johnson needed the support of Southern Democrats in the House and Senate to advance both his domestic agenda and his expanding war in Vietnam.

A new front opened that fall as the first wave of the Baby Boom hit the nation's campuses. On October 19, Jack Weinberg set up a card table near the entrance of the Berkeley campus of the University of California to recruit volunteers for CORE activities in the South. Since this was unauthorized, the administration summoned the campus police to remove him. Weinberg did not go peacefully and yelled for help. More and more students began to arrive, until 700 surrounded the squad car containing him. Mario Savio climbed on the car's roof and railed against the university's presumed *in loco parentis* guardianship of student politics and morality. Students refused to move for thirty-two hours, and when they finally dispersed, they knew this was only the first engagement in a new movement.

Weinberg became famous for uttering the caveat, "You can't trust anybody over 30," but Savio's oratory is what really galvanized the Free Speech Movement. Like the Port Huron Statement of two years earlier, his words expressed a mounting impatience among college students with the status quo on and off campus. He told an FSM rally on December 2: "There is a time when the operation of the machine becomes so odious, makes you so sick at heart, that you can't take part; you can't even passively take part, and you've got to put your bodies upon the gears and upon the wheels, upon the levers, upon all the apparatus and you've got to make it stop. And you've got to indicate to the people who run it, to the people that own it, that unless you're free, the machines will be prevented from working at all."

The paradox of Berkeley is that it was an attack on traditional liberalism, epitomized by the modern university, which coincided with liberalism's apotheosis in Lyndon Johnson. As the FSM was gaining force in October, Johnson was unveiling the broad outlines of his campaign for a "Great Society" and isolating Barry Goldwater as a political atavist. Goldwater and his "conservative" advocates, including a newly converted Republican named Ronald Reagan, were widely portrayed and viewed as right-wing extremists. This did not necessarily offend the hard core of Goldwater's support; they even printed buttons to this effect.

Many of these people were not traditional Republicans at all, but were moved by a deeper radicalism which sought an alternative to the hollowness and hypocrisy of the liberal state. More than a few Goldwaterites might have agreed with Mario Savio: "The reason liberals don't understand us is because they don't realize there is evil in the world." And many leftists secretly agreed with the line from Goldwater's famous—or infamous—acceptance speech declaring, "Extremism in the defense of liberty is no vice, and moderation in the defense of justice is no virtue."

Johnson exploited such utterances, and Goldwater's refusal to rule out the use of nuclear weapons in Vietnam, to paint him as a trigger-happy warmonger. These were dangerous times: On October 16, just three weeks before the election, China exploded its first atomic bomb, and the Soviet Politburu deposed Nikita Khrushchev. And it didn't hurt that Stanley Kubrick's acerbic send-up of the apocalypse, *Dr. Strangelove, Or How I Learned to Stop Worrying and Love the Bomb,* was playing packed houses. To Goldwater's slogan, "In your heart, you know he's right," most replied sotto voce, "and in your guts, you know he's nuts."

On November 3, America went "all the way with LBJ," with the exception of Arizona and the Deep South, and Johnson amassed a record popular majority of 61 percent. Johnson's coattails were long and sturdy, towing four new Democratic congressmen into office from Washington, including future Speaker of the House Tom Foley and future U.S. Sen. Brock Adams.

A few Republicans bucked the tide, most notably a state legislator and engineer named Dan Evans, who defeated two-term Democratic Gov. Albert Rosellini, and Seattle City Councilman Lud Kramer, who toppled the legendary band leader-politician Vic Meyers to become secretary of state. The rest of the GOP consoled itself with bumperstickers reading, "28 Million Americans Can't Be Wrong." Many more would come to agree over the next four years.

In Seattle, most readers followed these events in the pages of the *Seattle Times,* which defied convention to lead its morning rival in circulation by nearly 60,000. The *Times's* world view was then epitomized by Ross Cunningham, a militant establishmentarian in the tradition of publishing dynasts Alden and Clarence Blethen. "Fairview Fanny" did have some good writers, however, including Don Duncan, John Hinterberger, and Mike Wyne, who would play important roles in events to come.

The *Post-Intelligencer* took on an aggressive new stance when Dan Starr took over as *P-I* publisher in November 1964. He raided the *Times* the following spring and later made its arts critic Lou Guzzo his managing editor. The paper later adopted a stylish new typographical design and opened its pages to such unexpected commentators as Lorenzo Milam and architect-preservationist Victor Steinbrueck while giving crack journalists such as Hilda Bryant and Rick Anderson the freedom to expose Seattle's seamier side, allowing Emmett Watson the latitude to roam outre Seattle, and hiring the city's first full-time rock reviewer, Patrick MacDonald. Guzzo would even write sympathetically about the student movement (April 18, 1965): "A revolution is brewing in America and most of us are too sleepy or too busy to recognize it . . . . It is a battle of minds, young minds, troubled minds with high intellect and the deep wounds of disappointment in recent history."

The war in Vietnam finally won a permanent berth on the nation's front pages in 1965. The situation in South Vietnam had begun unraveling the previous August. Then, on February 7, Vietcong units attacked an American base at Pleiku. Johnson retaliated by bombing targets in North Vietnam for the first time. The fighting quickly spread, and the U.S. began to evacuate Americans from Saigon, while the administration insisted this was not a "war." SDS and other elements of the New Left could no longer ignore the issue of the war, but they were slow to take a hard line. The first "teach-in" in March at the University of Michigan featured a polite debate over the merits of U.S. intervention. SDS raised the temperature with a march on April 17. The streets of Washington, D.C., were filled with 20,000-plus marchers demanding "Negotiations Now."

Growing anxiety about the war was indirectly fed on April 28, 1965, when Johnson ordered 14,000 troops to the Dominican Republic to prevent the ascension of Juan Bosch, whom the U.S. regarded as a Communist sympathizer. Bosch had led a successful rebellion against the military rulers who had deposed him as president following free elections in 1962. (In 1966, Bosch lost to a conservative in U.S.-supervised elections—surprise!—and U.S. troops departed.)

Berkeley was then still in the throes of its Free Speech Movement, which expanded to protest the censorship of an off-campus literary magazine called *Spider*. On March 3, John Thomson staged a one-man protest by sitting down on the steps of the Berkeley Student Union building with the word "FUCK" pinned to his shirt. He was promptly arrested, and critics renamed FSM the "Filthy Speech Movement." One Berkeley wag tried to explain that FUCK was itself a movement "For Unlawful Carnal Knowledge," and even campus conservatives got into the act by printing signs reading, "Fuck Communism."

As the FSM continued to preoccupy Berkeley, Vietnam was not

invisible. More serious radicals (then at least) such as Jerry Rubin be-gan organizing a teach-in for May 21, 1965, under the ad hoc banner of the "Vietnam Day Committee." Tens of thousands jammed the campus stadium to hear speeches by independent journalist I. F. Stone, pacifist David Dellinger, pediatrician Dr. Benjamin Spock, Socialist leader Norman Thomas, comedian Dick Gregory, SNCC leader Bob Moses, Zen popularizer Alan Watts, novelist Norman Mailer, and *Realist* editor Paul Krassner, among others.

Events began to escalate rapidly in more ways than one. On June 17, Johnson ordered giant Boeing-built B-52 bombers to carry out their first raids over North Vietnam. Two days later, Air Vice Marshal Nguyen Kao Ky became premier of South Vietnam and brought its quarrelsome military under a measure of control. Meanwhile, Gen-eral Westmoreland demanded a minimum of 125,000 more U.S. troops to prosecute the war.

Johnson was poised on the brink of all-out war, and the CIA (of all people!) begged him not to take the next step. In a memo dated July 23, 1965, and only declassified in 1994, it warned the President that the war was unwinnable. The CIA noted with unwonted accu-racy that strategic bombing raids and troop deployments would not undermine Hanoi's confidence in ultimate "victory through a combi-nation of a deteriorating South Vietnamese army morale and effec-tiveness, a collapse of the anti-Communist government in Saigon, and an exhaustion of the U.S. will to persist."

The President did not listen to this advice. On July 28, Johnson finally told the nation that "this is really war." He gambled that it would be politically safer to double the draft than to call up reservists, most of whom were family men. On paper, it probably made sense.

Civil rights violence intensified during 1965. The most promi-nent victim of all was Malcolm X, shot and killed by Black Muslims as he addressed an audience in New York's Audubon Theater on Feb-ruary 21. The following month, Alabama police and bigots attacked Martin Luther King's Freedom March from Selma to the state capital of Montgomery, and President Johnson had to call out federal troops to protect them. Fifty thousand finally rallied in Montgomery on March 25, but their sense of victory was short-lived. Three Klansmen isolated Viola Liuzzo, a white organizer from Detroit, and killed her.

In the wake of the previous year's rejection of open housing legislation, race relations in Seattle were surprisingly calm. On the advice his new deputy, a savvy Irish pol from the East named Ed Devine, Mayor Braman had appointed the city's first black municipal court judge, Charles Z. Smith, the previous November. Braman began softening his early opposition to accepting federal antipoverty funds and tried to make peace with civil rights leaders. The cause of integration suffered a tragic blow on May 17, 1965, when a private plane piloted by Seattle businessman Sidney Gerber and carrying Seattle City Councilman Wing Luke and Gerber's secretary, Kay Ladue, disappeared over the Cascades. The wreckage was not found for years, and another Asian American was not elected to the City Council until 1969.

Race relations in Seattle took an ugly turn early on the morning of June 20, when an off-duty policeman shot and killed a black man, Robert Reese. The incident began in the International District's Linyen Restaurant at about 1:30 a.m. According to press reports, two white off-duty officers, Franklyn Junell and Harold Larsen, arrived well-liquored and armed for a late dinner with their wives. They looked at the mostly black and Asian clientele and began grousing loudly about having to eat with such people. Several blacks objected and fists started flying, in which the officers—whose identities were unknown to their antagonists—got the worst of the exchange. Both sides called for reinforcements. In a second confrontation outside the restaurant, Larsen fired on two blacks as they tried to drive away, killing the passenger, Reese. On August 1, an inquest ruled the homicide "excusable," and King County's Republican prosecutor, Charles O. Carroll, charged four blacks and one police officer with assault.

Only days later, on August 11, racial tensions in Los Angeles exploded. The arrest of Marquette Frye triggered a week of rioting in the Watts section of Los Angeles, killing thirty-four and causing $200 million in damage. The nation was stunned, and not a little frightened. But it didn't faze a King County jury which convicted four blacks of assault in the Reese incident on August 18, when the ruins of Watts were still smoldering. The police officer also charged was acquitted on August 26. Angry blacks occupied City Hall, and Mayor Braman promised a review of police training. The Rev. Peter Raible condemned the mounting evidence of official indifference to racial justice as "the shame of Seattle."

Other events captured the city's attention during the spring and summer of 1965, beginning with a serious earthquake, registering 6.5 on the Richter Scale, on April 29. The temblor killed five and caused millions of dollars in damage; among the casualties was the UW's venerable Meany Hall, which later had to be demolished.

And then there was Namu, an orca bull (originally misidentified as female) which some gillnetters snared on June 25 near the eponymous Canadian bay. Ted Griffin, who owned the "Seattle Marine Aquarium" on pier 56, bought the animal for $8,000 and began towing it to Elliott Bay in a floating pen. It arrived on July 27 and became a major attraction. Griffin went on to capture scores of additional killer whales over the years, which prompted growing public uneasiness and finally federal protection for the animals. It came too late for Namu, who died in his pen on July 9, 1966.

Boeing was beginning to feel like an endangered species itself. On September 21, 1965, Defense Secretary Robert McNamara announced that he was awarding the coveted contract for the C-5A heavy transport jet to Lockheed, not Boeing. It was the latest in a string of bidding rebuffs, beginning with the controversial rejection in 1962 of Boeing's bid to build a new "TFX" tactical bomber-fighter for both the Air Force and Navy. Later Congressional investigations, led by an irate Scoop Jackson, demonstrated that McNamara had overruled military experts to give the contract for the future F-111 to General Dynamics. Next, in December 1963, the Pentagon, under budgetary pressure from the White House, sent the "Dyna-Soar" project and 4,000 local Boeing jobs (including my dad's) into extinction. This vehicle was a winged, reusable space bomber to be launched atop a Titan II missile, and in some ways constituted a precursor of the Space Shuttle. Finally, in August 1965, Douglas was picked over Boeing for a $1.5 billion contract to build a Manned Orbiting Laboratory for the Air Force. This project was also later scrubbed in a policy decision which give NASA responsibility for all manned space projects.

The *Seattle P-I* complained that McNamara's Pentagon had never picked Boeing for a major weapons system. This was technically true, but the "Lazy B" still enjoyed substantial federal business from both the Pentagon and NASA. It was building the Minuteman solid-fuel ICBM which became the backbone of the nation's ballistic missile arsenal, and the giant Saturn V booster for the Apollo Project, among other rocket and satellite systems. The Navy picked Boeing to develop a fleet of hydrofoil patrol boats, the Air Force was buying scores of KC-135 jet tankers and constantly upgrading Boeing-built B-52s, and the Vietnam war provided a big customer for Boeing's Vertol Division, builders of the CH-55 "Chinook" transport helicopter. And Boeing was in the running for what was then the juiciest contract around, development of a national supersonic transport for NASA and civilian airlines.

Whatever McNamara's aversion to Boeing, he may have been doing the company a favor in the long run. Boeing made lemonade out of the C-5A loss by recycling preliminary design work into development of a new kind of civilian airliner, the 747 "jumbo jet." Meanwhile, Boeing's new 727 tri-jet was selling like hotcakes, and president William Allen announced that Boeing's Puget Sound payroll would increase to 75,000 workers in 1966.

Vietnam meant sales to Boeing, but student opposition to the war was escalating in lockstep with American involvement. In August 1965, the Berkeley Vietnam Day began a series of demonstrations trying to block the troop trains which rumbled through the city from the Oakland Induction Center. The war arrived at the UW on October 9, when some 200 students attended the first campus teach-in on the subject. A week later, the U.S. Senate Internal Security Committee linked the "teach-in movement" with the "Communist propaganda apparatus."

Actually, Communists had little to do with the early opposition, and the nascent movement couldn't even agree on whether its goal was negotiations or withdrawal or what. Participants decided they just wanted to "End the War Now," and this became the rallying cry for the first set of coordinated national demonstrations, beginning with a Vietnam Day march from Berkeley to Oakland on October 15. Oakland police turned back 10,000 protesters at the city limits.

They returned the next day and were confronted with good, red-blooded, patriotic Hell's Angels who beat the shit out of scores of marchers. At the same moment, in New York City, spectators attacked and beat some of 10,000 protesting the war. Among the latter was one David J. Miller who held up his draft card and set it afire for the benefit of attending news cameras. This act had become a federal crime the previous August 31st, and FBI arrested Miller two days later.

Also on October 16, Seattle experienced its first antiwar march, led by the UW SDS and "Seattle Committee to End the War in Vietnam" (SCEWV). I was among the nervous 350 or so who gathered in front of the Federal Court House that morning. We marched down two lanes of Fourth Avenue, herded by motorcycle police and taunted as Communists and traitors by passing motorists, to a noon rally beneath the old Monorail station at Westlake Mall. Our every move was photographed by men with crewcuts who aimed cameras at us from doorways and rooftops.

An ugly crowd surrounded us at Westlake, and they tried to drown out our speakers by singing the Mickey Mouse Club anthem. When UW professor Paul Brass began his remarks, a man rushed up and doused him with red paint. He later identified himself to the press as, paradoxically, "Joe Freedom." He turned out to be one of Brass' students. There were a few scuffles when the rally broke up, but all of us got home with our skin, if not our nerves, intact.

The press coverage was nasty and the public response was hostile. Both the *P-I* and the *Times* editorialized that students were allowing themselves to be duped and exploited by Communists. The Seattle Jaycees urged everyone to turn their lights on during the day to endorse the war, and 10,000 pro-war anti-protesters marched in New York City.

The violence in Vietnam took quantum leaps of intensity, as the U.S. engaged the Vietcong at Pleiku and Ia Drang. Westmoreland claimed victory, pointing to the swelling "body count" of enemy (and often civilian) dead. Americans were also dying: 240 fell in a single week in November, more than had died in the previous year. McNamara boasted, if that is the right word, that "we have stopped losing the war," but Sen. Edward Kennedy, passing through Seattle, warned, "We are deluding ourselves to think there is going to a quick solution in Vietnam."

The seeming depravity of American policy drove some to burn more than their draft cards. While sitting below McNamara's Pentagon window on November 2, Norman Morrison poured gasoline over himself and lit a match. Two other pacifists immolated themselves soon after.

On December 20, B-52s began bombing North Vietnam's primary seaport at Haiphong. Three days later, President Johnson halted all bombing in the north as a "gesture of peace." On Christmas Day, Tom Hayden and Quaker activist Staughton Lynd arrived in Hanoi on the first of many such pilgrimages.

The year ended with 184,000 U.S. troops deployed in Vietnam, and a combat death toll of 1,350 accumulated since the U.S. started counting in 1961. Most had fallen in the past six months.

Everyone knew much worse was to come. The national mood was summed up by the surprise hit song of 1965, written by P. F. Sloan and intoned in urgent, rasping tones by Barry McGuire: "And tell me over and over again, my friend, you don't believe we're on the eve of destruction."

Chapter 6:
On the Ave

*The hippies are acting out
what the Beats wrote.*

—Gregory Corso

By the fall of 1965, the inspiration of the Beatles and other rock stars had made long hair sufficiently popular among teenage boys that the Seattle School Board felt compelled to ban it. Shaggy locks and beards, for those who could grow them, also became more and more common on the UW campus.

A record 2,222 additional students—more than the G.I. Bill surge of 1946—matriculated that quarter at the UW. I was among the first wave of the 20 million Americans who would celebrate their eighteenth birthdays between 1964 and 1970 and commence their "higher education."

Our arrival was announced in the September 22, 1965, edition of the *University District Herald,* which warned of a new menace in the campus community: "beatniks."

Over the next several weeks, *Herald* publisher Lillian Beloine worked herself into a virtual froth over the growing numbers of idle, unkempt, possibly communistic youngsters loitering along University Way NE, the main business street near the UW better known simply as "the Ave."

I remember my first visit to the Ave one hot summer evening in 1963. My best friend John Moehring (later one of Seattle's most prolific psychedelic poster artists) and I stepped off the bus somewhere around 43rd Street. As we started to cross the Ave, two sandal-clad, bearded men strode past us. One had just inserted a crumpled cigarette into his mouth when the other commented, "Shit, man, that looks like a penis after the struggle." Not exactly Saul on the road to Damascus, but for me an epiphany nonetheless. I was home.

John and I became regulars in the District, commuting almost nightly from our north-end homes, he on a Honda 90, I on a Lambretta

TV-200 scooter, singing Verdi duets as we cruised the Ave. Our destinations were chiefly the Pamir House, which featured folk singing in an old house at the corner of 41st and the Ave, and the Eigerwand, then a tiny hole in the wall between 42nd and 43rd specializing in rancid coffee and fiery conversation. It had originally been founded by alpinist Eric Bjornstad and his partner Jim Walcott as a hangout for mountain climbers and other outdoor enthusiasts, but the District's small cadre of bohemians and artists soon took it over.

In 1965, the Eiger moved a block south into a larger space formerly occupied by the cabaret Queequeg (which moved across the University Bridge to become the Llahngaelhyn). The clientele expanded correspondingly, and began to get noticeably younger. On warm days and evenings, a large contingent would stretch out along the wall of the adjacent Adams Forkner Funeral Parlor parking lot, strumming guitars, peddling a little weed, and generally just "making the scene."

And we never called ourselves "beatniks." Anyone halfway hip knew that Herb Caen had coined that word as a put-down. If you were "beat," you didn't need a label.

It was really all quite innocent, but not in the eyes of the establishment. The assistant King County prosecutor denounced us as "unbelievable bums" and we began to attract police attention. Weekend nights became circuses as crusaders descended on the Eiger to save us all from Satan, and a growing number of dope dealers offered to save us from the Christians.

The student editors and writers of the *UW Daily* responded quickly to the *Herald's* alarum. Deb Das wrote a sympathetic column followed by an article headlined, "Beatnik Scare: Lower Ave Draws Beards Like a Magnet." On October 15, *Daily* editor Jerry Liddell urged "coexistence" with the "Fringies." That word was new to us on the Ave, and we liked it. Soon, some clever entrepreneur printed "Fringie" buttons to make it official.

In late October, the U District YMCA/YWCA convened a panel discussion of the Fringie problem. Lillian Beloine participated, sniffing that she couldn't find the word "Fringie" in her dictionary. Also present were Liddell, Eiger co-owner Walcott, a kid who called himself "Tran," attorney and U District business Brahman C. M. "Cal" McCune, and assistant professor of philosophy John Chambless, a relatively recent transplant from Berkeley (you will hear more about the last two). Chambless had the best line of the event: "Where do the people come from who give the District a bad name? They come from the newspapers."

They also came from the Narcotics Squad. On November 2, 1965, officers raided a house in the district and arrested thirteen suspects, including Walcott, for possessing and dealing marijuana. Seattle was in the big leagues—it had a "drug problem."

Nobody regarded marijuana as much of a problem until Prohibition, or more precisely, its repeal. During the dry years, a lot of folks discovered that this ubiquitous, freely growing weed delivered a perfectly pleasant high, equal to if not better than alcohol. Relegalized breweries and distilleries did not welcome this competition, and Congress declared marijuana a "narcotic" within four years of passage of the Twenty-first Amendment. Many drugs slipped through the net, particularly as modern chemistry churned out more and more exotic compounds to alter and manipulate moods and behaviors. In the case of Lysergic Acid Diethylamide-25, LSD, it was a total accident. On April 16, 1943, in Zurich, Albert Hofmann mixed up the twenty-fifth in a series of solutions derived from a rye fungus. In the process, he absorbed some of the chemical through his skin, and promptly took off on the world's first "acid trip." At the other end, he recorded in his diary, "a remarkable but not unpleasant state of intoxication . . . characterized by an intense stimulation of the imagination, an altered state of awareness of the world."

Word of Hofmann's excursion on LSD-25 spread slowly through scientific and academic circles. Interest heightened in the 1950s as psychic explorers such as Aldous Huxley sought a chemical philosopher's stone, and the CIA looked for a cheap way to zap the enemy without busting up all the furniture. The CIA began experimenting with LSD in 1953 under the code name "MK-ULTRA," and not every subject knowingly "volunteered."

By one route or another, the great and not-so-great were turned on. No less than Henry and Clare Booth Luce tripped out with Robert Isherwood, courtesy of Dr. Sidney Cohen, resulting in a "glowing" article on LSD in the May 27, 1957, edition of *Life*. In 1963, *Life* suddenly changed its mind and decided LSD was a menace (bum trip, Henry?). That same year, Harvard professor Timothy Leary and colleague Richard Alpert (the future Baba Ram Dass and author of *Be Here Now*) were canned by Harvard for dosing unsuspecting students. The CIA was still handing out free tickets to the beyond as late as 1965, when Abbie Hoffman took his first trip at its expense. "Say what you will about the CIA, but they had some damn good acid," he later commented.

Ken Kesey also got his first acid courtesy of the CIA in 1959, and the drug's revelations combined with his experience working in a mental ward to liberate *One Flew Over the Cuckoo's Nest*. The book's success financed a little ranch in La Honda, near San Francisco. From there, on June 14, 1964, Kesey and thirteen other "Merry Pranksters" launched off in a day-glo bus, with Neal Cassady at the wheel, on a transcontinental joy ride. On that same day the American boheme rolled over from the old hip to the new.

The beginning of the real psychedelic revolution might be most accurately dated February 21, 1965, when California narcotics agents raided an illegal meth-amphetamine laboratory operated by Augustus Owsley Stanley III. He beat the rap and decided it was safer to synthesize LSD, which was then legal. Soon, the Bay Area was awash in pure, exquisite "Owsley."

On (or about) November 27, 1965, Ken Kesey invited the world to his La Honda ranch for the first "acid test." Owsley supplied the "electric Kool-Aid," Hell's Angels mingled with would-be Miltons, and an impromptu band played rock and roll. The latter band members decided to call themselves "Grateful Dead" after a name for an ancient ballad Jerry Garcia had stumbled across in the dictionary.

By now something new was beginning to stir in the faded Victorian San Francisco neighborhood clustered around the intersection of Haight and Ashbury near Golden Gate Park. Young people promenaded in strange clothes seemingly picked up at a Global Village rummage sale: Medieval, Renaissance, Edwardian, Native American, Wild West, Navy surplus, and Grandma's attic. Odd stores and cafes were springing up with names like Blue Unicorn and Mnasidika. Roving actors calling themselves the San Francisco Mime Troupe staged impromptu, often political plays and skits in the park and on the sidewalks. Something called the Family Dog presented bands with names like Big Brother and the Holding Company and Jefferson Airplane (after blues musician Blind Thomas J.A.). They played a weird new kind of rock and roll blending pounding rhythms with floating, ethereal chords, while artists manipulated colored fluids and slides to project hallucinatory images on auditorium walls.

It didn't have a name yet, but as Charles Perry reports in his history of Haight Ashbury, what became known as "the San Francisco Style" was actually born in the spring of 1965 in Virginia City, Nevada, where Don Works, Chan Laughlin, and Mark Unobsky revived the Red Dog Saloon. The first significant band of the era, The Charlatans, got its start there, and carried the new style west to the Bay where it rooted like an alien weed.

When the Mime Troupe was busted for obscenity in August 1965, their manager, Bill Graham, was faced with the need to raise money for defense fees. He staged an "Appeal" concert dance in October, which was successful enough to inspire a second, larger event for which he rented the nearby Fillmore Auditorium. This too attracted huge crowds, which impressed photographer-activist Stewart Brand. He asked Graham to manage a January 21, 1966, event called a "Trips Festival." The concerts continued into 1966, getting wilder and weirder, and so did their posters. Wesley Wilson, a young printer without formal art training, devised a new flowing, almost organic alphabet for their posters. Later, Family Dog impresario Chet Helms started using another designer, Stanley "Mouse" Miller. Mouse briefly joined forces with Al Kelly to transform Mr. Zig-Zag into the presiding icon of the new scene and to produce several classic posters.

It all came together that summer of 1966 in the Haight—the music, the art, psychedelics, the idealism. This was the real "Summer of Love," when, in Theodore Roszak's image, the centaurs danced in the garden of the machines, celebrating a "counterculture" to transcend sterile technocracy. Many of San Francisco's older bohemians initially scoffed at these "hippies," a put-down for pseudo-beat poseurs, but the targets of their scorn adopted the name as a badge of honor.

Reports and artifacts of these wondrous developments began trickling north in 1966, borne mainly by hitchhikers and troubadours. The media, thank god, hadn't tuned in yet, but the authorities were also hearing rumors of bizarre happenings down south. Local poet Jan Tissot decided to have a little fun with establishment paranoia. He joined with John Spellman, a professor of Sanskrit at the UW, and artist Larry Van Over, among others, to announce that Seattle would host the Second Annual Bohemian Festival on March 17, 1966. The *Herald* responded with satisfying panic, as did the police and other guardians of public decency. It was a prank from the beginning (although Spellman tried to get Allen Ginsberg to Seattle) to the end, when the *Herald* reported, "Fringie Festival fizzles."

That June, the *P-I* dispatched Tom Robbins and cartoonist Ray Collins to Berkeley to attend and report on a UC-sponsored symposium on LSD. Others of us conducted our research closer to home. Bill H. (you'll understand my discretion in these matters), a washboard player living in the Pamir House, introduced me to LSD during the summer. It was wonderful, but the cliché is true: you really do see paisleys. Bill also introduced me to another chemical wonder, an oral amphetamine called "Desoxyn" which lit my brain on fire but, unlike acid, let me write and draw at the same time. It was a great remedy for what is now called "attention deficit disorder." Of course, I also sampled grass, but frankly, it usually put me to sleep.

John Moehring and I shared an apartment in the infamous "Monarch Annex" on Brooklyn. The Monarch and its adjacent building were decrepit but soulful piles which attracted an eclectic mix of tenants second in reputation only to "Roach Manor," another ancient apartment house demolished a few years earlier for the University Bookstore parking lot. I shuttled between the Monarch and the Eigerwand, with an occasional cameo appearance on campus.

My main accomplishment at the UW was to make a lifelong friend in one William Stonehill, known to all as "Fu" because of his mastery of Chinese and other Asian tongues (he has lived in Japan since 1979). Fu was a native Chicagoan and the eccentric offspring of a union between an ophthalmologist and an Adlerian psychiatrist. He was then recovering from a horrendous auto accident which had broken virtually every bone in his body. His skeleton was reassembled by an Armenian-born orthopedic surgeon who, by virtue of some bad experiences as a field surgeon during World War I, didn't believe in anaesthetics.

Fu and I were rivals in freshman English, but became fast friends off-campus. Of many adventures, one deserves telling:

In the Sixties, importation of goods made in the People's Republic of China to the U.S. was punished with stiff fines and imprisonment, but they were sold legally in Canada. I wanted to acquire the works of Mao and other Communist literature only available from Peking's English-language press, and Fu wanted to purchase some Chinese musical instruments, so we plotted a smuggling expedition to Vancouver, B.C.

At the time, I drove a strange little car called an Isetta, little more than a four-wheeled BMW motorcycle with a metal egg for a cabin. It had one door, which was the entire front of the vehicle. We decided that there was enough room under the seat to contain our contraband, and set off for Canada at a top speed of 50 mph.

In Vancouver, we tracked down the "China Store," and acquired our loot. Everything fit in our hidey hole except a banjo-like instrument, which we would have to declare upon re-entering the U.S. On the way south, Fu concocted a cover story involving a rare wood to "prove" that this instrument could only come from Taiwan.

The U.S. border guards at Blaine took one look at us and waved us over to the Customs office. Fu and I took the instrument and a handful of British Penguin editions and set them on a high counter for inspection. The guard opened the instrument case and studied its contents. "What do you call this thing?"

Fu gave a name which I no longer recall and explained, "As you can see, sir, it is made from the rare polonius wood found only on the island of Taiwan." The guard was unimpressed. "I've seen one of these things before, back when I was in India during the war. This is one of them see-tars."

I was delighted with this unexpected turn of fortune, but Fu was too proud of his cover story to let it drop. "No, officer, you are mistaken. This is definitely Chinese." By this point I was furiously kicking Fu's shin. He finally got the message and retreated. "Perhaps, you are correct after all. It appears I have been duped." We paid our $2.50 in duty and got the hell out of there as fast as the Isetta's tiny wheels could propel us. This was the beginning and end of our careers as smugglers.

The summer passed pleasantly in the District and the Haight, but things were not so peaceful in the Central Area, where the local CORE and the new Central Area Committee for Civil Rights were battling de facto segregation in the public schools. That spring, Seattle's population peaked at 574,000, of which blacks constituted more than 40,000. In just the past decade, the black citizenry had grown by more than 70 percent, compared to a 3 percent increase in whites, yet blacks found themselves confined to the Central Area and Rainier Valley, where the schools were widely acknowledged to be the worst in the district. Exasperated with the pace of reform under the new superintendent, Forbes Bottomly, activists announced a boycott for March 31 and April 1. They took a leaf from the successful Chicago and New York boycotts of 1963 and 1964 and set up ad hoc "Freedom Schools" to teach the kids who stayed away.

On the boycott's first day, 10 percent of the district's 93,000 pupils failed to attend school—but Central Area schools reported a 30 percent drop. On the second day, boycott participation rose to 11 percent overall, and 37 percent in the Central Area. It was enough to make the school board intensify efforts aimed at promoting voluntary busing.

Ironically, by this point many on the Left had now repudiated integration altogether, dividing the civil rights movement into two overtly hostile camps. The final split came in June, as James Meredith began his one-man pilgrimage from the Tennessee border to Jackson, Mississippi. One June 6, three days into his walk, he was felled by a sniper's bullet. Thousands took up the march and arrived in Jackson on June 21. There, SNCC director Stokely Carmichael shocked some and mobilized others by calling for "Black Power."

CORE's new director, Floyd McKissick, had also reached the conclusion that blacks would have to make their own civil rights revolution, and the organization endorsed black power on July 1. The next day, in Baltimore, the Urban League and SNCC formally signed on. The day after that, the NAACP loudly and officially rejected black power as reverse racism and "reverse Hitlerism."

Meanwhile, inner cities were erupting across the nation. During 1966, forty-three U.S. cities experienced riots in which eleven died, more than 400 were injured, and 3,000 were arrested. Not even M. L.

King Jr. escaped the violence: he was stoned by whites in Chicago during a civil rights march. As hopes for peaceful integration faded, black power's star rose. On October 15, the cause entered a new phase of militancy when Huey Newton and Bobby Seale joined in Oakland to establish the Black Panther Party.

The war in Vietnam continued to escalate as well. Johnson abandoned his "peace offensive" on January 31, 1966, and carried the bombing into the heart of Hanoi. The Selective Service System eliminated deferments for married men and began to scrutinize "2-S" deferments for college students more closely in order to sate Westmoreland's appetite for troops. The year ended with 385,000 in Vietnam, supported by another 90,000 at sea and in Thailand. Combat deaths doubled from the previous year and topped 5,000.

The cost increased in other ways. The budget for the war ran $10 billion over estimates, and the inflation fueled by massive spending for both "guns and butter" resulted in a 3.4 percent rise in the cost of living in the final two months of 1966. Yet, Gallup reported that 54 percent of Americans supported the war and Johnson's handling of it.

Chapter 7:
Medium Rare

*Freedom of speech is the
right to cry "theater" in a
crowded fire.*

—Abbie Hoffman

In the fall of 1966, two remarkable couples made their appearance
in Seattle: Jack and Sally Delay, and Robby and Susan Stern.
Jack Delay was a former Air Force cadet who resigned in disgust
with the war and the cheating scandals at the Air Force academy. He
was built like a pitbull terrier but had the sweet disposition of a slightly
manic Labrador. Sally was a thin, wiry beauty who matched Jack in
intelligence and compassion for the growing number of counterculture orphans beginning to assemble in the District.

When the venerable Mrs. Cutz relocated her stock and pride of
felines on the lower Ave as "Puss & Books," the Delays took over her
old "Bookworm" storefront on 42nd and turned it into an informal
day care center for the dispossessed. They also opened their home—a
former Navy refrigerator barge converted into an enormous floating
home and dubbed the *Rapid Transit*—to homeless kids.

Jack and Sally were inspired by San Francisco's "Diggers" (the
name comes from a communal sect in seventeenth century England),
who were then beginning to feed and counsel the Haight's growing
population of walking wounded. They incorporated a similar group
in Seattle called "The Brothers." Among the earliest members was an
inseparable pair, David Jensen and Dennis Stallings, who became fixtures in the Bookworm.

At about this same time, Robert and Susan Stern arrived from
Syracuse, he to take the law and she, social work. Robby was a natural
leader: handsome, serious but not humorless, who viewed the war,
civil rights, and the Ave with increasing concern but no particular
ideology. Susan was petite, vivacious, and a little wild. For a while, the

Sterns, Delays, and I became a close quintet, sharing dope, dreams, and ideas to set the world's problems right.

Ostensibly, I was attending college again, but most of my energy went into drawing cartoons for the *Daily* and studying drama at the Cornish Institute for the Allied Arts under the direction of Dale Meador. I briefly lived with Dale and his wife, a painter, in a sprawling Capitol Hill apartment (where the Safeway now stands) and got a taste of true bohemian life, complete with dinners of cheap red wine, baguettes, salami, and pepperoncini—the best dining experiences of my life.

I met Dale, who went on to found an experimental theater in Pioneer Square, via Bill Billings. Bill was what we shall call a street entrepreneur; tall, almost skeletally thin, he dressed entirely in black and dispensed his wares from a leather attaché case of the same color. He was both a fixture on the Ave and its spiritual proprietor. As the District began to fill with strangers, Bill surveyed the scene with apprehension. "Who are all these people," he demanded to know, "and what are they doing in my living room?!"

The reaction of others was even more negative. California legislators decided on October 6, 1966, to ground their high-flying citizens by ruling LSD a controlled substance. Washington followed suit in the new year (rebuffing a proposal from one legislator to establish centers where the drug would be dispensed for free to thwart a black market) as did other states and the federal government. Some found solace when the *Berkeley Barb* reported that you could get high smoking banana skins, but it was a hoax. This did not prevent the Dallas police from arresting two hippies for possession of dried banana skins. They told the police that they planned to inhale them for dessert after smoking a lamb chop.

Also in fall 1966, Republicans rebounded from the debacle of 1964 to post major gains in Congress. California voters elected Ronald Reagan governor that year, and voters here elected a Republican majority to the state senate. Many of the latter were a new breed of "conservative," led by King County GOP chair Ken Rogstad, which created enormous tensions with Governor Evans and his liberal state chair, Montgomery "Gummy" Johnson, who pressed for environmental laws and a state income tax.

That fall, the nation's campuses were unusually quiet. Mario Savio led Berkeley students in expelling Navy recruiters, and the UW SDS picketed Vice President Humphrey during a late September visit to inspect the mockup of the SST that Boeing had been selected to build for NASA. But for most, opposition to the war was an act of individual conscience, not political ideology, and the first students, including Russel Wills and Mike Leavy in Seattle, began choosing jail over induction. One hundred presidents of college student bodies (but not the ASUW's Judd Kirk) signed a letter on December 29 to President Johnson, telling him that "unless this conflict is eased, the United States will find many of her most loyal and courageous young people choosing to go to jail rather than bear their country's arms."

I registered my own protest with a display of political antiwar cartoons in the UW HUB, including a montage of Vietnam war images titled "A War Like No Other." As a result, I found myself being recruited by Stephanie Coontz to join the Young Socialist Alliance, which was beginning to guide planning for the following year's "Mobilization Against the War."

The main event that fall took place a block off campus, in a loft above the Coffee Corral on the corner of 42nd and U Way. There, on October 10, the "Free University of Seattle" opened for classes on everything from Anarchism to Zen. Its primary organizer was Miriam Rader, daughter of university professor Melvin Rader (target of McCarthyists in the 1950s) and then a Trot, with help from Ron Richardson, Deb Das, and Clay Grubb, among others. UW professors volunteered, including Alex Gottfried, Frank Williston, and historian Giovanni Costigan—the *éminence grise* of Seattle liberalism. Other lecturers included Unitarian minister Paul Sawyer, graduate student Paul Dorpat, biologists John Gallant and Henry Erlich, writer Tom Robbins, cartoonist Ray Collins, and an all-sorts collection of leftists. The Free University collected Seattle's dissidents into a critical mass for the first time in decades. It was too hot for the fire department, which shut the building down after one day. Repairs were made and the FUS initiated a chain reaction which energized the city's Left and counterculture.

By the beginning of 1967 the establishment media had begun to notice that something unexpected, possibly untoward was happening among America's youth. *Time* magazine named "Twenty-five and Under" as its "Man of the Year." The seminal event of January was the "Human Be-In," held in San Francisco's Golden Gate Park on the 14th. It was a communal celebration joining music, poetry, psychedelics, art, and politics, and bridging the beats, represented foremost by Allen Ginsberg, and the hippies, represented by a throng of 20,000 plus. Antiwar and radical leaders were also invited to speak, but most agreed that they laid a bum trip on the gathering.

News of the event inspired Abbie Hoffman, who was then running a store for SNCC selling handcrafts from the South in Greenwich Village, to organize a be-in in Central Park. Thirty thousand attended on March 26, and Los Angeles staged a be-in on the same day. The Brothers organized Seattle's first be-in at Cowen Park on April 1 (and the *Helix* newspaper sponsored the first of many such tribal picnics at Volunteer Park on April 30).

By now the San Francisco scene had developed its own cultural and economic infrastructure of head shops, coffee houses, musicians, impresarios, dope dealers, miscellaneous entrepreneurs, and "underground newspapers" to spread the news. Seattle was behind the curve, but not by much.

As 1967 began, KRAB-FM and the Free University constituted the institutional foundation for the local counterculture, and several strong bands were now performing regularly in local clubs, including the Magic Fern, Daily Flash, Time Machine, and Chrome Syrcus. The last achieved almost instant international fame by providing the music for Robert Joffrey's *Astarte,* the world's first "rock ballet." There was enough happening in town, and in the District especially, to warrant an independent medium to report it. Fortunately, technology stepped in with a new and cheap way to do it: the photo offset press.

Most newspapers and magazines at the time were printed the old-fashioned way, with type set either by hand or in lead slugs by giant Linotype machines. Compositors then assembled each page line by line, with etched plates for illustrations and photographs, which were reduced to "halftones" to create the illusion of shading via tiny dots of differing sizes and densities. It was a cumbersome, expensive, and time-consuming process.

In the Sixties, a new technology began to take hold, initially for low-quality business communications. This process began by taking a high contrast photograph of a pre-designed page. From this, the printer developed a negative in which "white" areas were opaque and "live" images were transparent. This was laid on top of a photo-sensitive aluminum plate and exposed to light, etching the imagery onto a chemical emulsion which would then hold ink. In the press, the image was transferred to the paper via a rubber "blanket" cylinder, hence the name "offset" printing. Half-toned images of photographs could either be "pasted up" on the master layout or "stripped in" as negatives before exposing the plate.

Photo offset dramatically reduced the cost and labor required for printing, and it greatly increased the designer's freedom. Anything which could be photographed could be printed. The frames holding type and photo plates no longer dictated the final design. Type and graphics could flow, swirl, and intermingle as the designer chose, so long as sharp contrasts were maintained between positive imagery and negative space.

As A.J. Liebling observed, "Freedom of the press is guaranteed only to those who own one," and the flexibility and low cost of photo offset printing made everybody a potential publisher. It also helped to revive an independent American press, which had been suffocated since the war by consensual politics and the myth of journalistic "objectivity." New York's *Village Voice,* founded in 1955 to combat "the pieties of liberalism," was just about the only major "alternative" newspaper to hit the streets before the mid-Sixties.

Things began to accelerate in May 1964 when Art Kunkin published the first *Los Angeles Free Press* in conjunction with KFPK-FM's Renaissance Pleasure Faire. Max Scherr came along in August 1965 and founded the *Berkeley Barb* in time to give the FSM and Vietnam Day Committee its own voice. In October 1966, the counterculture acquired its own newsletter with the debut of the *Oracle,* which exploited the freedom of offset printing with psychedelic zeal. Soon, "underground newspapers"—the term was coined by the "overground" establishment press—were popping up in every major city and on or near every campus like mushrooms after a spring rain.

Seattle's first brush with the phenomenon was a short-lived, mimeographed newsletter called the *Seattle Barb* published by four members of the UW SDS in January 1967. Only a few hundred copies of four editions saw the light of day, but the *Barb's* use of profanity and its endorsement of homosexual rights stirred a massive storm. SDS, then headed by Gordon Peterson, repudiated the paper, and its publishers in turn repudiated SDS for having no sense of humor or backbone.

The University launched an investigation but concluded that no rules had been broken. Even King County Prosecutor Charles O. Carroll got into the act. He demanded the names of the students so he could charge them with obscenity, but the UW refused to release them, prompting a blistering attack from the courthouse in March. As best as I can deduce from the public record, these pioneering publishers were Bernie Yang, Jim Brown, Dave Muga, and Brian Hodel.

Even before the *Seattle Barb* incident, the arrival of papers from the Bay Area had set members of the Free University thinking about publishing a paper of their own. The seed was planted in a winter 1966 conversation between Unitarian minister Paul Sawyer and Paul Dorpat. The latter is a friendly bear of a man who had just celebrated his twenty-eighth birthday and had all but abandoned finishing his master's thesis on the semiotics of Theodore Roethke's poetry. Dorpat had been seduced by the eclectic freedom of the Free U, and ended up virtually running the joint during its 1967 winter quarter. He set about trying to plan a newspaper, and the discussions widened to include Tom Robbins; *P-I* cartoonist Ray Collins; poet and song-writer John Cunnick; artists Maryl Clemmens, Karen Warner, and Gary Eagle; UW geneticist and KRAB co-founder Jon Gallant; Dan Murphy (fresh from Nathan Hale, where he published the *Swamp Fly*); Free University "janitor" Scott White; Seattle Folk Society founder John Ullman; Seattle Jazz Society leader Lowell Richards; writer-critic Gene Johnston; and *P-I* headline editor George Geazy. The group talked in circles: Where will the money come from? Who would read it? Who would write it? Who would print it? Should they just do one, or commit to an extended run?

They couldn't even agree on a name. Dan Murphy and Ray Collins pumped for "Peeping Fred," the name given to a voyeur-flasher then stalking the UW campus. Everyone else hated the name but had no other ideas. Finally, in February, KRAB's Nancy Keith and Lorenzo

Milam dragged Paul to the Blue Moon Tavern and told him, "Just do it." There was still the problem of what to call it. Paul Dorpat remembers John Reynolds, a student of UW Far East professor John Spellman, coming by at that moment and saying to him, "Why don't you call it the 'Helix'" (after Watson and Crick's description of DNA).

The name clicked. No one was sure what *Helix* meant, but the ambiguity was part of the name's appeal. And it was a lot better than "Peeping Fred." With the name resolved, Paul announced that he was going to publish a first edition in March, with the aim of coming out biweekly after that. Anyone who wanted to help was welcome.

Paul borrowed $200 and rented a storefront on Roosevelt Way near NE 45th Street. A handful of artists and writers, and some very brave typists, began knocking together a newspaper—something which most of them had never done before. Dorpat took the completed paste-up (the physical artwork and type from which the offset negative is made) to Grange Press. They took one look and demurred. At Grange's suggestion, Paul called Peggy Goldberg's experimental "Duck Press" in Bellevue, and they bounced him to Ken Munson.

Munson was then communications director for Lodge 751 of the International Association of Machinists and Aerospace Workers, the largest union representing Boeing workers, and a veteran of Democratic politics and liberal causes. He had just purchased a big Heidelberg sheet-fed press, hired Ed Wise to run it, and set up shop in Lynnwood as, simply, "The Printers." His equipment was not as efficient as Grange's "web press," which prints on a continuous roll of paper rather than individual sheets, but he had the right answer to Paul's question: "Yes, I'd be proud to print the *Helix*."

So, on the afternoon of Thursday, March 23, the first 1,500 copies of *Helix* rolled off the press. It was printed on pastel green and pink newsprint, and true to the confusion of its origins, the cover featured three mastheads: the letters "Helix" forming the trusses of a bridge with "Seattle's Hip Rag" beneath it; block letters with childlike cartoons; and Ray Collins' stencil lettering and squiggles with a final protest, "Peeping Fred Lives." The cover also offered this editorial manifesto:

> You have in your hand the first issue of a fortnightly newspaper. It is dedicated to no cause, no interests, no point of view; it is dedicated to you.

Helix is published at 4526 Roosevelt Way Northeast in Seattle by a group of volunteer workers. Although in the University District, *Helix* is a community newspaper in the human sense and expects to be a free printed forum in the Pacific Northwest.

"Underground" papers are appearing everywhere and *Helix* will be a member of the Underground Press Syndicate. Others in the UPS are the *Los Angeles Free Press*, *Illustrated Times* of London, *East Village Other* in New York, *San Francisco Oracle*. *Helix* will imitate none of these. It will be the free newspaper of Seattle and the Northwest and will answer to their needs. *Helix* will cover arts, politics, all kinds of unnamable scenes opening up in this last third of the Century. It will establish new pictorial values in print.

Friends, your help is needed. We have some devoted volunteers who brought out this first issue—we need many more to report and write the news, work on advertising and circulation, collect money, do all kinds of things to keep the young paper on its feet. Anyone who wants to give, see us at 4526 Roosevelt Way Northeast in Seattle, Telephone ME2-9320.

The paper was trucked in Paul's 1953 Chevy pseudo-woody station wagon from Lynnwood to the *Helix* office . Scott White grabbed an armful and headed up 45th toward the Ave. Along the way he ran into me and cajoled 15 cents out of my pocket. Thus, I became the first person to buy a *Helix*.

Chapter 8:
Fiat Lux

*Jefferson and Thoreau were
the secret heroes of the
Sixties.*

—W. J. Rorabaugh

I was not part of the *Helix's* founding team, although Paul and a contingent had come to the *Rapid Transit* to brief Jack, Sally, and the rest of "The Brothers" on their plans. Frankly, I wasn't impressed—but I was also very envious; I had dreamed of doing a magazine for many years. We were also very busy at that moment.

The Bookworm had just been given its walking papers effective March 31, 1967. At virtually the same moment, the dock owner told Jack that he would have to find new moorage for his houseboat. The Pamir House was demolished to make way for a Christian Science Reading Room, and Cal McCune bought the building housing the Eigerwand and promptly evicted the coffee house. We even lost our sacred "Hippie Wall" when Adams Forkner installed a steel pike fence to prevent unlawful perching along its parking lot.

On the Ave, the business community screamed blue murder to City Hall over the swelling numbers of street people and dope dealers, and the Seattle Police responded with their accustomed delicacy and sensitivity. It was open season on any male with hair longer than a crewcut, and any female without a beehive. You couldn't get served at any restaurant and the beat patrolmen would bust you for flicking a cigarette butt into the gutter. More than one hippie found himself the recipient of a late night free ride to the city limits in a police car, along with a few punches and kicks and a warning to keep heading north. I think they called it "law and order."

We called it harassment. Jack and Sally Delay, Robby and Susan Stern, myself, and our allies on and off campus organized a loose coalition called the "University District Movement." With the help of Mike Rosen, then director of the state chapter of the ACLU, we began collecting affidavits documenting police harassment and discrimination in food service and housing rentals. As the UDM gathered steam, another outrage occurred on April 3 at the Id Bookstore, which had been purchased by Reed College graduates Steven and Karen Herold a few months earlier and relocated to the U District.

Under the headline, "One Night of Hellenic Love," the second issue of the *Helix* reported on the "Id Bust": "'Hi, Steve. You're under arrest.' So went the cheery greeting given Steve Herold, owner of the Id Bookstore, by what must be one of the Ave's least successful khaki-clad undercover agents." Clerk Tony Tufts was "locked in the building" while eleven police officers "thumbed eagerly through the books in their never-ending battle against Gutenberg, smut and love. (After some discussion, two of them decided that there was no real chance of protecting the public against the corrosive influence of Simone de Beauvoir's Second Sex or even Lady Chatterly's Lover and sadly put them back on the shelves.)" Tufts was arrested on two counts of selling pornography, one for the Kama Sutra Calendar, featuring photos of Ron Boise's wiry sculptures copulating, and *Entrails,* a local poetry magazine. One charge was filed against Herold. Michael Rosen and William Dwyer (now U.S. District Judge) handled the case for the ACLU.

Two days later, Pacific National Bank, which owned the Id's building on 41st, evicted it. UDM added the cause of the Id to its lengthening list of demands and requested an audience with the U District Chamber of Commerce. Our cause received an unexpected boost when the *Seattle P-I* editorialized against "harassing the hippies" on April 7. Soon after, State Sen. (and future mayor) Wes Uhlman and Sen. Wilbur Hallauer of Oroville sponsored a resolution, partly tongue-in-cheek, advising the city council and county prosecutor to "practice tolerance" and "ignore inconsequentials." It didn't pass, but it made the front page of the *P-I.*

The Chamber met with us April 11, and its president Miles Blankinship grudgingly took delivery of petitions bearing 8,000 signatures in support of an end to harassment and discrimination against both hippies and racial minorities. One merchant summed up his group's attitude: "We have lots of tidelands. Why don't the hippies go pollute them instead of the U District." (A hundred years ago, many of the city's undesirables did, indeed, live chiefly in huts and house-boats along the shoreline.)

UDM held a rally the following day on campus, but no one was quite sure what to do next. The group was divided between trying to negotiate a settlement with the chamber or carrying the issue "to the streets." Exasperated, Robby Stern announced, "I'm marching down the Ave, and anyone who wants to join me is welcome to follow." More than 1,500 did, giving the U District its first taste of a major demonstration.

On April 15, the nation also got a glimpse of throngs to come as more than 200,000 marched in San Francisco and New York City in the first "Mobilization" against the war. I had played a tiny part in planning this event in San Francisco as part of a contingent of Young Socialists who motored 800 miles south in early April. The meeting was held just days after M. L. King Jr.'s emphatic denunciation of the war on April 4. He condemned the U.S. as "the greatest purveyor of violence in the world" and called for a common crusade between civil rights and anti-war movements. We were happy to try to oblige.

The ACLU was very busy that year. First, in January, the City of Seattle refused to rent the Opera House for a lecture by Timothy Leary (he joined an illustrious list of blacklisted speakers, including Paul Robeson and Gus Hall). The UW invited him to speak on campus instead and he gave a lecture at the Mountaineers Hall. Then the Se-attle School Board refused to allow Stokely Carmichael to speak at Garfield High School; the ACLU intervened and he did address audi-ences at Garfield and the UW, although some local civil rights leaders might have preferred it if he hadn't. The local CORE was one of the few in the nation to defy the national office and reject "black power."

The other big fight of that spring came over the issue of "light shows." The first such local exhibition was conducted by KRAB at a benefit concert held in Kirkland, a suburb east of Lake Washington, on November 5, 1966. The ASUW staged its own "Little Silly Dance" and light show in the HUB a week later, and Milo Johnstone orga-nized Seattle's first full-fledged light-show-concert-dance at the Frye Hotel on December 3.

The Free University rented the venerable Eagles Temple auditorium for a light show and dance on January 14, 1967, the same day as San Francisco's Human Be-In. The site was oddly appropriate: the Fraternal Order of Eagles had been founded decades earlier in Seattle as a self-help society for workingmen, and Franklin Roosevelt credited its activism for helping to secure passage of the original Social Security Act. Although the order had ossified over the years, and was currently in trouble for denying blacks membership, its ornate 1925-vintage hall provided a friendly setting for a new style of agitation.

In the third issue of *Helix,* Carol Burns offered a "True and Factual History of Union Light Company," founded by Ron McComb and a few friends. She noted, "The idea of a light show had been talked about around at least three kitchen tables. . . . Only two of us had ever seen a San Francisco light show, but KRAB put out a call for slide projectors, a dying strobe bulb was found at the Naval Air Station, and we did a light show.

"It might have ended there except that someone got the impression that the Union Light Company actually existed and hired us to do another show . . . for the U of W Parnassus Club. People were jumping up and down and waving their arms, grinning and having a wonderful time. And we got a call from Pat O'Day" (promoter and king of Seattle Top-40 radio at KJR). O'Day paired ULC with Merrilee (Rush) and the Turnabouts at Burien's Target Ballroom, with disastrous results. "The kids were not even what you'd call teenyboppers, couldn't dance, showed no visible response to the music, and were mystified by the light show. The boys, mostly drunk, rattled our scaffolding while the girls covered their eyes against the strobe and ran shrieking for the washroom." ULC decided to stick with known venues and audiences.

Meanwhile, the Free University reserved Eagles Auditorium for its January 14 dance and retained ULC to do the lights. Restrictions were daunting: current law prohibited anyone under eighteen from attending a public dance, the hall had to be licensed, a new dance permit was required for each event, and off-duty cops had to serve as chaperones. The power of life or death over such events was chiefly wielded by two men, Dance Squad officers Donald Parkin and Wayne Larkin (a future City Councilman)—yes, "Parkin & Larkin."

The Free U benefit was a huge success, but it left the police in the dark. Parkin & Larkin attended and wrote, "This is a weirdo-type dance with a way-out type of lighting effect. The patrons are a mixture of beatnik-type beardos, some intellectuals, non-conformists, and some spectators who just are curious." The manager of the Eagles saw no problem, commenting, "Hippies, schmippies, they don't fight or drink."

When ULC returned to the police for new dance permits, it was turned down. Meanwhile it performed at a "Lux Sit and Dance" party for Allied Arts at Seattle Center and for the Pacific Northwest Arts and Crafts Association in Bellevue. Neither group applied for a dance permit, and slipped under the anti-light-show radar. The Happening (a club in a former Jewish Bingo Hall on First Avenue) was not so lucky: light shows in connection with its dances were expressly banned.

ULC joined an abortive tour from San Francisco and made a disappointing foray into Vancouver, B.C., for that city's first be-in on March 26. It had better luck with spring shows at the UW, Bellingham's Western Washington State College, Mt. Vernon's Skagit Valley Community College, and the Jesuit-run Seattle University "where priests stood grinning at flashing images of Christ."

Curiosity and confusion hardened into opposition when 6,000 jammed into Eagles for Seattle's first "Trips Festival" on March 19. The event was staged by Trips Lansing and managed by Sid Clark, and featured music by The Seeds, Daily Flash, and Emergency Exit, plus a "Family Entertainment" staged by Tom Robbins and the Shazam Society (to be described in detail later).

The Dance Squad reported that the crowd was orderly, but Officer Elmer Wessalius painted a different picture: "The bearded beatnik types found in the majority around the unaccredited so-called Free U. of Seattle . . . have indicated a nearly complete disregard for our laws regarding conduct, narcotics, and drug abuse, etc." Alarm over hippies and their pagan rites was also spread by a modern-day Carrie Nation, Mrs. Ray Barger, and the ultra-rightist *Yakima Eagle,* who joined Wessalius in warning that a "Hippie Invasion" was imminent.

The police invoked a 1929 ordinance banning fire-prone arc lamps for "shadow dances" to deny permits for any more light shows. The

Free U, *Helix,* KRAB, et al. protested to the city council, which held a hearing in April. UW anthropology professor Monty West apologized to the council, "We strongly regret that hasty and petulant police action should have forced responsible citizens to impose upon the taxpayers and upon the valuable Seattle City Council time to debate the denial of constitutional rights when such pressing practical problems such as urban congestion, smog, water pollution, and ghetto segregation so urgently demand full attention." Notables including Tom Robbins and Paul Dorpat invited the council to attend a light show then scheduled for April 14 at the Vasa Ballroom on Lake Sammamish.

The police had different plans. A call from Seattle's Public Safety Building prompted the county sheriff to put the event off limits for off-duty officers, which rendered the light show illegal. Neat Catch-22, but the city ordinance did not apply on the UW campus, so the light show was shifted to the Edmonson Pavilion on April 23. Only one councilman, Charles "Streetcar" Carroll, attended but he had a good time and saw no peril to public safety.

As Carroll went to work on his colleagues and the ACLU readied a suit, Dorpat and friends returned to the police for a permit for a light show and dance at Eagles on May 7. Meanwhile, Police Chief Frank Ramon suggested to Monte West that an application might be more welcome if it were submitted by an "overall cooperative structure" which could be held accountable. So *Helix,* KRAB, the Free University, and the Union Light Company formed "OCS" to sponsor the next light show. Four days before the scheduled program, the city council decided that such events were not covered under the "shadow dancing" ordinance, and OCS got its permit. *Helix* celebrated with a special issue.

By May, I had overcome my own defenses and skepticism to become fully involved with the *Helix* as its "Rapidograph in Residence." The paper benefited from the talents of several excellent graphic artists, including Maryl Clemmens, Gary Eagle, Jacques Moitoret, Steve McKinistry (who went on to the *Seattle Times*), and, later, Billy Ward.

Putting out the *Helix* was less a journalistic enterprise than a communal celebration. The paper was almost a byproduct of a methedrine- and ego-fueled, anarchic gestalt. John Cunnick, the *Helix's* first "co-editor" described the bi-weekly layout process as "a sort of running be-in: during the last days before publication (when people are going 48 to 72 hours without sleep) the entire office turns into a single erratic [erotic?] organism. People go through changes, exchange ideas, get up tight, hear Kweskin for 97th time, and watch the door swing open and shut as the latest news about a God-sighting or police brutality comes in. It's a strained scene, with a lot of layers of mask rubbed off and an intense feeling of Yellow-Submarine-In-Unknown-Watersdom."

The medium was the mucilage that held us, and a growing number of readers, together. Our fourth issue topped 11,000 sales via street hawkers, head shops, and dirty book stores (more on that relationship later). What were they buying?

The covers helped: after the first two issues, these generally consisted of a single dominant illustration, often printed in black and a "split-font" which created a rainbow effect with only one additional pass through the press.

The interior design was never consistent nor what you would call "reader-friendly" today, but it was energetic. Type zigged and zagged, circled and spiraled, jumped forward and backward, and trampolined dizzily within and among an average of twenty-four pages, and sometimes as many as thirty-two pages. Every nook and cranny was filled with some kind of illustration or graphic bric-a-brac like a two-dimensional Victorian drawing room. Some illustrations even related to the adjacent article, but most were stream-of-consciousness selections clipped from old comic books, *Popular Science*, or *Life* magazine with cavalier disregard for copyrights or congruencies.

Then there were the stories. The *Helix* was a journalistic application of Parkinson's Law: the copy would fill the available space by deadline, so little forethought was put into story development or editorial planning. With varying degrees of quality, writers on and off the "staph" rewarded our faith in their verbosity, and artists, photographers, and paste-up volunteers took care of any space left over. The end product displayed the disorder, spontaneity, and random creativity of a community bulletin board.

The contents were an aggregate of nuggets and gravel: hard news on "the movement," local organizing, police harassment, and the past fortnight's outrages against the Constitution; meditations on eros, asthetics, theology, semiotics, and psychology, usually all in the same piece; stormy manifestos endorsing everything from anarchism to Stalinism; a rare thoughtful analysis submitted by some stifled expert who actually knew what he or she was talking about; some good poetry, but mostly not; reviews, criticisms, appeals, and diatribes. Most of it makes you wince today, but not all. A few samples from early issues:

Helix awarded its "first Tough Luck Award" to the *Seattle Times*, which had exploited a report of Vietcong using children as shields in a battle in the village of Truc Gian, forty miles south of Saigon, to rail against "The Double Standard in World Opinion" towards U.S. and NLF tactics. Unfortunately, the story proved to be false. Children had been killed and wounded during the battle in early January 1967, but not by the VC. They were victims of a midnight bombardment by South Vietnam artillery. The *Times* published the exposure of the hoax, but not as prominently as the first, erroneous report of the battle, and it never retracted or amended its editorial.

It reported that the Shazam Society, "perhaps the oldest and most mysterious of the Northwest's blossoming underground organizations," would surface again on April 1 at Attica Gallery, 426 Broadway, "First Official Exhibit of UFOs (Unidentified Funky Objects), Awesome Images Show, Better-Living-Through Sausages Display, and Brain Damage Festival." Shazam founder Tom Robbins dedicated it to "the tender and loving overthrow of established culture and to committing public and private acts of beauty, love and mystery." Co-conspirators included Georgia Pacific, George Schreiner, Larry Beck, and later Larry ("Captain Shazam") Heald and his brother Paul, as well as other innovative artists.

The ACLU detailed the cases of students interrogated by police at Roosevelt, Renton, Franklin, and Sealth high schools and at Asa Mercer Junior High. Parents were not notified of the interrogations, and several students were taken to the Youth Center without charges. The offenses consisted chiefly of suspicion of smoking pot.

Helix described the new Negro Labor Council formed in Seattle in March to fight discrimination in labor union hiring and apprentice programs in the building trades. This was the first move in a long and violent struggle by black construction workers and entrepreneurs to gain a foothold in the local market. A local study by the NAACP revealed that of 927 building trades apprentice slots filled since November 1965, only 7 went to nonwhite applicants.

Professor John Spellman revealed that his draft status was suddenly changed to 1-A, despite his being thirty-two years old and a professional scholar. Spellman had been forced out of the UW Far East Department by hawks and had just found a new professorship in Toronto. Shortly after the Id Bookstore Bust, owner Steve Herold, a graduate student at the time, also found his draft status magically transformed from 2-S to 1-A.

Paul Dorpat wrote the first of many long, often elaborately illustrated exegeses on love, psychology, and society, more influenced by Norman O. Brown's *Love's Body* than Herbert Marcuse's *Eros and Civilization.* Part contemplation, part celebration, these pieces sought to integrate id and ego in a new trans-Western, postindustrial moral equation. I must confess that at the time I didn't always understand what Paul was getting at, and John Cunnick had a good point when he commented, "Anyone who has time to write articles protesting sexual mores should fuck more."

Jon Gallant anticipated the antifreeway movement with the prescient observation that "long-range planning is the essence of progress, so Seattle's long-range planners should bear in mind that the expressway is only a temporary stage. The next step in the foreseeable future is clearly the *removal* of expressways." He proposed that "perhaps the master plan could coordinate the two activities, so that the demolition crew moved closely behind the construction crew, tearing down each section of the expressway as soon as it was built. That would be progress with a capital P." Gallant also suggested that rather than build new floating bridges, planners should just pave over Lake Washington with pontoons to create the "world's first floating parking lot." (Environmental and neighborhood opponents forced the cancellation of the R. H. Thomson Expressway in 1972 and stalled completion of the I-90 freeway and floating bridge for a decade.)

Speaking of roads—under the headline "Great Underground Freeway," the Vancouver-based Committee to Aid American War Objectors offered this advice: "Look straight. Hippies have been hauled out of buses and turned back. Be polite, cut your hair, and act like a tourist on short visit. (Hint: tourists do not take two TVs and a refrigerator on a four-day jaunt)." The article recommended taking the ferry from Anacortes to Sidney, on Vancouver Island, where "officials are a lot less suspicious" than at the Blaine border crossing on Interstate 5.

Eric Ramhorst reviewed the first Seattle concert by Country Joe and the Fish. He dubbed Country Joe McDonald "hippydom's greatest single musician [with] an almost Wagnerian concept of hippy synthesis of the arts, envisioning a combination of music, theater, light shows, electronics, and complete participation from the audience." The fish then included Barry Melton, Bruce Barthol, and Dave Cohen. McDonald and Melton started out as "folkies" at Berkeley's Jabberwock coffeehouse, and were recruited by SDS to tour campuses to attract new members.

U. Metcalf discussed the Llahngaelhyn's woes as a nonalcoholic venue for jazz and folk (immediately across from the old Red Robin on the south side of University Bridge). He lamented the loss of clubs such as Lake City Tavern, Pete Barba's Poop Deck, Noplace, Jazz'n' Jacks, and Town House (turned into the A-Go-Go) and noted that the Seattle scene had launched Paul Humphries, Dick Palumbi and Freddie Schreiber into national prominence. While eclectic and chancy in its acts, Llahngaelhyn attracted John Handy and McCoy Tyner for after-gig jams, and rock musicians such as Daily Flash drummer John Kelihor, Dean Hodges, Dave Lewis, Jabbo Ward, and Jordan Ruwe. Metcalf warned, "You may find four bass players and no drummer. Or a padlock on the door. Or a screaming session with all the best cats in town."

To promote the "Potlatch Power & Isness-in" in Volunteer Park on April 30, we published excerpts from Chief Seattle's stirring (if probably apocryphal) 1854 address to Gov. Isaac Stevens. It was then not well known, and closes, "At night when the streets of your cities and villages will be silent and you think them deserted, they will throng with the returning hosts that once filled and still love this beautiful land. The white man will never be alone. Let him be just and deal kindly with my people for the dead are not powerless. Dead, did I say? There is no death, only a change of worlds." Far out!

There was a hot flash that FBI director J. Edgar Hoover had told the *Christian Science Monitor,* "I regret to say that we of the FBI are powerless to act in cases of oral-genital intimacy, unless it has in some way obstructed interstate commerce."

And finally, there was this unusual complaint from the director of the Brecht Theater about casting a new play: "It's a lot easier to find talented, eager chicks to go to bed with you than to find talented, eager, young actresses." Oh, the suffering an artist must endure!

You get my drift. These stories were financed in part by an underground chamber of commerce of head shops, taverns, VW repair "clinics," record stores, porno shops, and a growing number of major record labels trying to penetrate the youth market. The porn later became an issue with the advent of feminism, but in the early years smut merchants were both reliable advertisers and, in the case of Art DeWitt's "Arts Adult Books," dedicated champions of freedom of speech.

And, of course, there were "unclassified ads" (what are today called "personals") for a dime a word. The *Helix's* very first unclassified ad was an archetype: "Hip spade wants to dig you." Future ads sought "swingers" to join menages of various sizes, kindred spirits for psychic voyages, buyers for ancient VW bugs or obsolete amplifiers, and rides to every point of the compass.

Circulation income was provided by stores and a legion of "dealers" who picked up bundles of papers and raced across the city to stake out their favorite corner. Interestingly, the heart of the downtown financial district was the best site for sales. It seemed that bankers and brokers couldn't get enough Marxism, or was it the naughty bits they liked?

Initially, we trusted dealers to return with our share of each fifteen-cent sale; not long after, we had to ask for upfront payment. Those of us who put the paper together earned our "wages" the same way, and lived comfortably on the $100 or so we took in each month. I rented a cozy little basement apartment on 12th NE for $25 a month, and had plenty of money left over for all the food, beer (fifteen-cent schooners!), cigarettes (thirty-five cents a pack!!), and sundries I needed. Before the war sent inflation into hyperdrive, it was remarkably cheap to live in Seattle, even with one of the nation's highest cost-of-living ratings.

By the official opening of 1967's "Summer of Love," the *Helix* was, perish the thought, firmly established. Unfortunately, the rest of the world was coming unglued.

Chapter 9:
Bummer of
Love

*The flower movement was
like a valley of thousands of
plump white rabbits
surrounded by wounded
coyotes.*

—Ed Sanders

The Brothers operation was evicted from the Bookworm on March 31, 1967, and relocated to 5824 Roosevelt. When Sally Delay applied for a business license at the new location, she was referred to the Police Department's bunco unit, where she was fingerprinted and detained for an hour. An officer informed her that "The Brothers is believed to be a front for the widespread distribution of LSD." Sally finally obtained a business license. The first meeting in the new headquarters attracted sixty participants and plans were laid for a variety of community services.

The Brothers held a "wake" for the Bookworm and the Eigerwand, which closed the same day, in Cowen Park at the north end of the Ave. This constituted Seattle's first be-in, and a hundred or so hippies picnicked inside a ring of police cars full of riot-equipped cops. Why didn't this make us feel safer?

Meanwhile, the Delays' giant houseboat still languished without power or water or prospects of new moorage. Jack discovered that the police had warned dock owners against renting to him, but he finally found one on Westlake who offered temporary moorage. Before he moved the *Rapid Transit,* Jack and I spent a last night aboard, dropping acid and rapping for hours in hopes of solving the world's problems, something we had done dozens of times before. As the sun rose and the electric tingle of the drug turned into a gauzy itch inside our craniums, an aquatic flying saucer floated past. Jack and I were suitably impressed, particularly when the hatch opened and a humanoid waved "Ahoy!" This was followed minutes later by a low rumble and the fractured notes of a distant brass band. It grew louder and a giant stern-wheeler dredge hove into view, its decks crowded with musicians in garish uniforms. As more ships cruised past—it was the opening day parade of the boating season—we concluded that the world could be even weirder than our psychedelic fantasies.

It could also be much more cruel. Days after the relocation of the *Rapid Transit,* somebody cut its mooring lines. Four hundred and eleven tons of barge blew gently across Lake Union and into some pilings between the Coast Guard and Geodetic Survey (now NOAA) station and Fairview houseboat colony. Jack finally found new moorage on the east side of Lake Washington, but the Bellevue Police beat him to shore. The dock owner reneged on his agreement, a fact reported in the *Seattle Times* before Delay was informed of it. "Our business has been taken away, now our home, what next . . . our son?" Jack asked in the *Helix*; he ultimately had to sell the *Transit* for salvage.

It wasn't all doom and gloom. By late spring, the District had developed into an alternative shopping center. Thanks to the UDM's efforts, the Id Bookstore found a new home on 42nd Street, where it thrived for many years. I supplemented my *Helix* earnings by clerking there, along with bibliophiles such as Joe Cain and Laura Besserman.

Over the next year, Robin Denny and Dick Leffel opened the Ave's first boutique, Arabesque, in the space occupied by the original Eigerwand. Not long after, Robin's ex, Monty Denny, opened a second boutique, Esoterica, next door to the Id in the former Bookworm space. A third boutique, Mnasidika-North, was located nearby, as was the innovative Random Sampler, founded by Danny Eskanazie to sell clothiers' seconds at low cost to students. (He has since made the transition from Funk to Punk through his "Dreamland" stores.)

Several blocks away on Brooklyn near 50th, Craig Imper established the equivalent of a psychedelic hardware store, Art Underground Unlimited, to provision inner space pioneers. Leather stores also cropped up, including the Infinite Sole and The Bench, where craftsmen such as Michael Green created and sold their wares.

With the publication of *Helix* number 4 in May, which featured my Freudian diptych of angels of war (with phallic mushroom cloud) and peace (castrated tank rusting amid labial flowers) and my earlier montage of Vietnam horrors, I decided to give the Haight a visit. I was joined by Fu Stonehill, District fixture and folk singer Jeff Jaisun, and a young woman whose identity I would protect if I could remember her name. We loaded papers and posters and our luggage into my 1950 DeSoto sedan, which I purchased from Dale Meador, and headed south on the new Interstate 5.

As the sun was setting, the radiator hose blew just outside Centralia, a farming town south of Seattle. I spent the next several hours wandering the streets in search of a replacement hose. Amazingly I found one; more amazingly, since my hair had long since passed my collar, none of the locals beat me to a bloody pulp.

We nursed the now chronically overheating sedan through the rest of Washington and Oregon, but when we began the long ascent near Mount Shasta, DeSoto gave up the ghost. We collected our samples and gear and trudged into the little town of Dunsmuir, which had a rail depot. I didn't have enough for the fare into San Francisco, so I signed over the title to my car to the station master for a ticket. After a hellish wait by the river amid clouds of hippie-eating mosquitoes, we finally boarded our train.

I did not expect to find paradise in the Haight. Jack Delay had recently visited and declared it a "can of worms." *Helix* reprinted the Diggers' warnings to kids to stay away, including Chester Anderson's bitter tract, titled "Uncle Tim's Children." He began with this story: "Pretty little 16-year-old middle-class chick comes to the Haight to see what it's all about and gets picked up by a 17-year-old street dealer who spends all day shooting her full of speed again and again, then feeds her 3000 mikes [micrograms of LSD] and raffles off her temporarily unemployed body for the biggest Haight Street gang bang since the night before last."

Anderson directed most of his wrath at "hip merchants" who ignored the human damage around them while exploiting the psychedelic mystique for profit, and at Timothy Leary, "who turned you on and dropped you into this pit." Such warnings were drowned out by the massive media hype and by pied pipers such as Scott McKenzie who exhorted thousands of runaways and day-trippers to "be sure to wear some flowers in your hair" in San Francisco.

What I found was even worse than the Diggers' psychedelic

dystopia: a cross between Peter Pan's Island and Devil's Island, awash in crime, violence, and misery. We crashed at the apartment of a woman friend who had moved to the Haight a few months earlier. A once rosy, bright girl now lived for just one thing: her next joint (yes, even marijuana can be addictive for the right personality). The pad was filthy and only acute hunger made me sample a foul communal stew. I promptly became a statistic in the salmonella epidemic then ravaging the district. Between visits to the bathroom, I dragged my increasingly frayed posters and *Helices* from one head shop to another, but found no one interested in any events north of Marin County. Fu took pity and lent me the money for air fare back to Seattle.

What I found back home wasn't much better. The Ave had degenerated into a circus, only these clowns had guns and knives. Heroin and injectable methedrine were now openly peddled where only grass and acid had formerly been sold. The authorities had gotten their wish: criminalization of relatively harmless drugs made everyone a criminal, and hard-core dealers flocked to the District eager to fulfill the prophecy that grass would lead to speed and crank.

As UW pharmacologist Dr. Lawrence Halpern later explained in a *Seattle Magazine* article, the real bridge for many of these junior junkies was the needle itself. Some needle-freaks were so addicted to the act of shooting up that "if there's nothing else available, they'll shoot distilled water. And if they can't get even that, they'll take the hypodermic, draw some blood out of their arm and then re-inject it—sometimes keeping this up for hours."

I witnessed something very similar when a young woman of my acquaintance openly talked of shooting up in her jugular vein, which, she knew, would be instantly fatal. That was part of the appeal: to die at the apex of the rush. I visualized her suicidal fantasy as Christ crucified on a hypodermic on the back cover of a July *Helix*. It was the right image, for she told me it made her clean up for a while at least. When, years later, I served on the board of Seattle's first methadone program, she was an early client and, I hope, has exorcised her demons.

The loss of one junkie would have no impact on the Ave. Hundreds of fresh recruits, some literally with flowers in their hair, began to migrate to the District, including many runaways. Gray Line "Hippie

Hop" tour buses and platoons of cars cruised the Ave on weekend evenings so straights and rednecks could gawk at the multicolored mobs crowding the sidewalks.

With the fall of the Eiger, the new hangout became "The Deli" on 42nd (later an Orange Julius outlet), which dispensed more pharmaceuticals than pastrami. When the Last Exit on Brooklyn coffee house opened on June 30, it gave us nonjunkies a place to go, and later occasioned a Mafia-like division of the U District between peddlers of narcotics and psychedelics.

By now the real heart of the scene was "Hippie Hill," a sward of campus shaded by giant trees, gently descending from Denny Hall toward the "T" of 42nd and 15th Avenue. Here the tribe could gather in relative security, chat, snuggle, trip, and maybe discreetly share a joint thanks to University President Charles Odegaard's steadfast refusal to permit Seattle Police on his turf. It was a gutsy stand, and it should be added that Odegaard, in stark contrast to Clark Kerr and many of his other peers at the time, took a generally tolerant view of the dissenters and nonconformists on and adjacent to his campus.

This, of course, drove the local constabulary bonkers. A teen curfew was in effect after 10 p.m. in Seattle, as were vagrancy laws. The police used these laws to harass denizens of Hippie Hill despite its status as state property. The UW, in the person of Assistant Attorney General James Wilson, formally objected to these SPD forays. Officer Larry Hart complained to the *Helix* (me, to be precise), "The Constitution of the United States will be our downfall in the next 20 years." Hart's partner Al Wilding added that Wilson "can go fuck himself," and that if the U didn't get the hippies off the hill, he would. One of UDM's last acts was to document hundreds of instances of police harassment and to present them to City Hall at a rally on May 18.

When not flouting the law, our local narcs worked the press to paint a picture even more grim than it actually was. *Times* columnist Don Duncan fell for their negative p.r. in the late summer, and I fired back a response in the *Helix* which demanded a more balanced coverage. My piece closed (in the typical rhetoric of the time), "They ask of a spontaneous people, 'What are your plans?' They ask of a moving people, 'Where are you?' They ask of a changing people, 'Who are you?' They never ask themselves, 'Why?'" To his credit, Duncan confessed that when the *Yakima Eagle* complimented his first few articles, he began to have second thoughts about what he had written, and described his first article as "blatant sensationalism" resulting from *Times* editorial policy and over-reliance on police. Duncan became a much more insightful observer of the District scene afterwards, and a friend as well.

There was no danger of Emmett Watson being duped: he loved the hippies from the start and gave their self-appointed spokesmen a prominent and frequent forum. Emmett sagely noted that the Heisenberg Uncertainty Principle was at work, and that "you can't know position and motion simultaneously" with a phenomenon as variegated and fluid as the counterculture. He also repeated a warning originally sounded by California Assemblyman Willie Brown, "THEY are not some horde of invading foreigners. They are our children, yours and mine, exercising their right to move freely about a country which will soon be very much their own."

The cause of counterculture music took a quantum leap nationally with the release of the Beatles' "Sgt. Pepper's Lonely Heart's Club Band" and the group's highly publicized dalliance with the Maharishi Mahesh Yogi. Locally, OCS brought the Grateful Dead and Country Joe and the Fish to Eagles, but it chiefly showcased local groups. The hall was later taken over by Boyd Grafmyre, who turned Eagles into a major venue on the national rock circuit. His shows were often advertised via posters designed by my old high school friend John Moehring, who was then heavily influenced by the style of Aubrey Beardsley. We welcomed Grafmyre's enterprise as competition for the despised Pat O'Day (né Paul Berg) who dominated the local music scene through his KJR and Northwest Releasing oligopolies. It turned out later that O'Day had quietly bankrolled Grafmyre. Oh, well.

In June 1967, a thousand miles to the south, Seattle-born Jimi Hendrix was catapulted into international stardom by his performance at the Monterey Pop Festival. He had already dazzled London with his revolutionary electric guitar stylings, and no less than Paul McCartney had urged festival promoters to book him, but Hendrix would not play his hometown until the following year. The festival and its documentary film also introduced Janis Joplin, Steve Miller, and the major San Francisco bands to national audiences.

That same June, the Seattle Symphony's assistant director, Richard Cornwell, found himself in a San Francisco jail for possession of drugs, along with ballet megastars Rudolf Nureyev and Dame Margot Fonteyn. They were at a party in the Haight when the police staged a raid; embarrassed authorities quickly released them.

The trial of Id Bookstore owner Steve Herold and clerk Tony Tufts reached a happy conclusion in July 1967 when Superior Court Judge Soderland dismissed the obscenity charges against both. In the original trial that spring, ACLU attorney William Dwyer demolished the prosecution's "expert witness," a self-anointed "art critic" named Bellamy who had "visited a number of museums," but couldn't say which or where. Under withering cross-examination, Bellamy managed to reveal his ignorance of such classical sexual exploits as Zeus's assumption of the form of a swan to seduce Leda and his rape of Europa, which Bellamy confused with the Latins' rape of the Sabines. As to the Kama Sutra, he denounced it as "an obscene sect," which prompted Sanskrit scholar John Spellman to retort, "Half the temples in India would violate this law."

Dwyer also attacked a Dr. Leavis's testimony on the poetry in *Entrails*. Leavis confessed to finding "some literary merit" in the magazine, which, of course, automatically protected the work under the Supreme Court's *Ulysses* test for obscenity. Dwyer also noted that the magazine had been used in UW poetry courses without eliciting complaints or charges.

This did not prevent District Judge Evans D. Manolides from promptly convicting Herold and Tufts in the first trial. Judge Manolides figured in that summer's other major trial, that of Floyd Turner for flag burning (see next chapter).

On appeal, Dwyer disposed of the prosecution's expert witnesses, a pastor of the University Lutheran Church and two professors from Seattle University (Jesuits and Lutherans, on the same stage!). After the dismissal, the prosecutor asked Judge Soderland how he expected police to control "pornographers" such as the Id. The judge replied "Don't arrest them."

The police continued hassling dispensers of unwelcome ideas, such as *Helix* dealers, but the paper thrived despite their best efforts. Circulation stabilized at 12,000 per issue, and the staff expanded. Among the additions: future co-editor Tim Harvey, photographer Roger Hudson, and poetry editors Henry Rappaport and Ed Varney (this honor later fell to me because my desk was closest to the dumpster).

We were later joined by Roger Downey, who first arrived in the office in his UW security guard uniform to warn us that the police were trying to recruit students to serve as undercover informers. He took over responsibility for our calendar of events and cultural coverage, and is today one of Seattle's most respected (or detested, depending on whose ox is being gored) performing arts critics.

Downey's appearance more or less coincided with that of two remarkable sisters, Sharma (just that and nothing more) and Roxie Grant. They started out setting our type on nifty new IBM computers at Stan Stapp's Outlook office. We were dazzled by this technology, which today would be dismissed as a glorified electric typewriter. Sharma and Roxie soon began writing and became key members of the collective, and Roxie and I later collaborated on many post-*Helix* projects.

Meanwhile, in Olympia, proto-gonzo-journalist Darrell Bob Houston launched his stylish but short-lived *Avatar.* He and I assembled the first issue (June 1, 1967) in a single, 24-hour burst of verbal and graphic frenzy—and we didn't need to drop speed.

The underground press was flourishing around the nation with the founding of Chicago's *Seed,* New York's *East Village Other,* Detroit's *Fifth Estate,* San Francisco's *Express Times,* Boston's *Avatar,* Portland's *Willamette Bridge,* Vancouver's *Georgia Straight,* and a number of particularly brave papers in the Deep South. Early in 1967, the first nineteen papers joined to form a copyright pool for sharing stories and graphics. The story goes that it was named the "Underground Press Syndicate," or UPS for short, when one of the participants noticed a United Parcel Service truck driving by.

The proliferation of these rags prompted the first national convention in Stinson Beach, California, on March 26, 1967. The delegates agreed to a manifesto which *Seed* editor and historian Abe Peck called "nothing less than a post-atomic, post-acid repeal of Western Civilization." This was as close to a unifying creed as the underground press ever came. New papers began springing up by spontaneous generation across the country (peaking at 500 in 1969) and by October 1967, the press was sophisticated enough to support its own Liberation

News Service, founded by Ray Mungo and Marshall Bloom on the eve of the Pentagon "levitation" (see chapter 13).

The most controversial new paper was San Francisco's *Rolling Stone,* first published on October 18,1967, by Jann Wenner, a former staff member of *Ramparts* (a liberal lay Catholic magazine) canned for smoking dope in the office. The *Stone* was almost exclusively devoted to covering the music scene. As such it was not the first—that honor belongs to *Crawdaddy* founded a year earlier—but Wenner openly disdained Left politics. Abbie Hoffman later denounced Wenner as "the Benedict Arnold of the Sixties," which is a little rough. Tim Harvey and I happened to be in San Francisco when the first issue hit the streets. It was pretty, but we didn't see much future for it.

Harassment of the underground press intensified apace. Canadian authorities temporarily closed the *Georgia Straight,* and Boston police drove Mel Lyman's *Avatar* out of business. British attempts to shutter London's underground press made a hero out of a civil liberties attorney and part-time writer named John Mortimer.

In September, the *Helix* was suddenly evicted from its office. We were rescued by Robert Eyre, an architect and leader in the city's new anti-freeway movement. We moved into two offices adjacent to his own at the intersection of Harvard and Eastlake.

Despite the best efforts of new self-help groups such as the Job Corp. ("Rent-a-Hippy") and the Basic Needs Company, the U District scene continued to degenerate. Overdoses and bad trips became routine, and powerful new drugs such as STP, a kind of extended-wear acid, and PCP, an animal tranquilizer derivative dubbed "angel dust" which made its users anything but, joined the old standbys.

Conventional agencies were at a loss over what to do, so social worker Lee Kirschner got busy trying to organize an alternative. She enlisted psychologists such as Ted Dorpat (Paul's brother) and Art Kobler, physicians such as Dr. Jim McDermott, and counselors such as Kord Roosenrung and Frank Lindsay, and assembled an impressive board including Judge Charles Z. Smith, Dr. David Bearman, Dr. James Dille, and Dr. Ed Severinghaus. The Urban Development League provided a rambling house at the corner of 12th NE and NE 38th, and the "Open Door Clinic" was true to its name by early October.

Open Door rendered The Brothers obsolete in many ways, which was good since the "organization" had disintegrated in a one-sided power struggle between Jack Delay and Monty West. The latter had decided that Jack was laying a bum trip on the scene with his columns in the *Helix* and repeated warnings about the perils of uninformed drug use. I should add that Monty had become something of a mega-lomaniac who resented anyone who might pose a threat to his own claim to the mantle of local Learyesque guruhood. The UW later dropped him and when I last saw Monty, some years later, he was on his way to a retreat to study "breatharianism" in order to subsist on air without eating or drinking.

Jack devoted himself to his *Helix* coverage. In November, he reported that tensions on the Ave had prompted the creation of an informal Vigilance Committee among dealers of pot and acid. Their targets were dealers of smack, who were breaking into other dealers' homes and selling cut-up phone books as "keys" (kilograms) of grass. When one of the thieves tried to sell a dealer a kilo of his own burgled boo, he was "detained" until he named the ringleaders in the original crime. A committee of forty pissed-off hippies descended on the Deli and "borrowed" three smackheads for a little chat in the alley. Meanwhile other smack dealers, including the masterminds of the ripoffs, got wind of the counteroffensive and arrived at the Deli armed with two rifles. Before they could load the guns, they were surrounded and hustled into the Pizza Haven for another friendly discussion. Narcs arrived at this point, but no one finked and the police had to be spectators to what became territorial negotiations.

Out of this came a peculiar detente in which pot/acid dealers decided to shift their operations to the Last Exit coffee house leaving the Deli to the junkies and what Delay accurately predicted was "its own miserable death." The division of the spoils was tacitly endorsed by the police. The Deli closed soon after, and the drug market moved to the "Burger Hut," on the lower Ave, much to the horror of its Korean owners.

Back in the Haight where it all began, the Diggers had imploded. Their successor social agencies held a symbolic funeral for "The Death of the Hippie" on October 6, 1967. It was premature.

Dope problems were not confined to the Haight and the District, of course. In a long piece in the September *Helix*, Gene Johnston related an interview with "Sergeant X" and other troops recently returned from Vietnam. Based on X's description, Johnston wrote, "Free tip to narcs: No need to rummage in campus dustbins. *Helix* tells you of an American city of 50,000 souls where 75 percent to 80 percent of the population smokes marijuana regularly." One officer complained, "This situation is incredible. We can't arrest colonels and doctors and lawyers and heroes. What would the folks back home think?" Johnston explained that the "Exploding Korean Doll Scare" of the previous Christmas also had its root in the Vietnam dope scene because the souvenir dolls sent home by G.I.s were routinely used to smuggle pot into the U.S. "Those dolls only exploded in your mind."

In the same article, a former medic-pharmacist, recently returned from Vietnam, described scenes staged for TV news crews in which four Vietcong prisoners in black pajamas were repeatedly rehearsed running across a rice paddy until the photographers were satisfied. Then, with cameras rolling, they were gunned down. "Black blots twitching in the Asian ooze."

Sergeant X defended the mounting civilian toll: "I don't blame guys for killing everyone in the Free-fire Zones. It's like this: we just can't fight them in their backyard. You bring them over and dump them in Spanish Harlem and see how long they last."

He also reported VD was rampant and related what became a famous rumor of the war. "There is a group of GIs with things nobody's ever seen before who will remain there until they are cured, or rot away."

Johnston's interviewees said there was no support for the war among enlisted men, but also no organized opposition. One said, "You don't care about anything but getting through the day." He described a training film: "They used to show us this movie with old Johnson sitting behind his nose with all these maps flashing, and he'd ask, 'Whaa Viet Naam?' Everybody'd break up. That's what we wondered, too."

Chapter 10: The Prosecution and Flagellation of Floyd Turner as Performed by the Inmates of the King County Court House under the Direction of the Hon. Charles O. Carroll

> *[The] freedom to differ is*
> *not limited to things that do*
> *not matter much.*
> —U.S. Supreme Court
> Justice Robert H. Jackson

O n the evening of May 12, 1967, several civil rights organizations threw a party for their pro-bono attorneys at the headquarters of the new Central Area Motivation Project, CAMP, which occupied a renovated mansion on 17th (it later moved into a converted firehouse). The event featured music by Clockwork Orange and, later, a "happening," during which several of more than 200 revelers took turns destroying a piano with sledge hammers.

The noise prompted Louis Scott, who lived across the street, to call police at around 6 p.m. and again at about 10:30 p.m. Before police arrived the second time, Scott watched through his binoculars as a man held up a small American flag. Another man, whose back was to his secret witness, set the flag afire with a cigarette lighter.

Twelve days later, Seattle police arrested Floyd Turner as the man who held the flag. King County Prosecutor Charles O. Carroll charged him under the state's 1919 Uniform Flag Law, which declared, "No person shall publicly mutilate, deface, defile, defy, trample upon, or by word or act cast contempt upon any [official] flag, standard, color, ensign or shield."

The enforcement of patriotic fetishism became a favorite pretext for police harassment during the Sixties. Milo Johnstone, who reigned as the uncrowned king of local hippiedom, was busted for upholstering his truck seat in bunting, and other hippies and Lefties were arrested for wearing flags as capes or hanging them for drapes. It reached such heights of silliness that the police arrested CAMP worker Kenno Carlos merely for explaining to students why some people felt compelled to burn the flag. Floyd Turner's case was the first of many flag flaps to come.

Floyd was a fixture in the District and the local Left, and well known to the police, whom he delighted in taunting. It is fair to say that he was one of a kind. Smallish and wiry, as well as wired with a manic energy, Floyd had arrived in Seattle from points unknown in the hope of getting a job at the World's Fair. In addition to any family or friends, Floyd lacked money, skills, the ability to read, or even much of a spoken vocabulary. To his great fortune, he happened to stumble into a meeting of the Seattle Committee of the Unemployed, headed by George and Louise Crowley (unrelated to the author), two former CPers turned anarchists. They took pity on Floyd and essentially adopted him. Floyd told the Crowleys (and anyone else who would listen) that he was a Doukhobor, a member of a Russian charismatic sect. Beginning in 1899, several thousand of these "Sons of Freedom" emigrated to British Columbia. Among their peculiarities was a habit of burning down their own houses and stripping off their clothes as a form of purifying protest. They also used guns, arson, and bombs to fight Canadian attempts to enroll their children in public schools and collect taxes, as well as to settle internal power struggles.

Via the Crowleys, Floyd was introduced to the Seattle Left and to Stan Iverson in particular. Stan offered this assessment of Floyd in a *Helix* article on his second trial in January 1968:

Now comes the question of the character of the defendant, Floyd Wayne Turner, Jr., of malformed imagination and, to say the least, an elusive sense of reality. "Doukhobor" he is called in some parts of Skid Road, and Doukhobor he regards himself. Nervous, exhibitionistic, individualistic, he loves demonstrations. In these, the unhappy and lonely child that is Floyd Turner can play a role. The little dishwasher and quasi-literate laborer can rise above the conditions of his life. He can bid defiance to the impersonal forces which have fallen athwart his life with such crushing force. No demonstrator is more daring than he. All eyes rivet on him as he unfurls a Viet Cong flag, or threatens to take off all his clothes, Doukhobor-fashion, against the menace of the police. And there are always police. Floyd attracts them like a magnet [attracts] metal filings.

Floyd lies. He lies habitually and indiscriminately. He lies to such an extent that it is a very real question as to whether he understands the difference between the true and the false in the ordinary sense of those words. Perhaps fictionalize would be a better word for it, for his vision is romantic and his reality is far from romantic, and he wanders between the two like a soul lost in limbo. And then there is this: if all of your life you have been so far toward the bottom of the heap that most of your experience has been a rain of invisible kicks emanating from forces that you do not so much understand as feel, the lie is one of your few defenses. You lie habitually and as a reflex. All really oppressed peoples have developed fantastic liars.

This last point was key, because the police were led to Floyd by his later boasting that he had burned a flag. They arrested him in late May, and Louis Scott identified him as the man he saw that night outside CAMP.

Floyd's first trial was held in District Court before Judge Evans D. Manolides. Edmund Wood Jr. (later Mayor Wes Uhlman's counsel and deputy mayor) represented Floyd courtesy of the ACLU. Wood undermined Scott's testimony and produced three pivotal witnesses. First, Stan Stapp, publisher of the *North Central Outlook,* testified that he had seen a dark-skinned man (who turned out to be a Filipino student at the UW), not Floyd, waving the flag around that night and threatening to ignite it. Quaker activist and sculptor Richard Beyer (now best known for carving Fremont's "Waiting for the Interurban") then testified that he would have seen the emblematic immolation had he been there—but he wasn't because he and Floyd were in his truck transporting the sacrificial spinet to CAMP.

The final defense witness was even more crucial: Stan Iverson took the stand and explained that he and another man (later identified as Mike Travers) had burned the flag. He did it because the aforementioned "dark-skinned man" was getting on his nerves and he decided that they should "just get it over with."

Judge Manolides personally interrogated Iverson on his motivations, beliefs, and morals. At the end of this he commented that "anarchists cannot tell right from wrong and cannot be trusted," and added, "There is too much of this going on in our country today. Freedom is a one-way street. Freedom is the right to do the right thing, not as someone pleases." Manolides pronounced Turner guilty and sentenced him to six months in jail and a $500 fine. He also set a punitively high appeal bond of $3,000.

Floyd Turner languished in jail for forty-five days, where the other prisoners scorned and beat him, before the bond could be assembled. In October, *Seattle* Magazine took up his cause. Its cover shocked the city with a photo of a burning flag, and James Halpin delved deeply into the case and tracked down Iverson's accomplices in the actual incident (the account above relies in part on his research).

Shortly after the magazine hit the stands, *Seattle* editor Peter Bunzel found himself subpoenaed to testify for the prosecution at Floyd's second trial, on the grounds that his magazine had "prejudiced this community against the state's case." Superior Court Judge J.W. Miflin denied the motion and quashed the subpoena as "legal palaver." Bunzel attributed the maneuver to "the arrogance which has so often characterized Prosecutor Charles O. Carroll and his underlings," and added, "Oh, yes. Carroll comes up for election in 1970."

Turner's second trial opened before a Superior Court jury in December 1967. Here is part of Stan Iverson's account:

> Comes then Louise Crowley to the stand. A one-time student of anthropology, very bright and enormously able, an anarchist, all of her life rebellious and compassionate, she collects strays, human and animal, mammalian and reptilian, like an institution for the preservation of unwanted life. The core of her testimony concerns the character of the

strangely alienated and inchoate personality that is Turner. When she first met him four years ago, he was totally illiterate and had a speaking vocabulary of about 200 words. She and George [Crowley] taught him to read and write. (How well can he read—how much can he understand? That's hard to say. Well, could he fill out a job application? Probably not without help.) She attempts to develop a picture for the jury of what Floyd Turner is actually like. They listen impassively.

In a daring maneuver, the defense puts Turner himself in the witness chair. No one, including his attorneys, can predict what Floyd will say. It is an effort to show by demonstration what little credence can be placed on any vainglorious brag he might [have made] during those weeks in May when there was a rash of flag-burning across the nation, conservatives were vociferously denouncing the desecrations, and Congress was busy drafting an act to penalize the desecrators. Flag-burning seemed quite the thing for a way-out demonstrator and if you hadn't burned one, you might at least say that you did or that you were going to. In putting Floyd on the stand, a great deal will depend on the perception and insight of the jurors. Perhaps too much.

Turner is sworn. [ACLU attorney Philip] Burton guides him gently through some of the story of his experiences in Seattle since his first arrival here during the World's Fair, and his relations with the Crowleys, and then, what organizations do you belong to, Floyd?

F.: Some civil rights organizations, CORE, Snick, the NAACP, and some others like SDS and UDM.

Burton: Are you a member of these organizations, Floyd?

F.: Well, no, but I've put out leaflets for them and I know some of the leaders.

Burton: What does CORE stand for?

F.: I don't know.

Burton: Do you know what SNCC stands for?

F.: No, but I know what NAACP means, National Association for Colored People.

And he doesn't know what SDS and UDM stand for either. The questioning continues, developing a picture of Floyd Turner's prejudices, his sympathies, his ignorance, his knowledgeability. At times it is faintly funny, at times a little pathetic, and sometimes embarrassing.

Turner denied anew burning the flag or boasting that he had. He admitted "that he had used some big words, some political words, some words that he didn't understand, but he never, never said that he had burned a flag or was going to burn a flag." It was Floyd's word and those of a motley crew of anarchists, protesters, and former Communists, against an apartment house manager and the police. It took the jury one hour and fifteen minutes to return a verdict of guilty on December 15.

Stan ended his report:

"His trial will continue. His case will be appealed; the constitutional issues will be raised. It is one trial in a life of trials. Franz Kafka smiles."

The case of Floyd Turner was not settled until September 3, 1970, when the State Supreme Court ruled in the matter. It reversed the conviction because Judge Albert Bradford Jr. had expressly instructed the jury "that it is not required that you find that the defendant intended to violate the law. You are only required to find that the defendant performed the physical act charged."

In a tortured review of flag desecration laws in various nations dating back to Kaiser Wilhelm, the Court found that "the acts must have been done knowingly and intentionally with an intent or purpose of defiling and desecrating [a flag] and holding it publicly up to contempt." Because the prosecution had not proved this, and the judge had excluded the issue, the Supreme Court remanded the case for retrial. By this time, Charles O. Carroll was in the political fight of his life. Two weeks later, he was defeated in the Republican primary by Chris Bayley Jr., who did not reprosecute Turner. Kafka got the last laugh.

In a way, Floyd Turner was orphaned anew by the Movement's disintegration in the early Seventies. He achieved a final burst of publicity by claiming to have climbed Mt. Rainier barefoot, as "documented" in a snapshot of him standing shoeless on the summit. To persuade skeptics, Floyd staged several demonstrations at U District street fairs during which he stood on a block of ice until his naked feet melted through to the pavement.

That is the way I saw him last.

Chapter 11:
From Protest to
Resistance

*In retrospect, the confluence
of Vietnam and the boom
generation seems eerily
exact, a hellish blind date
arranged by history.*

—Landon Jones

In the evolution of the antiwar movement, 1967 might be summarized as the year of the draft. Between 1964 and 1973, 26.8 million men passed through military draft age. Of these 11 million were called to duty (not all were baby boomers, by the way; only 6.5 million were born after 1945), and 1.6 million were ordered to Vietnam.

As Landon Jones notes, the U.S. was "able to fight the longest war in our history using only 6 percent of the eligible population." Because of this demographic bulge in the draftable population, the individual risk of being drafted in 1965 was actually lower than in 1959, and the 1965 monthly draft quota of 40,000 was half that at the peak of America's previous undeclared war in Korea.

But there were some wrinkles in the draft law which intensified its impact on eligible men. First, the law kept them dangling for eight years, from age nineteen to twenty-six—key years during which most started careers and families. This was offset initially by deferments for students and married men, which in turn increased the burden on working-class teens. Ironically, relatively high physical and mental standards actually shielded the poorest of the poor—including urban black teens—but the standards were later changed in the name of creating new "job opportunities" for inner city youth. Meanwhile, blacks began falling in combat in numbers seriously out of proportion to their participation in the armed forces.

The draft did not actually threaten that many of the war's loudest critics, who were protected by student deferments. Historian and former SDS president Todd Gitlin reports that of all troops sent to Vietnam, only 21 percent had graduated from high school and a mere 9 percent were college graduates. As Landon Jones noted, "One of the ironies of Vietnam is that the opposition to the war was led by college students, who were safely deferred, while its support came from young laborers—*The Deer Hunter*'s steel workers—who were doing the actual fighting."

The Selective Service System, headed by the suitably odious Gen. Lewis Hershey, tightened the noose a little in mid-1967 by eliminating deferments for graduate students, but many idealists had already responded like David Harris and willingly discarded their academic shields from the draft. For most who chose to avoid the draft, the motivation was not cowardice but annoyance with the dislocation of their lives and plans. Some became perpetual undergrads, some found sympathetic doctors to exaggerate old injuries or ailments, some suddenly discovered that they were queer. With so many compliant draftees, most draft boards didn't work overtime to snare the unwilling—unless they were being punitive.

Outright evasion was riskier, but not by much. Gitlin reports that over the course of the war, 570,000 men committed some kind of draft law violation, ranging from burning their cards to fleeing the country. Of these 9,750 were convicted, and Jones reports that only 3,250 served prison time—many willingly. An unknown number left the country, chiefly for Canada, and about 15,000 took advantage of President Carter's 1977 amnesty. Thousands qualified as conscientious objectors, passing a high hurdle which required proof of a long-standing, religiously premised opposition to all war and violence. The Supreme Court later reduced the theistic threshold, but maintained that an objector could not pick and choose which war he found morally repugnant.

The lot of the C-O was not to be envied. John Cunnick had received his dispensation from military service, but could not find a suitable assignment in Seattle. The draft board ordered him to Los Angeles County Hospital and "24 bedpan months." When he reported for duty with "the Enema Squad," he was told that hiring had been frozen due to "financial problems; I suspect Reagan." He volunteered later at the Open Door Clinic.

Things were much dicier for men who came to their convictions after enlistment. In *Reconciliation Road,* John Marshall, grandson of the great military historian S. L. A. Marshall, relates the terrible alienation he suffered in applying and obtaining discharge as a C-O after already winning his bars in the Army.

A particularly tragic fate befell PFC Michael Bratcher. A year into his tour as a medic, he realized that he was really just patching men up so they could get a second chance to kill or be killed. On April 10, 1967, he walked into his commanding officer's Fort Lewis office, stripped off his clothes, and announced, "I quit." He was imprisoned in the blockade for insubordination. There, he developed pericarditis as a result of a hunger strike and was transferred to Madigan Army Hospital.

ACLU head Mike Rosen represented Bratcher in his court martial and won an acquittal of the original insubordination charges. As soon as he could, Bratcher walked off base to write a C-O application and to contact the local Draft Resistance, recently organized by the UW SDS. Bratcher traveled to Seattle to hold a press conference at the Friends Center on June 22. MPs were waiting and bundled him into a car as news cameras rolled. In his written statement, which he never got to give, Bratcher noted that 80 percent of C-O applications were approved prior to 1967, but none had been okayed so far during the year. He was court-martialed anew and later sentenced to four years of hard labor.

It was less the physical threat of the draft than the idea that the government could willy-nilly reach down into a man's life and snatch him up to fight an absurd, undeclared war that offended so many. Even the conservative Young Americans for Freedom decried the "Selective Slavery System," before Vietnam became a litmus test of patriotism and anticommunism.

On April 28, events provided a perfect symbol of the inequity of the draft when Muhammad Ali was arrested for refusing induction after his draft board denied him C-O status on the basis of his new Islamic faith. Could a man who made his living beating others to a pulp morally "object" to war? The World Boxing Association thought not, and revoked Ali's championship. Ali was sentenced to five years in prison on June 20, but ultimately won his case on appeal; he also regained his championship in the ring.

In May 1967, the Student Mobilization Committee declared that this would be "Vietnam Summer." General Westmoreland agreed and told President Johnson he could win with a total deployment of 600,000 men. Soon after, the President authorized calling up an additional 70,000. Thus the draft and the related issue of Reserve Officer Training Corps (ROTC) programs seemed natural targets as the Left sought a strategy with which to build on the success of the April 15 Mobe. These objectives and intensifying campaigns against military and corporate recruiters on campuses helped realize a political transition from "protest to resistance," active engagement with "the enemy" to disrupt activities supporting the war. It was also an antidote to the white Left's isolation from the black power movement.

Campus leaders also needed a clear issue in order to reconstruct their credibility following the earlier *Ramparts* revelation that the CIA had secretly funded the National Student Association for years. It became very hard to find anyone on any campus who supported the war, the draft, or the ROTC, particularly at the UW, where, *Ramparts'* Sunday supplement had revealed, ROTC cadets had been recruited to spy on their fellow students.

Despite such ammunition, the UW SDS was still relatively small and hesitant in the spring of 1967. It had confronted an Air Force recruiter on campus in February and forced him to leave, and it organized an independent Draft Resistance–Seattle to counsel and assist men fighting induction.

A protest on May 12 at the Governor's Day review of the ROTC in Husky Stadium drew about seventy-five people. Police wouldn't let the protesters take their signs into the stands, so they carried flags and daffodils instead. Two burned their draft cards, and SDS president Gordon Peterson tried to outshout the p.a. to denounce the war. He was arrested for disturbing the peace during a military ceremony. Meanwhile angry spectators, including several women, attacked and beat Michael Turnsen and Cal Winslow (who with his wife Barbara would become important leaders in the UW Left).

The next day, several SDS members and allies staged an impromptu antiwar demonstration at the Pike Place Market, with similar results. The police arrested Robert Holley and David Wyatt for violating a 1907 ordinance against "refusing to separate from a crowd which annoyed citizens and travelers." The ACLU took up the case and challenged the constitutionality of such a law since "any speaker who causes a crowd to congregate will do so at the annoyance or disturbance of someone." That same day, 70,000 marched in New York City *for* the war.

Two events briefly distracted the nation from Vietnam. First, on May 30, the Nigerian province of Biafra declared its independence. This triggered a long, vicious tribal civil war which would ultimately kill hundreds of thousands through violence and famine. Five days later, Israel launched a stunning preemptive strike against its Arab antagonists. At the end of this "Six Day War," Israel controlled the former Jordanian territory of the West Bank, the formerly Syrian Golan Heights, and the formerly Egyptian Gaza Strip and Sinai Peninsula. Although the Left routinely portrays Israel as a U.S. puppet, Israeli leaders did not necessarily trust U.S. intentions during the war. On June 8, Israeli forces torpedoed an American intelligence ship, the USS *Liberty*, monitoring the war off the Sinai.

This war seriously divided the Left, which included many anti-Zionist Jews who nevertheless supported the survival of Israel, then nominally socialist under Prime Minister Golda Meir. When "anti-imperialist" rhetoric, particularly among black militants, was extended to endorse Yasser Arafat's Al Fatah and, later, the Palestine Liberation Organization, it opened deep wounds which still bleed in today's Jewish-black conflicts over anti-Semitism and racism.

On June 23, attention returned to the war in Vietnam, when Los Angeles police attacked 10,000 protesters who had rallied to hear a speech by Muhammad Ali and then marched on the Century Plaza Hotel, where President Johnson was addressing a fund-raising banquet. Police intercepted the procession, injuring seventy-five and arresting fifty, according to the *Los Angeles Free Press*. The incident became infamous within the Left as "Bloody Friday," but it was a be-in compared to what was to follow in July.

America's inner cities began exploding one after the other like a string of firecrackers. The first to go was Newark, on July 12. A week later, 26 were dead, some 1,500 were wounded, and more than a 1,000 were in jail—including black poet Leroi Jones, famed for such verses as "Up against the wall, motherfucker / this is a stick up." He was arrested and beaten by Newark police on the second day of the riots, and became an instant cause célèbre among left-wing intellectuals and a hero for black power advocates, who held their first national convention amid Newark's still-smoldering ruins on July 20.

The day that convention ended with a call for a "black revolution," Detroit blew. It took 13,000 federal troops and National Guardsmen a week to restore a semblance of "order." In the process 40 died, 2,000 were wounded, and 5,000 were left homeless.

While the Detroit riot was still raging, Maryland police arrested the new head of SNCC, H. Rap Brown, for inciting a riot in the city of Cambridge. On the same day, July 26, Stokely Carmichael delivered a speech in Havana calling for a "war of liberation" in the U.S. Riots followed in rapid-fire succession in Washington, D.C., Milwaukee, New York City, and seventy other cities. When the year ended, the death toll stood at eighty-three. President Johnson responded on July 29 by tapping Illinois Gov. Otto Kerner to head a special Commission on Civil Disorders. The big story in Seattle was the riot that didn't happen.

Helix interviewed two black activists, Les MacIntosh and Robert Redwine, who said establishment attempts to defuse tensions had actually inflamed the situation. Gov. Dan Evans had requested a meeting with young black activists from the SNCC and the Central Area Committee for Peace and Improvement. As a result, MacIntosh declared, "What the committee did was bring together a vocal nucleus that was pretty much committed to violence." Redwine explained, "This was the problem. We had people who wanted to see a riot, who were dead set on seeing a riot that Saturday night. There were 'volunteers' in our own group who would have gone down and gotten their brains blown out just to set the whole thing off."

So why didn't the riot "that all sides incited" happen? MacIntosh and Redwine credit Evans with responding immediately to "demands" for additional services and facilities. A new multiservice center came together within days of the meeting, an earned income credit of $50 a month was approved for the Central Area's 2,600 AFDC mothers, and Black History was added to the Seattle Public School curriculum for the coming year.

MacIntosh and Redwine were also extremely critical of NAACP counsel Herbert Hill—"a fraud"—for sidetracking the dispute with contractors into a demand for more trades union apprenticeships. They rapped the older Central Area Committee for Civil Rights for "still thinking in terms of integration, that is, knocking on the White Man's door."

The unnamed *Helix* interviewer noted that the Detroit riots were "racially mixed" and asked if there was an opportunity for "greater unity" among the oppressed in Seattle. MacIntosh replied that the "potential is here, but the difference also remains . . . I know for a fact that I won't get the same kind of justice you would if you had done the same thing."

The issue of potential black-white cooperation dominated the national Conference on New Politics held on August 29 in Chicago's incongruously posh Palmer House to plot the "New Politics." Among the participants were new SDS members Robby and Susan Stern. When black delegates found themselves outnumbered on the steering committee and encountered difficulties finding housing, they threatened to "tear down the Palmer House" if the problems were not solved. The conference split in two with a formal "Black Caucus" and a mostly white convention "plenary." CORE leader Floyd McKissick addressed the convention on "black liberation." In the *Helix*, Robby Stern described the presentation of thirteen Black Caucus resolutions to the steering committee during a session lasting from midnight to 4:30 a.m. The plenum adopted the resolutions in an emergency session by a vote of "17,000 to 6,000" (delegates cast more than one vote each). The Black Caucus also demanded and received a block of half of the convention's allotted votes. It was a monument to white guilt and a preview of ideological contortions to come.

Stern was in obvious awe of the "young black militants": "They said they are prepared to die to see their people liberated from American oppression. It became clear to many of the white people that the Black Movement is far more sophisticated than the white radical movement in recognizing the evils of the present American capitalistic system. They had perceived how the liberal American system inhibited and disenfranchised the people. And they set forth the need for immediate fundamental change in this society. They indicated that capitalism leads to racism and imperialism and they showed historically how this has been the case." The Sterns returned from Chicago and joined the UW SDS. Soon after, Susan helped to organize Radical Women with Clara Fraser—Seattle's own Emma Goldman—Jill Severn, and others.

The Conference on New Politics ended anticlimactically with a call for more local community organizing. This was the sort of left-handed circle-jerk which drove Abbie Hoffman mad. He had by now formed a partnership with Jerry Rubin which he likened to Fidel and Che—or Abbott and Costello. "The Left has the same smugness as the *New York Times,*" Hoffman complained, and it was just as obsolete in the new global village. His dictum was, "A modern revolutionary heads for the television station, not the factory." Hoffman argued, "We are the information on television, the rest is part of the rhetorical ground." His theory was to confront the news media with compelling, intentionally absurd images which they had to present undigested and unedited to viewers. Thus, the Left could communicate directly with a mass audience via a hostile medium, but the imagery had to express freedom and action, not "rhetoric," to young people. Hoffman variously called this technique "reverse manipulation" and "monkey warfare" in contrast to the heavy-handed "gorilla" variety.

He had honed his technique with a number of increasingly outrageous stunts. On St. Valentine's day, with money provided by Jimi Hendrix, he anonymously mailed joints to several thousand randomly selected New Yorkers. One of these was a TV newsman who showed off his gift on his program; police were there in minutes and arrested him on the air for possession. On August 24, he and Jerry Rubin threw 300 one-dollar bills from the gallery of the New York Stock Exchange, triggering a near riot on the trading floor.

For his next trick, Hoffman proposed to levitate the Pentagon as the climax of a week of demonstrations already scheduled for October's "Stop the Draft Week." Hoffman credits Ed Sanders with coming up with the idea, although historian W. J. Rorabaugh says Charlie Brown Artman, "Berkeley's original hippie," conceived the notion.

The national cycle of demonstrations began on October 16, and the main event was a return engagement at the Oakland Induction Center. Joan Baez and 123 other protesters were arrested during a sit-in on the first day. The police went berserk on the next day, dubbed "Bloody Tuesday," and the violence was repeated until Friday. The incidents led to the indictment of Frank Bardache, Terry Cannon, Reese Erlich, Steve Hamilton, Bob Mandel, Jeff Segal, and Mike Smith for "felonious conspiracy to organize followers to commit misdemeanors." They became the "Oakland Seven," the first of several "sevens" to be immortalized by local and federal prosecutors, usually for helping to organize demonstrations at which the police rioted.

Also on "Bloody Tuesday," seven protesters, including UW professor Alex Gottfried and his wife Sue, were arrested during a sit-in on the steps of the Federal Building in Seattle. UW president Odegaard chose the same day to hold his first "open door" session with students.

I missed the news of "Bloody Tuesday," since it happened to be the day I reported for my own induction. Stopping the draft had ceased to be a political abstraction since I received my "Greeting" a month earlier. Like any red-blooded American with better things to do than to languish in the Army for two years (the idea of seeing combat never occurred to me; basic training was a much more unsettling idea) I gathered up records of my sundry physical and psychological defects, which were numerous.

Mainly, I worked like a fiend. *Helix* had just moved into its new offices on Harvard, and I wrote and drew for days and nights. When the morning of my induction arrived, I was just finishing a suitably apocalyptic cover of nuclear devastation. I quickly penned a letter to my would-be new employers, "This is to clarify my political position, particularly in regards to your security codes, so that your files on me might attain some semblance of reality." I recited the tenets of my beliefs, concluding, "Yes, I oppose and will work to overthrow *your* America. No, you don't understand my philosophy because when you find out where it's at, it will have already moved."

John Cunnick added a note of his own:

Walt Crowley, 20-year old Trot . . . just stalked out of the office to report for induction into the Armed Forces of the these United States.

In front: the Army doesn't really want Walter. It is possible that Fidel

Castro, a folk hero of Walter's somewhat peculiar folk (he's the only one to the best of my knowledge) wouldn't want Walter, even cold and hungry in the Sierra. Walter is sarcastic, emotionally unstable even by UPS standards, and fully strung out on things that normal folk can't even get mildly dizzy on. . . .

He sped out the door wired like a generator factory . . . the light of battle glinting from his steel rims. He may return. Conversely, several generals may well appear at the office seeking sanctuary; one can never tell with Walter or ranking officers.

Dear Colonel Sir: Please excuse W. Crowley from your strange thing for the next duration or two as we need him badly here, and you can't use him anyway.

I reported to the gray, Bastille-like Induction Center off Alaskan Way with my files, a toothbrush, and a change of underwear, in order to be prepared for all contingencies. Outside, a sizable contingent of my comrades-in-arms chanted and marched. Inside, I almost flunked the weigh-in, barely registering 105 pounds at five-foot-seven. The officers took a great deal of interest in my letter, while a Navy physician fingered my groin, in search of hernia, with more than professional interest. I waited in my briefs alongside two teenagers who boasted nervously that they couldn't wait to "get over there and kill some gooks." At the end, I was handed a military-looking form and told to put on my clothes and get out. There on the paper were the sacred runes: 4-F.

The Army had taken Cunnick's advice. No reason was given, but *Helix* later printed a purported Selective Service memorandum advising local draft boards not to induct members of the underground press. They caused too much trouble in the ranks.

Abbie Hoffman's proposal to levitate the Pentagon attracted some 30,000 to the giant complex on the Virginia side of the Potomac on October 21. Assorted gurus and shamans, along with the Fugs, led the crowd in chants to "exorcise" the evil spirits, but it did not stir visibly. The confrontation did provide one of the Movement's enduring icons: a photo of a Berkeley hippie named "Super Joel" inserting a flower into the barrel of an MP's rifle.

After most of the press had departed, military and local police descended on the remaining crowd, injuring 47 and arresting 443, including Hoffman. The *P-I* headlined its account of the demonstration, "Troops Repel Attack on Pentagon." The problem with Hoffman's technique is that it required that observers possess a sense of humor, and what little there was of that would soon drain away.

Six days after the "Levitation," the Rev. Philip Berrigan and two other clerics walked into the draft board office in Baltimore and poured blood over their files. On the same day, a Fort Lewis court martial sentenced Michael Bratcher to four years of hard labor after he pleaded guilty to disobeying orders during his campaign for conscientious objector status. The day after that, October 28, Huey Newton shot an Oakland policeman during an arrest, and his defense became a long-running cause for the Left. Antiwar protesters battled police during major demonstrations in New York City in November and December, leading to hundreds of arrests, including those of Dr. Benjamin Spock and Allen Ginsberg.

Things were also happening in that other, "overground" world in which most people lived and toiled. That fall in Seattle, Jim Ellis's Forward Thrust Committee unveiled twelve bond issues to fund a host of civic improvements including rail transit and the Kingdome. King County began work on a new "home rule" charter, and Seattle took major steps toward sorely needed municipal reforms. The new Committee to Help Elect an Effective City Council, CHECC, won seats for two of its candidates, Phyllis Lamphere and Tim Hill, and State Rep. Sam Smith became the first black to join the council. The next month, Mayor Braman named Walt Hundley to head up Seattle's new Model Cities Program. We in the underground, of course, viewed these events as little more than changing the table linen aboard the HMS *Titanic*.

On November 22, General Westmoreland declared that U.S. victory in a twenty-day battle to take a hill named Dak To in the Central Highlands signaled "the beginning of a great defeat for the enemy." Johnson suspended bombing the North and renewed his "peace offensive" to get Hanoi to the bargaining table. He did not know that Ho was planning his own offensive a few months hence.

Eight days later, Minnesota Sen. Eugene McCarthy announced that he would run for the Democratic nomination for president.

Although most Americans still supported the war, President Johnson's approval rating had plummeted, and a majority of Democrats preferred New York Sen. Robert Kennedy, now a vocal critic of the war but not yet an official candidate for the nomination.

Events were beginning to converge; they would collide in August, in Chicago.

Chapter 12:
Dumping Johnson,
Dropping Pianos

All power to the
imagination!
—**French student slogan**

Nineteen sixty-eight was the defining year of the Sixties. It was truly the best of the times and the worst. It embraced the peak of the period's playfulness and the depths of its depravity and violence. If anyone had doubts that a genuine revolution was imminent, the events of early 1968 laid them to rest. If anyone hoped that a revolution could actually succeed, the events of late 1968 crushed their dream beneath the boot of repression.

Abbie Hoffman, Jerry Rubin, Paul Krassner, Dick Gregory, Ed Sanders, and others ushered in the new year by announcing the birth of the Yippies, designated as an afterthought as members of the "Youth International Party." For Hoffman, it was another experiment in monkey theater, the creation of a mediagenic "meta-myth" by which he hoped to unify the energies of the counterculture and New Left in a common cause. The climax was to be a collective "Festival of Life" in Chicago during August's Democratic National Convention. It sounded like fun.

The year's political circus opened on January 5, when Dr. Benjamin Spock, William Sloan Coffin, and three others were indicted in Boston for the mere act of "counseling" draft-age men on their rights and options. Two weeks later, the Pentagon announced that it would call up an additional 72,000 men. This same day, January 19, President Johnson named Clark Clifford to succeed Robert McNamara, who took over the World Bank, as Secretary of Defense. McNamara wouldn't slip away quietly. He was confronted with a new and final crisis on January 23 when the North Koreans seized a U.S. intelligence ship, the *Pueblo,* off their coast; the crew were imprisoned and tortured until December 22.

McNamara left the Pentagon utterly disillusioned with the war. In his final appearance before Congress, he warned, "No matter how great the resources we commit to the struggle, we cannot provide the South Vietnamese with the will to survive as an independent nation." Clark Clifford understood this as well and was committed to beginning America's disengagement from Vietnam.

Clifford needed time to neutralize the hawks, led by Secretary of State Dean Rusk, and persuade the President. As he prepared to move into the Pentagon, the situation in Vietnam seemed relatively stable. The troublesome Air Marshall Ky had stepped aside the previous year and allowed Nguyen Van Thieu to assume the presidency with an illusion of electoral legitimacy. General Westmoreland continued to send comforting body counts home from the battlefield, although "hot pursuit" forays into Cambodia had prompted its Prince Sihanouk in January to sever diplomatic relations with the U.S.

The U.S. Senate confirmed Clark Clifford on January 30, the eve of the Tet lunar new year festival and a brief truce with the VC and North Vietnamese. It was, therefore, a surprise as complete and devastating as Pearl Harbor when 70,000 Vietcong and North Vietnamese regulars launched nearly simultaneous attacks on scores of targets from Quang Tri near the Demilitarized Zone as far south as Camau. They captured the old capital of Hué, stormed presumably safe U.S. bases such as Danang, laid siege at the Green Beret base at Khe Sanh, and launched rockets into the U.S. port complex at Camranh Bay. Boldest of all, they carried the war onto the grounds of the U.S. Embassy in Saigon.

The battles raged for three weeks, costing the lives of 2,000 Americans, 4,000 South Vietnamese troops, and many more VC and civilians. When the fighting was finally suppressed, General Westmoreland claimed a victory. Technically he was correct, as VC Deputy Commander Tran Do later admitted. "We didn't achieve our main objective, which was to spur uprisings throughout the south." He added, "As for making an impact in the United States, it had not been our intention—but it turned out to be a fortunate result."

The Tet Offensive electrified the antiwar Left. For ordinary Americans it was perplexing and disturbing, coming after so much reassurance from the field and the Pentagon. For some it was horrifying, epitomized by Eddie Adams's photograph of South Vietnamese national police chief Nguyen Ngoc firing a bullet into the brain of a VC suspect on a Saigon street.

A lot more people, including many of President Johnson's "Wise Men" advisers, began asking themselves, what the hell are we doing in Vietnam? Some, like Senate Foreign Affairs Committee chairman J. William Fulbright, had been asking that question loudly for some time, and repeated it now louder than ever. Walter Cronkite traveled personally to inspect the situation in Vietnam, and devoted his entire February 27 broadcast to his report. He ended by calling for a negotiated withdrawal from the war. In mid-March, North Vietnamese Foreign Minister Nguyen Duy Trinh told another CBS correspondent, Charles Collingwood, that his government was ready to talk.

For the "Dump Johnson" movement, launched the previous year by Allard Lowenstein with quixotic prospects for success, the aftermath of Tet was a godsend. New Hampshire voters voiced their misgivings on March 13 by giving Eugene McCarthy 42 percent of the Democratic primary vote. Not all of these voters necessarily disapproved of the war, but none liked Johnson's handling of it. The next day King County Democrats gave the majority of their caucus votes to McCarthy, and they didn't like the war in any way, shape, or form. Two days after that, Robert Kennedy announced his own candidacy for the Democratic nomination, something Johnson had feared for months. No one knew then that on the same day, March 16, troops under the command of Lt. William Calley were machine-gunning scores of civilians in a little village called My Lai. The massacre wouldn't be exposed by Seymour Hersch for a year.

President Johnson could read the political writing on the wall. He kicked Westmoreland upstairs to Chairman of the Joint Chiefs of Staff, and later sent General Creighton Abrams to take command in Saigon. He was not looking for scapegoats, just tidying up for the balance of his term. He made a decision he had been considering since January. On March 31, the President addressed the nation. He announced a halt to bombing North Vietnam above the 20th parallel and invited the enemy to the peace table one more time (he had already signaled his agreement to Hanoi's key demand that the NLF also be seated). Then, at the close, he paused and explained he didn't want to embroil the conduct of his duties in "partisan divisions" and, "accordingly, I shall not seek, and I will not accept the nomination of any party for another term as your president."

Abbie Hoffman thought it was a plot to spoil his Yippie festival.

For *Helix*, 1968 marked something of a rebirth. Circulation fell from 16,000 the previous summer to a low ebb of barely 5,000 copies during the winter, and morale sank deeper. Maryl Clemmens moved away, John Cunnick's output temporarily dried up, and Jack Delay became embittered by the degeneration of the street scene in the District. I entered my "weltschmerz" phase of morbid adolescent omphaloskepsis.

Paul Dorpat kept us going. As I later wrote on the paper's second anniversary, "Paul provided the center and the drive of the paper. He alone had any concrete idea of what to do. Thus the paper radiated out from him. *Helix* was after all an alarmingly appropriate name, for Paul was Helios." Our survival was abetted by Tim Harvey's cool competence, Scott White's ego-deflating humor, and artist Billy Ward's indomitable cheerfulness. I wrote of Ward, a follower of Meher Baba ("Don't Worry. Be Happy"), "I wouldn't be surprised if Billy glows in the dark, a softly fluorescent Cheshire cat grin."

Roger Hudson, bearded with a slightly crazed look behind his wire-rims, was our chief photographer. Roger became a story in his own right later in the year when Highline Community College busted him for selling *Helices* on campus. The charge was "loitering without lawful purpose"; it took a judge to explain to the school that selling newspapers is regarded as a lawful purpose under the Constitution.

Harassment of *Helix* dealers did step up in the winter of 1967-68, which was attributed in part to my "Arresting Tales" cover featuring "Super Cop from the Pubic Safety Building," an image of a Marvel Comics–style cop wielding a phallic nightstick. Despite their public disapproval of the image, many cops pinned the cover to the inside of their lockers, I'm told. Another cover of mine ended our brief flirtation with Grange Press in 1968. It showed an exaggerated buxom woman swinging on a magnet between two penile missiles to illustrate Dick Tracy creator Chester Gould's dictum, "The nation that controls magnetism controls the universe." Grange Press didn't find it attractive, and we had to go all the way to Mount Vernon to find a new printer who'd take us—for cash on delivery.

"Not So Straight John" Bixler joined us that spring, and also began taking pix for us. (John's first appearance was an ad to sell his Bugati motorcycle; his next appearance was to beg whoever stole it to please bring it back.) *Helix* also printed many photographs taken by Gary Finholt and *Seattle Magazine* mainstay Frank Denman. Our poetry also took on more depth and polish with the words of Paul Hunter and Tom Parson.Courtesy of the UPS, *Helix* began publishing numerous cartoons: M. Rodriguez's violent, gritty action strips (which got the *EVO* busted); Ron Cobb's tight, barbed editorial cartoons from the *LA Free Press,* and R. Crumb's wry, erotic strips from Detroit featuring Mr. Natural, Flaky Foont, Whiteman, and Angelfood McSpade, a voluptuous black primitive who would send today's politically correct hall monitors into a self-righteous rage. Later came Gilbert Shelton's hapless Furry Freak Brothers, Rick Griffin's surreal world of winged eyeballs and mutating Mickey Mice, and S. Clay Wilson's brutal, sexually explicit visions of life among dykes and bikes. (Wilson later visited the *Helix* and drew an original strip for us, but I made him do a "soft-core porn" version for our sensitive readers.)

This marvelous work inspired Tim Harvey and me to concoct our own serialized strip, the adventures of "Omega-84," a biologically mutated revolutionary in a future dystopia. The strip ended after sixteen panels just as our hero was about to confront his creator, the evil Dr. Schwarzherz. Frankly, I didn't know how to get him out of the fix I'd put him in. Other notable cartoonists in our ranks included Zac Reisner, who illustrated many of Cunnick's pieces, and the British artist Michael Lawson, who painted deceptively childlike and very disturbing paintings but penned chatty, Feifferesque strips exploring the absurdities of modern life.

That spring, the Seattle counterculture founded its first permanent institution, the Experimental College at the UW. The College was promoted by Mike Mandeville, a dynamic student leader with an entrepreneurial bent, who had founded Lecture Notes in 1966. These printed reports of major lectures were sold to students too busy to attend class and initially faced stiff antipathy from professors. By spring

1968, the Free U had lost its "campus" above the Coffee Corral and was spinning apart, so Mandeville's imitation was viewed as a lifeboat, not a pirate raid.

Also that spring, UW students elected Thom Gunn as their new student body president. Gunn's candidacy was only one of many pranks, and he was as astonished as anyone by his victory over serious contenders. Upon his election, Thom jumped into Frosh Pond to wash off the "politics." Gunn was not trusted by militants, and for good reason: his antics threw cold water on their efforts to raise the temperature on campus.

In the meantime, *Helix* threw a little party of its own: The Piano Drop. The idea began with Larry Van Over, better known then as "Jug" for his musicianship as a member of The Willowdale Handcar jug band. One night while listening to KRAB-FM, Larry and illustrator Gary Eagle caught a replay of the CAMP benefit during which a piano was demolished with sledge hammers. They found the aural experience disappointing, which led them to speculate (with the aid of certain psychoactive chemicals) about dropping a piano from a building, or better yet, a helicopter. It might be considered an experiment in Zen acoustics: What is the sound of one piano dropping from a height of a 100 feet or so?

Sproinnnng? Charrrownnng? Brrrannnngggg? Kashwonngagaga?

Thus inspired, Larry enlisted the aid of Paul Dorpat. *Helix* and KRAB had already scheduled a benefit "Media Mash" for Sunday, April 21. The Piano Drop hooked on as a free premium the following Sunday. Those who did not attend the Mash were charged a buck each to see the Piano Drop and hear Country Joe and the Fish (or vice versa).

Larry tracked down an old upright piano and trucked it to his three-acre farm off Cherry Valley Road. He then contracted a helicopter service out of Boeing Field. The pilot didn't quite get the point, but he had moved pianos with his helicopter before. Having successfully not dropped pianos, he saw no special problem in doing the opposite. As Larry later recalled, "There were a number of Newton's laws that the pilot neglected to consider."

Assured of the feasibility of musical strategic bombing, Larry calmly dropped acid on Sunday afternoon and climbed into the helicopter to guide the pilot out to his farm. It was sunny and clear. As the helicopter passed Woodinville, Larry and the pilot noticed that the traffic below was getting heavier and heavier. "Gee, there are a lot of people out today," Larry commented over the engine's roar. By the turnoff to Larry's farm, he and the pilot realized that they had not been observing mere Sunday drivers. The roads around the farm were a parking lot—and then they saw a wall-to-wall carpet of humanity covering the drop zone. Instead of the 300 participants he had expected, the pilot estimated at least ten times as many filled the countryside below. At this moment, Larry got that special, tinny taste in his mouth indicating that his mental altimeter had exceeded the helicopter's.

"No way, no way, no way," the pilot muttered with mounting conviction as he set the helicopter down next to the waiting piano. "What exactly is your apprehension here?" Larry asked innocently.

"They're not going to get out of the way," the pilot explained.

"They'll move, man, they'll move," Larry pleaded with that persuasive power only true evangelists and zonked-out lunatics can muster. "Trust me, man, it'll be like the Red Sea all over again!"

For whatever reason—curiosity, fear of not being paid, or a contact high—the pilot relented. "Okay, but they gotta give me plenty of room, or no drop."

The pilot hitched the piano to a special harness and lifted off. He approached the target, a platform of logs, from an altitude of at least 150 feet. The machine hove into view and the crowd, as Larry had predicted, parted and retreated to a respectful distance.

The pilot brought his machine to a halt mid-air, but bodies in motion tend to remain in motion, and the 500-pound piano dragged the helicopter forward. The pilot panicked and hit the harness release, but nothing happened. He then hit the emergency cable release, and the piano snapped free. It described a lazy arc through the bright spring sky, overshot the target by several yards, struck the soft earth, and imploded with a singularly unmusical whump. "A piano flop," Dorpat later dubbed it.

The crowd was not disappointed and let loose a collective "Far out!" as it surged toward the remains of the piano. By the time Larry pushed his way to the piano's impact crater, not a stick, wire, ivory, or scrap of felt remained. "They devoured it," he recalls. The last he saw of the instrument was its steel harp being loaded into a VW microbus by two hippies.

As Country Joe and the Fish fired up their amplifiers, somebody said, "Hey, let's do that again," and so was born the idea for the Sky River Rock Festival and Lighter Than Air Fair.

Chapter 13:
To the
Barricades

I'm tired of reading history.
Now I want to make it.
—Mario Savio

D uring the winter and spring of 1968, the Black Panther Party emerged as the leading advocate of black power. Stokely Carmichael recognized its hegemony at a February 17 rally in Oakland where he joined the party's leadership. On April 1, SNCC—whose titular head, H. Rap Brown, had either been on the lam or in jail most of his tenure—formally merged with the Panthers.

At the February rally, Carmichael denounced socialism and communism as "an ideology not suited to black people" because they addressed class rather than race. "The question of race becomes uppermost in our minds," Carmichael exhorted the crowd, because "it is a question of how we regain our humanity and begin to live as a people" by overthrowing the institutions of racism. Carmichael's position received backhanded support from the Kerner Commission's report released on March 2. It faulted excessive police force in ghettos, called for spending $2 billion a month to revitalize inner cities, and warned that America "is moving toward two societies—one black, one white—separate and unequal." Thus, in the establishment view, race, not economics, was also the prime determinant.

The Rev. Martin Luther King Jr. had reached the exact opposite conclusion—that the cause of civil rights had to reach beyond race to encompass economic and social justice for all. He was no longer afraid of being Red-baited, and declared that when federal funds are "given to the white people, it's called a subsidy" for suburban home loans or new highways, but when it's given to blacks and the poor, it's called "welfare." In America, King said, there existed "socialism for the rich" and "rugged, free enterprise capitalism" for the poor.

In a bid to regain leadership of the Movement and to reassert an integrationist agenda along class lines, King had formulated a "Poor People's Campaign" the previous fall, which was to culminate in a another huge rally in Washington, D.C., in May. His new, overtly economic emphasis took King to Memphis in late March to aid a strike by mostly black sanitation workers. The scene in that city was confusing and violent, abetted by the FBI's new "Counter-Intelligence Program" (COINTELPRO) to disrupt the Left. King came close to abandoning the campaign, but his supporters encouraged him to press forward in Memphis and beyond.

There, in the early evening of April 4, King lingered on the balcony of his motel before going down to dinner. Shortly after 6 p.m. he was struck by a sniper's bullet and died minutes later. As King's life drained away, Andrew Young knelt beside him and wailed, "Oh my God, it's all over!"

The nation reacted with horror, and young blacks raged through the ghettoes of Washington, D.C., Chicago, and other cities in a week-long paroxysm of violence that left at least thirty-three dead. In Seattle, Central Area youths pelted buses and cars with rocks and torched four local businesses. In Oakland, police stormed the Black Panther office, killing Bobby Hutton and injuring Eldridge Cleaver and three others; four officers were also wounded by the Panthers' return fire.

Ten days after King's assassination, Bobby Seale visited Seattle. He met with a small group of young blacks including Aaron and Elmer Dixon. The Dixon brothers, along with Larry Gossett, Carl Miller, and Trolice Flavors, had been arrested on March 29 after staging a sit-in at Franklin High School to protest Flavors's expulsion. Attorney William Dwyer won their release the next day and the Dixons, Gossett, and Miller flew to San Francisco for the Western Black Youth Conference where SNCC and the Panthers merged.

After attending Bobby Hutton's funeral and hearing a call to action from Bobby Seale, they resolved to organize a local Black Panther chapter. Seale himself flew into Seattle in mid-April and appointed Aaron "captain" of the local party; Curtis Harris became "co-captain" and Elmer Dixon also joined the leadership, along with E. J. Brisker, head of the new Black Student Union at the UW. A meeting a few weeks later attracted fifty interested blacks, but not all joined, and some who did, like Carl Miller, were not active. Larry Gossett was another titular member, and the future director of CAMP and Metropolitan King County Council member decided to focus his energy on the BSU. The local party never had more than a few dozen reliable members, but it cast a long shadow—all the way to the downtown Public Safety Building.

Attention shifted back to the war with a new Mobe and national student strike on April 26 and 27. The strike "idled" as many as one million high school and college students, while 60,000 marched in New York against the war. Two thousand protested peacefully in Seattle, but police attacked 3,000 demonstrators in Chicago, foreshadowing events to come.

At the UW, Larry Baker organized a rally of some 2,000 students who presented a list of demands to president Odegaard dealing with academic governance, ROTC, corporate and military recruiting, and weapons research. He rejected them out of hand, but was more responsive to demands for increased minority student aid presented by BSU head E. J. Brisker on May 6.

The UW campus was downright peaceful compared to New York's Columbia University. After long agitation on and off campus to halt Columbia's plan to expand into the adjacent, mostly black Morningside Park neighborhood, SDS leader Mark Rudd and a separate contingent of black students occupied several campus buildings, and briefly took a dean hostage on April 23. Police cleared the buildings on May 1, triggering a full-scale strike by students and sympathetic faculty.

Two weeks later, presidential candidate Richard Nixon would call the Columbia uprising the "first skirmish in a revolutionary struggle to seize the universities of this country and transform them into sanctuaries for radicals and vehicles for revolutionary political and social goals." Mark Rudd could not have said it better, and such campus agitation was not limited to the United States.

Hundreds of thousands of snake-dancing Japanese leftists had staged repeated demonstrations against the war and the U.S. over the past several years, and tens of thousands of German leftists had booed Vice President Humphrey in West Berlin the previous spring. Virtual street warfare broke out in several German cities when a right-wing gunman shot and wounded student leader "Red Rudi" Dutschke on a West Berlin street on April 12.

Students in Czechoslovakia constituted one of the bulwarks of the "Prague Spring" movement for liberalization and "communism with a human face." Key reformer Alexander Dubcek took the reins of the party and government in January 25, carefully loosening restraints on civil liberties while assuring the Soviet Union of his loyalty. His position was steadily undermined as increasingly large and raucous rallies led chiefly by students demanded that "Ivan Go Home."

France's left-wing "Gauchistes" were also active. When police arrested six antiwar protesters at the University of Nanterre, near Paris, on March 22, a national movement began to coalesce around the leadership of Daniel Cohn-Bendit, who advocated opposition to both liberal capitalism and "obsolete communism." When right-wing forces threatened to attack the campus on May 2, the Gauchistes barricaded themselves in. When the administration scheduled disciplinary hearings on the Sorbonne campus of the University of Paris, thousands of students marched en masse. They were met on the evening of May 6 by club-swinging gendarmes, and the battle for Paris was on.

Thousands of students rallied to the barricades around the Sorbonne and fanned out across the city. On May 7, they raised the red flag of revolution over the Arc de Triomphe. It resembled a reenactment of the 1876 Paris Commune, only directed this time by Alfred Jarry, as "Situationists" and assorted anarchists papered the city with dada slogans.

How effective these were is debatable, but the spectacle of police beating students, who enjoy a status in France different and higher than in the U.S., shocked the public. Over the next several weeks, nearly ten million French workers staged wildcat strikes in sympathy with the students. Both President DeGaulle and the French Communists, who had lost control of the labor movement, scrambled to reassert their authority.

The impact of these events on the American student Left cannot be overstated. Across the world, the archipelago of academia was aflame with revolutionary fervor. Here, at last, was an example equal to that of the Black Panthers and Vietcong: white radicals engaged in hand-to-hand combat with the beast. As Todd Gitlin recalls in his history of the era, "Many of us had concluded that the problem wasn't simply bad policy but a wrong-headed social system, even a civilization. The weight of decades, or centuries, even millennia has to be thrown off overnight—because it was necessary."

All through May, participants in the Poor People's March trickled into Washington, D.C., and encamped near the Lincoln Memorial in a makeshift "Resurrection City." Coretta Scott King, Robert Kennedy, and the Rev. Ralph Abernathy, the new head of the SCLC, addressed the first arrivals on May 12, hoping to rekindle the dream. The tent city soon became squalid and dangerous, and a final "Solidarity Day" rally on June 12 drew a disappointing 50,000 attendees. Few protested when police cleared out the tent city, arresting scores, including Abernathy. Many of King's lieutenants, including Andrew Young and Jesse Jackson, decided to pursue different courses afterward.

The war continued to dominate the news that spring and summer. The Paris talks had stalled almost immediately after beginning on May 10, as delegates wrangled over "the shape of the table." The real issue was the status of the NLF delegation, whose participation was adamantly opposed by Thieu. There was no incentive for the North or the VC to compromise. The long siege at Khe Sanh and the VC's renewed attacks during the "Battle of Saigon," pushed American fatalities during the first half of 1968 to 9,557—more than had died during the entire previous year.

The antiwar movement gained new martyrs on May 17, when Father Daniel Berrigan, SJ, his brother, Father Philip Berrigan, and seven other Catholic protesters destroyed draft records at Catonsville, Maryland. Three days later, the trial of Dr. Spock and his three co-defendants began on charges of abetting draft evasion. Both sets of protesters were ultimately convicted, although the draft counseling charges were later overturned; along the way, five of the "Catonsville Nine," including the Berrigans, went "underground."

The nation was still bleeding from King's assassination when the next blow fell. On the night of June 4, Robert Kennedy and his supporters gathered in Los Angeles to celebrate his victory in the California primary. A self-styled champion of the Palestinian cause, Sirhan Sirhan, fired point-blank into Kennedy's skull; he died early the next morning. Jerry Rubin did his cause no favors when he declared "Sirhan Sirhan is a Yippie."

With Kennedy's death, Eugene McCarthy inherited the mantle

of the liberal antiwar movement, although radicals distrusted him. Fearing a successful challenge from the Left, Vice President Humphrey, campaigning for the Democratic nomination, began to distance himself from Johnson by calling for an immediate cease-fire. North Vietnamese General Giap's strategy of "bleeding" America's will to fight was proceeding well.

On July 1, riots broke out around Garfield High School following the conviction of Aaron Dixon, Larry Gossett, and Carl Miller for unlawful assembly at Franklin High during March's sit-in. *Helix* staffers Tim Harvey and Hillaire Dufrene drove out to cover the action, and were suddenly attacked and beaten by black youths. Only the intercession of another black activist, Michael Ross, saved them from more serious, possibly fatal injury.

The rhetoric and, more important, the mob psychology of black rage did not distinguish between friends and foes among white faces. Indeed, Leroi Jones had denounced white radicals as oppressors, although the Panthers locally and nationally strove to maintain connections with white sources of money and political credibility, deftly manipulating what Tom Wolfe dubbed the "radical chic."

Eight days after the Central Area riots, the Seattle School District designated Garfield as its first "magnet school" under a new plan to stimulate voluntary desegregation. This only acknowledged that Garfield had attracted many of Seattle's best and brightest—and most liberal—students of all races for many years under principal Frank Hanawalt, who later took over integration planning for the district.

In mid-July, the city announced that it would spend $2.3 million in federal funds to create 1,800 new jobs, chiefly for minority youth. If this was meant to cool tempers, it didn't work. Black kids rioted again on July 18, prompting City Councilman Sam Smith to call for a curfew in the Central Area. This was precisely the wrong remedy, since the real source of heat was friction between Seattle police officers and increasingly assertive black teens, led or inspired by the Black Panthers.

The fuse was lit on July 29, when fourteen Seattle police officers marched into the local Panthers' office and magically found a "stolen" typewriter (probably planted by an undercover agent). The police arrested Aaron Dixon and Curtis Harris. That night, seven policemen and two civilians were struck by sniper fire or rocks during rioting in the Central Area, despite Dixon's appeal from jail, delivered by attorney William Dwyer, that such a response "will only jeopardize the lives of masses of black people."

The Central Area erupted anew on July 31, and police swept up sixty-nine in a mass arrest. The Seattle–King County Bar Association protested police tactics, and a delegation of the Central Area's leading ministers and citizens met with Mayor Braman and demanded that he fire Chief Frank Ramon. Braman declined, but Ramon would be gone for a different set of reasons before the end of 1969. Mayor Braman named a "Police Liaison Committee" to investigate widespread allegations of police brutality—but the committee's all-white membership just set off more howls. The situation cooled for the moment, and Seattle could say that it had dodged a bullet: seven died in a clash between black nationalists and police in Cleveland on July 23 and subsequent riots claimed four more lives.

The reality of such violence, and the eagerness of more and more white radicals to emulate black militants and "off the pig," in Panther parlance, alarmed me. In August, I asked *Helix* readers, "Could you kill someone? Maybe, in the heat of the moment we could all kill a 'racist fascist motherfucking pig of a cop,' but even stereotypes bleed and moan and have wives who'll miss them. And anyway, isn't that part of this odious evil we supposedly oppose?"

I still thought of myself as a small "r" revolutionary but I began to put some distance between myself and the bigger-than-life "R" variety. In the spirit of a loyal opposition with the Left, I criticized the degeneration of the New Left into a comic-book parody of Leninism-Marxism: "The cliches we mouth about America originated in an analysis of an entirely different society a hundred years ago. . . . We haven't even thought up our own platitudes. . . . Were Che alive, he would laugh in our faces." Events would confirm my worst fears.

In the summer of 1968, I marked my twenty-first birthday. The *Helix* staff celebrated by carrying me around the block from our office to the old Red Robin, where I had been a regular customer for two years. This was Sam's Red Robin and it bears no resemblance to the fern conservatory built in its place in 1970 by tavern imperialist Jerry Kingen. Seedy, shady, ramshackle, disreputable, and thoroughly de-

lightful, the old Robin seemed to host nightly brawls, usually insti-
gated by Alfredo Arreguin, a Mexican-born painter of great ability
and then greater bellicosity (he's calmer now).

My birthday roughly coincided with the release of Stanley Kubrick's
2001, a Space Odyssey. As a longtime fan of both Kubrick's films and
Arthur C. Clarke's transcendental science fiction, I couldn't have asked
for a better present. Whoever did publicity for the movie knew it
would have special appeal for the counterculture, so I was invited to
the press preview in July at the Cinerama Theater. When the first
chords of Strauss' *Also Sprach Zarathustra* boomed out, I knew I was
in for one hell of a trip. It was so good I took it at least a dozen more
times.

The other great film of 1968, in my estimation, was Wojciech
Has' *Sargossa Manuscript,* which I described as Ingmar Bergman di-
recting Restoration Comedy and the closest thing to "an acid cycle
this side of pharmacopoeia." Also that year, Jane Fonda achieved stardom in the erotic-space fantasy, *Barbarella,* based on a French precursor of the Heavy Metal comic strip genre.

My majority signaled my move to political postgraduate study
under the tutelage of Stan Iverson, who presided over a running symposium at the District's other great tavern, the Blue Moon. Instead of
a class bell, Stan signaled the beginning of each lesson by bellowing,
"Wellll, Motherrrrfuckerrr," upon one's entrance (if he liked you, that
is) and motioning you to his table.

The Moon was (and still is, thanks to its owners, Three Fools,
Inc., and a preservation victory in 1990) the unofficial capitol of
bohemia in Seattle, serving generations of radicals, nonconformists,
the occasional genius—such as Theodore Roethke, among at least four
Pulitzer Prize winning poets who toped there with regularity—and
the rarer normal person. I count Stan among the genius category.

A former Communist organizer born in Montana, Stan had left
the party in disgust with its hypocrisies on civil rights and become a
freelance anarchist. His views boiled down a distrust of all organiza-
tional structure, except the most basic voluntary associations, as essentially coercive. He also demanded respect for the rights of all individuals, unless they were spouting tripe, as his friend and fellow anar-

chist John Severn recalls, in which case it was all right to take a swing at 'em.

Stan was not a pacifist by any stretch, but he taught me the most important principle: the end does not justify the means, the means ordain the end. As would-be social physicians, he advised, revolution-aries are subject to the Hippocratic injunction: first do no harm.

Had there been a few more like Stan Iverson, the Sixties might have turned out better.

Chapter 14:
Ceremonies of
Innocence

And I am awaiting
perpetually and forever a
renaissance of wonder.

—Lawrence Ferlinghetti

Not only had the Piano Drop proved to be a countercultural success, it actually made money: $2,137, most of which was split by KRAB and the *Helix*. "If 3,000 people come to hear *one* band," Paul Dorpat speculated aloud, "how many would come to hear a dozen, or two dozen, or . . . ?"

The discussions began informally, and no participant can point to a particular time or place when the idea of a rock festival germinated. The notion appealed to multiple circles which intersected at the *Helix*'s office. Social revolutionaries, hippie communalists, psychedelic evangelists, musicians and their fans could all see value in holding some kind of event—but what kind and, for that matter, under what name?

Larry Van Over had become obsessed with the idea of giving people rides on a giant tethered helium balloon and therefore advocated "The Lighter Than Air Fair." He believed that such a gimmick, not the music, would be the main draw, but this seemed, well, too flighty to the rest of us. I have a dim recollection of a meeting in a Wallingford home (Gary Finholt's?) one evening in May or June of 1968. Paul was there, and I think Scott White, Gary Finholt, and John Bixler, John Cunnick, and Tim Harvey were there, too, and maybe Tom Robbins, or at least his astral body. The agenda was picking a name for the festival.

We already had a location for the festival: Betty Nelson's "organic raspberry" farm just outside the town of Sultan, near the banks of the Skykomish River. Nicknamed the "Universal Mother," Betty had established her own reputation as a rural free spirit, and she had gladly donated use of a large pasture cradled in a natural amphitheater.

We squatted Japanese-style around a large, low table and tried to figure out what to call this thing we were planning. Candles illuminated the haze of burning hemp and incense. Somebody intoned "Skykomish River." Somebody else abbreviated this to "Sky River." And somebody else added "Rock." The group took up the elemental mantra: "Sky River Rock."

We now had a venue and a name. This left only the question of what the Sky River Rock Festival would actually be.

About this time, Cyrus Noe entered the scene. Cy is perfectly cast as that uncle your parents always advised you to avoid—round, bearded, gravel-voiced, and probably not thinking wholesome thoughts behind his impish eyes. He was then recently retired as director of the UW's noncredit extension programs, and he had appointed himself the *Helix*'s "Society Editor" in the vain hope of getting a press pass to Dave Beck's wedding.

Cy was intrigued by Sky River and introduced John Chambless to the group. John was, of course, not a complete stranger and had been a visible champion of the counterculture since his arrival from Berkeley. A scholar of Nietzsche and Wittgenstein, Chambless was also an enormously popular instructor at the UW. His introductory courses in philosophy were packed, and he scored at the top of unofficial student ratings of faculty—which, of course, totally alienated John's colleagues. What we didn't know was that he had served for many years as associate producer of Berkeley's Folk Festival.

A former bantamweight boxer who further compressed himself into a permanent shrug with his hands typically buried deep in his pockets, John exuded irony. He spoke with a slight drawl betraying his southern roots, and was quick to note the absurdity of any situation with a wink and slightly manic cackle. Dorothy, his wife and soulmate, offered a perfect counterpoint: petite with delicate Asian features, compassionate, and eminently organized, she made their home a virtual counterculture club house within earshot of the Woodland Park Zoo's hooting monkeys.

Chambless was a self-confessed "groupie on the grand scale," and he offered to direct the Sky River Rock Festival, with the help of Cy Noe and Dorothy. This was a blessing for Paul Dorpat, who found the logistical challenges more than daunting, and who, after all, had a newspaper to run.

The festival was incorporated as the New American Community, a name suggested by Cy, who joined John in co-signing notes for $40,000 in seed capital. NAC rented a small office next door to the *Helix,* and an expanding staff and coterie of volunteers went to work. Arrangements were made to donate any profits (perish the thought) to Native American organizations.

Larry Van Over reappeared on the scene, and repeated his skepticism about the attractive power of a bunch of bands in a cow pasture. At his urging, the festival incorporated his helium balloon rides, and thus the event's name expanded to "Sky River Rock Festival and Lighter Than Air Fair."

Like the rabbit in *Alice in Wonderland,* the planning was permanently behind schedule. Amid the scramble, any help proffered was welcome. This inevitably allowed con men and charismatics to insinuate themselves into the group, and a strange, Manson-like scene developed at NAC's quasi-official crash pad in a Queen Anne mansion.

Time was passing, and Sky River began selling tickets in mid-July before a single band had been signed. Advance prices were set at $6 for all three days, and $8 at the gate. Meanwhile, Chambless and his crew scrambled to sign up acts. The ever faithful Country Joe McDonald was one of the first and lent the festival credibility, but it proved an easier sell than one might expect: the idea of creating a temporary musical utopia fired the imagination, and my first poster for Sky River (published only two weeks before the event) was able to list forty confirmed acts.

This poster also got me into trouble. It featured a frog sitting on a rock, contentedly smoking a large joint. Cy Noe, who had to deal with the local Sultan and Snohomish constabularies, came unglued. He had been assuring the authorities that the festival would assemble the finest examples of American youth for a celebration of American values in the great American outdoors. Truth in advertising was unwelcome. I countered that if he could sell the locals that line of bull, he could convince them that the frog was smoking a fine American cigar. Knowing Cy, he probably did.

Unfortunately, Cy's persuasive powers did not extend to the weather. August 1968 proved to be one of the wettest on record. NAC staged a pre-event rite at Volunteer Park to placate the rain gods, but they were not appeased.

Meanwhile, on August 7, Republicans gathered in Miami to nominate or, better, coronate Richard Nixon for president. All of his potential opponents had withdrawn or self-destructed, including Michigan Gov. George Romney (pilloried in the press for truthfully stating that the government attempted to "brainwash" him on Vietnam), New York Gov. Nelson Rockefeller (too liberal for a party still dominated by Goldwaterites), and Pennsylvania Gov. William Scranton (simply too late). Nixon picked Maryland Gov. Spiro T. Agnew for his vice president and Washington Gov. Dan Evans delivered the keynote address.

A mass of several thousand Yippies camped near the convention, but there was no confrontation. Things were less peaceful in nearby, mostly black Liberty City, where two died in riots.

The main event was Chicago. As the first Yippies and more serious New Mobilization protesters began to arrive, they got a preview of events to come. Warsaw Pact troops, chiefly Soviet and East German, staged "maneuvers" in Czechoslovakia. On August 20, tanks rolled into Prague, crushing the reform movement and enforcing the "Brezhnev Doctrine" of Soviet hegemony over its Eastern European satellites. Meanwhile, thousands of Illinois National Guardsmen and regular Army troops poured into Chicago with well-publicized orders to "shoot to kill" in the event of a "disturbance."

Mayor Richard J. Daley's intention was to scare demonstrators away from the city, and he largely succeeded: no more than 10,000 assembled in the city. Jerry Rubin and Abbie Hoffman tried to recoup through publicity, by releasing the YIP presidential candidate "Pigasus," an authentic swine, in the Civic Center. Soon after, Rubin acquired a volunteer "bodyguard," a police agent named Bob Pierson disguised as a biker.

The pig prank was overshadowed when the police killed an American Indian near Lincoln Park a few days before the convention. Barely 2,000 Yippies collected there on Sunday to listen to the MC-5, a Detroit band led by "White Panther" John Sinclair. When the 11 p.m.

curfew fell, the remains of the crowd, possibly incited by undercover agent provocateurs, began taunting the police and pelting them with stones and trash. They replied by gleefully gassing and clubbing the stragglers.

The convention opened officially on Monday, August 26, in the International Amphitheater. Tom Hayden went to Lincoln Park to organize a protest march on police headquarters, and was promptly arrested. Mobe leader Rennie Davis led 500 or so to Grant Park, near Humphrey and McCarthy headquarters in the Hilton, where Dave Dellinger was speaking to a few thousand. When some protesters unfurled VC flags, the police waded in, but then retreated. That night, police made another sweep of Lincoln Park. Jerry Rubin missed it: he was recovering from an especially heavy hit of acid.

Tuesday, President Johnson's sixtieth birthday, was relatively quiet as delegates got ready to nominate Humphrey and Maine Sen. Edmund Muskie the next day. A last-ditch effort to "draft" Edward Kennedy collapsed, and McCarthy fell short. Our roving correspondent Scott White was in Chicago and reported that a small contingent from Lincoln Park went on a brief "trashing" spree in the Loop, ostensibly to support striking transit workers. Later in the park, a group of ministers conducted a "pray-in," and "the first canister hit near the cross held by the clergy."

On Wednesday, Mobe leaders Rennie Davis and Dave Dellinger decided to defy the police and lead a march from Grant Park to the convention where the delegates were casting their nominating ballots. Before the protesters could get moving, police attacked. Control of the crowd was lost, and thousands found themselves barricaded inside the park.

Finally, an unguarded exit was discovered, and a leaderless mass surged toward the Hilton. Along the way, they encountered a legal "Mule Train" march led by Ralph Abernathy. Simultaneously, about 2,000 McCarthy supporters collected in front of the nearby Hilton. As the throng pressed against the cordon of police guarding the hotel, under the lights of numerous news camera crews, protesters taunted, "The whole world is watching." It didn't matter: platoons of police unleashed their gas bombs and nightsticks. The fumes of the gas reportedly made Hubert Humphrey, high above in the Hilton, weep.

News of these events reached the convention, which was then casting its nomination votes for president. Connecticut Sen. Abraham Ribicoff took the podium and denounced the "Gestapo tactics on the street of Chicago." Live TV cameras cut away to Mayor Daley in the Illinois delegation. Face flushed, jowls flapping, he shouted something inaudible. Lip readers deciphered words to the effect, "Fuck you, you Jew son of a bitch!"

Democracy in action, and Abbie Hoffman was AWOL. He had been arrested earlier in the day for having written "FUCK" on his forehead with lipstick.

Jerry Rubin later boasted to historian Milton Viorst that the Yippies had succeeded in exposing "an America ruled by force," but polling showed little public sympathy for the demonstrators. Most thought the police had been "restrained," and it is significant that no shots were fired and no one died during the Festival of Life. Still, a formal investigation conducted by Chicago attorney and future Illinois Gov. Daniel Walker concluded that this had been "a police riot."

As television broadcast images of Chicago's police riots, we scrambled to put the Sky River Rock Festival together. A giant stage and assorted tents were erected, portable toilets (far too few) were rented, generators were fired up, miles of wire were strung, and gradually Betty Nelson's pasture was transformed into a bivouac for the expected Golden Horde.

And they came, 20,000 strong. Some even paid. First a trickle, the smart ones who scouted out the best camp sites, then the masses, eager but unprepared. It fell to Roger Downey to direct "security." As such, he displayed solid strategic judgment, and sounded a retreat within hours of the festival's opening on August 31. To do anything else would have been, in Cy Noe's phrase, "like trying to steer an avalanche."

The weather that first day was overcast but not hostile. Thousands of people poured through the gates and plopped down on the grassy slope before the stage. Meanwhile, Milo Johnstone and a relay of drivers shuttled bands and performers between Sea-Tac airport, their rooms in the Camlin Hotel (appropriately, home of the Cloud Room), and unsunny Sultan.

Larry Van Over dutifully filled his balloon with helium, tied it to a truck bumper, and ten minutes later watched it float away toward Ultima Thule. Frantic calls located a hot-air balloonist in Spokane, who trekked west with his gear. He could have skipped the trip, for contrary to Larry's skepticism people came for the music, not balloon rides.

Who played and in what order? Who knows? Some fifty groups had committed, but not everyone showed up. On the other hand, the Grateful Dead arrived unscheduled and unexpected. We know that Big Mama Thornton was there, and James Cotton, and Country Joe and the Fish, and Richard Pryor, Dino Valenti, Byron Pope, It's A Beautiful Day, Peanut Butter Conspiracy, Alice Stuart Thomas, the Youngbloods, Santana, New Lost City Ramblers, and local groups such as Juggernaut and Easy Chair. It really depends on who you talk to, for, as Cy Noe points out, Sky River quickly took on a Rashomon quality. Suffice it to say that enough bands came to keep the stage hopping eighteen hours a day for three days.

And the rain came, too, that first night: chill, fitful drizzle interspersed by cloud bursts. The vast field turned to mud, yet few attendees gave up their ground. The bands played on, and the view from the stage, looking out into the darkness, was of scattered fires and lanterns flickering in the mist like some prehistoric encampment, a spontaneous pueblo dug into the soft earth beneath a canopy of ancient trees.

The gods took pity the next day, and the mud baked briefly in bright sunlight. The denizens of Sky River Rock stirred from their huts and greeted the day. Blouses and bras, pants and briefs were discarded. A dance began and soon linked hundreds in a spontaneous ritual of purification around and within a deep pool of ooze.

It was magic. Even the drunken rowdies who intruded with the sole aim of kicking some hippie butt were swept up in the collective wonder of the thing. There was not a single fight that I know of, and when the festival ran short of drinking water, the Sultan townsfolk gladly trucked it in for free.

The clouds and drizzle returned but they had been defeated. They had no power over this community. The pervasive good cheer prevailed against every adversity and shortage. It was a triumph of—I cringe at the word but there is no alternative—love.

And so Sky River wound toward its final confluence with reality.

Three days had passed in an instant, or a millennium, and "It's a Beautiful Day" finished the last set on the afternoon of September 2. The stage was disassembled, the tents struck, the cables coiled, the litter collected, and a final caravan of beat-up trucks, VW buses, and vans headed south toward the real world.

All around us—in Chicago, Paris, Prague, China, Vietnam, on every campus and in every urban ghetto—the ceremonies of innocence were drowning in Yeats's blood-dimmed tide, but for a few of us there was a moment when the hour came round at last. The clouds parted, the sunlight streamed down, and we danced naked in the mud of Sky River Rock.

Chapter 15:
All Power to
the People

If it's a blood bath they want, then let's get it over with.

—Gov. Ronald Reagan

(1969)

N ews of Sky River galvanized the music world and was even reported, with due tut-tutting, by Establishment organs such as *Time* and the *Wall Street Journal.* NAC added up the receipts from 11,000 or so paying customers, dispersed gifts to the festival's Native American beneficiaries, and closed the books with credits and debits more or less equal. This was enough to start people thinking about the next festival.

The Left was also thinking about what to do for an encore to Chicago, but events had by now developed a momentum of their own. We were swept up in a vortex like leaves in a fall storm.

On September 17, Washington held its primary election. Under the state constitution, minority parties must hold their "conventions" on the same day for the purpose of placing candidates on the fall ballot. Among these was the Peace and Freedom Party. The PFP had begun life a year earlier as a pan-Left electoral coalition in Berkeley chiefly intended to protect the Panthers. It held a national convention in Ann Arbor in August and nominated Eldridge Cleaver for president over Dick Gregory. Cleaver surprised many by picking Jerry Rubin as his running mate. Before Chicago made him a national celebrity, Rubin was distrusted by the hard core in both the Left and the counterculture. Even afterwards, his egocentric recklessness was a frequent source of political peril and embarrassment.

The local PFP nominated Art DeWitt for U. S. Senate, UW economics professor Judith Shapiro and civil rights veteran Flo Ware to run for Congress from the 1st and 7th districts respectively, and tapped E. J. Brisker and Carl Miller to run for the legislature from the Central Area. Despite my apostasy on orthodox Marxism and revolutionary violence, I was also picked to run for the legislature from the U District. PFP's leaders C. van Lydegraf, a freelance Stalinist, and SDSers Cal and Barbara Winslow decreed that none of us should talk about anything remotely interesting to voters.

My "campaign" got me into immediate trouble. I adopted Martin Luther King's line, "Community, Not Chaos," and championed proposals such as rapid transit, police review boards, legalization of marijuana, and citizen control of neighborhoods. Such notions were too radical for liberals, and too liberal for radicals—and I was too much of either for the Kent School District. When a teacher invited me to address his history class, the local right wing burned up the phone lines with protest calls. The students confronted the Kent School Board and demanded the right to hear whomever they chose, so my "lesson" was delivered after all.

The most interesting candidate to emerge in the September primary was Richard A. C. Greene, a classics instructor, who entered the Republican primary for State Commissioner of Public Lands on a lark. To his and everyone else's amazement, he won. The new Republican standard bearer promised if elected to "go forth and commission the land, gently but firmly," and retired to Waikiki, from which he directed a beachfront campaign executed locally by Jon Gallant, Lorenzo Milam, and other members of the Greene Machine. While in Hawaii, Green was warmly embraced by vice presidential candidate Spiro Agnew. On the same trip, Agnew got in trouble for referring to someone as a "fat Jap." It was the first of many veepee witticisms.

On September 18, the UW experienced its first serious political arson fire when someone torched Clark Hall, which housed the Navy ROTC. A large crowd gathered as firefighters arrived, and chanted, "Let it burn!" Ten days later, a contingent from SDS and PFP attended a rally for Vice President Humphrey in the Arena. Several attempted to "arrest" Humphrey for "crimes against humanity" and traded taunts with him; I'm afraid Humphrey came off better in the exchange.

132 Fall Power to the People

Within the next two weeks, Humphrey called for an immediate halt to U.S. bombing in the North and faster "de-Americanization" of the war in the South. As his opponent began inching up in the polls, Richard Nixon hinted that he had a "secret plan" to end the war.

Violence was never too far off stage that fall. In Seattle, the Panthers and police resumed their deadly duet. In September, the Panthers staged an armed demonstration at Rainier Beach High School to protest the beating of several black students by whites. Curtis Harris was ordered to court, and there on September 18 allegedly threatened to kill a policeman. On October 5, a Seattle policeman killed Panther member Welton Armstead while attempting to arrest him on suspicion of stealing a car. The following day, bullets struck two police cars patrolling the Central Area. Two days after that, Harris was convicted of threatening an officer. Amazingly, the lid stayed on Seattle; Washington, D.C., by contrast, was ripped by riots the next day when a policeman killed a black man.

Thom Gunn and the local Chamber of Commerce tried to salve the growing friction in the District by staging a "Love-U" concert in the middle of the Ave on October 1. More than 10,000 filled the street and then retired to the campus to carry on until early morning. That same day, Jerry Rubin appeared before the House Un-American Activities Committee bare-chested and war-painted with a bandolier and toy assault rifle. Not to be outdone, Hoffman appeared the following day in a shirt sewn from an American flag. He was promptly arrested and later told a judge, "I regret that I have but one shirt to give for my country."

Also on October 2, ten days before the opening of the Olympic games in Mexico City, national police machine-gunned a student protest rally at the National Polytechnic Institute, slaughtering at least 200. The games went on, and on October 16, during the playing of the U.S. national anthem, black sprinters and medalists John Carlos and Tommie Smith lowered their gazes and raised their arms in a "Black Power" salute to protest racism.

On the same day, the Resistance Union held the UW's largest teach-in on the war yet, with speeches by Kathleen Cleaver, Todd Gitlin, David Harris, and former South Vietnamese ambassador Tran Van Dinh, among others. Two days later, Mayor Braman told the

University District Rotary to brace itself for "guerrilla warfare" led by the local SDS, PFP, and Panthers. Right on cue, Jerry Rubin rolled into town on October 24 and led 2,000 students in "liberating" the UW Faculty Club.

In hopes of putting Humphrey over the top, President Johnson halted all bombing of North Vietnam on October 31 and publicly agreed to NLF participation in the Paris talks, which prompted the South to walk. It almost worked. Humphrey lost to Nixon by barely half a million votes, but the latter carried thirty-two states and their electoral college ballots. George Wallace garnered 13 percent of the popular vote and carried five states in the Confederacy.

Humphrey carried Washington, and one of the votes he won was mine. The prospect of Richard Nixon being elected was too much for me in casting my very first ballot, so I broke ranks with the PFP and pulled the lever for the Politics of Joy. Dan Evans retained his governorship, defeating former State Attorney General John O'Connell, whose old job was won by Slade Gorton. PFP candidates registered protest margins of 1 or 2 percent, and Richard A. C. Greene also lost—much to his relief. On the third try in a decade, Seattle voters finally swallowed fluoridation.

The day after the election, San Francisco State College went on strike to protest the firing of a Black Panther instructor. The president was replaced by famed semanticist S. I. Hayakawa, who later confronted protesters and made national headlines (which helped make him one of history's least effective U.S. Senators). On November 27, Eldridge Cleaver, fearing that a return to jail would cost his life, fled the country. The author of that year's best-selling *Soul on Ice* reappeared two weeks later in Algiers, where Kathleen later joined him.

Finally, 1968 drew to a close on two somewhat cheerful notes in Seattle. A disappointed Senator Jackson announced that the Army would not build an antiballistic missile base at Fort Lawton, as he had hoped. And a King County jury acquitted Aaron Dixon in the case of the stolen typewriter.

The ghost of Chicago lingered into the new year. Liberal Democrats used the convention fiasco to force a top-to-bottom reform of party rules. New procedures were written by a commission chaired by South Dakota Sen. George McGovern. Chicago had also shattered the liberal-left coalition of the Mobe and the responsibility for leading the antiwar movement passed unchallenged to SDS. Within its ranks, the schism widened between orthodox Marxists and an emerging bloc which championed a Hoffmanesque fusion of counterculture and Third World revolutionism. The former were dominated by Progressive Labor and increasingly influenced by a new force, "Labor Committees" organized by a former Trotskyist calling himself "Lyn Marcus." His real name is Lyndon LaRouche.

For want of anything better to do, SDS and its allies returned to harassing ROTC and corporate recruiters and championing a potpourri of Third World causes. In January and February 1969, major demonstrations rocked the universities of Wisconsin, Pennsylvania, and Massachusetts; City College of New York; Berkeley and several other California campuses; and Howard, Duke, and Rice.

The first fatalities of 1969 fell on January 17, when two Black Panthers were murdered by rivals at UCLA. Five days later, person or persons unknown murdered Seattle Urban League director Edwin Pratt in front of his home. The police never identified a suspect, and the case remains unsolved to this day.

On January 30, the Third World Liberation Front launched a minority student strike at Berkeley, which was suppressed by National Guard troops. The following month, twenty-one Black Panthers were indicted for allegedly conspiring to blow up buildings and landmarks in New York City, and riots broke out in Chicago. On May 21, Black Panther members in New Haven allegedly beat to death one of their own, Alex Rackley, accused of being an informer. Bobby Seale was one of those indicted for the murder in August.

On February 24, SDS physically expelled a United Fruit company recruiter from the UW's Loew Hall, which prompted disciplinary action against Robby Stern, Ed Mormon, and three others. They returned on March 6 to lead 9,000 in a peaceful protest against ROTC, the UW's largest demonstration to date. The following week, SDS protesters disrupted the UW hearing on Stern et al., leading to eight more suspensions.

Meanwhile, Jerry Rubin published *Do It!* and Abbie Hoffman (now calling himself "Free") unleashed *Revolution for the Hell of It,* which became dueling manifestoes for future Chicagos. Among their most avid readers were new U.S. Attorney General John Mitchell and his staff. On March 20, Mitchell personally announced federal indictments against Rubin, Hoffman, David Dellinger, Rennie Davis, Tom Hayden, and lesser known organizers John Froines and Lee Weiner for interstate conspiracy to incite a riot in Chicago. Mitchell also threw in Bobby Seale, although he played no role in the New Mobe or Yippies. Collectively, they became known as the Chicago Eight; Seale was later separated from his codefendants for separate trial, leaving the "Chicago Seven."

Mitchell hoped that these indictments would decapitate the most dangerous leaders of SDS and the antiwar Left. His action had precisely the opposite effect: it sanctified them. The living martyrdom of Hoffman and Rubin in particular legitimized a gonzo activism that was indifferent if not hostile to history, rational debate, and any standard of practical political benefit. Mitchell ultimately achieved his goal in a backwards way: he destroyed the New Left by handing the keys to the asylum over to its worst lunatics.

On April 1, the U.S. deployment in Vietnam hit its all-time peak of 543,400 troops. Two days later, American fatalities surpassed the 33,629 who had died in Korea. By now, President Nixon had already begun the secret and illegal bombing of Cambodia while publicly announcing a new policy of "Vietnamization" by which the U.S. would begin to withdraw its troops. He also announced support for a new "draft lottery" to correct the system's inequities.

On April 9, SDS led an occupation of several buildings at Harvard. When the police cleared out students, injuring thirty-seven, it provoked a long strike. Black and Puerto Rican students effectively "locked-out" students and faculty at City College of New York for two weeks beginning April 22.

The next day, the UW put thirteen students, mostly SDS members, on probation. SDS roared back the day after that with a demonstration at Loew Hall protesting corporate recruiting. Conservative students wrestled with radicals at the building's entrance, and the melee turned into farce when angry bees poured from hives being transported across campus by two Eastern Washington farmers. They explained that it was an accident but nobody believed them. The bees, being both apian and apolitical, stung leftists, rightists, neutrals, and police with equal enthusiasm.

At this moment in Berkeley, students and hippies were in the process of transforming a UC-owned vacant lot into a "People's Park." They cleared away debris, began planting flowers and vegetables, and hauled in cast-off furniture and playground equipment. It was about as innocent an undertaking as anyone could imagine, yet the symbolism was very powerful. No less than Bobby Seale wondered aloud, "You mean you just took that land without asking anyone?"

Gov. Ronald Reagan, the land's ultimate owner, was not amused. On his orders, California highway patrolmen surrounded the park at 4:30 a.m. on May 15, and erected a chain-link fence around its perimeter. While a police helicopter hovered overhead, a bulldozer crushed the plantings and fixtures which the people had donated over the previous weeks. Word of the outrage spread quickly, and several thousand gathered for a rally at Sproul Hall. They resolved to retake the park and set off down Telegraph Avenue. They were met by state and San Francisco police units who first fired tear gas and then heavy gauge birdshot. The crowd scattered, and small groups engaged the police in running battles all during the day. The police continued firing their shotguns, wounding 110 by nightfall, including an artist, Alan Blanchard, who was blinded, and a rooftop spectator, James Rector, who died four days later.

Over the next four days, the confrontations built toward a new crescendo of brutality. State police sealed the area around the university, trapping thousands of students, faculty, shoppers, and bystanders. As these sought escape, a National Guard helicopter crossed slowly overhead, spewing nausea gas, which historian W. J. Rorabaugh reports "tortured polio victims hooked to iron lungs" at a nearby hospital and "caused skin burns to swimmers" more than half a mile distant.

The lid on the Central Area blew off that same May, when a long-simmering dispute at Seattle Community College boiled over. Frank Williams and other Black Student Union leaders had discovered plans to shift most of the college's academic programs to the North Campus, leaving only vocational programs for the mostly nonwhite students attending the Central Branch on Broadway. They demanded that one of the college's five trustees, all white, resign so a black named by BSU could be seated. "Negotiations" began but quickly led no-where, so BSU announced a student strike on May 8.

This was largely ignored by the student body, so BSU and its SDS allies stepped up the heat with a demonstration on May 22 in front of the old Edison Technical School (the new, fortress-like campus had not yet been built). A few hundred protesters stormed the building and occupied it until Seattle Tactical Squad members cleared them out.

The next morning, another group of about 200 assembled at Edison. From there they marched to the nearby Summit School and paraded noisily through its halls. When they returned to Edison they found the entrance blocked by the armor-vested Tac Squad. Rocks and bricks started flying, and a group charged the line of cops. They were driven back with squirts of "Federal Streamer," a hand-held Mace-like spray.

The leaders of the protesters then decided that we should all march to another SCC satellite, former Washington Junior High. Our ranks swelled en route with junior high students from the new Washington school. Police were waiting and let the tear gas fly. We retreated to Garfield, and the Tac Squad followed. The march degenerated into a melee of gas, clubs, Molotov cocktails, and shots from an unseen sniper who hit three policemen, all in the buttocks. A heavy rainfall that night finally cooled everybody down.

Marc Krasnowsky and I covered the event. He saw "the flame which may signal an early beginning to . . . long hot summer;" I saw it "fizzle," and more evidence for the folly of "revolutionary violence." Governor Evans interceded, and one of the trustees, Carl Dakan, re-signed. Evans refused to name a new trustee suggested by the BSU, and the BSU refused to sanction the appointment of black leaders such as attorney Gary Gayton and the Rev. Willie Jackson, who de-clined the honor under BSU pressure. The governor and BSU finally reached a compromise (or stalemate) with the appointment of Marvin Glass on July 24.

The national civil rights movement had taken a strange a new turn in May, when James Forman demanded $500 million from America's churches as "reparations" to blacks. Not to be undersold, CORE's Roy Innis raised the ante a month later by demanding $6 billion from U.S. banks as "recoupment for the earnings of black folk."

In contrast to such rhetorical extravagance, the Seattle Black Panthers applied themselves to building their local community base. They opened a Free Breakfast Program for Central Area school children in the spring and the Sidney Miller Free Clinic the following winter. Such practical organizing also contrasted starkly with the growing violence and mayhem in other Panther chapters.

The embattled national Panthers began pushing for endorsement of a "United Front Against Fascism," which was really an argument that the whole of the Left should dedicate itself singlemindedly to their defense. Their need for allies would play a key role in the destruction of SDS when nearly two thousand members collected in Chicago's dingy Coliseum for what turned out to be the group's last national convention beginning on June 18.

Chapter 16:
Stormy
Weather

*At this point, things do not
simply become ugly; they
become stupid.*

—Theodore Roszak

By the summer of 1969, SDS had fractured into three pieces: the Progressive Labor caucus, which advocated a new program to build "student-worker alliances"; an "action faction," which advocated building a "revolutionary youth movement"; and a whole lot of people in the middle who just wanted to end the war and racism.

Superficially, the distinctions between the two main camps seem very narrow. Both had, in historian Kirkpatrick Sale's words, "rushed pell-mell into the comparative safety of one or another variety of Marxism," but as you have seen, Marxists seldom if ever agree with each other, and the more picayune their differences, the more passionate their disputes.

Progressive Labor followed an orthodox line which entrusted sole responsibility for the revolution in the sainted industrial proletariat. SDS's proper task, therefore, was to go out among the workers and try to educate them to assume their proper historical role. As such PL adamantly repudiated racialists such as the Panthers, who used the rhetoric of "black nationalism" to advocate the liberation of domestic "colonies" of America's ghettos. Similarly, they scoffed at Rubin and Hoffman's glorification of counterculture militancy as bourgeois self-delusion, and they subordinated the issue of sexual discrimination, which was becoming a prominent topic within SDS, to class domination. More subtly, PLers were uncomfortable with the growing romanticization of Cuba, North Vietnam, and the NLF, which Maoists felt were too cozy with "revisionist" Russia.

The other camp had coalesced around Mike Klonsky's paper, "Toward a Revolutionary Youth Movement," published in December

1968. "RYM" also deferred to the working class key revolutionary role, but it targeted young proletarians through organizing lower-income students and teenagers. The real issue raised by RYM was one of style, an aggressive leadership by example in visible confrontations with police and other symbols of imperialist and racist power. Between the lines, it was a call for a permanent Chicago.

The SDS National Council endorsed RYM by a scant dozen votes in December. PL decided to fight another day, which came on June 18, 1969, in, appropriately, Chicago. The RYM advocates included most of the national SDS leadership, notably Columbia veterans Mark Rudd and Bernardine Dohrn. At the June convention, they circulated a manifesto which took a line from Bob Dylan for its title: "You don't need a weatherman to know which way the wind blows." This statement made long-evolving trends in SDS thinking bluntly explicit. The role of the American Left was to support national liberation movements outside the country and "black liberation struggles" within. The white Left had no other meaningful part to play but as a fifth column abetting other people's revolutions.

The statement dispensed with any effort to build support among liberals or the middle class, or even the masses. Instead it called for a "revolutionary party" of white, urban, working-class youth organized in "collectives" and guided by a "central organization" of clandestine, self-reliant cadres. Without apparent self-irony, the advocates of this line started calling themselves "Weathermen"—the people you don't need to tell you which way the wind blows.

It was Lenin on LSD. Veteran SDS theorist Carl Ogelsby complained, "Any close reading of the RYM's Weatherman statement will drive you blind." Susan and Robby Stern were in Chicago and had similar reactions. In her memoir, Susan confessed, "I tried to read it one day over lunch, but it was too long and theoretical for me to assimilate." She remembers, "Robby wasn't favorable. 'Who can relate to that thing!' he exploded. 'It puts everybody down. You either have to be a genius or a madman to support it.'" Not even Abbie Hoffman, who was one or the other or both, could make sense out of the debate at the convention.

Support for the Weathermen manifesto was not unanimous within the RYM caucus. Some saw it as an endorsement of "adventurism," a

Marxist codeword for activism for its own sake. Original RYM theorists Mike Klonsky and Les Coleman distanced themselves from the Weathermen statement, as did Bob Avakian, future leader of the quasi-Maoist "Revolutionary Communist Party." These dissenters called themselves RYM II, and advocated more traditional community organizing to recruit working-class youth.

As Susan Stern recalled the convention, "There wasn't a moment of harmony throughout the whole damn thing." The real issue was power: it was Bolsheviks versus Mensheviks all over again, and the test was to see who was more disciplined. RYM tried a preemptive strike by inviting Black Panthers, Young Lords, and Brown Berets—all anathema to PL—to address the convention. Illinois Panther Rufus "Chaka" Walls took the microphone and blasted "armchair Marxists," i.e., PL, but he didn't stop there. He rambled on to free love and "pussy power," which ignited roars of "fight Male Chauvinism" from the delegates. Still not getting it, Walls volunteered this nugget of wisdom: "Superman was a punk because he never even tried to fuck Lois Lane."

The plenum dissolved into pandemonium. The Panthers' sexism echoed back to Stokely Carmichael's SNCC dictum that the proper position for women in the Movement "is prone," and it confirmed PL's criticism of the revolutionary credentials of race-based movements. RYM beat a hasty retreat and the session ended.

The next day, June 20, another Panther spokesman, Jewel Cook, interrupted the convention to read an important announcement. The Panthers had decided that PL had "deviated from Marxist-Leninist ideology on the National Question and the right of self-determination of all oppressed people." If PL members didn't change their tune, Cook continued, "they will be considered as counter-revolutionary traitors and will be dealt with as such," and SDS "will be judged by the company they keep." Despite this ideological ultimatum, RYM leaders were still uncertain whether or not they had the votes in the room to formally expel Progressive Labor then and there. Mark Rudd called for a recess and led his supporters out of the hall. They returned the next day, and a defiant Bernardine Dohrn delivered the final word. Anyone who does not subscribe to RYM is "no longer part of SDS." She then leapt from the stage, and marched out of the hall with as many as 700 delegates, including Susan Stern, behind her. It was an audacious maneuver: RYM "expelled" PL by walking out itself.

That was the end. Technically, there were now two SDSs, PL's and RYM's, but in reality there was none. For PL in particular, it was fatal. As a symbiote living within the body of SDS, it could not survive independent of its host and quickly dissolved in the open air. Lyndon Larouche threw open the doors of his National Caucus of Labor Committees, and many of the more orthodox Marxists disappeared into the black hole of what became one of the most bizarre political cults in American history.

RYM continued to fragment. The most militant coalesced as the Weather Underground, including Susan Stern. Others such as Robby Stern couldn't take the next inevitable step to "bring the war home" via terrorism. In Seattle, they tried to salvage some semblance of the old SDS under the banner of the "Revolutionary Organizing Committee," but ROC proved less than solid. Nationally, RYMers outside the Weathermen scattered like leaves in the wind.

It was a genuine political tragedy. SDS, founded with such bright hopes for a New Left analysis and strategy for transforming America, had disintegrated in a parody of the most arcane Old Left dissension. A group whose salient virtue was the refusal to exclude anyone on the basis of ideology had torn itself apart over competing claims to "Marxist-Leninist" purity. A movement which began by seeing white, middle-class students as key to the solution of society's problems had decided that white, middle-class students were the problem.

Ironically, there were more of those students than ever before. By that June, SDS had more than 300 chapters, and perhaps as many as 100,000 avowed (if not dues-paying) members. Public opinion had finally shifted against the war, and the largest public demonstrations still lay in the future. A huge mass of motivated, intelligent members was waiting for its marching orders, but SDS leadership disdained its own followers. The final farce in Chicago brought SDS full circle, from its earliest adoration of black SNCC workers in the Deep South to the deification of Black Panthers in the ghetto as the sole representatives—and enforcers—of revolutionary authenticity. The long march from Port Huron to Birmingham to Chicago was over, and so was SDS.

But the body would twitch for a while longer. The Weathermen's alliance with the Panthers ended abruptly in July at the latter's Oakland conference for a United Front Against Fascism. Weathermen balked at the Panther principle of "community control of the police," which included whites as well as blacks. Such ungrateful impertinence outraged Panther chair Bobby Seale and chief of staff Dave Hilliard. They repudiated their former SDS allies as "jive bourgeois national socialists" and threatened "disciplinary actions."

For supporters and observers of this conference, the Panthers required increasingly painful intellectual contortions. Py Bateman, who later would become one of Seattle's ablest advocates of women's empowerment, found herself endorsing the Panthers' "realistic attitude toward the backwardness of women and the need for developing leadership abilities among women." At this point she was more horrified by the Panthers' open association with "revisionists" from the Communist Party, USA, such as Herbert Aptheker who dominated the conference.

Our *Helix* correspondent, Marc Krasnowsky, properly recognized that the Panthers' real problems stemmed not from repression, which was brutally real, but from their "position in the black community" and their reliance on the "lumpen" rather than workers for membership and support. In the Panthers' dalliances with the bourgeois Marxists of the CP on the one hand and the "wild-in-the-street boys" of RYM on the other, all chanting "Power to the People" together, Krasnowsky saw "a weird practical joke being played on the working people of this country."

At this moment, the Panthers came in for criticism from no less than Stokely Carmichael. He angrily resigned from the party, which he denounced as "dishonest and vicious." As Hugh Pearson documents in his biography of Huey Newton, the Panthers had already begun to degenerate into little more than a gang in Oakland, New York, and other cities (not Seattle), but of course few of the white Left believed it.

The growing tension with the Panthers could have been devastating for the "Weather Bureau," as the new leadership called itself, but it had other models and heroes. A trip to Cuba and meetings with Vietnamese revolutionaries fortified its sense of mission. A Weather report on the talks explained, "As people who are located inside the monster, revolutionary Americans are in a position to do decisive damage" to the American war effort and imperialism. It was official now: the job for white radicals was not to make a revolution for Americans, but to help others win their revolution against America.

Amid all this chaos, the more militant members of UPS gathered at a farm outside Ann Arbor for a "Radical Media Conference." I attended in the faith that of all the institutions of the Movement, the underground press was the healthiest (and sanest); I would leave with a different view.

My optimism may have been a projection since the *Helix* had regained its vigor that summer. Norm Caldwell and Mike Crowley (no relation, but there sure were a lot of Crowleys running around the fringes of Seattle) had brought new order and strength to our ad sales and circulation. Norm and Mike were a dynamic duo, the former tall and droll, the latter compact and utterly nuts.

At Norm's suggestion, we hired our first real employee, George Arthur, at the munificent salary of $50 per month. George was a student of journalism in the full sense of the word, and had put out a controversial newspaper for high school students, *The Advocate,* with his West Seattle chum, Marc Krasnowsky. He was a droll, insightful writer who fully understood the arcana of the Left but never took it too seriously. After journalism, history was his first love, and he brought a nicely rounded perspective and acid wit to his accounts of intra-Movement maneuvers.

That year we also gained the services of two terrific photographers, Paul Temple and Alan Lande. With the support of Roxie Grant and Sharma, we imposed new order on the paper's layout with radical innovations such as justified columns of type and page numbers, and Alan Lande and I became something of a reporter-photographer team over the months to come.

Another notable addition was an older gentleman who went by the initials "KC" and later "KS" (he never divulged his real name); his thoughtful columns reminded me of I. F. Stone. Robert Horsley began contributing his comic-morose explorations of "endless despair." Steve Shafer penned stunning ink drawings, and J. Allen Jensen and Mary Ida Hendrickson provided gorgeous charcoal and pencil portraits. Downey had turned *Helix's* reviews into a cultural force that even the establishment respected, and Ed Leinbacher began writing in-depth "Pop Oeuvres" reviews of music. Cunnick's writing was stronger than ever, and even Paul had acquired a more disciplined approach. In short, *Helix* was finally acting, looking, and reading like a real newspaper.

Many of us bonded closer than ever during an expedition south in January 1969. Paul, Norm, Mike, Tim, Scott, Alan, and perhaps a few others piled into the *Helix*'s "new" Ford panel truck and set off to visit our UPS cousins along the I-5 corridor. We broke bread with *Berkeley Barb* publisher Max Scherr (who tried to hire me away from the *Helix*) and gained entry through the security maze of the *LA Free Press*.

As we headed back north, a sudden storm buried I-5 in snow from Grants Pass to Tacoma. We didn't have enough money to stay overnight so we decided to press on. Mike Crowley was at the wheel, and he ran a State Patrol roadblock diverting traffic off the ostensibly impassable interstate. Possessed by the spirit of Neal Cassady (and heavy doses of Methadrine), Mike drove all night, skidding out of control only once.

On that expedition we met Marvin Garson, who had transformed San Francisco's earnest *Express Times* into the free-wheeling *Good Times*. He came up later in 1969 and introduced us to his special brand of anarchism. He printed greeting cards reading, "The System Does Not Work," to which Horsley added on the reverse, "You Lose."

The *Helix* was no longer alone in the Northwest. Bellingham now boasted two papers: the *Western Front* based at Western Washington State University, and the independent *Northwest Passage* (which would outlive *Helix* by nearly a decade). Portland's *Willamette Bridge* and Vancouver, B.C.'s, *Georgia Straight* were also going strong. We all held a little Northwest Underground Press Conference in Bellingham in June, but the stolid know-nothingism and bovine imperturbability of our "country hippie" hosts drove me to distraction.

No risk of that at the Ann Arbor media conference. It showcased all of the contradictions bedeviling the Movement at that moment. The gathering was hosted by the "White Panthers," an anarchic assemblage of the white lumpen proletariat dreamed up by John Sinclair. He was then a movement martyr, fighting a ten-year sentence for having passed a joint to a narc, and his band, the MC (as in Motor City)

5, was arguably the world's first "heavy metal" group. In a sense, the White Panthers were acting out the Weathermen's fantasy of revolutionary working-class youth, but close up they looked and behaved like glorified thugs.

Then there was Abbie Hoffman, who argued passionately for the underground press to punish the major record labels, particularly Columbia, for "ripping off the people's music." His remedy was a "boycott" of their advertising. That'll show 'em: we won't take their money any more! In truth, record advertising was already declining in the underground press, not because of some music industry cabal as Hoffman suspected, but because they had figured out that kids read more than just our rags. *Helix* was an exception to this; Norm and Mike had cut some innovative arrangements with local retailers which kept record ad revenue high. We were cocky enough that when Electra threatened to stop advertising because Cunnick had panned some of their artists, we dared them to go ahead so we could report the reason. They didn't.

The conference was then treated to a presentation from a Detroit Panther called, accurately, "Big Man," who lectured us on the United Front Against Fascism and demanded our fealty. He was interrupted when the women at the conference, well aware of the events at the previous month's SDS meltdown, confronted the Panthers (Black and White) and the rest of us with evidence of our sexism and chauvinism. Over the objections of the Panthers, we adopted a resolution pledging to treat women as equals and to eliminate exploitative ads and graphics from our papers.

The latter was easier said than done. Porno theaters, nudie clubs, dirty books stores, etc., had been financial mainstays of the underground press from the beginning, and they were political allies in the struggle against puritanism and censorship. Beyond this, "free love" had been a component of the bohemian scene and cultural underground since time immemorial, and the sexual revolution launched by oral contraception was an essential facet of the Sixties. Now our sisters seemed to be saying that this was somehow all wrong, perhaps even evil. It was a hard pill, pardon the pun, for us men to swallow.

Helix had already begun to wrestle with this issue, and maintained only a "token sex ad for the Rivoli [theater] as artifact of fading decadence." Just weeks earlier, the issue of pornography had contributed to the destruction of the *Berkeley Barb,* one of the founding rags of the underground press. Its staff became convinced (rightly it turned out) that Max Scherr was pocketing thousands of dollars in ad revenue each week, much of it from pornographers of one sort or another, while paying them peanuts. They demanded both a new division of the spoils and censorship of the most offensive advertising. They took over the paper and put out a "strike edition." Max Scherr, a former union organizer, finally agreed to negotiate if the staff would vacate the *Barb* office. When they were gone, he moved out all the equipment and started publishing again with a new staff and his nasty old advertisers. The original staff retaliated by founding a new paper, the *Berkeley Tribe.*

Events such as this and the previous year's split of the Liberation News Service into warring camps suggested to many of us that the easy, free-wheeling fraternity of the UPS was over. Jeff Shero, publisher of New York's militant *RAT,* proposed that the most political papers should form a new group, the Radical Press Movement. I liked the idea, but RPM didn't come to pass, and a few months later Shero lost control of his own paper. As a sop to women on the staff, he and his male comrades allowed Robin Morgan and her female comrades put out an issue of *RAT* on their own. They enjoyed the privilege so much they never gave the paper back.

The conference ground to a close as rumbling, flashing thunderheads gathered overhead. Alan Lande and Jim Emerson arrived in Jim's Barracuda, and we set off west. A few hours later, officers of the Michigan State Police's notorious "Red Squad" descended on the remaining conferees. Abbie Hoffman described the scene in his autobiography:

> In an early morning coordinated attack, troopers wielding shotguns stormed out of the woods surrounding our camp. Kicking in farmhouse doors on the pretense that we were training guerrillas, they roughhoused people. A few pot busts occurred, and we underwent the humiliating experience of being forced to line up naked under a row of shotguns. We left the conference determined to bring the war home.

Chapter 17:
Let It Bleed

The policeman isn't there to
create disorder. He's there to
preserve disorder.

—Mayor Richard J. Daley

In contrast to the darkening national scene, things in the local counterculture actually started to look up in early and mid-1969. In the spring, the community gained two important and enduring institutions. First came Morningtown Pizza on April 1, established as a worker-owned cooperative in a converted garage on Roosevelt by Tom Ninkovich, a refugee from Berkeley, and Warren Argo and Bob Owen, former engineers who quit their jobs to conduct R&D on a new "secret sauce."

In May, Art Bernstein and Jim O'Steen opened the Harvard Exit in the former Women's Century Club hall just off Broadway. This elegant little cinema became an instant hit, and Art or Jim introduced each film, be it a new release or revival, with an enthusiastic commentary. The Harvard Exit was a welcome complement to the limited film circuit which consisted of the Ridgemont on Greenwood, Edmonds' Edgemont, and film showings on campus. Meanwhile, cineaste Richard Jameson began organizing the first Northwest Film-Makers Festival and a Seattle film Society. (Randy Finley would come along a few years later to open his first theater, the Movie House, at 50th and U Way, and launch a revolution in independent film exhibition with his Seven Gables chain.)

By spring, Sky River Rock impresario John Chambless was jockeying discs on KOL-FM, where he succeeded Robin Sherwood. John was joined on the air by Max Baer, John Cunnick, and Pat MacDonald, and, in the most dire emergencies, by Robert Horsley and me. Retina Circus was now the undisputed ringmaster of Northwest light shows, and David "Doc" Eskanazie was the reigning wizard of sound engineering.

When not broadcasting or introducing UW freshmen to Nietzsche, Chambless was guiding the New American Community's plans for a second festival over the coming Labor Day weekend. In order to hone their skills (and earn some seed money), he and his NACkers managed Boyd Grafmyre's three-day Seattle Pop Festival in Woodinville in late July. The following month, NAC entered a "hippie float" in the Seafair Parade. It was a giant, creaking juggernaut-like affair that had to have scared the kiddies as it rumbled down Fourth Avenue with an entourage of long-haired freaks.

Our attention to these important events was briefly distracted by Sen. Edward Kennedy driving off a bridge, drowning his companion, and two guys landing on the moon. We took little note of the first, but *Helix* did celebrate "the last rising of a virgin moon" on July 20.

The summer's relative calm on the UW campus ended at 3:30 on the morning of June 29, when a bomb equivalent to a case of dynamite exploded in the foyer of the Administration Building, causing $100,000 in damage but no injuries. No culprit or reason for the explosion was ever identified (although I have been told unofficially that a disgruntled employee was a prime suspect; given later events, I tend to suspect police agents), and no radical group claimed credit or even tried to exploit the incident.

The Ave itself was grimmer than ever. Heroin and speed were openly dispensed from the Burger Hut, while a particularly brutish contingent of beat cops devoted themselves to harassing teenyboppers and *Helix* dealers. The local merchants demanded more, and the police obliged. Even the most laid-back hippies were getting annoyed. All the Ave needed by August was a spark, and it came from an unexpected direction.

On the warm evening of Sunday, August 10, some two thousand people gathered for a long-planned rock concert on the beach at Alki in West Seattle. Many lined up along the esplanade, which was already crowded with its usual population of bikers and low-riders. The music began at 6 p.m. and was scheduled to continue for three hours as allowed by a city permit.

Around 8 p.m., half a dozen patrol cars appeared and parked opposite the beach. A member of the last band scheduled to play crossed the street to ask the police if it was okay to perform. A sergeant told him to go ahead. As the band fired up its amps, the police began to hassle some of the spectators on the periphery of the crowd for drinking in public. Somebody, allegedly a biker, strolled up to one of the unattended police cars, emptied a bottle of gasoline in the back seat, and threw in a lighted match. The police, understandably, took offense. The fire was quickly doused and the officers began opening up their car trunks and taking out riot gear. Being focused on the band, few in the crowd were aware of what was coming down. Even fewer could hear the police loudspeaker when it suddenly barked, "This is an illegal gathering. You have one minute to disperse."

Almost immediately, the air filled with a pungent, nauseating gas— not ordinary tear gas, but the "CS" type which sickened its victims. With clubs swinging, the police waded into the crowd, which was trapped against the bay. Some fought back with fists and rocks, damaging several police cars.

Grenade after grenade exploded along the whole length of Alki. A brisk evening breeze carried the fumes inland, choking families in neighboring homes as they watched TV or ate a late Sunday dinner. One grenade rolled into a "mom and pop" grocery, gassing the owners, their infant child, and several customers.

The police eventually cordoned off the strip and arrested six for rock-throwing or public drinking. The air was still thick with gas when I arrived to interview witnesses from the concert and neighboring homes and shops for KOL-FM and the *Helix*. Not one could understand or justify the police tactics. The following day, Police Chief Frank Ramon (who was trying to get out of town on vacation) defended his men against complaints of "over-reaction" and "excessive force." He hinted of a planned provocation since "most people don't ordinarily carry firebombs to a concert," and explained that tear gas was the "best alternative" in such a situation. Ramon didn't convince very many listeners, particularly reporters, as eyewitness reports piled up. The official story of why the police had descended on a legal concert in the first place changed from noise complaints to reports of windows being broken, none of which was verified. Many suspected that the police had by their own presence and actions precipitated all that followed.

The backs of a lot of necks in the University District were already "gettin' dirty and gritty," when news of the Alki fracas began to spread.

While the newspapers paid little heed to the incident, TV and radio reports were much fuller. Rumors and anecdotes raced up and down the Ave.

At about 9 p.m. on Monday, August 11, a young man, for reasons known only to himself, kicked over a trash can at the corner of NE 42nd and U Way. Beat cops immediately grabbed and handcuffed him. As they tried to bundle the struggling man into a patrol car, his girlfriend began berating "the pigs" and pleaded for the growing crowd of spectators to do something.

When the cops grabbed her, Jim Emerson, mow a self-declared White Panther, decided he had had enough. He landed a haymaker on the jaw of Officer Mike Bolger, and spectators began throwing everything they could get their hands on. Two officers, Marvin Queen and Tom Grabicki, were struck by bricks (the latter suffered a concussion), and a stray missile shattered the window of the Coffee Corral. The original offender escaped in the confusion but was later re-apprehended.

More police quickly arrived along with a TV news crew. The crowd and the cops glared at each other but there was no more trouble that night. Eventually the spectators drifted away and the police withdrew. The next day, the Ave was electric with news of the previous night's incident. The police wisely kept a low profile and let street people celebrate their "victory" unmolested.

On Wednesday, August 13, two flyers circulated on the Ave. One urged calm in the name of the New American Community; the other was unsigned and much more militant. A sketch of a pistol bore the caption, "We're looking for people who like to draw," parodying the matchbook come-ons for art school. Word spread that there would be a "community meeting" on Hippie Hill. About fifty gathered on the lawn at 7:30 p.m. The session was organized and chaired by Jan Tissot, who had succeeded Jack Delay as chief advocate for the street people. Scores spoke, and while much anger was vented about "the pigs" and harassment, the dominant tone was that people should be cool and avoid further confrontations.

As we filed off the Hill around 8:30, two things became immediately evident: there were no police in sight, and the Ave was filled with hundreds of teenagers, white and black, whom no one had ever seen before. The warm night air was saturated with the hormonal energy of kids looking for trouble. They found it at about 9:30, when a small group of black teens began looting Bluebeard's boutique on the 4200 block of U Way. Several Ave regulars tried to intervene, explaining that Bluebeard's wasn't "the enemy," but the break-in had nothing to do with class dialectics. Amazingly, no police appeared. Somebody dragged a trash can into traffic and lit it afire. Still no police came.

Precisely at 10 p.m., a banshee wail erupted from atop the Adams Forkner Funeral Home, where police had installed a "howler." The machine emitted a focused beam of disorienting sound which strafed the Ave like a sonic machine gun. Moments later a loudspeaker announced, "You are ordered to disperse. If you do not disperse, you will be removed by force."

The police might as well have cried "Havoc! and let slip the dogs of war." Rocks immediately flew in the direction of the speaker. CS gas grenades began popping, and scores of Tactical Squad officers in full riot gear charged onto the Ave from nearby alleys. Amid the screams, explosions, and otherworldly howling, clots of kids pelted the police. When the latter advanced, the kids retreated, rearmed, and attacked anew. Along the way, trash cans were ignited to bait the police, parking meters were smashed, and stores were looted. A mobile crane parked along 15th NE was set afire, and when firemen arrived they had to withdraw under a hail of stones from campus.

At the height of the violence, around 11 p.m., the Neptune Theater's performance of *Romeo and Juliet* ended, and hundreds of moviegoers exited into the middle of the war zone. Astoundingly, the police never blocked off traffic, and scores of motorists on U Way and NE 45th found themselves trapped in clouds of tear gas and swarming masses of teens and police.

The battle, really a series of running skirmishes, continued until 3 a.m. The night ended with twenty-one rioters in jails and three officers in the emergency room. *Helix* photographer Alan Lande and a KING-TV reporter nursed bruises received from police batons, as did an unknown number of other bystanders and participants.

On the morning of Thursday, August 14, the *Helix* hit the street with news of Sunday and Monday's events, heralded by the headline: "Police Riot: Pigs Declare War on Youth." I interpreted the riots as an "episode in the second American Revolution." So, from a different point of view, did Police Chief Ramon, who claimed that the riot was a product of "deliberation and planning and was violence for violence's sake." He also denied that police had used CS gas, despite ample physical evidence to the contrary.

The *Seattle Times* harrumphed that the same "agitators" (moi?) were present at Alki and on the Ave, "suggesting a preconceived plan to create chaos." U District merchants blamed the street people, and mayoral candidate Wes Uhlman saw a link with the September 1968 arson at the UW's Naval ROTC building and the June 29 bombing of the Administration Building.

In truth, few of the participants were habitués of the U District and even fewer were politically motivated. Susan Stern, a newly inducted Weatherman fresh from the SDS convention in Chicago, was quickly disillusioned with the crowd's revolutionary potential when one of her street-fighting comrades declared gleefully, "I don't know who I hate more, the niggers or the pigs." Other than a handful of rads trying to earn their off-the-pig merit badges and George Crowley, a favorite foil of police paranoia, nobody had an agenda on Wednesday night beyond some good old-fashioned American teenage fun at the expense of cops and property.

In fact, it was such good fun that a lot of kids decided to do it again. As the afternoon turned to dusk on August 14, the Ave filled with a couple of thousand teenagers from every quarter of Seattle and even from the suburbs. The word had gone out on some kind of pheromonal telegraph that it was going to come down in the District again— so let's get it on!

Those of us who actually lived and worked in the neighborhood became alarmed that our turf was being turned into an arena for ritual combat between pigs and punks. John Chambless joined with ASUW president Steve Boyd to convene an emergency community meeting. Business was represented by attorney Cal McCune, and John Mitsules, a recent Vietnam vet who managed Bernie's, a "mod" men's store on the Ave. Jan Tissot spoke for the street people, and I was there ostensibly as a reporter. We set aside our grievances to beg the police to close off the Ave to traffic and let volunteers patrol the street. The police replied huffily that they had the situation under control and didn't need help from amateurs.

Famous last words. Promptly at 10 p.m., the events of the previous night began to replay when a group of black teens broke into a TV repair shop on the corner of NE 43rd and U Way. Squads of police appeared from the north and south, surrounding a crowd of a couple of hundred, while a truck-mounted howler swept the street. Police told the encircled mass to disperse but there was nowhere to go when the officers waded in. finally the police line opened a narrow gap onto 43rd, and people ran out through a gauntlet of truncheons and fists.

Another gang of people collected at the corner of NE 42nd, blocked traffic and ignited a bonfire of trash cans (it never occurred to the city to remove these ready sources of radical fuel). The police arrived, fired gas, and pursued people down U Way and 15th NE and even onto campus. Another mob coalesced at NE 45th and 15th and trashed the brand-new plate glass windows in the Pacific National Bank building before the police chased them away.

Again and again, clusters of rioters scattered and reassembled to do battle. In the course of the night, the police arrested twenty-one and roughed up five reporters, including KOMO-TV's Don McGaffin and Brian Johnson. Finally weary of these hit-and-run engagements, the police shut U Way to traffic and systematically gassed the street from 42nd to 45th with foggers and grenades. "Order" was restored shortly before 1 a.m.

By Friday morning it was clear to all that the police could neither prevent nor contain the violence, and the weekend promised to supply thousands of fresh recruits for the next rounds of street fighting. The city was considering ordering a curfew and summoning the National Guard when a delegation from the U District met with Acting Mayor Floyd Miller (he was filling out the term of Dorm Braman, who had joined the Nixon Administration) and veteran Deputy Mayor Ed Devine. Since the police had no better ideas, they agreed to let the community try to handle the situation.

The police closed U Way to traffic at dusk and parked several hundred Tac Squad members out of sight, while scores of volunteers wearing "peace" armbands spread out. Whenever a significant number of teens collected, street monitors plunged in to throw cold water on any ideas for looting or vandalism. It was a long, nerve-racking night, but every spark of potential violence was successfully doused. The tactic was repeated Saturday night with equal success. By Sunday, the Ave was too cool to reignite and the police withdrew. The success of the Ave's self-pacification led to months of "negotiations" among street people, merchants, residents, clergy, students, police, and city officials to reduce police harassment and establish a community center.

Meanwhile, 2,500 miles away on Max Yasgur's farm near Bethel, New York, nearly 400,000 kids turned a rural rock festival into a temporary—and peaceful—city.

It was called the "Woodstock Music and Art Fair and Aquarian Festival" in honor of a little town in the low Catskills, home to Bob Dylan and legendary counterculture pranks, although the planners originally chose a site near the town of Wallkill ("Wallkill Music and Art Fair and Aquarian Festival" doesn't quite cut it). A month before the event, the town of Wallkill changed its mind, and the promoters found an alternative site near White Lake.

Contrary to all the nostalgic tripe published on the twenty-fifth anniversary of Woodstock, the initial reports were quite unflattering. On August 21, *Helix* published an unsigned article, possibly an LNS feed, describing the "Aquarian Festival" as "one of the biggest bummers of this year's rash of rock festivals" and blamed "greediness on the part of the promoters." The article counted one death (a sleeping man run over by a tractor) and more than 1,000 injuries. The anonymous reporter was particularly shocked by concessionaires "selling water for 10 cents a glass, beer for 75 cents, and soft drinks for 50." Only later did Andrew Kopkind launch the festival's romanticization, and Abbie Hoffman appropriated it for his latest meta-myth, "Woodstock Nation."

Woodstock's organizers were not the only promoters receiving closer community scrutiny. Seattle's Boyd Grafmyre came under fire for allegedly netting $125,000 from the Pop festival, a figure he disputed. Several of the Crowley Kids (George and Louise's) helped to organize an Eagles Liberation Front to demand a reduction in "outrageous" ticket prices of $3.50 each. I later ended up mediating a settlement for lower prices on selected concerts, and the Crowley Kids ended up going to jail for disturbing the peace during a demonstration at Eagles.

For a moment in August, it looked like the Second Sky River Rock Festival wouldn't come off. Under intense pressure from police, conservatives, and the Catholic Archdiocese, virtually every county passed laws prohibiting or severely restricting rock festivals. A site in Enumclaw was offered and then withdrawn, and Chambless scrambled to find an alternative. He ended up with a strange locale: the Rainier Hereford Ranch, a stretch of dry grassland dimpled with miniature hillocks (left behind as some glacial prank) near Tenino, south of Olympia. The Tenino Chamber of Commerce and several adjacent property owners obtained an injunction blocking a Thurston County permit, but a sympathetic judge required the plaintiffs to post a $25,000 bond against NAC's anticipated losses. They couldn't, and at the last possible second the festival was cleared for takeoff. An estimated 25,000 attended over three days, but NAC still lost money.

With so much news to report, *Helix* decided to start publishing weekly on September 26. The new deadline imposed some discipline on us, and the paper began to look positively journalistic. It still came together, however, in a single twenty-four-hour orgasmic rush fueled by meth, pizza, and beer, so our integrity was not totally compromised.

The romance of rock festivals would take a mortal blow a little more than three months later, when Hell's Angels, hired to provide security, beat and killed a fan at the Rolling Stones' Altamont concert in Los Angeles. It closed a circle begun six years earlier when Ken Kesey invited Allan Ginsberg's "motorcycle saints" to attend his first Acid Tests.

Three days before Altamont, Charles Manson and three members of his "family" were arrested for torturing, murdering, and mutilating actress Sharon Tate (the wife of Roman Polanski), coffee heiress Abigail Folger, and three others at Polanski's estate, and supermarket magnate Leno LaBianca and his wife the previous August 9.

No amount of myth-making could disguise the brutal reality of these incidents, and they sounded the first chords in the Sixties' violent coda.

Chapter 18:
Daze of Rage

*The real dead end was the
dream that this was a
blessed generation, immune
to the darkness of the heart
that has always caused
violence and oppression.*

—**Charles Perry**

On September 3, Ho Chi Minh died in Hanoi of natural causes. The U.S. had by now dropped more ordnance on Vietnam than was used in all of World War II, and still they managed to miss him.

As another record enrollment—32,600, up by 1,300 from a year ago—streamed into the UW that fall, the campus looked as if it had been bombed by a stray B-52. The former lawn stretching between the Administration Building, Suzzallo Library, and Parrington Hall was now a deep pit spanned by rickety bridges. Construction of the underground parking lot and future "Red Square," Meany Hall, Kane Hall, and the Undergraduate Library became a battleground in a new civil rights struggle.

For more than a year, black construction workers led by Tyree Scott, Eddie Rye Jr., Mike Ross, and others had been agitating and negotiating to win a fair share of jobs and apprenticeships in the building boom then reshaping the city's skyline. They formed the Central Area Contractors Association in May and had been able to reach agreement on most points with the Association of General Contractors, but the county's conservative building trades unions balked.

CACA turned up the heat in August. Members picketed county-managed construction projects, including the new Administration Building, and secured a new ordinance in September mandating training for black workers, but the unions refused to accept them. At this point, CACA attorney Lem Howell filed suit to force union members to work with the new apprentices, and he found an ally in Arthur Fletcher, a black Republican from this state whom President Nixon had named Assistant Secretary of Labor. It was a delicate maneuver because the unions regarded the matter as a collective bargaining issue; Howell wanted it treated as a civil rights case to apply federal power in mandating compliance.

As hearings began on the CACA suit on September 23, Scott led pickets to the UW. Fights broke out, and picketers sent a bulldozer and two trucks toppling into the pit of the future parking garage. They returned the next day, and the contractors quickly shut the project down. Scott then led his supporters to Sea-Tac Airport to halt the major terminal and parking expansion underway there, which led to scuffles with police.

Governor Evans interceded on September 26, while the Port of Seattle (which manages Sea-Tac) and the UW filed suit both to force the unions to accept trainees and to prevent further work stoppages. Evans negotiated a settlement, prompting thousands of angry white workers to picket both the County Court House and State Capitol in several ugly rallies. Evans bravely faced down the bigots at the latter, and the unions grudgingly accepted twenty new trainees, but the war was far from over. Alan Beasley, chronicling this struggle in some of the *Helix*'s best reporting, commented that "some fat cat was sitting there smiling and thinking: 'Good, if these dumb workers keep fighting themselves, we sure as hell aren't going to have any trouble with them.'"

Despite this agitation in the UW's front yard, the war in Vietnam remained the foremost issue on campus. President Nixon did everything possible to divert public attention from the war, signing the new draft lottery law, lowering the draft quota, and withdrawing 60,000 troops. This did not prevent the deaths of more than 8,000 additional Americans during the year, nor did it cool student agitation to end the carnage.

The antiwar movement was now divided into two hostile camps. In the wake of Chicago and SDS's suicide, a New Mobilization Committee was patched together from surviving liberal and leftist war critics. Its leadership was dominated by the safe-and-sane Socialist Workers Party/Young Socialist Alliance, which insisted on an inclusionary, nonideological movement around the simple message, "Bring the troops home Now." The New Mobe scheduled mass Moratorium demonstrations for October 15, a national student strike on November 14, and a national "Mobilization" the next day.

The local Student Mobilization Committee was headed by my old comrade, Stephanie Coontz, who was roundly castigated and even physically attacked by Weathermen and their allies for being insufficiently "anti-imperialist." She replied in *Helix,* "I fail to see what can be more 'anti-imperialist' than building a mass movement against an imperialist war."

Even this was too radical for some, and the Trots had to beat back an internal coup by some New Mobe elements who wanted to eliminate all political content. On the other side, the Weathermen and RYM II joined to plan to "Bring the War Home" during a "national action" in Chicago between October 8 and 11. Abbie Hoffman says he suggested the demonstration's name, "Days of Rage."

The female members of Seattle's Weathermen collective gave their own answer when they rampaged through Air Force ROTC offices in a portable building. They spray-painted the walls, threw ink bombs, and scuffled with ROTC cadets who tried to detain them. Susan Stern recalls that the "FBI was totally baffled," and "SDS men of all factions were flabbergasted." News of the attack helped to attract 300 to an "SDS" (most still did not understand the effect of the June split) rally on October 2, followed by an attack on Navy ROTC offices in Clark Hall. The UW later banned nonstudents Judith and Trim Bissell, Jerry Ganley, Pat Ruckert, Alan Shafer, and Jeri Detweiler (who was in Harborview Hospital at the time of the incident) from campus.

This was all drill for the main event in Chicago. After months of organizing "jail breaks" in local high schools, the Days of Rage were supposed to test of the readiness of "revolutionary youth" to follow the Weather banner into battle. They flunked: no more than 600 participated in two separate trashing sprees and slug-fests with police. The first began late on the night of October 8, when a few hundred Weathermen, shivering in Lincoln Park, charged surrounding police and broke out toward the "Gold Coast," where they smashed the windows of expensive shops. Police shot six protesters and arrested sixty-eight; twenty-two police were injured.

An attempted march by the "Women's Militia" was quickly halted the next day and most of the seventy participants were arrested (including Susan Stern). Meanwhile, RYM II theorists Mike Klonsky and Noel Ignatin joined with Panthers and Young Lords to stage a march "of such an orderly and peaceful nature," comments Kirkpatrick Sale, that police "must have been left dumbfounded as to what the initials 'SDS' really meant." The Weathermen rallied for one more set-to on October 11, which injured 38 cops and sent 128 protesters to jail. In all, 287 protesters found themselves cited or incarcerated by the end of the Days of Rage; so much for "Bringing the War Home"!

In contrast, as many as a quarter million marched in peaceful Moratorium demonstrations around the country on October 15. Four thousand rallied at Westlake Mall in Seattle. Four days later, Vice President Agnew blasted the antiwar movement's leadership as an "effete corps of impudent snobs who characterize themselves as intellectuals."

Amid all this agitation, the trial of the Chicago Eight "progressed" in the court room of Judge Julius Jennings Hoffman. The hearing opened on September 24, and the first weeks were dominated by the testimony of police undercover agents such as Bob Pierson. The senior Hoffman traded bon mots with the junior Hoffman and his second banana, Jerry Rubin, while Bobby Seale demanded with mounting vehemence that he be separated from his codefendants and allowed to pick his own counsel. Exasperated by these demands for justice in his courtroom, Judge Hoffman ordered Seale bound and gagged on October 29. Seale got his wish on November 5, when Hoffman sentenced him for contempt (for mumbling and rattling his shackles in a disrespectful way). The Chicago Eight shrank to Seven.

On November 15, the national Mobilization attracted a quarter of a million people to Washington, D.C., for the largest single demonstration in the nation's history. Twenty Vietnam vets led 85,000 in San Francisco, and hundreds of thousands, possibly a million in all, marched in other cities. Four thousand assembled in downtown Seattle. An otherwise peaceful march was disrupted by two dozen Weathermen who split off from the main mass and went on a trashing spree, breaking the windows of a travel agency, stores, and the "Minute Chef" at Westlake. Ten Weathermen were arrested, and Susan Stern suffered a concussion from a nightstick.

Helix mocked the action with a "communiqué" from Hanoi noting "the strategic importance of the Minute Chef installation." I lamented that the madness of SDS left the mass of antiwar movement participants "doomed to betrayal, despair and defeat because they have no generals," while immobilizing experienced radicals "because they have no army."

Back at the UW, Coontz joined that fall with ASUW president Steve Boyd in one of the more audacious gambits of the campus movement. On November 25, they convened a "corporate meeting" of the student body in the Hec Edmonson Pavilion to repeal bylaws giving the UW Administration a veto over student government. Unfortunately, the required 3 percent quorum of the student body drifted away, and UW counsel Gary Little declared the action meaningless.

That same day, the UW Committee on the Environmental Crisis sponsored an "Environmental Fair" at the HUB. Environmentalism had been groping toward self-awareness as a movement through most of the year, and *Helix* now published extensive and detailed articles on pollution, overpopulation, and the destruction of wilderness and habitat. Also that week, Radical Women and other groups held the first major lecture series on women's liberation. The defining movements of the Seventies were stirring in the wings, but the Sixties weren't quite ready to surrender center stage.

On December 1, local Weathermen staged another assault on ROTC, this time in Savery Hall. Among those arrested was a new recruit, Horace "Red" Parker, an undercover police agent who would figure in later events. This was the last straw for the UW administration, which canceled SDS's accreditation as a legal campus organization. SDS, of course, had already ceased to exist as an organization.

Four days later, Chicago police burst into the apartment of Black Panther leader Fred Hampton and machine-gunned him and Mark Clark in their beds. Who could doubt that it was war, now?

On December 12, the remains of the "Weatherbureau" leadership convened in the grim factory town of Flint, Michigan, and declared that it was done trying to mobilize an army of revolutionary youth. Now was the time to go "deep underground." The bombings had already begun.

The mood that winter was captured by a single film, Dennis Hopper's *Easy Rider,* which made stars of Peter Fonda, Jack Nicholson, and himself. Hopper visited Seattle and a *Helix* team interviewed him. We were disappointed that he had manipulated our paranoia without the benefit of a detailed dialectical analysis, but this did not diminish the movie's gut impact. After seeing it, I remember retreating to Tim Harvey's apartment with him and his paramour of the time, Pat Churchill (now a Hollywood producer). We grimly evaluated our options: emigration or rifle practice with the Weathermen.

Helix came under increasing pressure during these months. The first incident was downright comical. Our printers were then the *Skagit Valley Herald,* owned by rock-ribbed Republicans and staffed by even less liberal folks, who took our business only because we paid cash (traditional values, you know). We had had trouble before when one of the "strippers" (who prepare the printing negatives) decided to stick tape over all of the exposed body parts in photos of the second Sky River Rock Festival. The owner of the press had to take over the job of doing our negatives.

In pasting up the October 9 edition, we discovered an old *Life* magazine article on U.S. currency through the ages. We clipped out the pictures, about the size of postage stamps, and used them to illustrate a couple of articles. When the strippers in Mount Vernon saw these, they figured they had caught us red-handed counterfeiting the sacred U.S. dollar. They called the Treasury Department, which confiscated our paste-ups and the completed press run, and then drove to Seattle to arrest me as the titular editor.

A tiny, rotund man, named Special Agent Elmer something, wearing a porkpie hat, and his larger, silent companion closed in on me in the *Helix* office. Informed that I was being arrested for counterfeiting, I protested, "For whom, Munchkins?" I demanded to make a phone call, and luckily ACLU director Mike Rosen was in his office to answer my appeal. He asked to speak to the agent, who held the phone about a foot from his ear as Rosen explained the law. Rosen told him not to move until he called back.

We sat in silence amid the post-paste-up chaos of the office for about a minute. The phone rang, and I answered. This time the caller was Stanley Pitkin, the U.S. Attorney for Western Washington, and he wanted to speak to the Special Agent. This time Elmer held the phone as far from his ear as his pudgy arms would permit, bringing it closer only to mumble an occasional, chagrined "yes, sir," and "no, sir." At last he hung up. He was not going to arrest me after all, but I should take this as a lesson to show more respect for the paper currency of Lilliputia. He released the papers but retained the paste-up boards as "contraband" (still stored in a federal warehouse somewhere with the lost Ark of the Covenant, no doubt). He gave me a green receipt. I regret that I have since lost it, because it would prove that his last name was, as I remember it, Fudd.

The next incident was not so funny. Somebody poured gasoline on our office door and set it afire. Since we were in the back, we quickly doused it. A few weeks after this, I was alone in the office when the phone rang. "The *Helix* and its Commie-Red Faggot Gook-Lovers [or words to that effect] will be blown to kingdom-come in twenty minutes." I thanked the caller for the courtesy of the warning, and called a few friends.

Within ten minutes, the office and adjacent rooftops were bristling with more weapons than an NRA picnic: shotguns, rifles, pistols, and something that looked a lot like an M-16. We positioned cars, motors running, in each direction to give hot pursuit, and waited. Fortunately, our would-be bomber never showed up, because he surely would have died that night.

SDS's final plunge into madness cast all but of its hardest-core adherents adrift, including Susan Stern. Her dalliance with the Weathermen had shattered what remained of her marriage, and Robby moved to California. Meanwhile, three other orphans of the Weather storm arrived in Seattle, the former Cornell "Sundance Collective" of Chip Marshall, Jeff Dowd, and Michael Abeles.

At this moment, a new BMOC of the Left asserted himself at the UW: Assistant Professor Michael Lerner. Bug-eyed, bewhiskered, his mouth twisted into a congenital sneer, Lerner was the man who would lead us into the worker's paradise, or at least one to his own liking. As a student, Lerner had participated in the Free Speech Movement and Vietnam Day Committee at Berkeley. He first achieved prominence when, dressed in a tux, he gained entry to a 1967 Democratic gala featuring Robert Kennedy, which the VDC was picketing. According to W. J. Rorabaugh, Lerner waited in the receiving line and when Kennedy reached him, shouted, "Get out of Vietnam" to his face. Security guards quickly ejected him.

Lerner arrived in Seattle in fall 1969 to teach Philosophy 110, an introduction to Marx, Marcuse, and the gang. He quickly surveyed the wreckage of the local Left, and visited the *Helix* one day to demand to know what we were doing to advance the people's struggle. He found our efforts wanting.

Meanwhile, John Chambless found himself under attack, both from his colleagues and from Art Linkletter, of all people. Linkletter had achieved fame for such early TV shows as "People Are Funny" and his "Houseparty," which featured a segment called "Kids Say the Darndest Things." Tragically, his daughter committed suicide while on acid on October 4. A few weeks later, he visited Seattle. When he was introduced to a UW student, Linkletter told her, "Say, if you see that professor who staged the festival at Tenino, would you kick him in the face for me?"

The campus was also shaken that fall by dissension on its sainted football team. As *Helix*'s "Rip Randell" reported, black players had long chafed under what they regarded as Coach Jim Owens's racist remarks and treatment. Black alumni had staged a boycott of May's varsity-alumni game, and things only got worse. Owens retaliated on October 30 by suspending four players for "lack of commitment." Two days later, the remaining nine black members of the squad refused to travel south for a game with UCLA, which proceeded to crush the all-white Huskies by a score of 57 to 14. The administration reinstated three of the suspended players eight days later, and the writing was clearly on the locker room wall for Coach Owens.

There was some good news in the real world that fall. On November 4, Seattle voters chose a thirty-four-year-old liberal, State Sen. Wes Uhlman, over the establishment-blessed Mort Frayn. The City Council elections offered mixed results: While CHECC candidate George Cooley won, former Police Dance Squad hoofer Wayne Larkin defeated liberal journalist Don Wright. Former King County Democratic chairwoman Jeanette Williams would prove to be a reliable advocate for women and minorities, but Liem Tuai, the council's first Asian-American member since Wing Luke's death, turned out to be an implacable foe of the new mayor and most of his reforms.

Helix had given Uhlman a limp endorsement in the election, but we were not prepared for his action on December 19 when he personally greeted César Chavez, in town to organize grape boycotts, and named him a "first Citizen" of Seattle. It was the first of many surprises Wes had in store for us.

That same fall, the noose began tightening around the police-courthouse gang. Reporters for the *P-I* and KING-TV exposed massive payoffs, and linked Prosecutor Charles Carroll with known gamblers. Chief Frank Ramon was forced to take early retirement in October, and his interim replacement, M. E. Cook, lasted only a few weeks before accusations forced him out. Frank Moore became the new chief, but the scandal was far from finished.

The year ended with Seattle laying claim to the dubious distinction of being the nation's "bombing capital," with sixty-nine explosions and arson fires (not all or even most politically motivated) and damage estimated at $3.5 million. An economic bomb was also ticking that fall, as Boeing's local employment declined by 30,000, despite the introduction of the 747 Jumbo Jet and rosy predictions for the new SST.

Things would get much worse.

Chapter 19:
Things Fall
Apart

*Watch the man who throws
the first rock. He may be a
cop.*

—Todd Gitlin

As 1969 closed, the mainstream media hailed the end of a decade variously described as tumultuous, violent, traumatic, etc. They were technically a year premature, and their sense of the zeitgeist was as bad as their arithmetic. We weren't done with the Sixties yet, and they weren't done with us.

President Nixon opened the new year with a flourish by signing the new National Environmental Protection Act, whose passage had been pushed by Sen. Henry Jackson. Environmentalism was actively promoted by the establishment as a harmless alternative for youthful radicalism, as witnessed by the broad support for the first Earth Day the following April. It didn't work out as planned. NEPA's token requirement for "environmental impact statements" would soon backfire on its authors by giving opponents of highways and other major projects new legal leverage to delay and mitigate harmful construction and policies. No good deed goes unpunished.

Michael Lerner had spent his first winter at the UW rounding up potential adherents for a new organization to fill the void left behind by the implosion of SDS. He asserted his hegemony over the ruins of the local Left by inviting his former Berkeley comrade Jerry Rubin to speak on campus on January 17, 1970. Some 4,000 turned out, and two days later Lerner hosted the first formal organizing meeting for the "Seattle Liberation Front."

The philosophy of the SLF was a Whitman's Sampler of New Left goodies: anti-imperialism, working-class organizing, psychedelic evangelism, Third World solidarity, environmentalism, women's liberation, tenants' rights, student and community control. Recruits were invited to pick their favorite flavors and chew on them. There was no underlying philosophy except a mushy Marxism adaptable to every issue, nor was there any strategic coherence—except to avoid the kind of self-destructive violence which had undone SDS.

None of this was necessarily bad. Indeed, several of us at *Helix* were initially intrigued by SLF, but we quickly saw problems. Like the Weathermen, it emphasized a central cadre organized into a network of "collectives," intended to concentrate organizing activity among like-minded people on specific goals, e.g., health care, women's rights, housing, etc. This loose, theoretically participatory democracy was an open invitation to a dictatorship of the ego-tariat. There was no process for deciding what was more or less important, correct, or practical; it all rested on the enthusiasm and persuasive force of individuals and internal caucuses. As in Orwell's *Animal Farm,* some collectives soon proved more equal than others—particularly the transplanted Sundance Collective from Ithaca—and some individuals were more equal than all the rest, and none more so than Lerner.

More conservative Marxists in the SWP/YSA and other groups viewed SLF with scorn, and the remnants of the Weathermen and their wanna-bes sneered at SLF's antiviolence. They were still up to their old tricks: the day before SLF's organizing meeting, Trim Bissell (scion of the floor-sweeper family and former draft resister) and his wife were captured planting a crude incendiary bomb under the steps of the Air Force ROTC portable, and both went underground soon after. The day following Lerner's conclave, a contingent of Weathermen broke away from an otherwise peaceful antiwar rally at the UW and trashed the ROTC office in Clark Hall.

Most UW students simply ignored SLF and the other loonies as best they could, but there was still a sizable group of activists orphaned by SDS who, if not ready to join a collective, at least welcomed some kind of leadership. In the marketplace of leftist ideas that winter, SLF at least had a new stall. One marketing ploy backfired, however.

On February 11, SLF made headlines when five of its members invaded Henry Bluechel's Economics 200 lecture to demand that he talk about something more important, "like the war in Vietnam and the Chicago." He told them to shut up or get out. When they declined to do either, he and several students chased them from the lecture hall. SLF may have thought that it had struck another blow for liberation, but all it did was give Hank Bluechel his fifteen minutes of fame and make itself look like a bunch of bullies.

In February, the Kafkaesque trial of the Chicago Seven ran its course. In anticipation of the verdict, Abbie Hoffman et al. called for supporters to organize demonstrations for "The Day After" the jury handed down its judgment. SLF answered the call and began planning a "TDA" do at the Federal Court House. Since no one knew exactly when the verdicts might come, this was a unique organizing challenge. Like the Weathermen before them, Susan Stern and other TDA recruiters focused their outreach in local high schools.

Chip Marshall, the one SLF leader with certifiable charm and charisma, came to the *Helix* with copy for a floating manifesto for a "Stop the Courts Day" at 2 p.m. in front of the courthouse on whatever date constituted TDA. While Marshall's copy never explicitly called for a violent action, it all but invited it, and this made us very nervous. *Helix* labeled the piece as a "Paid Off Political Advertisement" and we appended an ironic headline taken from Fidel Castro: "History will absolve us."

The same February 12 issue of *Helix* contained an incredulous headline, "Uhlman Spares Panthers?" Six days earlier, Mayor Uhlman had publicly spurned a request from federal Alcohol, Tobacco and Firearms agents for Seattle Police support in "serving a search warrant" on the Seattle offices of the Black Panthers. Uhlman expressed disapproval of "midnight raids" against the Panthers elsewhere, and left us lefties scratching our heads.

While the Chicago Seven jury was still out on the morning of Saturday, February 14, Judge Hoffman launched his own preemptive strike by sentencing all of the defendants and their lead attorneys, William Kunstler and Leonard Weinglass, for contempt. Added to Bobby Seale's previous sentence, Hoffman sentenced the original Chicago Eight and their defense team to nineteen years and ninety-three days. This was the cue for TDA three days hence.

On the appointed afternoon, about 2,000 people collected in front of the courthouse along Fifth Avenue. At the head of the sloping lawn, police and U.S. Marshals stood guard in front of the doors; other police hid out of sight at the Seattle Public Library across the street and in nearby alleys. As Susan Stern recounts the incident, many in the crowd "believed Lerner" in his earlier, written pledge "that we have no intention of introducing violence into the demonstration," but that she and others—particularly a large number of teens—came prepared for something else.

Whatever "leadership" there was dissolved almost instantly, when some in the crowd began to shout "Free Bobby" and the air filled with rocks and paint bombs. Hundreds surged up the lawn, and some made it to the doors. At least one managed to lob a police gas bomb into the courthouse lobby, but most were repulsed with clouds of tear and nausea gas and chased back down the lawn.

At this point, Chip Marshall leapt atop a car to speak. Suddenly the police charged from every direction. The chant went up, "Downtown! Downtown!" and the mass of people fled downhill toward the waterfront or north toward the retail district, with uniformed and plainclothes officers in hot pursuit. The more experienced berserkers broke off into "affinity groups" and began trashing store fronts and police cars. Police, meanwhile, isolated individuals and beat the living shit out of them. When it was over, scores had been injured, eighty-nine were in jail, and $75,000 in damage had been done.

The account above is constructed from newspaper accounts, including the *Helix*, because I wasn't at TDA. That day I lectured a large class at Mercer Island High School on the environmental movement. As I drove back on I-5, I could see white clouds rising behind the slab-like courthouse and felt sick to my stomach, but not from the gas.

Susan Stern reported that a great time was had by all. The next night, she sat in the living room of a friend's house as a man who turned out to be a police agent helped two others assemble bombs from stolen dynamite. A different set of bombs was planted three nights later on the construction site of the new UW architecture building, but only one worked.

A few days later, reality began to sink in. SLF ejected Stern because she was the most visible link to Weathermen militancy (ironically the Weathermen expelled her for not being militant enough). The police searched the Sundance house and confiscated a shotgun. On March 3, despite a confrontation with angry SLF supporters, Michael Lerner's colleagues in the Philosophy Department voted not to extend his contract.

That same night, Jan Tissot, Jon Van Veenendaal, Michael Reed, and Jeff Desmond, a notorious police informer, set off a bomb next to the U District Post Office. It left a black stain on the concrete wall and flattened one tire of a postal jeep. Police descended instantly and scooped them up.

I later asked Tissot how he, the organizer of 1967's Second International Bohemian Festival, could have turned to violence. He replied, "I was very angry at the time." As to associating with someone known to all as an informer, if not a paid agent, he blamed arrogance. He and his comrades later pleaded guilty to reduced charges; Jan says federal attorneys didn't want to reveal that the dynamite they used had been stolen earlier by a federal agent.

The UW succumbed to a new round of demonstrations beginning March 5. BSU and SLF members briefly occupied Thomson Hall after meeting with acting UW president John Hogness (Odegaard was in Europe) and a rally of 2,000 supporters. Their goal was to compel termination of all athletic and other arrangements with Brigham Young University, whose parent Church of Latter-Day Saints (Mormons) formally discriminated against blacks. This was a me-too issue which emerged the previous November when Stanford University severed ties with BYU; the next BYU-UW event was nearly a year away.

The next day, roving gangs of demonstrators invaded several buildings. The havoc prompted the UW to finally abandon its longstanding prohibition of Seattle Police on campus. Seeing no point in pulling Brigham Young's wagon, the UW announced on March 8 that it would sever all athletic ties with BYU when current contracts expired. This was not enough for BSU and the SLF, who again invaded buildings and classrooms. Two hundred Seattle Police occupied the campus on March 12, and BSU canceled further demonstrations. Nothing had been accomplished except to violate the UW's status as a sanctuary.

That night a colossal explosion leveled a posh Greenwich Village townhouse. The police literally pieced together the identities of three individuals, Diana Oughton, Ted Gold, and Terry Robins, all Weathermen. They had been assembling bombs in the basement, but there were others to take their place.

At the *Helix,* we watched these events with leaden hearts, which was too bad, because the paper had actually managed to cheer itself up since the gloomy winter of 1969. Tom Robbins wrote one of his funniest pieces, relating his attempt to call Pablo Picasso collect from the Blue Moon's pay phone; Picasso declined to accept the charges. John Cunnick pulled off a masterful hoax in December with a counterfeit interview between Paul Krassner and Bob Dylan—a seamless flow of increasingly hallucinogenic non-sequiturs—which was reprinted nationally via UPS. Dylan never reacted, but Krassner went ballistic; I guess the man who portrayed LBJ fucking JFK's corpse can dish it out, but he can't take it.

Roger Downey at least equaled Cunnick's achievement with another put-on in January: "The Great Electron Crisis." Downey had been annoyed by Frank Herbert's (the author of *Dune* was then a *Seattle P-I* reporter) pseudoscientific brand of environmental alarmism, so he concocted a plausible sounding report claiming that with the spread of industry and appliances, we were using up the world's supply of electrons. *Helix* received two kinds of letters over the next few weeks: those who demanded to know why the Establishment wasn't addressing the electron crisis, and those who inquired somewhat sheepishly as to when the laws of thermodynamics had been repealed.

By the paper's third anniversary in March 1970, such antics seemed a thousand years in the past. Paul and I wrote dueling bum trip essays. His explored the metaphor of the Second Coming and a second crucifixion: "Civilization is chugging up Golgotha like a tired train. It's a life and death matter. Progress is weary and wants to be crucified. The tracks behind have all been twisted by saboteurs. No one knows why. They are dropping bombs off the caboose."

I concluded my piece, "*Helix* for me was an experiment in freedom. Eccentric, anarchistic, creative: when *Helix* began, those were the qualities which dominated the movement and the community. Those values, however, have been supplanted with new principles whose legitimacy I accept but do not celebrate. *Helix* has lost its context. Within *Helix,* I have lost mine. I think the time has come for a revolution in the REVOLUTION."

Happy birthday to us.

On April 16, the federal government, in its infinite wisdom, beatified eight more Movement leaders when Mike Abeles, Jeff Dowd,

Michael Justesen, Joe Kelly, Michael Lerner, Roger Lippman, Charles Clark "Chip" Marshall III, and Susan Stern were charged with conspiracy to incite a riot at the February 17 "TDA" demonstration. The FBI arrested Abeles, Dowd, Kelly, Lerner, and Stern immediately; Lippman was picked up in Berkeley; and Marshall was nabbed two days later, while drinking a beer in the Century Tavern on the upper Ave. Justesen disappeared underground, so the "Seattle Eight" became the more mellifluous "Seattle Seven."

On the same day, the ASUW elected small "r" radical Rick Silverman as its new president, along with two sidekicks, Bill Felice and Dave Graybill. Silverman looked like a human torch: wild-eyed, hyperenergetic, and topped by a mane of flaming red hair. He was also a very astute campus politician, and very, very funny. Silverman's chief ally on campus was the *Daily's* new editor, Bruce Olson, who was almost immediately accused of taking a hard Left in coverage and editorial stance.

On April 18, as if for comic relief, the road production of *Hair* opened in the refurbished Moore Theater. The troupe hit the stage nearly three months before their originally planned opening because the cast (they called themselves a "tribe") astrologer found June to be unpropitious.

In the *Helix*, Roger Downey praised the production's energy, because "it's the only thing that makes the show bearable," and then ripped into millionaire-producer Michael Butler, the script, and the whole premise as "another lie for profit." My girlfriend of the previous two years was a tribe member. She held me personally responsible for the slam, and dumped me.

Two weeks later, on April 30—the fabled "Walpurgis Night" of witches and demons—President Nixon announced that he was sending U.S. troops into Cambodia. Their ostensible mission was to cut the so-called "Ho Chi Minh trail" via which North Vietnam bypassed the DMZ to supply its troops in the south, but the move was also intended to support a right-wing coup which deposed Prince Sihanouk a few weeks before. Nixon also resumed heavy bombing of North Vietnam, which had been suspended for nearly a year and a half. Virtually every campus in the nation rose up in fervent protest. At the UW, Weather-types conducted a ritual trashing of ROTC, and a downtown demonstration attacked the Boeing Employment Center. Students at Ohio's Kent State University went further, and burned their ROTC building down. On May 3, the call went out from antiwar and campus government leaders for a national student strike. No one was prepared for the next day's events.

Ohio dispatched National Guard troops to the Kent State campus to prevent further arson and vandalism. They took a position on a low hill in a formation not unlike a British Square, with their guns aimed at the surrounding clots of chanting, jeering students as though they were Zulus about to attack. Suddenly, the troops began firing. Four students fell dead or mortally wounded (William Schroeder, Allison Krause, Jeffrey Miller, and Sandra Scheuer), and fifteen more were injured.

The entire nation gasped. Push had come to shove, and shove had come to shooting. In a decade drenched in blood, nothing had quite the impact as the deaths of these four white students, alive one second amid the sunshine of a spring day on a midwestern campus, sprawled dead or dying the next, their bodies ripped by the bullets of American soldiers no older than their victims. It had come to this: America's children were killing each other.

And it had to stop. The presidents of thirty-seven U.S. universities, including Dr. Odegaard, sent telegrams to President Nixon urging immediate withdrawal from Southeast Asia. The nation's campuses ground to a halt, some in silence, some in chaos, but the business of education could not continue. Some schools such as Boston University and Princeton shut down for the balance of the spring quarter.

On May 5, Stephanie Coontz and Rick Silverman presided over a rally of some 7,000 students, who "voted" to strike. The leadership decided to lead the mass through the U District. Perhaps 5,000 marched off campus and up the Ave. When they reached NE 45th, a spontaneous cry went up, "Freeway!" and it multiplied into a collective roar. Some separated or returned to campus, but most veered west, and then south on Interstate-5.

A crowd of 3,000 inched onto the highway, filling the right lane, then the next, then the next, slowing and finally halting traffic behind a human barricade across the south-bound half of the Freeway Bridge.

Amazed and elated at their own power and audacity, individuals cavorted on pavement reserved for rubber tires, not human soles. Then the mass began to ooze south.

At Roanoke, they were met by a line of no more than a dozen very nervous police officers. Having left their official leaders far behind, the vanguard of the crowd hesitated. They decided that they were having too much fun to fight that sunny afternoon, so the crowd poured off the freeway and proceeded downtown via Eastlake. Most made it to the hated Federal Court House, where they listened to speeches and most congratulated themselves on their great victory. The rally broke up without a single gas bomb exploding, a single club swinging, or a single store window shattering.

The next day would be different. President Odegaard closed the UW and Mayor Uhlman ordered flags on city buildings lowered to half mast in memory of the Kent State victims during an official "day of reflection." Some 10,000 rallied downtown and several hundred decided to retake I-5 for the march north. This time they were met by riot police who used tear gas and clubs to force them off at the Roanoke and Mercer exits. A young reporter for KOMO-TV, Norm Rice, watched the mayhem and called the police behavior "unmitigated brutality." Meanwhile, in Washington, D.C., President Nixon met with six Kent State students and promised to investigate the shooting.

May 7 began peacefully. Students and faculty milled around the idle campus, and police kept out of sight. That evening, several thousand marched off campus and through the U District. Most chanted "Peace Now," but a handful had other objectives. When the parade reached the Applied Physics Laboratory near 12th and 40th, rocks and bottles suddenly exploded from the crowd and began ricocheting off the fortress-like building's gray concrete. This was what the police were waiting for.

Suddenly, scores of riot-equipped police roared out of the shadows and began beating everyone in sight. I was standing a few yards apart from the main mass, describing the scene on a tape recorder for KOL-FM, when one cop spotted me and charged. I am not athletic, quite the contrary, but I think I set a new world's record for the 100-yard dash, and I left the panting policeman far behind.

As I paused to catch my own breath, Dave Wood, an aide to Mayor

Uhlman, walked past on his way to the melee, and I joined him. We entered Lander Hall, a highrise dormitory near the Physics Lab, and we watched dumbfounded as a dozen or so cops began beating a rackfull of students' bicycles with their clubs. Unsatisfied, they invaded the lobby and chased everyone, including Dave and me, upstairs or outside. At about this point, Cal McCune and U District Chamber of Commerce President Dick Coppage walked out of the former's office and on to the Ave. They were immediately confronted by police who told them to get off the street. Cal and Dick made the mistake of arguing that they had every right to be there, and were cuffed and hauled downtown for their trouble.

It was clearly time to get indoors, but the police were now between me and my apartment. I decided to take refuge in the Id Bookstore, where I worked part-time. This, upon reflection, was a strategic error. I headed east to 15th and then north. As I passed the intersection at the new Schmitz Hall, I could see a man also walking north about fifty feet ahead. Suddenly, several dark figures burst out from the bushes along 15th and began beating him. I yelled, "Hey!" and he broke free and ran toward me. When he came into the light, I could see his face covered in blood.

I helped him back to Campus Parkway, where a single police officer stood by his car, blocking traffic from entering University Way. "Help this man," I said. "There are thugs on 15th beating people up." The policeman looked at me, looked at my bleeding companion, and turned his back on us without saying a word. My companion chose to head south toward a friend's apartment, but I declined his invitation to come along.

I sidled up the Ave and found another refugee along the way. He reported that he had seen groups of men ambushing people on side streets and on campus. He thought they might be cops in plain clothes. When he and I turned the corner at 42nd, we faced a squad of uniformed police standing abreast in front of the Id. In my single greatest act of courage or stupidity, I walked up to them, politely asked to pass, and unlocked the door.

Ten minutes later, the police marched off. Another ten minutes later, a car drove by and loosed a fusillade of rocks which smashed the store's front windows. Not wanting to wait for the next act, I called

Steve Herold and he drove into the District in his vintage Morris Minor coupe. How he got past the roadblocks, I don't know, but we bundled into the car and escaped with our skins intact. Many that night were not so lucky.

The next day, after lamely denying that these thugs were policemen, Chief Frank Moore finally admitted the obvious and denounced the "vigilantes" (I don't think any lost their badges, but Seattle Police Tactical Squad commander Major Ray Carroll was later demoted for "over-reaction"). Mayor Uhlman closed the I-5 express lanes to traffic and opened them to 15,000 protesters who marched from the UW to a rally at the courthouse. This time, the police taped daffodils to their nightsticks.

President Nixon tried to sound a conciliatory air in addressing the nation that night, but the furor would not die down. More than 100,000 rallied in Washington, D.C., on May 9, and a sleepless president drove to the Lincoln Memorial for a midnight "rap session" with some of the encamped protesters. Not everyone sought an end to the turmoil.

Two days later, six blacks were killed by police and National Guardsmen in Augusta, Georgia, during riots provoked by the earlier death of a black prisoner beaten to death by guards in his cell. On May 15, state police fired into a dormitory at Jackson State College, killing two black students.

That same night, Seattle Police Officer John Hannah fired three shotgun blasts into Larry Ward, a black veteran only recently returned from the war. Ward, who had no political connections or axe to grind, had become swept up in a scheme to bomb either the Central Area offices of the Model Cities Program or Hardcastle Realty, which was notorious among blacks. The following sequence is condensed from a chilling account written by Ardie Ivie for *Seattle* magazine.

Ward fell into an acquaintance with one Alfie Burnett, a petty crook and suspected police informer. Burnett had developed a sudden interest in bombs, following a trip to New York, and he tried to recruit several people to assist him. Early on the morning of May 15, he roused Ward from bed to help him bomb the real estate office on the corner of Union and 24th. Ward did not know that Alfie had first called the FBI, and that they had called the Seattle Police. They were waiting, but not for Larry Ward. The FBI told them to expect Black Panther leader Curtis Harris.

While Burnett waited in the car, Ward knelt to place the bomb against the realty office door. At this moment, John Hannah fired his shotgun from a squad car parked half a block west on Union. A single, massive slug, used to disable fleeing vehicles, smashed through the window next to Ward's head. He started to run toward Alfie's car, but Alfie was already driving away. Hannah's partner swung the car onto 24th and Hannah fired a load of shot.

Several pellets struck Ward in the shoulder, but he did not fall and stumbled north on 24th, in the direction of his mother's home a few blocks away. Ward could no doubt see a second police car racing south toward him, but he kept on running. As Ward approached this second car, Hannah leaned out of his window and pumped two cartridges of heavy gauge pellets into his quarry. Several steel balls ripped through Ward's heart and lungs, and he crumpled up on the sidewalk and bled to death. As Ivie reported, the time was 2:38:50 a.m.—24 seconds had elapsed from the first shot to the last.

Twelve days later, an inquest jury voted 3-2 that Ward had died by "criminal means," i.e., that Hannah, who said he fired the final fatal shots in self-defense, was not justified. Charles O. Carroll declined to prosecute, because the verdict was not unanimous, and the press howled for reforms of the inquest system. Despite the best efforts of attorney Lem Howell, Ward's family never obtained justice.

The city, and indeed, the nation had lost its capacity for shock, grief, or remorse. Two weeks into May, the university began to clamp down on dissent. The first targets were KUOW-FM, which had become a virtual NPR of revolution during the strike, and Bruce Olson. *Daily* "publisher" (really an adult supervisor) William Asbury demanded that his name be removed from the masthead, and six staff members, including future *P-I* cartoonist Dave Horsey, resigned in protest of the paper's "Marxist line." The *P-I* and right-wing KIRO editorialist Lloyd Cooney demanded Olson's head, but he hung on to it to finish the quarter. When Eric Lacitis was named editor for the fall quarter, he dismissed the attacks against Olson as nonsense and praised his journalistic integrity.

On May 29, some 3,000 Seattle residents rallied to defend the honor of the police under the banner of "Help Eliminate Lawless Protesting," and the Police Guild threatened to strike if investigations of police misconduct were pressed further. On June 3, Vice President Agnew denounced the "charlatans of peace and freedom [who] eulogize foreign dictators while desecrating the flag that keeps them free" before a cheering throng of Annapolis graduates. The national mourning period for Kent State was officially over, and things were back to normal.

For the survivors at *Helix,* it was more than we could bear. Tim Harvey had already departed for New York City, and Jack Delay, John Cunnick, and Billy Ward had headed for the hills. Paul and I no longer partook of the communion of paste-up, and Sharma, Roger Hudson, and Roxie Grant were bushed. Roger Downey had inherited responsibility for the paper, and he was visibly melting down. Not even Scott White, newly returned from harvesting Cuban sugar cane with the Venceremos Brigade, could muster much enthusiasm. So the "collective" gathered for a last meeting. We added up our receivables and payables and found them more or less equal. It was as good a time as any to pull the plug.

Larry Heald penned a sweet illustration of a closed door for the cover of the 125th and final *Helix,* issued on June 11. On the back cover, we published a brief farewell acknowledging the media rumors of our impending demise and thanking everyone. The reason was stated simply: "It is time. We are tired. Three years is a long time for an experiment to last."

The letter closed, "The era, the page, has turned. The *Helix* is dead. We are growing, we are winning."

ALL POWER TO THE PEOPLE,

The Helix Staff

(Signed) *Bob A., Alice, Sharma, Otis, Scott White, Roger Hudson, Alan, Roxie, Bart Thrall, Maurie, Norman Caldwell, Mark, Kaaren, Brian, Nils, Sonny, Paul, Mike Crowley, and Walt Crowley.*

Previous page: The author taking notes at Garfield High School during 1969 riots (Alan Lande)

Top left: David Jensen on the Rapid Transit, 1966 (photographer unknown)

Middle left: Unidentified hippie, left, and Joe Cain, 1967 (Laura Besserman)

Bottom left: Author and Jack Delay on the right, 1966 (unknown)

Top right: Robert Horsley, left, and Doc Eskanazie, 1969 (A. Lande)

Top: Country Joe and the Fish at the Piano Drop, 1968 (unknown)

Middle: John Chambless at KOL-FM, 1969 (A. Lande)

Right: View from stage of second Sky River Rock Festival, 1969 (A. Lande)

Top: The "mud dance" at the first Sky River Rock Festival, 1968 (un-known)

Bottom: Black Snake performing with Retina Circus light show at Eagles, 1969 (A. Lande)

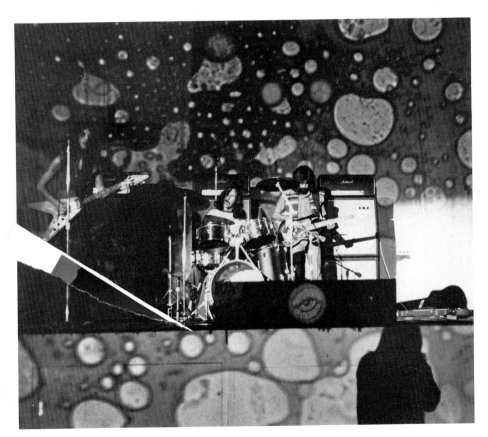

Top: Author addressing 1968
Black Panther Party convention
(Roger Hudson)

Middle: Paul Dorpat announcing light show permit, 1967
(unknown)

Lower Middle: Jerry Rubin at
the UW, 1970 (A. Lande)

Bottom: Floyd Turner, 1967
(M. Mates)

Opposite: Beginning of the May
5, 1970, Freeway March
(A. Lande)

Top left: Federal Marshall, left, and Mayor Wes Uhlman, 1970 (R. Hudson)

Top right: Aaron Dixon, 1970 (A. Lande)

Middle and bottom: Police and demonstrators clashing at 1970 TDA demonstration (A. Lande)

Opposite top: Laura Besserman at the head of 1969 Moratorium march (A. Lande)

Opposite bottom: Susan Stern being arrested during Loew Hall protest, 1969 (A. Lande)

Top: Six of the Seattle Seven in 1970: Michael Lerner, far left, Chip Marshall, Susan Stern, Mike Abeles, Jeff Dowd, and Joe Kelly (A. Lande)

Bottom: Rick Silverman, center, facing camera, trying to manage UW strike rally, 1970 (A. Lande)

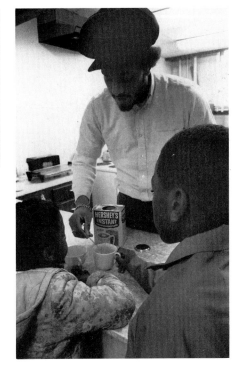

Top: UW Pres. Charles Odegaard, with bullhorn,
and Stephanie Coontz, to his immediate left, at
1970 strike rally (A. Lande)

Middle: Abbie Hoffman, left, and Tom Hayden,
rear, with Mike Abeles at UW, 1970 (A. Lande)

Bottom: Elmer Dixon staffing Black Panther
Breakfast Program, 1970 (A. Lande)

Top: U District Center staff in 1970: Clay Grubb, left, Gilda Traylor, author, Bill Billings, Roxie Grant, and "UDC" (adapted from a photo by Harald Sund, courtesy of US West)

Middle: Cal McCune, 1969 (A. Lande)

Bottom: 1969 University District "negotiations" session with Ed Devine, far left, Chief Frank Ramon, Asst. Chief Tony Gustin, rear, Jan Tissot, and the author (A. Lande)

Chapter 20:
The Center
Cannot Hold

*Nothing indicates that it
will be a good end.*

—Herbert Marcuse

A few days before the *Helix* folded, I was approached by Cal McCune, Steve Boyd, and the Rev. David Royer, a minister with the Campus Christian Ministries, to take over as director of the new University District Center. It didn't take much to persuade me.

My ascent from the underground had really begun nearly two years earlier with my "candidacy" for the Peace and Freedom Party. I began to follow small "p" progressive politics with greater interest, albeit also with condescension, as folks like Jim Ellis struggled to fund obvious public improvements such as rail transit (it failed in both the 1968 and 1970 Forward Thrust bond elections). Of course, these plans were never good enough for the *Helix* or our readers, and the Left never noticed that it was siding with the Right, which viewed such things as creeping socialism. Creeping too slowly for us, I guess, and without the proper vanguard in front.

The elections of 1969 pulled me further upwards toward the surface, and I was not alone. *Helix* by then enjoyed the occasional services of television reporters Don McGaffin and Mike James (writing collectively as "Gabby Hayes"), who gave us an above-ground perspective. This helps to explain why *Helix* ended up endorsing Wes Uhlman, limply, granted, for mayor, and cheering on CHECC reformers.

We began to see that the campus and the ghetto did not have monopolies on meaningful political issues. Movements opposing further freeway construction and for environmental quality, neighborhood control, citizen participation, women's rights, arts funding, historic preservation, and abortion law reform originated in the living rooms of ordinary citizens, not in left-wing self-criticism sessions. Perhaps people like Jim Ellis, Annie Gerber, Phyllis Lamphere, Alice Rooney, Lee Minto, Margaret Tunks, Walt Hundley, Roberto Maestes, Bob Santos, Bob Block, Victor Steinbrueck, Fred Bassetti, Ibsen Nelsen, Richard Anderson, and a thousand others I could name were the real "radicals," not the army surplus jacketed, black bereted poseurs. They at least were making positive changes in people's real lives, not just talking about some remote, unobtainable utopia.

Indeed, the campus Left was utterly indifferent to a community issue right in its own back yard: the plight of the street people and transients in the U District. As early as 1968, Jan Tissot began agitating for a community center to help address this population's social needs as the Open Door Clinic addressed its medical needs. At the *Helix,* we were besieged daily with pleas for food, spare change, and a place to crash by a growing army of homeless hippies. When we appealed to the pre-RYM SDS for help, we were told that junkies had no place in the revolutionary order; as for the post-RYM Left, these kids were just demo-fodder.

This is where things sat when the August 1969 riots erupted in the District. In covering the ensuing "negotiations," I found myself acting as interpreter and then mediator among the main factions. These included the "street caucus," led by Jan Tissot, Bill Harrington, and Bob Shupe; the business community represented by Cal McCune, John Mitsules, and Andy Shiga; the "residents," led by Roger Pense and Alan Fox, who would go on to found the U District Community Council; the ASUW, led by Steve Boyd and then Rick Silverman; the local clergy, represented chiefly by Dave Royer; the police; and the mayor's office, represented first by Mayor Miller's deputy Ed Devine, and then by Mayor Uhlman aides Dave Wood and Tim Stander. It was a remarkable assemblage of talent (even the police were at least interesting), and I want to comment on a few individuals.

First and foremost was Ed Devine. He kept the police on a short leash, but also demanded that everyone make practical proposals, not the sweeping, non-negotiable demands typical of the time. Ed really gave me my first and best lesson in politics as "the art of the possible."

I've mentioned Cal McCune before, chiefly as a villain; now, it's time to rip off the mask and reveal a sentimental, generous, and progressive would-be-bohemian turned business Brahmin. Cal is tall, patrician, gruff, and very smart; he is also very honest, loyal, and determined. I value him today as one of my best friends.

John Mitsules, along with Cal, became something of a mentor for me. Built like the proverbial fireplug, John was fresh from Vietnam when he took over managing the Bernie's men's store on the Ave. He could talk to the cops and hips with equal ease, and earn the trust of both. He was also Wes Uhlman's main man in the District, a role which became crucial.

Andy Shiga was a Japanese American pacifist, who drove a dairy truck and earned enough to open his own store on the Ave. He was "peace and freedom" personified, and his legacy to the community is the annual U District Street Fair.

Dave Wood and Tim Stander made an interesting team at the bargaining table. Dave was cool, intellectual, and a committed organizer who helped to found CHECC and elect Wes Uhlman (they later fell out, and I ended up succeeding Wood as head of the Citizen Service Bureau). Tim was a gonzo go-fer who only used his extensive political connections to help others and, when bored, to stir up a little trouble. Not surprising, Tim soon gravitated into Mitsules' orbit, although Dave was his titular boss.

Dave Royer constituted my first real exposure to a man of god, and he was one of the best. Dave always translated issues into benefit for human beings and truly practiced what he preached. He and his colleagues at Campus Christian Ministries opened up a whole new world of human experience and intellect to me which had been closed by the antireligious fervor of my upbringing.

My failure to expand on the personalities of the others at the table is not intended as a slight, but they played lesser roles in the story to follow.

Initially, all issues were before us: police harassment, dope dealing, a community center, commercial exploitation of students, discrimination, even land use. At first, everyone took turns pounding the table and walking out, even mild-mannered Roger Pense. The discussions sometimes dissolved into unintended comedy, as in this exchange reported in the *Helix:*

Officer [Dennis] Falk, who at an earlier session accused Jan Tissot of being a "known agitator or semi-organizer," became quite upset when another member of the Caucus made a passing reference to "The Revolution." The good officer wanted to know what kind of revolution was meant and whom was the Caucus taking its orders from.

The Caucus member growled back, "The sun goes down, the flowers suck up oxygen and that's The Revolution." He never did explain this strange correlation between botany and social change, so Falk and the rest of us were left to ponder another mystery. In any case, I'm sure that the police now observe the nocturnal activities of plants with a great deal more caution than before.

It became clear that no progress could be made with such a jumble of issues and personalities, so the group narrowed the issues to "community-police relations" and the idea for a community center, and formed subcommittees to pursue each.

Through months of hard bargaining, the Community-Police Relations Committee came up with a "code-of-conduct" for the Ave. They agreed on most points except the sensitive issue of "detainment" without arrest, which prompted dueling walkouts by both Tissot and Police Captain Mel Matheson, head of community relations for the department. The group finally agreed to disagree. This committee was chaired with Job-like patience by Barney—whose last name, I regret, has been lost from both memory and the record.

The progress of the CPR Committee was aided by several factors. First, *Seattle Times* reporter Mike Wyne attended virtually every session and his reports helped to keep all sides honest. Second, the reputation of the police was sinking fast due to daily exposures of the extent and depth of the police payoffs from gambling interests. The new State Attorney General, Slade Gorton, had started this decades-old web of corruption unraveling when he declared that there was no ambiguity in the law: gambling was illegal and could not be "tolerated" by any city, formally or otherwise.

This made Chief Ramon uncharacteristically cooperative. He even removed two of the District's most obnoxious beat patrolmen at our request, not that those who remained were exactly sweethearts. Such concessions helped keep the peace, but they didn't save Ramon's job; he was gone before Uhlman took the oath as mayor on December 1,

1969. Not long after, Ramon and County Prosecutor Carroll were indicted for graft by a grand jury, along with two dozen other officers and officials, but the charges were later voided.

I focused my energy on the community center issue, which was closest to my heart from having to turn down so many appeals for aid at the *Helix* office. Progress here was smoother and faster, and not marred by as much grandstanding. Basic agreement was reached on the "U District Center," its functions, and its governance by a board of trustees to be elected annually at an open, come-as-you-are community meeting. This last feature proved troublesome later on.

The founding board located a house on the corner of NE 56th and U Way that winter. The upper Ave was no longer off limits for long-hairs since the drug revolution had thoroughly infiltrated and converted Frat Row. This opened up new culinary vistas at the Hasty Tasty, and a new watering hole at the Century Tavern.

The center was operating after a fashion by January 1970 under the part-time direction of Dick Leffel, who was co-managing Arabesque. Funds were cobbled together from local churches, businesses, and individuals. It held a formal opening on April 15, with the mayor in attendance, and Dick departed for Greece with his new wife, Robin Denny, not long after.

The board took a long look at the center while Dick was gone, and it didn't like what it saw. Programs were virtually nonexistent, and the physical environment was filthy. The center was essentially an indoor sidewalk. No one blamed Dick—his error was to trust the wrong people to deliver on their promises—but a full-time director was clearly needed. Cal McCune, Dave Royer, and Steve Boyd asked me to take over.

Why me? I had no administrative training or experience, but I talked a good line and it seemed that I would work with all sides. On this basis, I was named Executive Director on June 8, three days before the *Helix* published its last issue.

I may not have known what I was doing, but I wasted no time doing it. My first step was to fire all of the "staff," dismiss the volunteers, and close the center for a good douche. I recruited a new staff of people I knew and trusted: Roxie Grant, who had become my right (left?) hand at the *Helix;* Gilda Traylor, an able and imaginative promoter; Clay Grubb, who had helped to found the Free U; John Kahila, former *Helix* staff astrologer and a smart, hard worker; and a contingent of superb volunteers (one of whom became my significant other for many years). The street promptly denounced us as elitists, but we were used to that by now.

We reviewed what the center then offered, which wasn't much, and what our clientele really needed. We agreed that the most pressing need was temporary housing, "crash pads" in the parlance of the day. We then did something that was incredible at the time—and unthinkable today: we fanned out over the district, knocking on doors in search of basements, spare bedrooms, garages, any shelter where someone might sleep. More than a hundred homeowners and renters volunteered for our new summer "Shelter Referral Program."

Our side of the bargain was to screen our referrals carefully so we would not send out any dopers or creeps, at least not twice. To this end, we developed an elaborate data base (by hand in those days), recording names, origins, and demographics on shelter applicants. We called the shelter volunteers the next morning, and the card of anyone who caused trouble was marked with the dreaded "SRX"—Shelter Referral Canceled. In my two years with the program, we needed to do this only a handful of times (we also had to "X" a few houses whose owners hassled our referrals for sex or drugs).

An unintended benefit of this program was to paint a portrait of the large number of transients then passing through Seattle. That first summer we made 939 referrals. On the busiest night, June 22, we handled 30 people, and we averaged 90 a week between June and the end of August. Their demographics surprised even us: average age 22, 80 percent from out-of-state, with at least one year of college completed on average. Not surprisingly, only 23 percent were women. (This was a very elite group in contrast to the bands of poor and homeless teenagers who loiter on the Ave today.)

The following year, we expected an even larger influx, so we decided to augment our private housing with a summer youth hostel. We approached the District's several "liberal" churches who had contributed funds to the center, but we found there was "no room at the inn." Finally, in desperation, we went to the last congregation on our list, the notoriously conservative University Baptist Church.

I vividly remember traveling with Roxie, Gilda, and other staff to a house on View Ridge to meet the church elders. They listened silently to our pitch, and I don't recall anyone asking a single question. At the end of our presentation, one of the church elders asked aloud, "What would Jesus do?" Someone answered, "He'd let them sleep in His house." And that was it. (This congregation later sheltered scores of Central American refugees in the 1980s.)

The city gave us some money, the National Guard donated cots, and we went to work bringing the church basement up to code to house, bathe, and feed as many as 100 people a night. My old friend Bill Billings coordinated the effort and served as the hostel manager, for which he and his future wife Diane (an MSW who was a terrific volunteer) received a little apartment converted from an office.

Fortunately, the door of this room had a small window at eye level. A few days after the hostel opened, I led the elders on a tour. Bill and Diane weren't in the main hall, so I figured that they were in their digs and led the elders down the narrow hall terminating in the chaperones' apartment. Just as I was about to open the door, I looked through the window and saw Bill and Diane buck naked doing what lovers like most to do. "Oh, I see Bill and Diane aren't in," I announced sharply, turned, and herded the elders back down the hall as quickly as possible.

By the end of 1971 we had provided shelter to more than 3,000 people and had generated a solid set of demographics to rebut the old chestnut about most hitchhikers being felons or psychopaths (data based, by the way, on a survey conducted in the early 1950s by the Arizona State Patrol a mile down the road from a state prison). We organized a "Committee to Reform Anti-Hitchhiking Laws" (CRAHL) with the ASUW, and State Reps. Jeff Douthwaite and Bill Burns and State Senate leader John Bagnariol carried our banner in Olympia. As a result, hitchhiking became legal (except on the interstates and certain dangerous intersections) in Washington on May 23, 1972.

Meanwhile, back in the Sixties, little changed. The trial of the Seattle Seven began on November 23, 1970, in the Tacoma courtroom of Judge George Boldt. He would later hand down the historic ruling affirming Indian fishing rights, but he was not in a liberal mood when the Seattle Seven defied the decorum of his court. He sentenced them on contempt and declared a mistrial on December 10; the defendants later won temporary freedom on bail.

The original "unity" of the Seattle Liberation Front was frayed by the trial and its impacts on the defendants' personal lives. While celebrities of the Left, only a few of the Seattle Seven, notably Chip Marshall and Jeff Dowd, exercised any real leadership. Individual collectives fragmented but a few stayed together to do some good work, notably establishing the Country Doc Free Clinic on Capitol Hill and helping to launch what would become *The Seattle Sun, Helix's* legitimate heir.

A number of attempts were made to fill the communications vacuum left by the *Helix.* Eric Lacitis got out a few issues of *The New Times Journal* in the summer of 1970, and an SLF collective established *Sabot* in the fall. The latter folded in December, when female activists such as Py Batemen and Kathy Severn decided that they had had enough of SLF male chauvinism and blew what was left of the Front apart.

An environmentally oriented rag, *The Seattle Sound,* debuted in 1971 but quickly became extinct. In March 1972, Thom Gunn ran *The Seattle Flag* up the pole, and a lot of people saluted, particularly when he published a purported interview with the skyjacker D. B. Cooper. Stunts were not enough, however, and the paper folded in December after 20 issues. The *Sun* came along a year and a half later, and Alec Fiskin and Dick Clever turned it into a real newspaper (before the *Sun* folded in the early eighties, several of its staffers launched *The Rocket,* which is still going strong). David Brewster's *The Weekly* didn't appear until 1976, and it owes its journalistic chromosomes chiefly to the old *Seattle* magazine (which folded in December 1970), not to the underground press.

Returning to 1971—Seattle was following Boeing in a steep nosedive. The 1970-71 recession hit the airlines hard, and they began canceling airplane orders in droves just as Boeing was trying to recoup the cost of developing the new 747. Then Congress, led chiefly by Sen. William Proxmire, shot the SST and 25,000 Seattle-area jobs out of the air. Boeing's payroll plummeted from 110,000 to barely 35,000 in eighteen months, and volunteers like Peggy Maze organized "Neighbors in Need" to feed a growing army of unemployed workers and their families.

The city was in a virtual economic panic, and two young realtors, Bob McDonald and Jim Youngren, decided to mock the doomsayers. On April 16, they posted a billboard message on Aurora at NE 167th reading, "Will the *last person* leaving Seattle *turn out the lights.*" It made international news, but few in Seattle saw the humor, and the sign was removed after two weeks.

At this moment, the ASUW and U District Center was hosting "The Community Conference" on campus. Rick Silverman was coming to the end of his term as ASUW president, and he and his allies did not want to leave their conservative successors the $30,000 surplus which they had amassed during the year. So Rick and I came up with a weeklong community organizing extravaganza which would bring major radicals to town and pump thousands of dollars into local community groups. The major speakers included "Dump-Johnson" mastermind Allard Lowenstein, historian Harold Cruse, social critic Michael Novak, feminist poet and activist Robin Morgan, new Berkeley City Councilmember Penny Jackson, and economist William Domhoff, plus a few token conservatives.

The conference was almost hijacked by the Black Panthers. After the money had been budgeted and the contracts signed, a squad of the local Party came pounding on our door to demand that we sponsor a speech by Bobby Seale. His fee was a mere $5,000, at least five times what we were paying our top speakers. Silverman and I responded with our best political judo, by which you let your opponent's momentum overcome his own balance.

"Delighted," we replied. "There's only one problem: we and the university cannot accept responsibility for his security." These were dangerous times, after all, and the Panthers would have to indemnify us and finance their own police protection for Seale's appearance. The Panthers decided that the Chairman was too busy to come talk to a bunch of jive-ass honkies in Seattle.

That summer, Gilda Traylor and I paid a visit to the mayor's office to pitch another idea. We were ushered into a conference room to meet two other people, Ann Focke and Rolon "Bert" Garner, founders of and/or gallery, who had the same great notion: the city should sponsor an arts fair. Some other folks, notably Seattle Center director Jack Fearey and his aide C. David Hughbanks, had similar thoughts, and out of it all came what is today called "Bumbershoot." To round things out, John Chambless, having finally been exiled from academia, came to direct the festival. Some hippies led by Norm Langill, who called themselves "The One Reel Vaudeville Show" and had a funky truck and a ton of talent, are still running it today.

The U District Center was an accidental beneficiary of the recession when we qualified for Emergency Employment Act funds to hire additional staff. We hired Milo Johnstone and my old friend "Fu" Stonehill, among others, to spruce up the center. Among other improvements, Milo painted a huge copy of the Hokusai wave on the center's north wall, where it remained for many years.

By now Cal had roped me into chairing the Citizens Advisory Committee to support University District Development Council plans for a pedestrian mall on the Ave. It was a replay of the early post-riot "negotiations," except now the chief warriors were the new Community Council and the Chamber of Commerce. Despite this, we came up with a fine plan, thanks to Development Director (and former Tacoma city manager) Dave Rowlands; UW Vice President Ernie Conrad; UW community development advisers Ken Nyberg, Fred Fortine, and Patricia Shiner; my vice chair Ron Denchfield; and CAC activists such as Donna Gordon and Mary Ellen McCaffree (yes, the former state legislator I had challenged in 1968); city staff John Alley, Jim Hornell, and Joe MacKechnie; and the architects of TRA, Richard Haag and Joyce Copland Vaughn.

It was sabotaged in the end by Don Kennedy, a major property owner whose practices had helped to spark UDM 1966. Implementation of the mall required District land owners, most of whom lived out of state, to "vote" for raising their own property taxes to pay for construction. Kennedy got to them first, and we lost.

When I say "we" I'm lumping myself in with a pretty establishmentarian group, notwithstanding hair down to my fanny at the time. I had gone "overground" by the fall of 1971, and it showed. My antennae were tuned too high to detect the subterranean rumbling on the lower Ave. On November 10, we convened the U District

Center's first (and only) annual "membership meeting" to elect ten trustees to the Center's twenty-one-member board. A rump group calling itself the "New American Movement" packed the room, and elected eight of its own. We had never seen most of these people before, either as clients or supporters of the center, and we were stunned. NAM, for its part, fantasized that the center was rolling in dough; in truth, our major source of funding, ironically a Law Enforcement Assistance Administration grant, was due to expire in a few months with no chance of renewal.

The community rallied on November 22 to reverse the election. It was a gratifying response, but try as I could I could not find a legal basis for voiding the previous vote. The meeting was tense, and there was real risk that the NAM contingent might attack the two hundred or so citizens who turned out to defend the center, so I begged the majority to affirm the election. They did, reluctantly.

I was done. I resigned soon after, and John Mitsules hired me as his assistant in the new North Seattle Model City Program branch in Ballard. Thus began a five-year career as a city official, and the rest of my life. Roxie took over the center and tried to keep it afloat; she couldn't, and it folded in mid-1972. The hostel, however, ran for a few more years as an independent agency.

The Sixties were not quite done with me. On March 28, 1972, I appeared in my new guise as a City Program Coordinator to speak as a character witness for Susan Stern and Joe Kelly, who volunteered at the UDC, in the Seattle Seven's sentencing hearing. There was no cheering crowd, no restless masses waiting outside the courthouse, not even any unusual degree of security. Just seven very nervous young people who decided that the legal limbo of their lives was a worse prison than anything the Feds had.

The hearing was really pro forma, as most of the defendants had cut their losses by agreeing to six months behind bars in exchange for the government forgetting the original charges. Roger Lippman, who was only obliquely involved with SLF and the demonstration, got one month. Michael Lerner was let off completely.

This latter fact embroiled me in one final controversy. I wrote an article on the hearing for the *Seattle Flag* which commented, "Whatever solidarity he [Lerner] might have felt with his fellow defendants seemed to have collapsed under the weight of a wife, a new baby, a promising career, and the alternative prospect of prison. On the stand, he all but recanted the revolution in whose cause he willingly accepted leadership, if not martyrdom."

This elicited an angry rebuttal that was so long the *Flag* serialized it. Lerner called my description of his testimony "a bald-faced lie" and went on to explain how he had always been dedicated to the cause of democratic socialism, in contrast to a "domestic pacifier" like me. The revolution had degenerated, as I later wrote in the *Flag*, into "the pathetic spectacle of two washed up Lefties trying to throw each other on the rubbish heap of history."

Because the warning is still relevant to those who would undertake radical change in America, I will close with the last words I ever wrote for *Helix*, the conclusion of a long meditation on revolution titled "Vegematic Blues":

> The proper mission of the revolution is to liberate a people from their oppression. In America, the nature of a revolutionary movement is to conceive an industrial community, a transformation of the American social experience and the organization of American society.
>
> This can be accomplished only by a movement which acts in sympathy and harmony with the people. Until we are reconciled with the American people, we will only be a source of further confusion and pain for them. So long as this movement continues to reject the American people, it risks both the destruction of itself and the frustration of any meaningful revolution in America. Whether we succeed or fail in this, we hold the potential salvation of America in our grasp.
>
> There is no future for either Americans or revolutionaries as long as they stand in suspicion of each other. Unless we change, we will be consumed by a final and cruel irony in which the American people are unloved even by their own liberators.
>
> The revolution must itself be revolutionized if it is to succeed. In this moment of gathering repression, we can no longer afford the folly of adolescence.
>
> Saint Paul sounded this same warning in A.D. 63. Imprisoned during the first major repression of the Christian movement, he urged in an epistle to the Ephesians, "That we, henceforth, be no longer children, tossed to and fro, and carried about with every wind of doctrine . . ."

Epilogue: History Will Dissolve Us

Lifelong dissent has more than acclimated me cheerfully to defeat. It has made me suspicious of victory.

—I. F. Stone

At the conclusion of Milton Viorst's fine survey of the Sixties, *Fire in the Streets*, the author makes an odd and, I believe, erroneous assertion: "The Sixties ended as they began, abruptly."

He is wrong on both counts. The Sixties gathered force gradually, but with an exponential acceleration, and they ebbed away equally quickly but never quite completely.

It is conventional wisdom now to speak of the Sixties as a failed revolution. This is accurate in terms of the comprehensive, absurdly ambitious goals many of its leaders and philosophers articulated at the time, but it ignores the many solid victories and gainsays the truly extraordinary courage of so many during the period.

The beginnings, Abbie Hoffman rightly says, "were filled with the cry of a movement at its purest moment. People who had never sung a note in their lives gained perfect pitch overnight. People ventured into the streets, faced down police dogs, endured beatings, and grew stronger. The war against racial inequality was by no means won, but legal segregation was defeated."

This goal had eluded America a full century since the collapse of the radical Republican experiment of Reconstruction, yet this generation achieved it within a single decade—not singlehandedly, not without the momentum of earlier agitation—but at least it broke through the barriers of de jure racism.

And American military involvement in the war in Vietnam did

end, and with it American faith in the ability and legitimacy of military intervention to coerce an unruly world into conformance with our national interests. Does anyone really believe that this would have come about if hundreds of thousands of Americans had stayed quietly at home, instead of charging noisily into the streets?

Yet a few have suggested this, and many more have repeated the slander that the movement against the war was motivated by cowardice and selfishness. This last does not stand empirical scrutiny: the draft was already largely defanged and thousands of troops on their way home in 1971 when the largest single demonstration against the war paralyzed Washington, D.C.

Without the antiwar movement, the machismo of East-West confrontation would have kept the United States in the domino game until the last tile was played. If Lyndon Johnson couldn't extricate us, Richard Nixon was certainly not going to, unless and until domestic politics forced him to walk away from the gaming table. In the end, I believe, American withdrawal was a moral, not merely a strategic, choice. We did not have the stomach for the protracted brutality, the Conradian "horror" entailed in that kind of war in that kind of place, and this testifies not to the American people's weakness but to their spiritual strength.

"The Vietnam Syndrome" of aversion to military force persisted for almost two decades. Even now, when we have supposedly recovered from our involvement in Indochina, Pentagon policy makers pointedly prefer one-night stands to extended commitments. Some relish the irony of the first baby boomer and antiwar demonstrator to serve as president being hoisted on this same petard in attempting (legitimately, in my opinion) to use military power to address the injustices in Haiti, a de facto American colony orphaned by the end of the Cold War.

Other legacies of the Sixties are more problematical. In the case of mass culture, the Right portrays the Sixties as America's fall from grace, with Dr. Spock and other "permissive" liberals cast as the serpent supplying the apple of sex, drugs, rock and roll, and do-your-own-thing situational ethics and cultural relativism. Without this evil temptation, presumably, we would all be still be perfectly content with a little premarital necking, a Coca-Cola, and Pat Boone.

The Sixties did not invent sex, drugs, or even rock and roll, and the folks who marketed them to young Americans were good old-fashioned capitalists, not communist Fifth Columnists or fellowtravelers. As morals declined, profits rose.

The national pandemic of illegal drug use cannot be denied or minimized, but the drugs themselves did not cause this—the law caused it. The prohibition of drugs, just like the prohibition of alcohol, has only undermined the authority of lawful government, established and perpetuated a vast black market, separated hundreds of thousands of citizens from society, and condemned many of them to lives of addiction, crime, and misery.

The impact of television on the Sixties (and vice versa) remains largely unexplored. Marshall McLuhan hoped that TV would revive dormant preliterate sensibilities in western civilization through an "electronic implosion" of a fragmented world view, but he also saw perils. He warned, "Once we have surrendered our senses and nervous systems to the private manipulation of those who would try to benefit from taking a lease on our eyes and ears and nerves, we really don't have any rights left." As I put it in 1969, "America has cleverly turned Orwell's telescreen inside out. Who needs to watch the people if all of the people are watching television?"

McLuhan anticipated the effects on history's first TV generation in both a new activism ("since TV, the drive to participation has ended adolescence") and the rise of a conservative counterculture, commenting, "When the technology of a time is powerfully thrusting in one direction, wisdom may well call for a countervailing thrust." Thus, he forecast the cultural revolutions—and counterrevolutions—which would rock the Global Village.

The New Left did not blow itself up in one great Weatherman bombing. Many of its leaders went "overground" and entered local and state government and the Democratic Party. Ten years after the Port Huron Statement, SDS's original mission of radicalizing the Democratic Party was accomplished with the nomination of Sen. George McGovern. That this precipitated the party's worst defeat since the eve of the Civil War did not prevent the Democratic Party from becoming in structure, values, and style the purest institutional descendant of the old New Left.

New Left values survive in other settings and forms, notably in academia and much of the public education establishment, in the movement for women's liberation and sexual minority rights, in the environmental movement, and in a host of campaigns for neighborhood and ethnic self-determination. Some of this activity is creative and exciting; too much remains bogged down in ideological nitpicking.

Beyond these specific organized activities, American politics has been transformed by three New Left innovations: the politics of identity, citizen participation, and the rhetoric of values.

The first is exemplified by the disintegration of the civil rights movement into campaigns for "black power," "brown power," "red power" and the rest of the ethnic rainbow. Every hue has its cry, and identity politics has evolved beyond race and ethnicity to embrace the causes of women, gays and lesbians, the elderly, and virtually any other grouping large enough to demand its own census category. It is chaotic, but such assertions of independent cultural identities are essential components of the broader resistance to technocratic hegemony. They allow people to define themselves in their own ways, not as mass marketing or media might dictate.

On the negative side, not even a charismatic evangelist like the Rev. Jesse Jackson has been able to forge identity politics into a transcendent populism able to attract and motivate enough people to address their shared grievances. The politics of identity is by definition centripetal, and resists any effort to pull it toward the center (ask President Clinton, if you doubt this). The politics of identity also has the collateral effect of pitting groups against each other as supplicants before a higher authority. They compete to prove their superior "authenticity" and while each is strong enough to "mau-mau" policy makers into granting special rights or benefits, none can compel fundamental change. Hence, the halls of government and media echo with the incessant whine of Robert Hughes's "culture of complaint."

Citizen participation is the New Left's most subtle and subversive contribution to American governance. The principle that the people affected by decisions deserve to have a voice in them has so thoroughly permeated government over the past twenty years that we forget how really radical an idea it is. Citizen participation is antithetical to the hierarchical conventions of government and business, and their elites are still groping for ways to manipulate and co-opt it.

The principles of citizen participation revolutionized local politics in Seattle. It has become a national leader in routinizing public consultation and involvement in its municipal administration under Mayors Wes Uhlman, Charles Royer, and Norm Rice and a solidly liberal and remarkably diverse City Council. Unfortunately, most examples of effective citizen participation are reactionary, e.g., halting a freeway or unwelcome development. As citizen participants, we have become very good at stopping bad things; we are not so practiced at starting good things.

Finally, there is the rhetoric of values introduced so eloquently by Martin Luther King Jr., Tom Hayden, and kindred theorists, and carried ad absurdum by the Weathermen and other self-appointed moral avengers. It is not so odd then to find the likes of Patrick Buchanan and Newt Gingrich picking up the Left's melody of values, if not the lyrics. Moral certitude is the *sine qua non* of any movement by a political minority, but you can have too much of a good thing. The stridency, self-righteous elitism, and fanaticism of the Moral Majority, Operation Rescue, and the Christian Coalition echo the Leninist conviction that worthy ends justify any means. In the New Right's drift toward terrorism, we see mirrored the madness which finally undid the New Left.

There is another legacy of the Sixties which is often neglected: tens of thousands of individuals who won the revolution at least in their own lives. They live within "the system" but they are not part of it. They organize their work and existences by their own rules, and have achieved a personal independence of thought, action, and moral choice which does not require social sanction. They are free men and women, and their examples might be the most subversive influences extant today.

In short, a quarter of a century later the Sixties are still with us, because they changed America—and millions of Americans—for better and for worse. Yes, the revolution did not overthrow the system, but it did make it react to indigenous, spontaneous movements of the people "in the belly of the beast." If nothing else, it gave the technocracy indigestion. The forces of oppression and alienation which prompted the Sixties are still at work, creating conditions which cry out for resolution and, perhaps yet, revolution.

It is up to a new generation now.

The Sixties Day by Day

A Chronology of major
international, national, local
and cultural events of 1960
through 1972

Warming Up for the Sixties: 1943–1959

1943

April 16: Swiss chemist Albert Hofmann accidentally takes the world's first acid trip while mixing a batch of lysergic acid diethylamide (LSD) 25.

1947

May 12: President Truman outlines the "Truman Doctrine" to combat Communist-led revolts in Greece and Turkey.

June 20: The author is born in Ferndale, Michigan, one of 3.8 million births in the highwater year of the early postwar baby boom.

June 24: Local pilot, Kenneth Arnold, reports spotting "flying saucers" (the first use of the phrase) over Mount Rainier.

July 26: President Truman consolidates U.S. armed forces under a single Department of Defense.

Also in 1947: Great Britain grants independence to India and Pakistan; thepolicy of "containment" is first articulated, and the Marshall Plan is proposed to rebuild Western Europe

1948

April 1: Soviet forces blockade land routes from the west to Berlin; U.S. and Britain airlift supplies to the city until the roads re-open in September; the Cold War begins.

May 14: The State of Israel is declared in Tel Aviv.

November 2: Harry S Truman squeaks past New York Governor Thomas E. Dewey to be re-elected president.

1949

March 8: France declares Vietnam an "associated state" within its empire, but re-

tains control of the military and treasury. Bao Dai, puppet ruler under Japanese occupation, remains titular head of state.

July 1: Bao Dai establishes his capital in Saigon.

August 24: Most western powers join North Atlantic Treaty Organization (NATO).

October 1: After expelling Nationalist forces from the mainland, Mao Tse-tung declares the People's Republic of China.

1950

January 14: After nearly a decade fighting the French and Japanese and after repudiation of his attempts to form an independent Vietnam, Ho Chi Minh declares a Democratic Republic of Vietnam from his rural stonghold outside Hanoi. His forces are called the League for the Independence of Vietnam, or Viet Minh for short.

June 25: North Korean forces cross the 38th parallel to invade the south. President Truman commits U.S. forces to a "police action" under UN auspices (the Soviets were boycotting the UN at the moment and could not veto the operation).

July 26: President Truman gives France $15 million to fight Ho Chi Minh.

November 20: Chinese army counterattacks UN troops, which had pushed North Korean forces back to the Manchurian border.

1951

April 11: President Truman sacks Gen. Douglas MacArthur for challenging policies guiding Korean operations (MacArthur wanted to drop atomic bombs on China, among other things).

April 30: UN forces push Chinese and North Korean armies north across 38th parallel and the front settles into a stalemate.

June: Cleveland disc jockey Alan "Moon Dog" Freed coins the phrase "rock and roll" to introduce white audiences to rhythm and blues.

1952

July 23: Military revolt deposes Egypt's King Farouk.

November 1: U.S. detonates world's first hydrogen bomb at Eniwetok atoll.

November 4: Gen. Dwight D. Eisenhower soundly defeats Illinois Gov. Adlai E. Stevenson for president.

1953

March 5: Joseph Stalin dies.

May 8: President Eisenhower reveals that U.S. has given France $60 million to support its forces in Indochina and pledges more aid to come.

July 27: Korean "Police Action" ends with armistice.

Also in 1953: James Watson and Francis Crick describe the "double helix" structure of DNA. Chuck Yeager pilots the Bell X-1 through the sound barrier. Hugh Hefner begins publishing *Playboy* magazine. William Burroughs' (a.k.a. William Lee) *Junkie*, Richard Wright's *The Outsider*, Arthur Miller's *The Crucible*, and James Baldwin's *Go Tell It on the Mountain* are published.

1954

May 7: French Army defeated by Vietminh at Dienbienphu after a seven week battle.

May 14: In *Brown v. Board of Education* of Topeka, Kansas, U.S. Supreme Court rules "separate but equal" public education unconstitutional under the 14th Amendment.

December 2: U.S. Senate censures Sen. Joseph McCarthy and ends his probes into alleged Communist infiltration (but the House and many states continue their own investigations).

June 16: Bao Dai names Ngo Dinh Diem as his prime minister (bad choice).

July 22: With the mediation of China, French and Vietminh agree to temporary partition of Vietnam at the 17th parallel, to be followed by elections within two years. U.S. and South Vietnam do not sign the accord.

September 8: U.S. forms Southeast Asian Treaty Organization (SEATO) for "mutual defense."

December 2: U.S. Senate votes to "condemn" Sen. Joe McCarthy for abuse of power and insults to diginity of the institution.

Also in 1954: A. G. Nasser seizes power in Egypt; Puerto Rican nationalists open fire from the gallery of the U.S. House of Representatives; William Golding publishes *Lord of the Flies.*

1955

April 12: Dr. Jonas Salk's polio vaccine declared a success.

May 14: First Dash-80 prototype of the 707 civilian jetliner rolls out of its Boeing hangar in Renton; the "Jet Age" begins (although 707s did not enter regular service until late1958).

October 26: Ngo Dinh Diem ousts Bao Dai and declares Republic of Vietnam with himself as president.

December 1: Rosa Parks refuses to surrender her bus seat to a white man in Montgomery, Alabama, and the Rev. Martin Luther King Jr. launches the modern civil rights movement with a city-wide transit boycott.

December 5: American Federation of Labor and Congress of Industrial Organizations merge to form AFL-CIO.

1956

January 28: Elvis Presley makes his television debut on the Jackie Gleason Show.

February 14: Nikita Khrushchev denounces "excesses" of Stalin at 20th CPSU Congress, which helps to fracture what's left of the "Progressive Left" in the U.S.

July 26: U.S. refuses to support British and French forces in launching a Mideast War to depose Nasser and sieze the Suez Canal.

September 9: Elvis Presley appears on Ed Sullivan's "Toast of the Town." On his second appearance, October 28, the camera discreetly avoids his swiveling hips.

October 23: "De-Stalinization" does not prevent Soviets from sending troops to crush uprisings in Hungary and Poland.

Also in 1956: Elvis Presley rockets to the top of the charts with "Ain't Nothin' but a Hound Dog" and other hits; City Lights Books publishes Allen Ginsberg's *Howl.*

1957

August 5: ABC begins national broadcast of Dick Clark's "American Bandstand" (televised in Philadelphia since 1952).

September 24: President Eisenhower dispatches Army troops and federalizes the Arkansas National Guard to enforce court-ordered desegregation of Little Rock's Central High School.

October 4: Soviet Union launches the world's first artificial satellite, Sputnik, and the "Space Age" begins. "Leave it to Beaver" debuts on CBS.

November 3: Soviets launch "Mutnik" with a dog, Laika, aboard.

December 6: The Navy-built Vanguard, bearing what was to be America's first satellite, explodes on the launch pad.

December 17: U.S. tests its first ICBM, the Atlas.

December 31: The U.S. baby boom crests with a record 4.33 million births, a rate of 25.3 per 1,000 Americans.

Also in 1957: Committee for a Sane Nuclear Policy (SANE) and Southern Christian Leadership Conference (SCLC) founded. America's stumbles in the first lap of the Space Race prompt the passage of National Defense Education Act which helps fuel dramatic increases in college enrollments in the 1960s. Jack Kerouac publishes *On the Road.*

1958

January 31: U.S. finally gets a satellite, Explorer I, off the ground.

March 24: Elvis Presley reports for induction into the Army.

December 17: NASA announces Project Mercury to orbit a man.

Also in 1958: Committee for Non-Violent Action founded to protest nuclear arms. Linus Pauling organizes scientists to petition the UN for an end to nuclear testing.

1959

January 1: Cuban dictator Juan Batista flees the island. Fidel Castro's forces enter Havana the next day, and Castro himself arrives January 8. He assumes full state powers on February 16.

January 3: Alaska Territory granted statehood; Hawaii follows on August 21.

February 3: Buddy Holly, Ritchie Valens, and The Big Bopper die in a plane crash.

March 31: The Dalai Lama flees Tibet to India.

June 8: X-15 rocket plane conducts its first flight test.

June 9: First Polaris missile submarine is launched.

July 8: Vietnamese guerillas ambush two U.S. "advisers," making them the first American casualties of "The Vietnam War" (although a U.S. agent was killed in 1946).

July 24: Vice President Nixon and Premier Khrushchev conduct their "Kitchen Debate" in a U.S. trade exhibit in Moscow.

July 30: Pathet Lao guerillas launch revolt in Laos.

Fall Season: The debut of "The Many Loves of Dobie Gillis" on September 29 introduces impressionable minds to their first beatnik, Bob Denver's Maynard G. Krebs.

September 15: Nikita Khrushchev begins two-week tour of the U.S. and promises "to bury you" economically.

October 4: On the second anniversary of Sputnik 1, the Soviet's Luna 3 circumnavigates the moon and takes the first photographs of the dark side. Three U.S. lunar probe launches ended in disaster before Pioneer 4 reached the moon's vicinity on March 3, 1960.

October 6: Congress opens hearings on the rigging of TV game shows.

October 7: Rod Serling's "The Twilight Zone" debuts on CBS.

1960

January 2: UW Huskies upset Wisconsin 44 to 8 in the Rose Bowl.

February 1: "Greensboro Four" sit in at North Carolina Woolworth's lunch counter and focus national attention on segregation of public accommodations.

February 11: Jack Paar quits "Tonight Show" after NBC censors a joke involving a "water closet." Steve Allen later takes over as host.

February 19: During a visit, former Seattle Symphony conductor Sir Thomas Beecham "withdraws" his 1942 description of Seattle as an "esthetic dustbin," but says the phrase fits the entire U.S.A.

March 1: United Airlines inaugurates first jet airliner service between Seattle, San Francisco, and Los Angeles.

March 5: A French freighter loaded with munitions explodes in Havana harbor; Castro later blames the U.S. Seattle mayoral candidate Gordon Newell's car explodes in the U District; police blame "pinball" interests.

March 7: Fourteen thousand members of the Screen Actors Guild strike to secure residuals from the rebroadcast of films and television programs.

March 8: Gordon Clinton is elected mayor of Seattle.

March 11: Congress rejects President Eisenhower's proposals to strengthen civil rights protections and desegregation.

March 17: CBS fires actor William Talman, who played Lt. Tragg on Perry Mason, on the same day he pleads innocent to "morals charges" stemming from a Hollywood party involving nudity and marijuana. Talman calls the action "ironic."

March 21: South African police kill eighty-nine protesters in Sharpeville and other towns during protests of apartheid pass laws.

March 31: Pope John XXIII makes the Bishop of Rutabo the Catholic Church's first black African cardinal.

April 5: John Kennedy defeats Hubert Humphrey in Wisconsin primary for Democratic nomination for president.

April 15–17: Veterans of sit-ins and protests at southern universities organize the Student Nonviolent Coordinating Committee (SNCC) during a conference at Shaw University.

April 27: Student protests in the wake of rigged elections force the resignation of South Korean President Syngman Rhee.

May 1: U.S. U-2 spy plane is shot down over the Soviet Union, and the pilot, Gary Powers, is later tried for espionage. President Eisenhower's refusal to apologize for the incident aborts plans for the first major East-West summit in five years.

May 2: California sends Caryl Chessman to the gas chamber, twelve years after his conviction for kidnaping and rape.

May 9: The FDA approves the first oral contraceptive pill, G. D. Searle Company's Enovoid 10, for prescription sale. Meanwhile, the world's population goes over 3 billion.

May 13: San Francisco police attack students protesting a local hearing of the House Un-American Activities Committee (HUAC). The incident is later documented in a film, *Operation Abolition,* for the purpose of proving HUAC's effectiveness.

May 23: Israeli agents capture Adolf Eichmann, main architect of Hitler's "Final Solution," in Argentina.

May 27: Military coup overthrows civilian government in Turkey.

June 16: Leftist student demonstrations in Tokyo compel President Eisenhower to skip Japan during his Asian tour.

June 17: Students for a Democratic Society, formerly named the Student League for Industrial Democracy, holds its first convention in New York City and elects Alan Haber as its president.

June 21: Nobel laureate Linus Pauling defies Congress by refusing to name signers of petitions calling for total halt of nuclear testing.

July 1: Soviets shoot down a U.S. RB-47 reconnaissance plane over their territorial waters in the Arctic.

July 14: After a brief and sentimental surge of support for Adlai Stevenson, Democrats nominate John Kennedy at Los Angeles convention. Kennedy picks Texas Sen. Lyndon Baines Johnson as his running mate the next day, and calls for a "New Frontier" in his acceptance speech.

July 27: Richard Nixon triumphs over Nelson Rockefeller and Barry Goldwater to secure the Republican presidential nomination and names UN Ambassador Henry Cabot Lodge as his running mate.

Fall Season: Hanna-Barbera's "The Flintstones" debuts on September 30 (became extinct in 1966).

August 7: Fidel Castro announces intention to nationalize all U.S. firms in Cuba.

August 17: Trial of U-2 pilot Gary Powers begins in Moscow.

September 10: Creation of the North Cascades Wilderness Area, comprising nearly 460,000 acres of forest, is announced in Seattle.

September 14: Organization of Oil Exporting Countries (OPEC) meets for the first time.

September 19: While visiting New York to attend the UN General Assembly, Fidel Castro and his entourage reject a fancy hotel and take rooms in Harlem.

September 24: U.S. Navy launches the first nuclear-powered aircraft carrier, the USS *Enterprise*.

September 26: Massachusetts Sen. John Kennedy and Vice President Richard Nixon duel in first of four televised presidential debates (October 7, 13, and 21).

October 12: During a UN General Assembly address by a Philippine delegate, Premier Khrushchev pounds the desk with his shoe.

October 17: Charles Van Doren and thirteen other TV quiz show contestants are arrested for perjury during grand jury investigation of rigged shows.

October 19: U.S. imposes a trade embargo on Cuba following nationalization of U.S.-owned enterprises.

October 25: M. L. King Jr. is jailed in Decatur, Georgia.

October 26: Military coup deposes El Salvador President Jose Marie Lemus.

November 8: After campaigning on the issue of an alleged "missile gap," Sen. John F. Kennedy defeats Vice President Richard M. Nixon (who carries Washington state) for the presidency by a scant 119,000 votes. Washington voters refuse to repeal "Alien Land Law" provision of the state constitution barring Asians from owning property despite the fact that it had been nullified years earlier. Gov. Albert Rosellini narrowly defeats GOP challenger Lloyd Andrews, and Seventh District Congressman Don Magnuson squeaks past GOP challenger John Stender in a recount.

November 24: Leftist Venezuelan students riot in Caracas.

December 6: Soviet Union and China agree to disagree in ideological disputes over de-Stalinization and the inevitability of war with capitalism.

December 8: Seattle Mayor Gordon Clinton names Frank Ramon as new Police Chief.

December 11: Soviet-backed Quinim Polsena takes power in Vientienne, Laos. French paratroopers fire on rebel mobs in the streets of Algiers, killing at least sixty-five.

December 15: U.S. backs right-wing counter-coup in Laos.

December 20: National Liberation Front is organized to fight the South Vietnamese government. Its members are nicknamed "Vietcong," meaning Vietnamese Communists.

December 22: Annual Debutante Ball at the Olympic Hotel introduces forty-two young ladies into Seattle society.

Zeitgeist: Elvis Presley ends his tour in the Army in March; the "Howdy Doody Show" is canceled; Ken Kesey drops LSD courtesy of the U.S. Army. *Camelot* opens on Broadway. Paul Goodman's *Growing Up Absurd* and Harper Lee's *To Kill a Mockingbird* are published. Federico Fellini's *La Dolce Vita,* Ingmar Bergman's *Virgin Spring,* and Stanley Kubrick's *Spartacus* are released. The Hollywood Argyles' "Alley-Oop" is the top single and Bob Newhart's "Button-Down Mind" is the top album. Burt Lancaster wins the Oscar for *Elmer Gantry,* and *The Apartment* is voted best movie.

1961

January 1: Great Britain retires the farthing.

January 2: UW Huskies defeat Minnesota's Golden Gophers in the Rose Bowl.

January 3: U.S. severs diplomatic relations with Cuba following further nationalization of properties owned by American companies. (Trade embargo is extended to all goods on February 3, 1962.)

January 10: First black students enroll at the University of Georgia, leading to a riot the next day.

January 17: In his farewell address, President Eisenhower warns America against "the acquisition of unwarranted influence, whether sought or unsought, by the military-industrial complex." Patrice Lumumba, former premier of the newly independent Republic of the Congo, is assassinated; CIA involvement is widely suspected.

January 20: "The torch is passed to a new generation" as John Kennedy takes the presidential oath of office.

January 25: Military coup topples previous junta in El Salvador.

February 1: Boeing tests its first Minuteman solid-fuel ICBM.

February 9: President Kennedy outlines first proposal for what will become Medicare.

February 20: President Kennedy outlines major new federal aid for elementary and high schools.

March 1: President Kennedy establishes the Peace Corps by executive order.

March 15: South Africa withdraws from British Commonwealth.

March 25: President Kennedy threatens to intervene in Laos.

April 12: Soviet Cosmonaut Yuri Gagarin becomes first man to orbit the earth. He is followed on August 6 by Gherman Titov, who stays aloft for two days. The best the U.S. can do is shoot Alan Shepard 115 miles into the air on May 5. Gus Grissom follows on July 21, but his capsule sinks on splash-down.

April 15: Anti-Castro (possibly CIA) pilots bomb Cuban airfields in preparation for Bay of Pigs landing.

April 17: Cuban insurgents are abandoned by their U.S. backers during a landing at the Bay of Pigs, and most are captured by Fidel Castro's forces.

April 22: French troops in Algeria and France mutiny against President DeGaulle's intention to grant the colony independence.

April 29: Actress Vanessa Redgrave is among 826 British antinuclear protesters arrested during a London "sit-down."

May 1: Fidel Castro declares Cuba a "socialist republic."

May 4: Congress of Racial Equality (CORE) organizes "Freedom Rides" to integrate southern bus terminals and services.

May 9: FCC Chairman Newton Minow decries television as a "vast wasteland."

May 10: Federal highway officials reject proposal of First Hill Improvement Club and architect Paul Thiry to "lid" Interstate 5 through downtown Seattle.

May 13: Police stand by while pro-Castro protesters are beaten by opponents during a "Fair Play for Cuba" rally in downtown Seattle.

May 14: Segregationists attack and burn a "Freedom Rider" Greyhound bus near Anniston, Alabama, and stone protesters at the Birmingham Trailways Depot.

May 16: South Korean military coup deposes Prime Minister John Chang.

May 17: Fidel Castro offers to trade Bay of Pigs prisoners for bulldozers.

May 20: Attorney General Robert Kennedy dispatches U.S. Marshals to Montgomery, Alabama, to protect blacks.

May 25: President Kennedy tells Congress, "This nation should commit itself to achieving the goal, before this decade is out, of landing a man on the moon and returning him safely to Earth."

May 30: Dominican Republic dictator Rafael Trujillo is assassinated.

June 3: President Kennedy and Premier Khrushchev meet in Vienna for a disastrous summit, but Jackie is a big hit in Paris. The failure of the Vienna Summit intensifies tensions over the status of Germany and Berlin.

June 9: Boeing tests its first jet thrust hydroplane on Lake Washington.

June 12: Army Maj. Gen. Edwin Walker is disciplined for indoctrinating his troops with John Birch Society propaganda. Walker resigns on November 4.

June 15: U.S. Army completes Nike Hercules anti-aircraft battery on Vashon Island.

July 2: Ernest Hemingway blows his head off with a shotgun in Ketchum, Idaho; Emmett Watson is the first reporter to reveal that the "accident" was actually a suicide. Great Britain dispatches troops to protect Kuwait from "aggression."

July 3: President Kennedy invokes Taft-Hartley Act to halt national maritime strike.

July 5: Seattle City Council and state legislature announce probes of incidents of local "police brutality."

July 24: The first of many U.S. airliners is hijacked to Cuba.

July 25: President Kennedy addresses the nation on the "Berlin Crisis" as U.S. and Soviet forces confront each other.

August 12: East Germans close the border between the Eastern and Western zones in Berlin and begin to build a permanent wall to halt mass emigration. The Hood Canal floating bridge opens.

August 20: First U.S. troop reinforcements enter Berlin.

August 25: U.S. orders 76,500 reservists to active duty as Berlin crisis worsens. An additional 73,000 are activated on September 19.

August 31: The Soviet Union announces that it will resume nuclear testing, ending a three-year hiatus during which only France tested atomic weapons. The first new Soviet test is conducted on September 2.

Fall Season: "The Defenders" with E. G. Marshall debuts on CBS on September 16 and runs until 1965. It tackles several hot issues, including abortion, euthanasia, travel restrictions, civil rights, and the 1950s Blacklist. Edward R. Murrow's "Person to Person," begun in 1953, is aired for the last time on September 15 (Charles Collingwood had replaced Murrow in 1959).

September 15: U.S. conducts its first underground nuclear test since October 30, 1958.

September 18: UN Secretary-General Dag Hammarskjold dies in a plane crash over Rhodesia during a mission to the Congo.

September 28: Following a coup, Syria breaks away from the "United Arab Republic" formed with Egypt in 1958.

October: The Seattle branch of CORE launches "selective buying" campaigns to compel major downtown retailers to increase minority hiring. CORE stages "shop-ins" at grocery stores and "shoe-ins" at Nordstrom's to extend this effort to other stores over the next three years.

October 1: Yankee slugger Roger Maris' 61st home run breaks Babe Ruth's season record.

October 11: President Kennedy sends Gen. Maxwell Taylor to Saigon to bolster the faltering Diem-Ngo regime.

October 27: U.S. and Soviet tanks face off in Berlin. NASA launches first Saturn I booster, then the world's largest rocket. Richard Nixon visits Seattle to raise funds for his campaign for California governor.

October 30: The Soviets explode the largest bomb in history, with a yield of at least 60 megatons. Joseph Stalin's body is removed from public display in Lenin's Tomb and buried along the Kremlin Wall.

November 1: Fifty thousand American women join protests across the nation against the resumption of atmospheric nuclear tests, leading to the formation of Women Strike for Peace. Interstate Commerce Commission forbids segregation on buses.

November 3: UN General Assembly rejects Soviet proposal for "troika" leadership and elects Burma's U Thant as General Secretary. President Kennedy publicly rejects idea of sending combat troops to South Vietnam.

November 8: Attempted Army coup fails to prevent installation of leftist president in Ecuador.

November 12–13: M. L. King Jr. pays his only visit to Seattle.

November 26: P-I reports on teenagers sniffing "glue balls" for kicks.

December 11: First U.S. air cavalry helicopter units arrive in Vietnam.

December 10: USSR breaks diplomatic relations with Albania, which aligns itself with Mao Tse-tung in widening Sino-Soviet ideological split.

December 16: M. L. King Jr. and 266 others arrested in Albany, Georgia.

December 18: India invades Goa and other Portuguese enclaves.

Zeitgeist: Pete Seeger writes "Where Have All the Flowers Gone?" The Supremes sign with Motown; Robert Heinlein publishes *Stranger in a Strange Land;* and Francois Truffaut's *Jules et Jim,* John Huston's *The Misfits,* and Robert Rossen's *The Hustler* are released. Chubby Checker invents "The Twist," the Beatles play the Cavern Club in Liverpool, and Bob Dylan gives his first concert in Greenwich Village's Gerde's Folk City. *West Side Story* wins Best Picture and "Moon River" is the top song.

————————————

1962

January 18: Louisiana's black-only Southern University closes amid demands for integration. President Kennedy submits a balanced federal budget totaling $92.5 billion.

January 19: Seattle Mayor Clinton calls for ban of pinballs and punchboards.

January 24: U.S. Navy confirms plan to build Polaris submarine base at Bangor.

January 29: King County Commissioner Howie Odell resigns amid charges of official misconduct.

February 2: UW bans campus speech by Gus Hall, head of the Communist Party, USA.

February 8: U.S. establishes military command structure in Vietnam.

February 10: U.S. exchanges Soviet spy Rudolf Abel for U-2 pilot Gary Powers and a student held in East Berlin.

February 12: A military transport with eight U.S. troops aboard crashes during a "propaganda mission" in South Vietnam.

February 14: President Kennedy announces that U.S. "advisers" in Vietnam may return fire if attacked.

February 20: U.S. finally gets an astronaut, John Glenn, into orbit.

February 26: Mutinous South Vietnamese pilots bomb the presidential palace in Saigon.

March 3: President Kennedy announces resumption of U.S. nuclear tests in the atmosphere.

March 9: Elizabeth Taylor drops Eddie Fisher for Richard Burton.

March 13: Wing Luke becomes the first non-white to be elected to the Seattle City Council and the highest Asian American elected official in the continental U.S..

March 15: Gus Hall and other U.S. Communist Party leaders are indicted for failing to register as subversives.

March 19: France and Algerian rebels sign a cease-fire in their seven-year war. An odd-bedfellow coalition of Communists and Peronists sweep Argentinian elections.

March 28: New military coup in Syria topples leaders of previous coup.

March 29: Seattle City Council is deluged with complaints of rent gouging and forced evictions by landlords hoping to cash in on World's Fair visitors (a law "licensing" apartments was passed on April 16). Military coup topples civilian government in Argentina.

April 11: President Kennedy confronts U.S. Steel over price increases; steel blinks.

April 12: Department of Agriculture announces that it will expand "food stamp" distribution in the wake of successful pilot programs.

April 21: Seattle comes of age with opening of the Century 21 World's Fair. Igor Stravinsky and Van Cliburn join the Seattle Symphony in its first Opera House concert. The festivities are marred when an Air Force jet taking part in aerobatics crashes in the Lake Forest Park area, killing two residents.

April 25: U.S. resumes nuclear testing in the atmosphere. Seattle Board of Theater Supervisors censors the "Girls of the Galaxy" revue on the World's Fair "Gay Way."

May 3: Congressional Republicans make an issue of alleged federal favoritism toward Texas entrepreneur Billie Sol Estes, a chum of many high-ranking Texas Democrats. Estes is convicted of fraud on November 7.

May 7: Cosmonaut Gherman Titov visits Seattle and tweaks Christians by stating that he didn't see god in space. John Glenn arrives two days later, along with Vice President Lyndon Johnson and New York Governor Nelson Rockefeller; all affirm their faith in a higher being.

May 16: U.S. dispatches Marines to Thailand in response to Pathet Lao gains in neighboring Laos.

May 18: Federal grand jury indicts Teamster head Jimmy Hoffa for accepting kickbacks from truckers.

May 21: Israel hangs Adolf Eichmann.

May 22: U.S. Attorney Brock Adams and FBI agents conduct gambling raids at the Turf, Green's Cigar Shop, and Pennyland Arcade in downtown Seattle.

May 28: New York Stock Exchange suffers its worst drop to date since the 1929 Crash.

June 1: Britain's Prince Philip visits Seattle. Lorenzo Milam, Gary Margason, and Jon Gallant incorporate the "Jack Straw Memorial Foundation" to operate an "alternative radio station" in Seattle.

June 2: Jimmy Hoffa addresses a Teamsters convention in Seattle.

June 3: A chartered Boeing 707 carrying most of Atlanta's civic and cultural leadership crashes on take-off at Paris' Orly Airport, killing 130 in the worst single-plane accident to date.

June 7: Seattle Symphony stages "Aida" in the Opera House; bailing out the resulting debt leads to the creation of Poncho (Patrons of Northwest Cultural, Civic and Charitable Organizations).

June 11-15: Students for a Democratic Society (SDS) convene at a Michigan resort and prepare the "Port Huron Statement," the seminal manifesto of the "New

Left." The Republican National Committee meets in Seattle.

June 20: Former Teamsters president Dave Beck begins serving a sentence at McNeil Island for misuse of union funds.

June 25: U.S. Supreme Court rules official prayers unconstitutional in public schools.

July 1: Algeria wins independence.

July 6: William Faulkner dies of a heart attack.

July 9: U.S. explodes a nuclear warhead 200 miles in space above the Pacific Ocean. Billy Graham and Bob Hope visit Seattle.

July 10: Telstar 1, the first telecommunications satellite, is placed in orbit.

July 17: U.S. Senate rejects President Kennedy's Medicare bill.

August 1: Birth defects resulting from the German-made tranquilizer Thalidomide lead President Kennedy to propose stricter FDA testing.

August 5: Marilyn Monroe dies of a drug overdose.

August 7: Attorney General Robert Kennedy visits Seattle.

August 14: Soviet Union launches two Vostok capsules during a 24 hour period and their crews maneuver close enough to see each other

August 29: President Kennedy nominates U.S. Labor Secretary Arthur Goldberg to succeed the ailing Felix Frankfurter on the U.S. Supreme Court.

September 5: Elvis Presley arrives in Seattle to begin filming *It Happened at the World's Fair.*

September 11: Auto Club opposition helps to defeat Metro bid to take responsiblity for mass transit.

September 13: In *Gideon v. Wainwright*, U.S. Supreme Court mandates right to counsel for all criminal defendents.

September 15: Amid mounting tension over Soviet military aid to Cuba, President Kennedy wins Congressional authority to call 150,000 reservists to active duty.

September 23: Philharmonic Hall, the first unit completed of New York's Lincoln Center, opens.

September 25: Sonny Liston flattens Floyd Patterson in the first round of their heavyweight championship bout.

September 28: A rare tornado strikes homes on Seattle's View Ridge.

October 1: After the deployment of 10,000 federal troops to quell segregationist violence, James H. Meredith begins classes at the University of Mississippi as its first black student. Johnny Carson takes over NBC's "Tonight Show" from Steve Allen.

October 9: President Kennedy announces plan to visit Seattle for World Fair's closing day on October 21.

October 11: Pope John XXIII convenes the Second Vatican Council to prepare a comprehensive liberalization of Catholic policy and liturgy.

October 12: Hurricane-force winds buffet Seattle and the Northwest, killing 32. The "Columbus Day Storm" also flattens millions of board-feet of timber which are later sold to Japan in the region's first export of raw logs.

October 17: Two U.S. Congressmen are indicted over savings and loan bank deals.

October 18: James Watson and Francis Crick win the Nobel Prize in Chemistry for their earlier work in discovering the "double-helix" molecular structure of DNA.

October 21: President Kennedy pleads illness to cancel Seattle visit on Fair's final day. Chinese and Indian troops clash in the Himalayas.

October 22: President Kennedy announces a naval blockade of Cuba to compel the removal of Soviet missiles.

November 1: Boeing completes assembly of the 744th and last B-52 airframe in Wichita, Kansas.

November 6: U.S. Senator Warren G. Magnuson narrowly wins re-election over Richard Christensen.

November 7: After losing his bid for the governorship of California, Richard Nixon tells the press that they won't have him "to kick around anymore"; alas, another lie. Eleanor Roosevelt dies.

November 14: AFL-CIO and NAACP feud over discrimination in labor unions.

November 20: U.S. lifts Cuban naval blockade in exchange for Khrushchev's pledge to remove medium-range bombers and missiles.

November 24: Defense Secretary McNamara stuns Seattle when he overrules the Air Force and awards a $6 billion for the TFX (F-111) tactical fighter bomber to General Dynamics instead of Boeing. At the urging of Senator Jackson, Congressional hearings were held in March 1963 but McNamara prevailed; the plane was a lemon.

November 27: Boeing rolls out its first 727 at Renton.

November 29: California court convicts three Navajos of the crime of consuming peyote during a religious rite.

December 11: U.S.-U.K. relations sour when President Kennedy suddenly cancels development of air-launched Skybolt missile, which had been key to British nuclear strategy.

December 13: Lorenzo Milam, Gary Margason, Robert Garfias, et al. assemble in a converted donut shop at 9029 Roosevelt NE to broadcast Seattle's first "alternative radio" programs over KRAB (107.7 FM).

December 15: The Port of Seattle dedicates the Shilshole Marina.

December 18: Washington State opens the Freeway Bridge and first Seattle sections of Interstate 5.

December 21: American interests pay Cuba a ransom of $53 million worth of medicine and supplies to liberate 1,113 prisoners held since the Bay of Pigs invasion.

Also in 1962: César Chavez, Dolores Huerta, et al. found the United Farm Workers to organize seasonal and migrant agricultural laborers. *Ramparts* magazine begins publishing as a liberal Catholic quarterly based in San Francisco under the editorship of Warren Hinckle III.

Zeitgeist: Guy Carawan copyrights "We Shall Overcome." Stanley Kubrick directs *Lolita*. Anthony Burgess' *Clockwork Orange*, Joseph Heller's *Catch-22*, Ken Kesey's *One Flew Over the Cuckoo's Nest*, and Rachel Carson's *Silent Spring* are published; Edward Albee's *Who's Afraid of Virginia Woolf* debuts in New York; Bob Dylan records "Blowin' in the Wind"; the Essalen Institute is founded at Big Sur. Marshall McLuhan posits that "the medium is the message" in *The Gutenberg Galaxy*, and socialist Michael Harrington details Appalachian poverty in *The Other America*. The Beatles release their first record, "Love Me Do," and Vaughn Meader's send-up of "The First Family" wins the Grammy for best album.

1963

January 1: Under orders from Mayor Clinton, Seattle's "tolerance policy" on gambling ends—officially, at least.

January 7: The price of a first-class stamp rises to five cents.

January 9: UN forces finally subdue Katanga, the former Belgian Congo's breakaway province, and arrest rebel president Moise Tshombe.

January 23: Boeing employees reject company's final offer and prepare to strike. President Kennedy immediately invokes Taft-Hartley to prevent a walkout.

January 30: The Kennedy Administration defends its tax cut and resulting $11.9 billion deficit as necessary to stimulate economy.

February 7: Bellevue School District names Donald Phelps, later chancellor of the Seattle Community College, as its first black principal.

February 8: Military coup in Iraq topples regime of Abdel Karim Kassem.

February 14: City planners reveal a scheme to build "ring roads" and parking garages around downtown Seattle. The plan would have destroyed most of Pioneer Square and all of Pike Place Market.

March 1: *P-I* editorializes in favor of permitting Frank Krasnowsky of the Socialist Workers Party to speak at Ballard High School; he does so later.

March 9: Clyde Shields becomes the first patient treated with an "artificial kidney" dialysis machine developed at the UW by Dr. Belding Scribner.

March 12: Seattle voters flush proposal to fluoridate water down the toilet.

March 15: Governor Rosellini vetoes bill which would have permitted the Meany

Hotel to sell alcohol inside the dry zone around the UW.

March 18: U.S. Supreme Court requires provision of counsel to all criminal defendants and excludes illegally obtained evidence.

March 31: Military coup exiles Guatemalan president Miguel Fuentes. New York City's 114-day newspaper strike ends. Boeing wins study contract for supersonic transport (SST).

April 3: M. L. King Jr. launches a voter registration drive in Birmingham, Alabama. Police Chief "Bull" Connor responds with fire hoses and attack dogs.

April 5: Soviet Union agrees to U.S. proposal for a "hot line" to expedite communications during crises. The system goes into operation on August 30.

April 10: Pope John XXIII issues his "Pacem in Terris" encyclical.

April 11: U.S. nuclear submarine *Thresher* sinks in the Atlantic with 129 crewmen aboard.

April 27: PONCHO holds its first auction to benefit the arts.

May 1: Seattle alpinist Jim Whittaker becomes the first American to reach the summit of Mt. Everest (but word doesn't reach Seattle for nine days). Jack Jarvis reports on "revolt" of UW female dormitory residents who are subject to an 11 p.m. curfew while men are not.

May 12: President Kennedy dispatches federal troops to Alabama as Birmingham disturbances continue.

May 18: President Kennedy delivers strong civil rights speech at Vanderbilt University in Nashville, Tennessee.

May 23: Congress passes first legislation intended to ensure women equal pay for equal work. The original bill was submitted in 1947.

June 1: U.S. Supreme Court bans formal prayers and religious exercises from public schools. A civil rights march in Jackson, Mississippi, leads to arrest of 531, including NAACP executive secretary Roy Wilkins.

June 3: Pope John XXIII dies.

June 5: John Profumo resigns as Secretary of State for War after his affair with "model" Christine Keeler undermines the Tory government in London.

June 7: Century 21 fairgrounds rededicated as the "Seattle Center."

June 11: Alabama National Guard is federalized after Gov. George Wallace blocks enrollment of two black students at the University of Alabama. President Kennedy tells the nation that segregation is morally wrong. Buddhist monk Quang Duc immolates himself on a Saigon street to protest the Catholic-led regime's treatment of Buddhists.

June 12: NAACP leader Medgar Evers is gunned down in front of his house in Jackson, Mississippi. His murderer is not convicted until 1994.

June 14: Second SDS convention formulates "America in the New Era" manifesto calling for "the re-creation of a popular left opposition."

June 15: The Rev. Mance Jackson and other black ministers lead 1,000 from Mt. Zion Baptist Church to Westlake Mall in Seattle's first civil rights march.

June 16: The first woman in space, Valentina Tereshkova, rides Vostok 6 into orbit. David Ben-Gurion resigns as Israel's prime minister.

June 17: U.S. Supreme Court declares public school readings of the Lord's Prayer unconstitutional.

June 19: President Kennedy proposes an "omnibus civil rights act."

June 24: Washington Secretary of State staff discover that petitions for a referendum on gambling tolerance are missing from a Capitol vault. The petitions, organized by gambling opponents, bore more than 82,000 signatures which were waiting for validation.

June 26: President Kennedy declares "Ich Bin Ein Berliner."

July 1: Following a brief sit-in by the Central District Youth Club, the Seattle City Council votes to approve creation of a Human Rights Commission and to consider an open-housing ordinance within 90 days.

July 4: Baltimore police arrest 283 civil rights demonstrators. Participants at a Chicago NAACP rally boo Mayor Richard Daley.

July 17: Seattle mayor appoints first members of the Human Rights Commission and names Jackson Street Community Council leader Y. Philip Hayasaka as its first director.

July 25: Police arrest 23 young blacks following a Seattle City Council sit-in to protest the inclusion of only two blacks (the Revs. Samuel McKinney and John Adams) on the new Human Rights Commission. The charges are dismissed on August 14.

August: The Nation of Islam (Black Muslims) organizes its first Seattle chapter. Gregory X becomes the local leader.

August 1: Poet Theodore Roethke dies.

August 3: U.S. and North Korean troops clash.

August 5: U.S., Soviet Union, and Britain agree to ban atmospheric nuclear tests. U.S. chemist Linus Pauling (who had won the Nobel Prize in Chemistry in 1954) is later awarded the deferred 1962 Nobel Prize for Peace in recognition of his protests against nuclear weapons testing.

August 9: The third child of John and Jacqueline Kennedy dies shortly after his birth.

August 16: Buddhists stage protests across South Vietnam and a monk immolates himself in Hué. James Meredith graduates from "Ole Miss" without incident.

August 21: South Vietnam declares martial law to contain expanding Buddhist protests.

August 23: Seattle City Council approves the city's first Urban Renewal project, which calls for redevelopment of the "Northlake" area for expansion of the UW campus.

August 27: W. E. B. Du Bois, black sociologist and founder of the NAACP, dies in Ghana.

August 28: "March for Jobs and Freedom" attracts 200,000-plus to Washington, D.C. Some 1,500 Seattle citizens rally for civil rights at the Federal Court House. Seattle School Board votes to permit student transfers to schools outside their neighborhoods in order to address segregation. Evergreen Point Floating Bridge opens.

Fall Season: "Leave It to Beaver" leaves the air on September 12. CBS and NBC expand evening newscasts to 30 minutes.

September 1: *P-I* headlines AP report, "Nightmare in Vietnam: $2 Billion, 8 Years Down the Drain?" The article reports 14,000 U.S. troops in Vietnam.

September 2: President Kennedy criticizes Diem regime for "repression" of Buddhists. The Administration virtually endorses a coup to remove Diem.

September 4: First black students enroll in formerly segregated Birmingham schools.

September 10: Federal government intervenes to integrate public schools in Alabama.

September 12: Protesters scuffle with police during House Un-American Activities Committee hearings in Washington, D.C., on student travel to Cuba.

September 15: Four children die when the Sixteenth Street Baptist Church in Birmingham, Alabama, is bombed during celebrations for its annual Youth Day. Two other children are killed during the day.

September 19: President Kennedy proposes $11 billion tax cut to stimulate economy.

September 26: Governor Rosellini names Randolph Carter to head State Board Against Discrimination.

October 2: Local NAACP, led by Jack Tanner, files suit to block a referendum on Tacoma open housing ordinance.

October 5: Saigon policemen beat three American journalists, including David Halberstam.

October 7: Hearst correspondent Marianne Means reports that U.S. will escalate Vietnam support to win "quick victory."

October 10: Limited Test Ban Treaty, barring nuclear explosions in the atmosphere, takes formal effect.

October 11: U.S. Senate kills proposal for joint U.S.-Soviet mission to the moon,

which was proposed by President Kennedy at the UN on September 20.

October 20: Between 3,000 and 5,000 supporters of open housing rally at Garfield High School in Seattle's largest civil rights demonstration to date. They chiefly protest the City Council's failure to enact an open housing ordinance.

October 22: More than 200,000 students boycott Chicago's public schools to protest de facto segregation.

October 25: Seattle City Council refers open housing ordinance to the voters on March 1964 ballot.

October 26: Premier Khrushchev takes the Soviet Union "out of the moon race," but nobody believes it.

October 29: U.S. Senate begins investigation of scandals centered on former Majority Secretary Bobby Baker.

November 2: Rebel South Vietnamese Army forces assassinate Ngo Dinh Diem and his brother Ngo Dinh Nhu in Saigon. Madame Nhu is in Beverly Hills at the time, where she denounces U.S. complicity in the coup.

November 4: Soviets block U.S. military convoy from driving through East Germany to West Berlin. The blockade is lifted two days later.

November 17: White House announces that President Kennedy will tour five cities in Texas.

November 21: Administration announces that it will reduce Vietnam troop strength from 16,300 to 15,000. Cambodian Prince Sihanouk bars further U.S. military aid, which he says benefits his enemies. Betty Friedan visits Seattle.

November 22: Person or persons unknown assassinate President Kennedy in Dallas. Lee Harvey Oswald is apprehended later in the day, after allegedly killing a policeman during flight. Vice President Lyndon Johnson takes the oath of office as President while flying back to Washington, D.C., with Kennedy's body and widow in Air Force One.

November 24: While cameras televise the scene nationwide, Jack Ruby murders Oswald in the garage of the Dallas police headquarters.

November 29: President Lyndon Johnson appoints special commission headed by Chief Justice Earl Warren to investigate Kennedy assassination.

December 2: U.S. renews offer of joint lunar manned expedition made three months earlier by President Kennedy.

December 4: Nation of Islam censures Malcolm X for saying he was "glad" about Kennedy's assassination. Bolivian rebels take four Americans hostage.

December 9: *P-I* reports that Boeing's Dyna-Soar contract and 4,000 local jobs are headed for extinction under President Johnson's proposed budget.

December 21: Boeing wins NASA contract to build lunar orbiter.

December 26: President Johnson wins his first Congressional victory by obtaining approval for a stalled plan to sell wheat to the USSR.

December 31: By year's end, more than 15,000 U.S. military "advisers" are stationed on Vietnamese soil. The Southern Regional Council tallies 930 civil rights demonstrations involving 20,000 arrests in 11 Southern states during the year.

Zeitgeist: Tony Richardson's *Tom Jones* and Federico Fellini's *8 1/2* released; James Baldwin's *The Fire Next Time,* Kurt Vonnegut's *Cat's Cradle,* Sylvia Plath's *The Bell Jar,* and Betty Friedan's *The Feminine Mystique* published. Timothy Leary and Richard Alpert ejected from Harvard for LSD experiments; Roche laboratories introduce Valium to the market; the Beatles soar to the top of the Top 40 with "I Want to Hold Your Hand"; Elvis Presley stars in *It Happened at the World's Fair;* and Frankie Avalon and Annette Funicello go surfing in *Beach Party.*

1964

January 3: Arizona Sen. Barry Goldwater announces his candidacy for the Republican nomination for President. Fred Hutchinson, former Seattle Rainiers star and manager of the Cincinnati Reds, reveals that he has cancer.

January 4: Pope Paul VI begins the first papal tour of the Holy Land in the history of the Church.

January 8: President Johnson "declares unconditional war on poverty in America" and an $11 billion tax cut. Johnson's program includes what becomes VISTA and Model Cities, and is to be funded by reductions in defense spending.

January 10: David Frost's American version of England's satirical "That Was the Week That Was" (TW3) debuts on NBC (it lasted until May 4).

January 11: U.S. Surgeon General Luther Terry issues report linking cigarette smoking and lung cancer.

January 14: Alabama Gov. George Wallace addresses a packed hall at UW.

January 17: U.S. and Panama break off diplomatic relations in dispute over the flying of the Panamanian flag inside the Canal Zone.

January 22: An Okanogon jury awards Former State Rep. John Goldmark a historic $40,000 libel judgment against local publisher Ashley Holden and former State Rep. Albert Canwell. (The defendants had labeled Goldmark a Communist during his 1962 re-election campaign; Goldmark was represented by William Dwyer.)

January 24: *P-I* reports that Indiana Gov. Matthew Welsh had recently claimed that the Kingsmen's version of "Louie, Louie" contained obscene words when played slowly.

January 29: NASA successfully launches first Saturn V booster.

February 3: Black students boycott New York City public schools.

February 6: Castro cuts off Cuban water supply for Guantanamo Bay base.

February 7: The Beatles arrive in New York City to start their first American tour. They appear on the Ed Sullivan Show two days later.

February 17: U.S. Supreme Court establishes principle of "one man, one vote" for Congressional redistricting.

February 24: Sufficient states ratify Twenty-fourth Amendment to ban poll taxes.

February 25: Cassius Clay knocks out Sonny Liston to win the world heavyweight championship. He declares himself a Muslim, having been converted by Malcolm X, and takes the name Muhammad Ali.

March 2: Marlon Brando and Bob Satiacum are arrested during Puyallup "fish-in" at Frank's Landing to support Indian fishing rights.

March 3: King County Commissioners approve open housing ordinance.

March 10: Seattle voters elect Dorm Braman mayor over Lt. Gov. John Cherberg, and reject COMET initiative for electric trolleys and open housing referendum by two to one margins. (Ray Eckmann is later appointed to serve the balance of Braman's term on the City Council.) Soviets shoot down U.S. reconnaissance plane near the German border and capture three airmen.

March 12: Malcolm X splits from the Nation of Islam (he founds the Organization for Afro-American Unity on June 28). UN dispatches troops to Cyprus to quell Greek-Turkish clashes.

March 13: New Yorker Kitty Genovese is stabbed to death while her neighbors ignore her screams.

March 14: Jack Ruby is convicted of murdering Lee Harvey Oswald.

March 17: Dr. Louis Leakey displays oldest hominid remains yet unearthed in Tanganyika's Olduvai Gorge.

March 25: Arkansas Sen. J. William Fulbright declares that the "master myth of the cold war is that the Communist bloc is a monolith."

March 27: An earthquake measuring 8.6 on the revised Richter scale flattens Anchorage, Alaska. The quake and aftershocks kill 117 and cause $750 million in damage. The temblor is felt in Seattle and tsunamis pound the Washington coast.

March 31: A right-wing revolt spreads against Brazilian president Joao Goulart. He flees the country April 3.

April: King Broadcasting publishes first issue of *Seattle* magazine.

April 5: Gen. Douglas MacArthur dies.

April 7: Alabama Gov. George Wallace wins 25 percent of the vote in the Wisconsin Democratic presidential primary.

April 13: Sidney Poitier becomes the first black to win a major Oscar with best actor honors for *Lilies of the Field.*

April 14: UW students picket Subversive Control Board hearings in Tacoma.

April 20: Blacks boycott Cleveland school system. Two weeks earlier, a white minister, the Rev. Bruce Klunder, had been run over by a bulldozer while protesting at a school construction site.

April 21: Congressional Republicans accuse the administration of downplaying U.S. involvement and casualties in Vietnam.

April 25: President Johnson names Lt. Gen. William Westmoreland to succeed Gen. Paul Harkins as chief of U.S. forces in Vietnam.

May: Crisis Clinic opens, offering phone counseling for people considering suicide.

May 1: Students clash with Communist authorities in Prague on May Day. Seven hundred participants in a Communist Party rally in New York City demand an end to the war in Vietnam.

May 2: On "Loyalty Day," the Progressive Labor Party (a Maoist splinter of the U.S. Communist Party and later a major faction within SDS) stages an anti-war demonstration in New York City. Vietcong sappers are blamed for sinking a U.S. aircraft transport at anchor in Saigon; the cause turns out to be a mechanical fault.

May 4: President Johnson distresses animal lovers by picking up his beagles "Him" and "Her" by their ears during a White House press conferences. Burke Museum opens on the UW campus.

May 5: Alabama Gov. George Wallace wins 30 percent of Indiana Democratic primary.

May 7: The Seattle Opera, directed by Glynn Ross, makes its debut with *Tosca.*

May 15: New York Gov. Nelson Rockefeller pulls off a surprise victory in Oregon Republican primary, besting Henry Cabot Lodge and Senator Barry Goldwater.

May 20: Boeing and Lockheed are chosen to vie in a "design-off" for the coveted federal contract to build the first U.S. civilian supersonic transport (SST).

May 23: Art Kunkin publishes the first issue of what becomes the *Los Angeles Free Press* for distribution at KPFK-FM's Renaissance Pleasure Faire near Los Angeles.

May 27: Indian Prime Minister Jawaharlal Nehru dies.

May 28: Congress of Racial Equality chairman Floyd McKissick speaks in Seattle. The following day, American Nazi Party Führer George Lincoln Rockwell addresses a packed crowd in Meany Hall.

June 1: The Rolling Stones arrive in New York to begin their first U.S. tour. U.S. Supreme Court strikes down Washington state law imposing loyalty oaths on state employees and university faculty.

June 2: Senator Goldwater ekes out narrow win over Governor Rockefeller in California primary and clinches Republican nomination. He wins all but two of Washington's 24 delegates at the state party convention on June 6.

June 5: Seattle Coliseum, remodeled after the World's Fair, opens as a sports arena.

June 7: U.S. jets strafe Pathet Lao positions after rebel fire downs U.S. aircraft.

June 10: U.S. Senate breaks Southern filibuster of Civil Rights Act. A later proposal to submit the bill to a national referendum is also defeated.

June 14: With Neal Cassady at the wheel, Ken Kesey and his 14 "Merry Pranksters" set out from La Honda, California, in a day-glo International Harvester school bus for history's longest joy ride around the United States.

June 15: U.S. Supreme Court imposes "one man-one vote" standard on state legislative districts. The Court scraps Washington's 1957 redistricting law on June 22, and thereby undermines long-

standing rural domination of the legislature.

June 17: Senator Goldwater announces opposition to Civil Rights Act.

June 19: Edward Kennedy, Birch Bayh, and his wife are injured in plane crash which kills the pilot and Kennedy's administrative assistant.

June 21: Civil rights volunteers Michael Schwerner, Andrew Goodman, and James Chaney disappear near Philadelphia, Mississippi.

June 25: White mob attacks integrationist march in St. Augustine, Florida.

July 2: President Johnson signs Civil Rights Act barring discrimination in public accommodations, employment, and voting.

July 6: The Beatles' *A Hard Day's Night* opens in London.

July 7: Gen. Maxwell Taylor succeeds Henry Cabot Lodge as U.S. Ambassador to South Vietnam.

July 10: The Republican Party nominates Arizona Sen. Barry Goldwater for president. He taps New York Congressman and future Trivial Pursuit teaser William E. Miller as his running mate.

July 18: Riots rock Harlem, followed two days later by riots in Bedford-Stuyvesant. Over the next two weeks, riots break out in Rochester, New York; Jersey City, Patterson, and Elizabeth, New Jersey; Philadelphia; and the Chicago suburb of Dixmoor.

July 19: Governor Wallace withdraws from race for president.

July 31: Ranger 7 broadcasts the first close-up photos of the lunar surface.

August 2: USS *Maddox* exchanges fire with North Vietnamese patrol boats in the

Gulf of Tonkin. (A second incident reported two days later involving the *Maddox* and *C. Turner Joy* is now regarded as bogus.) Blacks riot in Jersey City, and a week later in Paterson and Elizabeth, N.J.

August 4: The mutilated bodies of civil rights workers Michael Schwerner, Andrew Goodman, and James Chaney are found buried in a Mississippi swamp.

August 5: U.S. aircraft attack North Vietnamese naval installations.

August 7: Congress passes the Gulf of Tonkin Resolution authorizing the president to take "all necessary steps" in Vietnam. Only two senators dissent: Oregon's Wayne Morse and Alaska's Ernest Gruening. Passage does not rate the front page of the *P-I*.

August 10: Turkish aircraft attack Greek positions on Cyprus.

August 11: Congress passes first legislation for President Johnson's "War on Poverty" and expands Food Stamp program.

August 14: Charles Berrard and other blacks returning from a visit to Cuba announce creation of the "Black Liberation Front."

August 16: Riots break out in Dixmoor, a Chicago suburb. General Nguyen Khanh deposes General Duong Van Minh as head of South Vietnam.

August 18: Riots rock North Philadelphia's ghetto. The Beatles begin their second U.S. tour in San Francisco.

August 20: President Johnson creates Office of Economic Opportunity, which institutionalizes "citizen participation" in many federal programs.

August 21: The Beatles perform in the Coliseum.

August 25: Democratic National Convention begins in Atlantic City, New Jersey. President Johnson, hoping to hold the South, refuses to allow the seating of the Mississippi Freedom Democratic Party delegation in lieu of all-white representatives. Johnson and Minnesota Sen. Hubert Humphrey are nominated on August 27.

August 29: A week of student riots and U.S. pressure force General Khanh to relinquish control of the South Vietnamese Government to an interim premier, Nguyen Xuan Oanh, while elections are organized. Khanh maintains de facto control, however.

Fall Season: "The Man from U.N.C.L.E." begins his four-year battle with THRUSH starting September 22. Jim Nabors enlists as "Gomer Pyle, USMC" on September 25 (discharged in 1970). Bob Denver is marooned on "Gilligan's Island" beginning September 26 (the audience is rescued with the show's cancellation in 1967).

September: Victor Steinbrueck and Robert Ashley found "Friends of the Market" to promote preservation of the Pike Place Market.

September 11: Navy commissions Bangor Polaris submarine base.

September 13: Gen. Lan Van Phat leads a counter-coup against Khanh.

September 14: General Khanh leads counter-counter-coup.

September 15: Dan Evans bests Richard Christensen for the Republican nomination for governor, and Brock Adams defeats Norm Ackley for the Democratic nomination for the Seventh Congressional District.

September 27: Warren Commission issues final report and declares that Oswald acted alone in killing President Kennedy.

October 1: The Free Speech Movement is born when University of California police attempt to arrest Jack Weinberg for manning an unauthorized table to raise funds for CORE on the Berkeley campus.

October 4: Sen. Warren Magnuson weds Jermaine Peralta.

October 10: Olympic Games begin in Tokyo.

October 12: Soviets launch first three-man Voskhod capsule.

October 14: Johnson aide Walter Jenkins resigns after being charged with "indecent gestures."

October 16: Leonid Brezhnev and Aleksi Kosygin depose Nikita Khrushchev. China announces test of its first atomic bomb. Great Britain elects Labour government headed by Harold Wilson.

October 19: Seattle CORE launches a boycott of downtown retailers to protest their lack of minority hiring; the campaign fizzled out in January 1965 with limited gains.

October 20: Herbert Hoover dies.

October 31: President Johnson promises to create a "Great Society" in speech in Madison Square Garden.

November 1: Vietcong damage or destroy 27 U.S. aircraft parked at Bien Hoa near Saigon.

November 2: Saudi Arabia's Prince Faisal deposes King Saud.

November 3: Lyndon Johnson buries Goldwater under the greatest presidential landslide registered up to that time: 61 percent of the popular vote and all but Arizona and the Deep South go "All the Way with LBJ." Bucking the national Democratic tide, liberal Republican Daniel J. Evans defeats two-term Gov.

Albert Rosellini, Republican Lud Kramer topples long-time Secretary of State Vic Meyers, and Seattle Congressman Tom Pelly retains his seat easily. Senator Jackson crushes Lloyd Andrews to win reelection, and Brock Adams defeats Bill Stinson to become a Congressman. State Initiative 34 to liberalize gambling laws is rejected overwhelmingly. Floyd Hicks, Lloyd Meeds, and Tom Foley win their first terms in Congress.

November 5: Thousands of Berkeley students rally and occupy Sproul Hall, prompting president Kerr to call in the police.

November 10: Rainier Brewery head and baseball team owner Emil G. Sick dies. Fred Hutchinson, who got his start with Sick's Seattle Rainiers, dies the following day.

November 17: Mayor Braman appoints Charles Z. Smith to the Municipal Court, making him Seattle's first black judge.

November 23: U.S. Supreme Court refuses to strike "under God" from the Pledge of Allegiance.

November 24: U.S. airlifts Belgian paratroopers into Stanleyville, a rebel stronghold in the Congo, but they arrive too late to save white hostages from being slaughtered.

December 1: President Johnson approves U.S. military operations against Vietcong "sanctuaries" in Laos and Cambodia.

December 3: Police raid Berkeley's Sproul Hall and arrest 773 to end Free Speech Movement sit-in begun the day before. A strike the next day effectively shuts U.C. down.

December 5: Army Capt. Roger Donlon receives the first Congressional Medal of Honor awarded during the Vietnam war.

December 10: M. L. King Jr. accepts the Nobel Prize for Peace in Stockholm.

December 11: Anti-Castro protesters fire a bazooka at the UN Building during an address by Che Guevara to the General Assembly; they miss.

December 13: Governor-elect Evans and other Republican moderates fail to prevent election of ultraconservative Ken Rogstad as head of the King County GOP. (Evans had better luck with the State GOP, which elected C. Montgomery "Gummy" Johnson as its head on January 9.)

December 14: West Seattle public relations consultant Ted Best is appointed to the City Council seat vacated by Lud Kramer.

December 19: Military coup overthrows South Vietnam's provisional legislature. A King County Superior Court judge invokes the U.S. Supreme Court's recent *Sullivan v. New York Times* ruling to void the Goldmark libel judgment for failure to prove malice.

December 24: Vietcong sappers set off a bomb at Saigon's "Brink's Hotel," bachelor quarters for American personnel, killing two and wounding 58.

December 31: 1964 marks the final year of the baby boom with 4.07 million births; 75 million Americans have been born since 1945. Except for "boomlets" around 1970 and 1980, birth rates generally decline from a peak of 25.3 per 1,000 in 1957 to about 15 per 1,000 in the 1990s.

Zeitgeist: Ford introduces the Mustang; U.S. Post Office introduces zip codes; Marshall McLuhan's *Understanding Media,* Hubert Selby's *Last Exit to Brooklyn,* Eric Berne's *Games People Play,* and Herbert Marcuse's *One Dimensional Man* are published; Peter Weiss' film of *The Persecution and Assassination of Marat as*

Performed by the Inmates of the Asylum of Charenton under the Direction of the Marquis de Sade debuts; Stanley Kubrick's *Dr. Strangelove, or How I Learned to Stop Worrying and Love the Bomb,* Michael Cocoyannis' *Zorba the Greek,* Emile de Antonio's *Point of Order,* and John Frankenheimer's *Seven Days in May* are released; topless bathing suits and bars both appear (disappear?). The Beatles share top ten singles honors with the Supremes ("Baby Love"), Roy Orbison ("Oh, Pretty Woman"), the Animals ("House of the Rising Sun"), the Beach Boys ("I Get Around"), and the Dixie Cups, the Four Seasons, and Bobby Vinton. Petula Clark and Barbra Streisand win Grammys for "Downtown" and "People," respectively. Frank Zappa creates the Mothers of Invention.

1965

January 4: In his State of the Union address, President Johnson proposes to create "The Great Society."

January 10: Governor Rosellini pardons former Teamster head Dave Beck for state grand larceny conviction (Beck served his state and federal sentences concurrently at McNeil Island).

January 15: Bill Speidel begins leading informal tours of "Underground Seattle," the maze of abandoned sidewalks and storefronts beneath the elevated streets of Pioneer Square.

January 18: A segregationist assaults M. L. King Jr. in Selma, Alabama, as he registers as the first black guest in a hotel built a century earlier with slave labor.

January 19: U.S. Air Force reveals widespread cheating among cadets at its Colorado Springs Academy.

January 24: Winston Churchill dies. President Johnson submits his "Great Society" federal budget for 1965: $99.7 billion, with an annual deficit of $6.3 billion.

January 27: General Khanh leads another military coup to depose the leaders of the December military coup in Saigon.

February 1: M. L. King Jr., and 770 others are arrested during voter rights demonstrations in Selma, Alabama. The arrests rise to 2,600 before the end of the week.

February 3: Interstate 5 opens from Everett to downtown Seattle. Huge traffic jams soon develop at Mercer as commuters try to exit onto city streets.

February 7: Vietcong attack American base at Pleiku, and the U.S. retaliates with bombing raids against targets in North Vietnam.

February 15: Canada retires its British imperial ensign and unfurls its new flag featuring a red maple leaf. Soviets give SAM anti-aircraft missiles to North Vietnam. Five bills are introduced in the State Legislature to ensure equal rights for women.

February 19: A military coup led by Tran Thien Khiem deposes General Khanh. City Council rejects proposal for police review board.

February 21: Malcolm X is murdered in New York City by followers (agents?) of Elijah Muhammed. California narcs raid an alleged methamphetamine lab operated by Augustus Owsley Stanley III; he later beats the rap and decides to synthesize LSD rather than speed.

February 24: U.S. aircraft begin continuous bombing ("Operation Rolling Thunder") of North Vietnam south of the 20th parallel. Administration sources declares that no effort will be made to begin negotiations.

March 3: John Thomson sits down on the steps of the Berkeley Student Union building with the word "FUCK" pinned to his shirt. He is promptly arrested and the "Filthy Speech Movement" is born.

March 7: State Police teargas and beat participants in Freedom March from Selma to Montgomery, Alabama.

March 8: Two Marine battalions—first "combat troops"—land at Danang.

March 9: Three white Unitarian ministers are beaten in Selma; one, the Rev. James Reeb, dies two days later. Clark Kerr resigns as chancellor of the University of California. Boeing completes Space Center in Kent.

March 16: Montgomery, Alabama, police attack civil rights marchers.

March 18: Cosmonaut Alexei Leonov leaves his Voshkod capsule to become the first human to "walk in space."

March 19: University of California bans "Spider" magazine at Berkeley for using dirty words. In its first major act of civil disobedience, SDS organizes 700 pickets to blockade the entrance of Chase Manhattan Bank's New York headquarters to protest loans to South Africa.

March 20: President Johnson federalizes Alabama National Guard to help protect Freedom Marchers.

March 22: Pentagon admits that U.S. troops are using "nonlethal" gas against Vietcong.

March 23: Gus Grissom and John Young pilot the first Gemini capsule into orbit.

March 24: First Vietnam "teach-in" held at the University of Michigan. Four thousand Freedom Marchers and their military escort finally reach Montgomery. Jim Whittaker leads Robert Kennedy and others in an ascent of the newly renamed Mt. Kennedy in Alaska.

March 25: A victorious Montgomery rally attracts 50,000, following which, a white organizer, Viola Liuzzo, is murdered by three Klan members.

March 30: A bomb explodes at the U.S. Embassy in Saigon, killing 20.

April 7: President Johnson offers to begin "unconditional talks" on Vietnam and pledges $1 billion in aid; North Vietnam rejects the carrot.

April 17: SDS mobilizes 20,000-plus for a march in Washington, D.C., at the first national demonstration against the war. *New York Times* describes SDS as "a radical but non-communist group with chapters on 63 campuses."

April 21: Soviet basketball team defeats Americans in exhibition game at the Seattle Coliseum.

April 24: Bob Dylan and Joan Baez perform at the Arena.

April 28: President Johnson dispatches 14,000 troops to the Dominican Republic to prevent the ascension of Juan Bosch.

April 29: An earthquake, registering 6.5 on the Richter scale, rattles the greater Seattle area, killing five and causing $15 million in damage.

May 6: Britain nationalizes its steel industry.

May 12: Seattle School Board rejects Urban League's "Triad Plan" to desegregate schools.

May 15: National Teach-In is conducted on some 100 campuses.

May 17: A private plane piloted by Seattle businessman Sidney Gerber and carrying Seattle City Councilman Wing Luke and Gerber's secretary, Kay Ladue, disappears over the Cascades.

May 21: The Vietnam Day Committee holds Berkeley's first Vietnam teach-in.

May 25: Sonny Liston folds one minute into the first round in his rematch with Muhammad Ali (whom the press insists on calling Cassius Clay).

May 31: The Industrial Workers of the World ("Wobblies") close their Seattle hall, first opened in 1908, in the Prefontaine Building.

June: Sidney Pollack films *The Slender Thread* in Seattle, which is based on the Crisis Clinic's suicide intervention program and stars Sidney Poitier and Anne Bancroft.

June 3: During Gemini IV mission, Astronaut Edward White becomes the first American to "walk in space."

June 7: U.S. Supreme Court establishes right of marital privacy by overruling Connecticut's ban on birth control.

June 14: Soviets unveil their TU144 SST.

June 17: B-52s conduct the first of many bombing raids in Vietnam.

June 19: Air Vice Marshal Nguyen Kao Ky becomes premier of South Vietnam. Coup topples Ahmed Ben Bella's government in Algeria.

June 20: Following an altercation with black patrons provoked by off-duty policemen in an International District restaurant, one of the officers, Harold Larsen, shoots and kills a young black man, Robert Reese, as he drives away. The homicide is ruled "excusable" ten days later.

June 25: Gillnetters capture a killer whale which is later exhibited on the waterfront as "Namu." Vietcong bomb a Saigon cafe popular with U.S. personnel, killing 42.

June 29: "A Contemporary Theatre" (ACT) debuts with Greg Falls's production of *Oh, Dad. . . .*

June 30: UW closes the original Meany Hall as unsafe due to seismic damage.

July 4: "Big Daddy" Tom Donahue establishes a new kind of rock and roll club called Mother's in San Francisco. An August performance by the Lovin' Spoonful puts the joint on the map.

July 5: CORE national convention adopts and then rescinds resolutions calling for U.S. withdrawal from Vietnam and the Dominican Republic.

July 6: King County Labor Council readmits Teamsters Union, which had been expelled in October 1958.

July 12: Jack Hazzard announces a "Free the Whale" rally on the Seattle waterfront, but only eight people show up.

July 14: UN Ambassador Adlai Stevenson dies in London. President Johnson later appoints Supreme Court Justice Arthur Goldberg to replace him.

July 15: Mariner 4 relays the first close-up photos of Mars. King Constantine of Greece dismisses Georges Papandreou as premier, triggering riots.

July 26: M. L. King Jr. leads protests in Chicago against housing segregation.

July 28: President Johnson reports on Vietnam and tells the nation "this is really war." Johnson doubles the draft quota to supply 125,000 troops for Vietnam.

July 29: The Beatles' *Help!* premieres in London.

July 30: President Johnson signs Medicare into law.

August 4: President Johnson asks Congress for $1.7 billion in additional funding to prosecute the war in Vietnam. The Vietnam Day Committee begins obstructing troop trains passing through Berkeley.

August 6: President Johnson signs Voting Rights Act.

August 9: Singapore secedes from the Federation of Malaysia.

August 10: A Titan II ICBM explodes in its Arkansas silo, killing scores. State Sen. Ed Riley, a white, is appointed to fill out Wing Luke's term.

August 11: Arrest of Marquette Frye triggers a week of rioting in the Watts section of Los Angeles, killing 34 and causing $200 million in damage.

August 13: Max Scherr publishes the first *Berkeley Barb.*

August 15: The Beatles launch their third U.S. tour in New York's Shea Stadium.

August 20: A part-time sheriff's deputy in Hayneville, Alabama, kills a civil rights worker and wounds a priest.

August 21: Canadian antiwar demonstrators stage a sit-in in Vancouver, B.C., during a visit by Prime Minister Lester Pearson.

August 24: California narcs bust Ken Kesey for marijuana at his La Honda ranch.

August 31: President Johnson signs law criminalizing destruction of one's draft card. Premier Ky snubs peace overtures from Hanoi and the UN.

Fall Season: Don Adams mocks the current James Bond rage in "Get Smart" beginning September 18 on NBC (canceled 1970); CBS finds humor in a Nazi POW camp with "Hogan's Heroes" beginning September 17 (to 1971). Bill Cosby becomes the first black to star in national dramatic series: "I Spy" debuts with co-star Robert Culp on September 15 (to 1968). TV comedy drives off the deep end with the debut of "My Mother the Car" on September 14 (recalled after one season).

September 2: China Defense Minister Lin Piao calls for a "People's War" to encircle and strangle the West, and Mao Tse-tung launches "Great Proletarian Cultural Revolution" to purge China of "bourgeois influences." Indian and Pakistani troops clash in Kashmir.

September 3: President Johnson averts steel strike.

September 4: Albert Schweitzer dies.

September 7: As schools reopen, Seattle School District bans long hair for boys.

September 10: Governor Evans blasts Birchers and their "satellites" at State GOP Convention in Port Angeles.

September 16: Boeing IAM members strike.

September 22: In the first of several articles, *University Herald* attacks the U District's growing population of "beatniks."

September 31: The Pentagon spurns Boeing's bid and awards the $2 billion contract to design and build the C-5A military jet transport to Lockheed.

October: Walter Bowart launches the *East Village Other* (*EVO*) in New York City.

October 1: An attempted coup against Indonesia's president Sukarno precipitates the systematic extermination of more than 100,000 Communists and leftists. Ben and Rain Jacopetti found the Open Theater in Berkeley, where they stage the first true light shows, called "Revelations."

October 3: Congress dramatically raises the immigration quota for Chinese and other Asians.

October 4: Boeing machinists vote to return to work. Pope Paul VI arrives in New York City; he is the first Pope to visit the "New World."

October 8: President Johnson undergoes surgery for his gall bladder.

October 9: Two hundred attend the first Vietnam Teach-in at the UW.

October 10: A mass exodus of Cuban refugees begins with tacit blessing of Fidel Castro. U.S. and ARVN troops begin massive offensives in the central highlands and the "Iron Triangle" near Saigon.

October 12: At a banquet at the Pacific Science Center, UW President Charles Odegaard tells the National Academy of

Science that academia suffers "a want of attention to current moral issues encouraged by scientism run riot" and that young people "have the courage and forthrightness" to point out the neglect.

October 14: U.S. Senate Internal Security Subcommittee issues report linking "the teach-in movement" with the "communist propaganda apparatus." Puget Sound Governmental Conference study endorses construction of rapid rail transit in Seattle.

October 15: A Vietnam Day Committee march to Oakland attracts 10,000, who are turned back by police. Demonstrations also take place at the University of Chicago, University of Michigan, Wayne State University in Detroit, UC Santa Barbara, University of Colorado, University of Texas, and in both Portlands, Oregon and Maine.

October 16: In San Francisco, a new group called "The Family Dog" stages a concert with the Jefferson Airplane and Charlatans.

October 17: Seven hundred march without incident from San Francisco's Golden Gate Park to the Civic Center to protest the war.

October 18: In the first such charge, the FBI arrests David Miller for burning his draft card two days earlier in New York. The Justice Department announces its intention to investigate SDS for encouraging draft evasion.

October 20: The UW reports that fall enrollment increased by 2,222 to a total of 25,152, the largest increase in a single year since 1946, when the GI Bill financed college educations for returning veterans. Freshman enrollment alone grows by 18.6 percent. Undergraduate tuition is $115 a quarter for Washington residents.

October 24: President Johnson shows newsmen and photographers the scar from his gall bladder surgery.

October 26: U.S. and ARVN troops break week-long siege of base at Pleiku. Selective Service announces that the draft, which had been limited to single men, will be widened to include married men without children in January 1966.

October 28: Great Britain abolishes the death penalty.

October 29: U.S. detonates an H-bomb underground on the Aleutian island Amchitka. It is the second such test, originally described as needed to "calibrate" detectors for test-ban enforcement but later linked to the development of an antimissile system. Ted Griffin's second captured killer whale dies, but he tells the press it escaped.

October 30: Ten thousand march in New York City to support U.S. policy in Vietnam.

October 31: Court-martial proceedings begin against an ARVN officer whose "mapping error" led U.S. planes to bomb a "friendly" village and kill 42 Vietnamese civilians.

November: Detroit's *Fifth Estate* begins publication. Seattle's movie censorship laws are ruled unconstitutional by Superior Court Judge James Mifflin.

November 1: Selective Service lowers draft intelligence test standards in order to increase induction rates. ASUW publishes its first "Course Critique" of professors; only 34 out of 600 rate an "A." San Francisco Mime Troupe founder R. G. Davis is convicted of offering theater in public parks without a permit.

November 2: Liberal Republican John Lindsay is elected mayor of New York City.

While sitting below Defense Secretary McNamara's Pentagon window, Norman Morrison douses himself with gasoline and sets himself afire to protest the war. Two other pacifists immolate themselves soon after. Ted Griffin reports that a third captured killer whale "escaped"; it turned out she died, but her calf survived. The latter, dubbed "Shamu," is sold to Sea World in San Diego.

November 3: Seattle attorney James R. Ellis tells the Downtown Rotary that King County's unplanned growth has become a "cause for rebellion" and outlines a series of major capital improvements including rapid rail transit. This program is later dubbed "Forward Thrust."

November 4: Police raids in the U District net 13 suspects for possession of marijuana, including James Walcott, co-owner of the Eigerwand Coffee House.

November 6: Five more protesters burn their draft cards in New York City. San Francisco Mime Troupe publicist Bill Graham stages the first light show–concert–dance as an "Appeal" to raise funds for the group's legal costs.

November 8: Seattle Artificial Kidney Center is dedicated.

November 9: Northeast power grid fails, blacking out power for 30 million people in New York City and much of the Eastern Seaboard.

November 11: UN General Assembly condemns Rhodesia, which had declared independence from Great Britain in order to preserve its own form of apartheid. A World War II veteran is arrested in Lake City, for tearing down a Revolutionary War-era American flag and walking on it.

November 13: Administration policy defenders fail to appear at a conference on Vietnam held in the Meany Hotel.

November 15: *Look* Magazine reveals that the U.S. rebuffed a North Vietnamese proposal for peace talks in late 1964.

November 17: U.S. troops win a Pyrrhic victory in their first major battle with North Vietnamese regulars at Ia Drang. Body counts rather than civilian loyalty become the measure of future U.S. combat "successes," encouraging a false optimism for the outcome of the war.

November 25: The Pentagon reports that 240 Americans died in Vietnam during the previous week. The *P-I* later reports that 1,082 Western Washington men are to be drafted in December 1965, compared with 49 one year earlier.

November 27: Ken Kesey announces the first "Acid Test" at his La Honda ranch.

November 29: Returning from Vietnam, Defense Secretary McNamara declares, "We have stopped losing the war."

November 30: Vietcong release two U.S. prisoners, who condemn the war effort.

December: East Lansing, Michigan's, *Paper* begins publication.

December 2: KJR presents the Rolling Stones, Ian Whitcomb, Paul Revere and the Raiders, and the Liverpool Five at the Coliseum.

December 4: Vietcong sappers blow up a U.S. military hotel in Saigon, killing 10. Bob Dylan scandalizes purists by introducing amplified music into his repertoire. Ken Kesey holds the second Acid Test in San Jose.

December 10: Bill Graham stages the first light show–concert–dance held in the Fillmore Auditorium.

December 15: U.S. bombs Haiphong in first raid on an urban center in North Vietnam. AFL-CIO, led by George Meany, pledges "unstinting support" for the war.

After several launching delays, U.S. achieves first orbital rendezvous when Gemini VI comes within six feet of Gemini VII, which had been launched 11 days earlier.

December 17: Ferdinand Marcos is elected president of the Philippines.

December 20: Shamu, an orca calf, is flown from Seattle to San Diego's Sea World. Seafair cancels the 1966 Aqua Follies at Green Lake.

December 22: Boeing president William Allen announces that the company will add 15,000 jobs, raising its Puget Sound area employment to 75,000.

December 23: U.S. suspends bombing for Christmas truce; after peace bids fail, bombing resumes January 31, 1966.

December 25: SDS leader Tom Hayden and Quaker Staughton Lynd visit Hanoi, the first of numerous pilgrimages by U.S. radicals.

December 31: U.S. forces in Vietnam total 184,300. U.S. combat deaths since 1961 reach 1,350.

Zeitgeist: Barry McGuire records P. F. Sloan's "Eve of Destruction" and the Rolling Stones record "Satisfaction" (as in "I can't get no"); Grateful Dead, Big Brother and the Holding Company (pre-Joplin), and Simon and Garfunkle come together; the Beatles, the Rolling Stones, the Byrds, the Beach Boys, the Supremes, Herman's Hermits, Sonny & Cher, and Sam the Sham & the Pharaohs record the top singles while Roger Miller wins a Grammy for "King of the Road." International Society for Krishna Consciousness ("Hare Krishna, Hare") is founded in New York; Timothy Leary's *The Psychedelic Reader* and Alex Haley's *Autobiography of Malcolm X* published; Andy Warhol paints a Campbell's Soup can; Mary Quant intro-duces the mini skirt in London; macrobiotic diet claims first official victim (Beth Ann Simon); "Op Art" appears; Gino Pontecorvo's *The Battle of Algiers* and Sidney Lumet's *The Pawnbroker* released, while *The Sound of Music* wins Best Picture. During the first half of the decade, the mostly black populations of 10 former European colonies gained their independence, including Zaire, Zambia, Mali, Kenya, Uganda, and Jamaica.

1966

January: Paul Williams founds *Crawdaddy,* first magazine devoted to rock and roll.

January 1: Transit strike paralyzes New York City for the next 12 days. Cracks and mudslides slow I-5 construction in Seattle.

January 3: Floyd McKissick succeeds James Farmer as director of CORE. Although President Johnson continues to press his "peace offensive," the holiday truce effectively ends with fierce ground engagements across Vietnam.

January 12: President Johnson vows not to "abandon Asia to conquest" in his State of the Union address, and proposes $1 billion in higher taxes to finance the war. The original *Batman,* with a pudgy Adam West as the Caped Crusader, introduces America to the idea of "camp" on ABC.

January 13: Robert Weaver becomes the first black to serve on the Cabinet when President Johnson appoints him head of the new Department of Housing and Urban Development (HUD). Ted Griffin proposes building an aquarium at Seattle Center.

January 15: A military coup in Nigeria triggers weeks of turmoil.

January 17: Defense Secretary McNamara proposes to enlist 113,000 additional troops as part of a $12.3 billion supplemental budget to fund the war. A B-52 armed with nuclear weapons collides with a KC-135 tanker while refueling over Spain; it takes the Air Force two months to find an H-bomb which fell into the Mediterranean during the crash.

January 19: Indira Gandhi becomes prime minister of India. Georgia State House of Representatives refuses to seat Julian Bond because of his opposition to the war in Vietnam; he is not admitted until January 9, 1967.

January 20: Spokane attorney and civil rights leader Carl Maxey calls for federal investigation of discrimination in labor unions.

January 21: Bill Graham and Stewart Brand stage the first "Trips Festival" in San Francisco; a young printer by the name of Wesley Wilson designed the poster.

January 23: People's Republic of China MIGs reported operating over North Vietnam.

January 28: Arkansas Sen. J. William Fulbright, chair of the Foreign Affairs Committee, questions the legality of U.S. intervention in Vietnam. The next day, Sen. Wayne Morse calls for repeal of the Gulf of Tonkin Resolution.

January 31: U.S. resumes bombing of North Vietnam.

February 3: Soviet's Luna-9 probe achieves the first "soft" landing on the moon. Seattle-First National Bank unveils plan to build 50-story office building at Fourth and Madison.

February 6: *P-I* profiles Seattle's "Invisible Community" of homosexuals.

February 15: U.S. aircraft begin dropping defoliant chemicals to expose North Vietnamese supply routes.

February 18: The UW lures the Philadelphia String Quartet from its resident orchestra, but legal conflicts delay the move for many months.

February 19: Sen. Robert Kennedy suggests that the Vietcong be seated at any negotiations. Chet Helms takes over the Family Dog and introduces a new logo featuring a top-hatted Indian smoking a giant joint.

February 24: Russel Wills and David Miller become the first in Seattle to refuse induction into the armed forces in protest to the war.

March 1: Congress approves an additional $4.8 billion for the war. Soviets' Venus 3 becomes the first earth-made object to land on another planet.

March 9: General Motors admits in a Congressional hearing that it hired private detectives to tail and investigate Ralph Nader, leading champion of federal auto safety standards (GM president James Roche publicly apologized on March 22). President DeGaulle pulls France out of NATO.

March 10: South Vietnamese Buddhists protest against discriminatory policies in Saigon and Hué. King County Assessor Tony Steen is indicted on bribery charges.

March 12: General Suharto ends the pretense that Sukarno is in charge and takes over Indonesia. His purge of leftists ultimately kills 400,000.

March 15: A day-long riot in Watts leaves two dead.

March 17: Jan Tissot et al. convene the Second International Bohemian Festival in the U District, but the "fringie frolic" fizzles; it was all a gag. Following the first successful docking in space, Gemini 8 mission is cut short by technical malfunctions.

March 21: U.S. Supreme Court upholds an obscenity conviction against Evergreen Press publisher Ralph Ginzburg in the case of his *Eros* magazine.

March 22: Air Force launches investigation of repeated sightings of UFOs near a swamp in Hillsdale, Michigan. Dr. H. Allen Hynek later concludes the phenomena resulted from ignis fatuus, or "swamp gas." Later still, Hynek repudiates his own findings.

March 26: Antiwar marches in New York, Rome, and other U.S. and European cities attract thousands. The following day, the Pentagon announces that 2,762 U.S. troops have died in fighting so far in 1966 alone, twice the tally from the previous five years.

March 28: Britain's "The Avengers," featuring the unflappable John Steed (Patrick Macnee) and lithe Emma Peel (Diana Rigg), debuts on ABC.

March 29: Seattle City Council votes to launch a long-planned Yesler-Atlantic Urban Renewal project in the Central Area.

March 31: CORE and Central Area Committee for Civil Rights launch two-day boycott of Seattle schools to protest de facto segregation.

April 1: U.S. troop strength in Vietnam reaches 230,000. Vietcong bomb a U.S. officers billet in Saigon, killing 6 and injuring 100. Seattle's population peaks at 574,000, as calculated by the State Census Board.

April 2: Some 100,000 Vietnamese demonstrate in Da Nang against the U.S. and the Ky government while local officials rebel against Saigon control. Civil unrest spreads to Hué and Saigon.

April 4: As Congress debates imposing the first mandatory safety standards on automobiles, General Motors announces the first "recall" to repair faults in 1.5 million Chevelles and all new Chevrolets with automatic transmissions.

April 6: Forward Thrust steering committee elects James Ellis as its chair.

April 8: The cover of *Time* magazine asks, "Is God Dead?"

April 9: The Vietnam Day Committee office in Berkeley is dynamited.

April 12: B-52s launch their first bombing missions over North Vietnam. General Ky pledges to hold elections in South Vietnam.

April 13: Vietcong bombard Saigon airport with mortar fire. Pan Am places orders for the first 25 Boeing 747s.

April 14: Sandoz Pharmaceuticals announces that it will no longer market LSD-25 in the U.S. as the FDA begins to crack down on hallucinogenic drugs.

April 17: U.S. aircraft attack missile sites and railways on the outskirts of Hanoi.

April 18: Bill Russell becomes the first black to coach a major pro basketball team when he takes over the Boston Celtics. The Robert Joffrey Ballet Company, fresh from a triumph in New York City, offers to locate in Seattle if sufficient funds can be raised. Forward Thrust approves its articles of incorporation drafted by attorney Marvin Durning. Fundamentalist ministers file suit to prevent the UW from teaching the Bible "as literature."

April 21: South Vietnam expels six members of the U.S. Committee for Non-Violent Action (CNVA), including the Rev. A. J. Muste, who had attempted to stage a peace march in Saigon.

April 23: Allied Stores and Marshall Field & Co. announce plans to build South Center shopping complex.

April 25: At the Western Governors Conference, Governor Evans launches campaign to thwart Southwestern ambitions to tap Columbia River water.

April 28: IAM members approve new contract with Boeing, which reforms its "totem" system for rating employees.

May 1: U.S. artillery fires into neutral Cambodia in order to disrupt flow of supplies along the "Ho Chi Minh Trail." South Vietnamese troops disperse thousands of anti-U.S. demonstrators in Saigon.

May 5: Senator Fulbright attacks American "arrogance of power" in Vietnam.

May 13: U.S. aircraft down a People's Republic of China MIG.

May 15: South Vietnamese troops quell Da Nang rebellion. SANE, Women March for Peace, and the Quaker American Friends Service Committee rally 10,000 to picket the White House in antiwar protest. PRC Defense Minister Lin Piao emerges as the real power behind Mao Tse-tung.

May 16: As fighting continues in Hué, 50,000 workers strike in Saigon to protest General Ky's crackdown.

May 17: UW announces that it will police chemistry labs to ensure that LSD is not being manufactured on campus.

May 20: UW hosts forum on LSD.

May 22: Buddhist resistance collapses in Da Nang, but anti-Ky riots continue in Saigon and Hué. Six Buddhists, including a nun, kill themselves during the following week.

May 25: Arthur Kleps, "Chief Boohoo" of an alleged LSD cult, tells a U.S. Senate hearing his followers will "flood" the country with acid if Timothy Leary is ever arrested.

June 1: Students sack U.S. consulate in Saigon. Surveyor 1 lands on the moon.

June 3: People's Republic of China begins to purge "capitalist roaders" as a part of the "cultural revolution."

June 6: James Meredith is wounded during a "pilgrimage" from the Tennessee border to Jackson, Mississippi, which began June 3. Civil rights groups complete Meredith's march on June 26, when SNCC head Stokely Carmichael issues first call for "Black Power." A conference at Seattle University protests Soviet mistreatment of Jews.

June 7: Seattle marks the centennial of the death of Chief Seattle.

June 8: Seattle School District announces that it will begin busing 500 students the following fall to promote integration and relieve crowding in Central Area schools. The XB-70 prototype supersonic bomber collides with its chase plane, killing two pilots.

June 10: Navy Seabee Glen Shields dies in Vietnam. He becomes the first Seattle resident to receive the Congressional Medal of Honor for his actions in Vietnam.

June 13: In *Miranda v. Arizona*, the U.S. Supreme Court strengthens rights of criminal suspects during police investigations.

June 14: Superior Court Judge W. R. Cole rules that the UW's course on the Bible as literature does not constitute "religious instruction" and is permitted under the First Amendment.

June 17: Stanley Miller, who later collaborates with Al Kelly in "Mouse Studio," designs his first poster for the Family Dog. Mouse later makes the Zig-Zag Man the unofficial totem for the Haight-Ashbury scene.

June 18: Former Democrat and actor Ronald Reagan delivers a stemwinder for conservatism in the Seattle Arena.

June 20: Boeing begins construction of 747 plant at Paine Field. Aerial trackers count 76 Soviet fishing vessels off the Washington coast.

June 21: Seattle Transit Commission announces plan for "Blue Streak" commuter express between Northgate and downtown Seattle; it becomes the area's first "park and ride" service.

June 23: Premier Ky crushes Buddhist protests in South Vietnam.

June 28: Annette Buchannan, a Seattle native attending the University of Oregon, is fined for contempt of court for refusing to reveal the names of students she profiled in a campus newspaper article on drug use.

June 29: U.S. aircraft begin bombing Hanoi anew after long lull during which North Vietnam repeatedly spurned U.S. "peace feelers."

July 1: CORE national convention in Baltimore endorses "black power" agenda. Three days later, the NAACP, meeting in Los Angeles, rejects the same tenets, formalizing a long-simmering division in the civil rights movement. Medicare becomes available to senior citizens.

July 2: France resumes above-ground nuclear testing in the Pacific. Blacks riot in Omaha, Nebraska. Leaders of SNCC, CORE, and the Urban League endorse "black power" during a convention in Baltimore, which estranges them from integrationists based in the NAACP and SCLC.

July 4: President Johnson signs first Freedom of Information act giving citizens access to government records. Four hundred CNVA members gather in Philadelphia to protest the war.

July 8: Seattle City Light Superintendent John Nelson endorses construction of a nuclear reactor to supplement power generation.

July 9: Namu dies in his pen at Pier 56.

July 11: A Louis Harris Poll reports that 54 percent of Americans support President Johnson's handling of the war, up from 42 percent prior to U.S. bombing raids on Hanoi and Haiphong.

July 12–19: Riots erupt in Chicago and Cleveland.

July 13: Richard Speck slaughters eight student nurses in Chicago.

July 15: Boeing celebrates its 50th anniversary.

July 16: Washington State Democratic Party convention in Spokane refuses to either endorse or criticize the war.

July 19: Frank Sinatra and Mia Farrow wed.

July 20: Racial rioting spreads to New York City.

July 23: Local CORE chapter rejects black power "dictum" from its national parent.

July 25: To counteract rumors of Mao Tse-tung's infirmity, New China Press Agency publishes photos of the Great Helmsman swimming in the Yangtze River.

July 28: White Power rally triggers rioting in Baltimore. Seattle smog reaches a new record.

July 30: Soviet Union agrees to U.S. inspection of its fishing boats off the West Coast.

July 31: FBI director J. Edgar Hoover reports that the Communist Party will exploit the New Left to wage class warfare.

August 1: Charles Whitman opens fire from a tower at the University of Texas, killing 12 bystanders.

August 3: Lenny Bruce dies at age 39.

August 10: Mayor Braman and Ben Ehrlichman, president of the Urban Corporation, unveil plan to flatten most of Pioneer Square and develop new parking garages and office towers. Allied Arts and Victor Steinbrueck immediately express opposition.

August 12: The Beatles begin a fourth and final U.S. tour in Chicago. Their controversial album cover for "Yesterday and Today," featuring butchered baby dolls, is pulled from shelves and repackaged during the summer.

August 14: Boeing-built Lunar Orbiter begins mapping the surface of the moon.

August 18: Red Guards launch month-long rampage in major Chinese cities.

August 19: Berkeley activist Jerry Rubin, dressed in a American Revolutionary War uniform, disrupts HUAC hearings on the antiwar movement in Washington, D.C.

August 25: U.S. jet accidentally napalms U.S. troops, killing seven. Lunar Orbiter transmits first photograph of an "Earthrise" from the moon. The Beatles perform in the Seattle Center Coliseum. Seattle Planning Commission blasts proposal for Pioneer Square "urban renewal."

August 31: Richard Nixon and other leading Republicans express reservations about continuing escalation of the war. Mayor Braman proposes to rebuild most of central Seattle with federal "Demonstration [Model] Cities" funds.

Fall Season: "Star Trek" goes "boldly where no man has gone before" on September 8, but NBC jettisons the Enterprise after three seasons (fortunately, Capt. Kirk and crew escape to the parallel universe of syndication where their orbit shows no sign of decay). NBC releases "The Monkees" on September 12; they are rounded up after only two seasons.

September: French president DeGaulle visits Cambodia and calls for U.S. to leave Vietnam. The Puget Sound Regional Transportation Study calls for major new freeways, including a cross-sound bridge via Vashon Island, and dismisses rail transit as not viable. The Seattle Folklore Society is founded.

September 4: National Guard confronts white supremacy mobs in Cicero, Illinois.

September 6: Riots shake Atlanta over five nights. South African Prime Minister Hendrik Verwoerd is assassinated. Sen. Henry Jackson endorses "standby" wage and price controls and a tax increase to tame inflation created by the war.

September 11: Legislative elections are carried out in South Vietnam.

September 13: White mobs attack civil rights marchers in Grenada, Mississippi.

September 14: Powered by a special booster with which it rendezvoused in orbit, Gemini 11 sets a new altitude record of 853 miles above Earth.

September 15: Controversial Episcopal Bishop James Pike loses his diocese.

September 18: Lincoln County officers bust 17 residents at Tolstoy Farm, a large commune near Davenport, Washington, for growing the wrong kind of grass.

September 19: At a Greenwich Village press conference, Dr. Timothy Leary announces creation of the "League for Spiritual Discovery" to encourage people to "turn on, tune in and drop out." An intruder enters the home of Charles Percy, Republican candidate for U.S. Senate from Illinois, and murders his daughter.

September 20: Allen Cohen and Ron Thelin publish the first *San Francisco Oracle*. A $36 million bond issue to build a King County domed stadium fails.

September 24: James Meredith speaks before a virtually empty hall in Seattle.

September 23: UW student Russel Wills is sentenced to two years in prison for refusing induction.

September 26: Garfield graduate Rafael Stone becomes the first black freshman to pledge to a UW fraternity (Psi Upsilon).

September 28: National Guard quells riots in San Francisco's Hunter's Point and Fillmore neighborhoods. Vice President Humphrey visits Seattle and gets a private tour of Boeing's SST mock-up; several dozen antiwar demonstrators picket his address at the Olympic Hotel.

October 5: Ruling that his confession was not "spontaneous," the Texas Court of Criminal Appeals throws out Jack Ruby's conviction for killing Lee Harvey Oswald in front of a nationwide TV audience.

October 6: California makes possession and use of LSD a felony.

October 10: Miriam Rader et al. launch the first classes of the Free University of Seattle (FUS) above the Coffee Corral at U Way and NE 42nd.

October 15: Huey Newton and Bobby Seale form the Black Panther Party for Self-Defense in Oakland, California. President Johnson signs bill creating new Department of Transportation.

October 17: The Diggers hold their first free feed in Haight Ashbury.

October 26: At the conclusion of the Manila Summit, President Johnson pays a surprise visit to Cam Ranh Bay, before continuing his 17-day Asian tour. U.S. troops in Vietnam now exceed 331,000. Ho Chi Minh rejects renewed U.S. and Soviet peace overtures.

October 29-30: National Organization for Women holds its founding convention in Washington, D.C., and the 30 attendees elect Betty Friedan as NOW's first president.

October 31: Seattle homicides so far in 1966 rise to 24, twice 1965 rate. Boeing wins contract to build Short-Range Attack Missile (SRAM).

November 1: North Vietnamese kill six U.S. soldiers during President Johnson's visit to Seoul.

November 5: President Johnson signs spending bills totaling $14 billion, including new Model Cities program and first legislation promoting truth-in-labeling and consumer protection in children's products. The area's first light show is presented at a KRAB benefit in Kirkland.

November 8: State voters rummage through a passel of initiatives and referenda, and repeal the "blue law" limiting entertainment and retail sales on Sundays. John Spellman's election gives Republicans control of the County Commissioners and voters send a GOP majority to the State House. Ronald Reagan wins election as governor of California, and Edward Brooks of Massachusetts becomes the first black to be elected to the U.S. Senate since Reconstruction. Republicans gain 50 seats in the House of Representatives, marking a dramatic recovery from the Goldwater debacle of two years earlier.

November 10: Second Lunar Orbiter reaches the moon.

November 13: In the *P-I*, Jack B. Robertson advocates development of a countywide system of greenbelts.

November 14: Charles Z. Smith is sworn in as Washington's first black Superior Court judge.

November 15: U.S. Catholic bishops and cardinals accuse the Johnson Administration of promoting abortions among the poor.

November 16: The Gemini program concludes its twelfth and final mission. The following day, Seattle-born astronaut Richard Gordon Jr. is feted by his home town. The new Seattle Folklore Society hosts its first concert featuring Mance Lipscomb and Fred McDowell.

November 18: Catholic Church lifts ban on eating meat on Fridays effective December 2.

November 23: The ASUW hosts a "Little Silly Dance" featuring the Daily Flash and a light show in the HUB.

November 24: Police bust San Francisco bookstores for selling Lenore Kandel's "The Love Book" while turning a blind eye toward the city's topless and bottomless bars.

November 25: Catholic Seattle high school students picket downtown bookstores for selling "smutty" literature.

November 26: Peter Fonda is among 100 persons arrested on LA's Sunset Strip during a protest of enforcement of a 10 p.m. curfew.

November 28: Trial of comedian Dick Gregory and his wife begins in Olympia on charges stemming from their participation in a "fish-in" the previous March. The Gregorys, represented by Jack Tanner, are convicted on December 1.

November 31: A Norwegian freighter unloads 300 tons of PRC-made goods at the Port of Seattle for transshipment north on Canadian trucks; "Red Chinese" products were then prohibited in the U.S.

December 1: UC students led by Mario Savio expel Navy recruiters from the

Berkeley campus and begin a strike. Seattle police shoot and kill a 19-year-old black suspected of car theft.

December 3: Vietcong launch ground and mortar attacks against Saigon. Milo Johnstone stages Seattle's first true light show–dance–concert in the Frye Hotel.

December 6: President Johnson reports that Vietnam War costs are running as much as $10 billion over the original estimate of $58 billion for the fiscal year ending June 30. Nobel Laureate Linus Pauling speaks in Seattle and predicts that Vietnam will "peter out" like Korea with no U.S. victory.

December 9: Following acquittal of a white for killing a black student, 700 Tuskegee Institute students riot.

December 10: The Puget Sound Oceanographic Commission, chaired by Dixy Lee Ray, unveils plan for a giant research center and aquarium at Golden Gardens.

December 13: The authoritative journal *Jane's Fighting Ships* reports that the Soviet navy has surpassed that of Great Britain and is second only to the U.S.

December 15: Walt Disney dies. M. L. King Jr. tells a Senate committee, "The bombs in Vietnam explode here at home; they destroy the hopes and possibilities for a decent America."

December 16: For the first time in its 21-year history, the UN votes to impose mandatory economic sanctions. The target is Ian Smith's all-white rebel government in Rhodesia. The following day, the UN General Assembly approves an international treaty banning nuclear weapons from space.

December 17: Forward Thrust unveils 18 pieces of state legislation for which it will lobby to support regional growth controls

and capital improvements (17 ultimately pass).

December 21: Jacqueline Kennedy succeeds in compelling *Look* magazine to excise what she says are unauthorized passages in William Manchester's book, *The Death of a President*, a gritty account of JFK's assassination.

December 22: Statistics are published showing that Seattle-area consumer prices rose 3.4 percent in September and November alone.

December 23: Holiday truce takes effect in Vietnam for two days.

December 25: *P-I* reveals secret state plans to build fourth and fifth floating bridges across Lake Washington (a new I-90 bridge was already included in official road schemes). Pentagon admits that civilian targets are being hit "accidentally" during bombing raids over North Vietnam.

December 27: *P-I* honors Seattle's beloved but star-crossed boxer Eddie Cotton as its "Man of the Year" in sports.

December 28: Bettina Aptheker convenes a national conference in Chicago to organize opposition to the war in Vietnam; participants later merge with Spring Mobilization planners to create a permanent Student Mobilization Committee. Western Hotels announces plan to build a 39-story circular hotel on the site of the Orpheum Theater.

December 29: One hundred presidents of college student bodies protest war in Vietnam in a letter to President Johnson. An acoustics engineer in Phoenix tells the press that exposure to rock and roll could cause deafness. State Supreme Court rules that Seattle failed to prove that the "Northlake Urban Renewal Area" was blighted as required under law; the decision throws the city's redevelopment planning into chaos.

December 31: Boeing beats out Lockheed to win FAA approval to develop the SST. U.S. forces stationed in Vietnam total 385,000, augmented by 30,000 in Thailand and 60,000 naval personnel offshore; U.S. combat deaths reach 5,008, more than double the 1965 toll. During the course of 1966, 43 U.S. cities experience major racial rioting in which 11 die, more than 400 are injured, and 3,000 are arrested. Seattle experienced 32 homicides in 1966, up 33 percent from 1965 and 146 percent from 1960, attributable chiefly to the growing number of young males in the population.

Zeitgeist: Penney's and the Bon Marche report that while "GI Joe" is the season's hottest new toy, overall sales of war toys are down 95 percent. *Quotations of Chairman Mao* ("The Little Red Book"), Truman Capote's *In Cold Blood,* Konrad Lorenz's *On Aggression,* and Thomas Pynchon's *The Crying of Lot 49* are published. Michelangelo Antonioni's *Blow-Up,* Lewis Gilbert's *Alfie,* Karel Reisz's *Morgan!,* and Norman Jewison's *The Russians Are Coming! The Russians Are Coming!* are released. California imposes first exhaust limits on automobiles. U.S. Department of the Interior issues first list of endangered species. John Lennon tells the London press that the Beatles are "more popular than Jesus Christ" and later meets performance artist Yoko Ono at a London gallery. George Harrison takes sitar lessons from Ravi Shankar. Former "Animal" Chas Chandler discovers Seattle-born Jimi Hendrix and brings him to London to form "The Experience." The Mamas and the Papas debut with "California Dreamin'." Staff Sgt. Barry Sadler's "The Ballad of the Green Berets" is the top selling single, Jefferson Airplane takes off, the Beatles launch "Yellow Submarine," and Donovan (Leitch) turns "Mellow Yellow" into gold. First bank cards and pants suits for women introduced. "Dark Shadows," which debuts on June 27, pumps new blood into soap operas during its five-year run.

1967

January 3: Jack Ruby dies in prison.

January 5: Governor Evans proposes a single-rate income tax and corresponding cuts in sales and business taxes.

January 8: Red Guard excesses trigger counter-riots and strikes in Shanghai. The rebellion spreads during the following weeks.

January 10: President Johnson proposes 6 percent surtax on income tax to finance "guns and butter." Seattle Urban League attacks United Good Neighbors as offering more "middle class welfare" than help for the poor.

January 12: UW coeds vote to eliminate women-only dorm curfew.

January 13: Immediately after dying, a Los Angeles man is put into a cryogenic chamber in the hope that future physicians might be able to revive and cure him. This is the first such experiment with a human being, assuming that the rumors about Walt Disney's body being frozen are false.

January 14: *Oracle* et al. sponsor "Human Be-In" at San Francisco's Golden Gate Park. Free University of Seattle stages first light show ever held at Eagles.

January 15: The *Sunday Ramparts* reports that UW ROTC members are being directed to spy on "disloyal" students.

January 17: Boeing rolls out the first 737 twin-jet.

January 18: UW SDS members publish the first of four issues of the irreverent *Seattle Barb*. While denying rumors of rampant Seattle police payoffs, Chief Ramon suddenly suspends five officers.

January 20: University of California regents dismiss president Clark Kerr. Former Green Beret Don Duncan criticizes the war in Vietnam during a UW speech.

January 22: Protesters interrupt Mass at New York's St. Patrick's Cathedral to protest Francis Cardinal Spellman's hawkish pronouncements on the war.

January 23: Seattle City Council votes to deny Dr. Timothy Leary use of the Opera House for a planned lecture on February 5.

January 24: President Johnson proposes $172 billion federal budget for FY '67. Of every tax dollar, 16 cents is allocated to the Vietnam War. Ralph Nader speaks at the UW.

January 25: A study by the Seattle–King County Youth Commission finds that 60 percent of area teens are partaking of alcohol or illegal drugs.

January 27: U.S. astronauts Gus Grissom, Ed White, and Roger Chaffee burn to death inside their Apollo capsule during tests at Cape Kennedy. (The tragedy led NASA to assign Boeing responsibility for overall coordination of the moon-landing project.) UW History Department declines to renew Professor John Spellman's contract, which he views as the "price" for his iconoclastic views on the war, drugs, and society.

January 29: Senate aide Bobby Baker is convicted of income tax evasion and other charges stemming from political abuses. High winds damage the new Evergreen Point Bridge.

January 30: President Johnson proposes new federal programs to combat air pollution. State Rep. Mark Lichtman proposes that the state establish an "LSD Center" to distribute the drug and freeze out illegal sales.

January 31: U.S. Department of Labor announces plan to help 700 unemployed workers move to Seattle to help relieve labor shortage. Last remaining section of

Interstate 5 between Everett and Tacoma is opened. ACLU protests forced interrogation of local high school students by police.

February 3: Dr. Timothy Leary and Dr. Sidney Cohen debate LSD at the UW. Communist Party announces arrival of "pure communism" as Red Guards terrorize purged leaders and whole regions.

February 5: The debut of "The Smothers Brothers Comedy Hour" on CBS proves to be a network censor's nightmare.

February 7: Four-day Tet truce begins in Vietnam.

February 10: Sufficient states ratify the 25th Amendment providing for presidential succession.

February 11: Disc jockey Larry Miller introduces album-length rock and roll over the air on San Francisco's KMPX-FM.

February 12: U.S. suspends bombing raids over North Vietnam to stimulate peace talks; bombing is renewed the next day.

February 13: After months of an escalating propaganda war, the Soviet Union and PRC exchange gunfire on the Manchurian border. National Student Association president Eugene Grove confirms *Ramparts Magazine* revelation that the CIA had secretly subsidized the NSA for years. Harvard students protest the war during UN Ambassador Goldberg's visit to the campus. In Olympia, Seattle Police Chief Ramon advocates a 48-hour waiting period for gun sales.

February 14: President Johnson proposes federal open-housing law. Third Boeing Lunar Orbiter broadcasts clearest photos yet of the moon's surface. Abbie Hoffman, with financing from Jimi Hendrix, anonymously mails joints to several thousand New Yorkers as Valentine's Day gifts.

February 16: SDS protesters force a U.S. Air Force recruiter to leave the UW campus.

February 17: University of Puget Sound informs Professor Robert Lee, a public critic of the war, that his contract will not be renewed; student protests lead to his reinstatement on March 1.

February 18: New Orleans District Attorney Jim Garrison announces that he has begun investigating a possible conspiracy behind the Kennedy assassination.

February 22: Barbara Garson's *MacBird* (in which Lyndon Johnson plays Macbeth to JFK's Duncan) debuts in New York City. Meanwhile in New Orleans, David Ferrie, a key suspect in the Garrison investigation, dies as an apparent suicide.

February 24: Chinese Communist Party begins to rein in the Red Guards.

February 25: First 24 cadets resign in a new cheating scandal at the U.S. Air Force Academy in Colorado Springs.

February 28: President Johnson names Ramsey Clark to succeed Nicholas Katzenbach as Attorney General. Time-Life publisher and reformed acid head Henry Luce dies.

March 1: Congress refuses to seat Adam Clayton Powell, a black minister and activist elected from New York City, over allegations of financial misconduct. New Orleans District Attorney James Garrison orders the arrest of Clay Shaw for conspiracy to assassinate President Kennedy.

March 2: Sen. Robert Kennedy calls for cessation of the bombing of North Vietnam. U.S. Coast Guard seizes a Soviet trawler fishing in U.S. waters off Alaska.

March 3: The *Berkeley Barb* reports that you can get high by smoking banana skins.

March 4: A presidential commission proposes creation of a "draft lottery."

March 7: James Hoffa enters federal prison.

March 8: State legislature passes law allowing liquor sales within one mile of UW campus.

March 10: English narcs bust the Rolling Stones for possession of marijuana.

March 11: Switzerland grants asylum to Svetlana Stalin, Josef's daughter, who had defected earlier at the U.S. Embassy in New Delhi. Governor Evans signs state Open Housing law.

March 15: President Johnson names Ellsworth Bunker to succeed Henry Cabot Lodge as U.S. ambassador to South Vietnam.

March 16: *Science* magazine reports that LSD causes chromosomal damage in lab rats.

March 17: New Orleans court indicts Clay Shaw.

March 19: Six thousand attend Seattle's first "Trips Festival" at Eagles.

March 21: Howard University students heckle Selective Service chief Gen. Lewis Hershey off the stage during a speech.

March 22: National Municipal League and *Look* magazine honor Seattle as an "All-America City" (the city had first won the award in 1959). Jack Delay incorporates "The Brothers" despite facing eviction from his Bookworm storefront on March 31.

March 23: First *Helix* is published.

March 24: State legislature votes to establish community college system.

March 25: M. L. King Jr. leads 2,000 antiwar marchers through Chicago.

March 26: First gathering of underground press convenes in Stimson Beach, California. Abbie Hoffman et al. stage New York's first be-in at Central Park with as many as 30,000 attendees; Los Angeles also stages its first be-in. Brothers/*Helix* hold a benefit concert aboard the *Virginia V.*

March 28: Lt. Elmer Wesselius of the Seattle Police Dance Detail tells the City Council that a vanguard is working "to pave the way" for an exodus of hippies from California to Seattle.

March 29: Seattle School Board rejects Stokely Carmichael's application to speak at Garfield on April 19.

April 1: The Brothers organizes Seattle's first "be-in" at Cowen Park, attracting 300 for a Bookworm "wake." Shazam Society shows "psychedelic art" at Attica Gallery.

April 2: Allied Arts presents "Occurrences," a demonstration light show at the Pacific Science Center.

April 3: After another court reversal, U.S. government abandons 14-year campaign to compel the U.S. Communist Party to register as a "foreign agent." In Seattle, Id Bookstore owner Steve Herold and his employee Tony Tuft are busted for selling the "Kama Sutra Calendar" and *Entrails* poetry magazine.

April 4: M. L. King Jr. denounces the U.S. as "the greatest purveyor of violence in the world" and calls for a common crusade between civil rights and antiwar movements. Jerry Rubin garners 21 percent of the vote in his race for mayor of Berkeley. Future Congressman Ron Dellums is elected to the Berkeley City Council. "Friends of the Free University" testify before the City Council to win a permit for light show and dance benefit. Owsley is busted for possession while driving from

Timothy Leary's mansion in Millbrook, New York.

April 5: The Gray Line Bus Company inaugurates "Hippie Hop" tours of Haight Ashbury. Marvin Jordan of "Nature's Green Oratory" invites the Seattle City Council to attend a benefit light show in Hec Edmonson Pavilion on April 8, but the event is postponed until the 23rd.

April 6: Tens of thousands of Germans protesting the Vietnam War jeer Vice President Humphrey in West Berlin. Superior Court Judge Mifflin orders the School District to permit Stokely Carmichael to speak at Garfield; the ruling is affirmed on appeal on April 11.

April 7: "The Pill" makes the cover of *Time*. Sen. Ted Kennedy calls the draft "unjust" in a speech in Seattle.

April 8: Teamsters walk off their jobs in a national trucking strike. Abbie Hoffman and former Digger Emmett Grogan organize a "sweep-in" on New York's Lower East Side.

April 9: Boeing 737 makes maiden flight. Blacks riot in Nashville, Tennessee. University of Iowa student body president Don Smith refuses to resign after revealing that he smokes grass regularly.

April 10: Seattle City Council denies the Free University its dance permit. First U.S. Court of Appeals in Boston rules law against mutilation or destruction of a draft card to be unconstitutional.

April 11: University District Chamber of Commerce rejects University District Movement petition, with 8,000 signatures protesting harassment and price gouging. Jerry Rubin's candidacy for mayor of Berkeley garners 22 percent of the vote.

April 12: Following a UDM rally on campus, Robbie Stern leads 1,500 in a march down University Way.

April 13: Richard Kirkpatrick becomes the first president of the ASUW in a decade who does not belong to a fraternity; Mike Mandeville, who later founds Lecture Notes, is elected vice president. Former UW Committee Against the War president Deborah Leonard and University Lutheran Church pastor William Hershey urge opposition to "immoral" war in Vietnam.

April 15: More than 200,000 march in Spring Mobilization demonstrations against the Vietnam War in San Francisco and New York City (the original and current sites of the UN).

April 17: Two UC Medical Center physicians report that loud rock and roll music can cause permanent hearing damage.

April 19: Stokely Carmichael speaks at the UW and Garfield. With tongue planted firmly in cheek, New Jersey Congressman Frank Thompson Jr. introduces the "Banana Labeling Act of 1967" and the "Other Odd Fruit Disclosure and Reporting Act of 1967."

April 20: The dismissal of liberal theologian the Rev. Charles Curran sparks a student strike at the Catholic University of America in Washington, D.C. President Johnson authorizes Boeing to proceed with construction of an SST prototype. Washington State Patrol swears in its first black trooper.

April 21: Right-wing coup in Greece deposes civilian government a month before new elections were expected to reinstall Socialist George Papandreou as prime minister. (King Constantine II fled on December 14. Repression and suspicion of CIA involvement in Greek fascism inspired the film *Z*.) Joseph Stalin's daughter, Svetlana Alliluyeva, moves to the U.S from her Swiss exile.

April 22: The United Auto Workers threaten to bolt the AFL-CIO in protest of the latter's conservative head, George Meany.

April 23: Free U stages light show "demonstration" at Hec Edmonson Pavilion. City Councilman Charley Carroll attends and likes what he sees.

April 24: Soviet Cosmonaut Vladimir Komarov dies on re-entry during the first test of the Soyuz spacecraft. The accident brings known Soviet space fatalities to four. Peter LeSourd and Camden Hall announce creation of "Choose an Effective City Council" (CHECC) to promote reform candidates.

April 28: Muhammad Ali is arrested for defying the draft after his claim for conscientious objector status is rejected and the World Boxing Association revokes his heavyweight championship. Ali is convicted on June 20 and sentenced to five years in prison. World's Fair opens in Montreal.

April 30: *Helix* sponsors first be-in at Volunteer Park. Eigerwand coffee house closes in the U District.

May: Chicago's *Seed* begins publication. *Realist* publishes "The Parts That Were Left Out of the Kennedy Book," a vicious parody of Manchester. National Mobe begins organizing "Vietnam Summer."

May 2: General Westmoreland asks for deployment of 600,000 troops in Vietnam. Lord Bertrand Russell opens "International Tribunal on War Crimes" in Stockholm to investigate U.S. actions in Vietnam. Armed Black Panthers "lobby" the California Assembly in Sacramento in opposition to a bill banning the carrying of unconcealed weapons.

May 4: Prodded by an ACLU law suit and by Charles M. Carroll, the Seattle City Council reverses its ban on light shows.

May 9: NASA taps Boeing to coordinate the stalled Apollo program. Pentagon reports that 146 Washingtonians had died in Vietnam since January 1, 1961.

May 12: Someone burns an American flag during a party at the Central Area Motivation Project, for which Floyd Turner is later arrested. Seventy-five antiwar protesters are blocked from participating in a public "Governor's Day" review of the UW ROTC at Husky Stadium, and several are attacked by war supporters. H. Rap Brown succeeds Stokely Carmichael as head of SNCC.

May 13: Dave Wyatt et al. hold antiwar protest at Pike Place Market. In New York, some 70,000 march down Fifth Avenue *for* the war. Young blacks riot in San Francisco's Playland by the Pacific while the Diggers host a "love feast" in Haight Ashbury.

May 15: U.S. Supreme Court accords juveniles the same rights as adults in criminal proceedings.

May 17: Fifteen U.S. Senate "doves" led by Idaho Democrat Frank Church outline their own peace strategy. Julian Bond speaks at Garfield High School.

May 18: UDM rallies 160 at the Seattle Public Safety Building to protest police harassment and present a list of demands to Chief Ramon, who reports that 183 juveniles have been arrested or detained for marijuana since the previous November—compared to a total of three such busts over the previous 40 years.

May 20: Black UW alumni conduct a quiet but nearly unanimous boycott of the alumni-varsity football game to protest discrimination by Husky coach Jim Owens.

May 21: Jim Garrison outlines his theory that five anti-Castro operatives, not Lee Harvey Oswald, actually killed President Kennedy to avenge his abandonment of Bay of Pigs invaders. Followers of Malcolm X riot in Chicago. Major battles in and near the Demilitarized Zone push U.S. war fatalities past 10,000.

May 24–25: Some 200 members of rival gangs "rumble" along Alki Beach before police intervene.

May 25: The Beatles form Apple Music (later Apple Corps Ltd.) and John Lennon takes delivery of his psychedelicized Rolls Royce. Some 1,000 UW students march in support of the U.S. war effort.

May 26: The Beatles release *Sergeant Pepper's Lonely Hearts Club Band* in England.

May 29: Puerto Ricans and white hippies clash in New York City's Tompkins Square Park. Pro- and antiwar students clash on the UW campus.

May 30: Breakaway "Republic of Biafra" triggers a civil war in Nigeria and the near starvation of the Ibo people.

June: Mel Lyman founds *Avatar* in Boston.

June 1: Darrell Bob Houston publishes first issue of *Avatar* in Olympia.

June 2: Blacks riot in Boston.

June 5: After months of saber-rattling and skirmishes, Israel preempts an Arab invasion with lightning air and armor attacks led by General Moshe Dayan and Itszak Rabin. Seattle City Council adopts a new loitering ordinance to replace one declared unconstitutional.

June 7: Michael Leavy and Stanley Banks report for induction with the intent of refusing to serve, but their plan goes awry when military police order them off the premises because they would not surrender their antiwar leaflets, all of which creates a very convoluted legal problem for the government. Under new state law giving budget authority to the mayor, Seattle hires its first budget director, George D. Smith. Dorothy Parker dies and leaves most of her estate to M. L. King Jr. and NAACP.

June 8: Israelis torpedo USS *Liberty,* which was monitoring "Six Day War" off the Sinai Peninsula. The Woodland Park Zoo's first elephant, "Wide Awake," dies at age 54.

June 9: Douglas Barnett and Dale Meador's Ensemble Theatre opens in Pioneer Square with a production of D. H. Lawrence's *The Fight for Barbara* (years later the Pioneer Square Theater took over the same space, in which it unleashed "Angry Housewives" and other hits).

June 12: U.S. Supreme Court overturns a Virginia statute banning interracial marriage. Blacks riot in Tampa.

June 13: President Johnson nominates Thurgood Marshall to the U.S. Supreme Court. California Assembly passes bill to legalize abortion and Governor Reagan promises to sign it into law. Blacks riot in Cincinnati.

June 14: The Renton Eagles ejects two black teachers attending an educational conference in the fraternal order's hall.

June 15: M. L. King Jr. launches targeted boycotts of Cleveland, Ohio, bakeries to promote minority hiring.

June 16: First Monterey Pops Festival makes stars of Jimi Hendrix, Janis Joplin, Quicksilver Messenger Service, Steve Miller Band, and a host of others.

June 17: People's Republic of China detonates its first H-Bomb. Blacks riot in Atlanta.

June 18: During interviews marking his 25th birthday, Paul McCartney admits that he has taken LSD.

June 20: Israeli delegates walk out of the UN General Session to protest Soviet President Kosygin's denunciation of Israeli "aggression" in the Six-Day War. Right-wing organizers announce that Alabama Gov. George Wallace will campaign for president in 1968 as the candidate of a new "American Independent Party."

June 23: Presidents Johnson and Kosygin hold a "mini-summit" in Glassboro, New Jersey. Johnson then flies to Los Angeles for a fund-raising dinner at the Century Plaza Hotel, where police battle 10,000 protesters. U.S. Senate censures Thomas Dodd of Connecticut.

June 25: Abbie Hoffman and SF Diggers crash the SDS national convention in Denton, Michigan.

June 27: *P-I* trumpets the appearance of the super-psychedelic STP with this headline: "Seattle Hippies Warned of New Killer Drug."

June 28: Israel formally annexes Jerusalem, which it had captured earlier in the month.

June 29: General Ky rescinds his bid for the South Vietnam presidency in favor of Nguyen Van Thieu. Mick Jagger and Keith Richards are convicted of narcotics possession in London. NASA names Robert H. Lawrence as its first black astronaut (he died in an airplane crash on December 8, 1967).

June 30: Last Exit on Brooklyn coffee house opens at 3930 Brooklyn NE.

July 2: Joint Chiefs of Staff tell President Johnson that 70,000 additional troops must be dispatched to Vietnam immediately to retain the "initiative." Congress passes a new draft law eliminating deferments for graduate students.

July 4: Britain's House of Lords votes to decriminalize homosexual acts between consenting adults.

July 7: "The Hippies" make the cover of *Time*. Defense Secretary McNamara tells the press, "We are winning the war slowly but steadily." Seattle police harass the Id Bookstore over its sandwich-board sign.

July 9: Joffrey Ballet arrives in Seattle to establish its new home, but later end up at Tacoma's Pacific Lutheran University.

July 11: Rudolf Nureyev, Dame Margot Fonteyn, and Richard Cornwell, assistant director of the Seattle Symphony, are busted for possession at a party in Haight Ashbury; they are quickly released and not charged.

July 12: A week of riots begins in Newark, New Jersey, ultimately leaving 26 dead, 1,500 wounded, and more than a 1,000 in jail. Poet Leroi Jones is arrested and beaten by police on July 14.

July 15: Boeing christens its first operational Navy hydrofoil gunship, the *Tucumcari*.

July 22: Carl Sandburg dies. The Woodland Park Zoo's new baby elephant is officially christened "Bamboo."

July 23: A week of riots begins in Detroit, ultimately leaving 40 dead, 2,000 wounded, and 5,000 homeless. (It required nearly 13,000 troops and National Guardsmen to restore "order.") Black Power Convention rallies 1,000 delegates in Newark who call for "black revolution."

July 26: H. "Rap" Brown is arrested for inciting a riot in Cambridge, Maryland, the previous day. President DeGaulle endorses Quebec independence while visiting Expo '67 in Montreal. In Havana,

Stokely Carmichael calls for a war of liberation in the U.S. In New York, looters trash Fifth Avenue.

July 28: The Bellevue Arts and Crafts Fair holds the first Northwest "Underground Film Festival." The Basic Needs Co. hosts a "feed-in" for hippies in the U District.

July 29: President Johnson appoints a special Commission on Civil Disorders chaired by Illinois Gov. Otto Kerner. Fist fights break out when the Spartacist League leads a demonstration at the Pike Place Market in "solidarity" with urban blacks.

July 30: Four die during riots in Milwaukee, Wisconsin.

August: Andy Stapp and members of Youth Against War and Fascism found American Serviceman's Union.

August 1: Riots and arson flare in Washington, D.C.

August 2: Governor Evans meets with black leaders in Seattle's Central Area.

August 3: President Johnson asks for a 10 percent surtax on the income tax to finance the war, which Congress enacts later in the year.

August 5: Supreme Court Justice William O. Douglas and wife Cathleen lead a "camp-out" in the Glacier Peak Wilderness to protest a proposed open pit mine.

August 6: Demolition of the Orpheum Theater begins.

August 9: In the first defection by a Northwest Democrat from President Johnson, Congressman Brock Adams formally declares his opposition to further escalation in Vietnam.

August 14: B'nai B'rith accuses SNCC of anti-Semitism for its "anti-Zionist" rhetoric. Observers report intensifying perse-

cution of Soviet Jews. President Johnson loosens limits on U.S. bombing missions over North Vietnam. Governor Evans and Mayor Braman promise quick action on Central Area "grass roots" proposals.

August 15: M. L. King Jr. denounces war in Vietnam at SCLC convention.

August 17: Stokely Carmichael calls for "total revolution."

August 20: For the first time since the advent of state prohibition laws in 1916, it becomes legal to sell and serve alcohol on a Sunday in Washington State—but you can't buy meat!

August 24: Abbie Hoffman and Jerry Rubin throw 300 one-dollar bills from the gallery of the New York Stock Exchange, triggering a near riot on the floor. The Norman Bel Geddes–designed *Kalakala* ferry is sold to a cannery which tows it north to Alaska.

August 25: The Beatles are introduced to the Maharishi Mahesh Yogi, known as the "Giggling Guru," at a lecture in Bangor, Wales. A former aide murders American Nazi Führer George Lincoln Rockwell outside an Arlington, Virginia, laundromat. Mayor Braman opposes design of R.H. Thomson–520 interchange in the Arboretum as too big and complex.

August 27: The Beatles' impresario Brian Epstein dies of an overdose of barbiturates.

August 28: Local SNCC and other activists endorse retention of Garfield High School Principal Frank Hanawalt, whose removal was urged by the Central Area Committee for Peace and Improvement (CAPI) as part of a program for school reform.

August 30: U.S. Senate confirms Thurgood Marshall for the Supreme Court.

September 1: First *P-I* "Seattle Sound" index of local album sales rates Sgt. Pepper number one.

September 2: Be-in at Volunteer Park collects gifts for migrant workers.

September 3: After a succession of military regimes, Nguyen Van Thieu is "elected" president of South Vietnam. Former dictator Air Force vice marshal Nguyen Cao Ky becomes vice president.

September 4: Michigan Gov. George Romney, a leading contender for the Republican nomination for president and a critic of the Vietnam war, invites media attacks by saying, "I just had the greatest brainwashing that anyone can get when you go over to Vietnam."

September 8: Defense Secretary McNamara orders construction of an "electronic fence" across South Vietnam to cut infiltration and supply routes from the north. Metro urges addition of rapid rail transit to planned third Lake Washington floating bridge.

September 9: UW President Odegaard publicly rejects a citizen's plea that he expel hippies from campus as "unthinkable."

Mid-September: U.S. radicals meet with North Vietnamese and NLF leaders at Bratislava, Czechoslovakia, or as Raymond Mungo later put it, "I slept with the Vietcong." *Helix* is evicted from its office on Roosevelt Way.

September 10: Lynda Bird Johnson announces engagement to Marine Capt. and future Virginia Senator Charles Robb.

September 15: After months of rumors and Sino-Soviet clashes, observers confirm presence of Soviet troops in ostensibly independent Outer Mongolia. U.S. Sen. Warren Magnuson publicly criticizes President Johnson's request for tax increase to finance the Vietnam War. San Francisco Health Director Ellis D. Sox (his real name!) warns that hippies might spread hepatitis and other diseases through jobs and sex.

September 17: Episcopal Church opens national general convention in Seattle and seats the controversial Bishop Pike, but without a vote. While in Seattle, Bishop Pike demands a heresy trial (later recanted) and announces that he has "talked" to his dead son.

September 18: Defense Secretary McNamara proposes development of an antimissile defense against Chinese attack.

September 20: Women March for Peace demonstrators tussle with police in front of the White House. U.S. Senate approves President Johnson's budgets for Model Cities and low-income housing.

September 23: National convention of Americans for Democratic Action adopts a resolution opposing the war and President Johnson's reelection (ADA president Allard Lowenstein later led the 1968 "Dump Johnson" drive).

September 26: Forward Thrust unveils initial plan for 12 capital improvement programs, including rail transit and a domed stadium, totaling $815 million in local bonds.

September 29: Shelby Scates reports on growing boycott by black athletes targeting UW football coach Jim Owens. Private investors offer to build domed stadium in Kent, but officials favor options at Seattle Center or Pioneer Square. British Columbia authorities shut down the underground newspaper *Georgia Straight* for "gross misconduct" (it resumes publication on October 6).

October 1: Gallup poll reports that voters prefer Robert Kennedy over President Johnson by 51 to 39 percent.

October 2: Thurgood Marshall is sworn in as the first black justice to sit on the U.S. Supreme Court. Mayor Braman presents a $49 million city budget.

October 6: Haight Ashbury social agencies stage a wake marking the "Death of the Hippie."

October 8: Ernesto "Che" Guevara is captured in Bolivia and summarily executed, although his death is not confirmed for several weeks.

October 15: *Helix* moves into new offices at 3128 Harvard E. Chas. Talbot leads ACLU challenges to new state motorcycle helmet law.

October 16: Joan Baez is arrested along with 124 protesters during sit-in at the Oakland induction center on the first day of "Stop the Draft Week." Police go berserk the next day, "Bloody Tuesday," and violence continues until Friday, which leads to indictments against the "Oakland 7."

October 17: Soviet probe makes a soft landing on the surface of Venus. FDA Administrator Dr. James L. Goddard declares that he doesn't think marijuana is any more dangerous than alcohol. I report for induction but the Army declines my services.

October 18: The first issue of *Rolling Stone* hits the streets in San Francisco. Demonstrators at the University of Wisconsin block campus recruiting by Dow Chemical. American League offers Seattle a baseball franchise if it can build a suitable stadium.

October 20: Marshall Bloom, Ray Mungo, and other underground journalists meet in Washington, D.C., and begin planning the "Liberation News Service." The antiwar movement makes the cover of *Time*. Seattle police announce addition of Mace to officers' arsenal. A Meridian, Mississippi, federal jury convicts seven in the 1964 murder of three civil rights workers. U.S. Court of Appeals in San Francisco upholds conviction of Russel Wills for "willful refusal to possess" his draft card, which he had burned in Seattle.

October 21: Abbie Hoffman and Jerry Rubin lead 30,000 in an "Exorcism of the Pentagon"; 443 are arrested and 47 are injured.

October 23: Open Door Clinic opens at 3800 12th NE.

October 25: UW *Daily* estimates that 20 percent of student body smokes grass "regularly" and advocates decriminalization of possession. In New York, a Harvard medical student is found innocent by reason of insanity for stabbing his mother to death while he was high on LSD.

October 26: Ohio police use tear gas and fire hoses to disperse 100 Oberlin protesters who held a Navy recruiter hostage in his car for four hours.

October 27: The Rev. Phillip Berrigan and two other clerics pour blood over draft records in Baltimore, Maryland. A Fort Lewis court martial sentences Michael Bratcher to four years of hard labor after he pleads guilty to disobeying orders during his campaign for conscientious objector status. Seattle Public Schools announce that Jack Delay, who addressed a West Seattle High School health class on October 24, would not be invited back.

October 28: South Vietnamese police crack down on Buddhist protesters waiting for a visit by Vice President Humphrey. Huey Newton is arrested for murder following an Oakland shoot-out in which a policeman died. Architect Ibsen Nelsen and the Seattle Chapter of AIA propose creation of a 52-acre Denny Regrade park bounded by Denny and Lenora streets and Second and Fifth avenues.

October 29: Local meat cutters end 29-day strike and approve sale of meat after 6 p.m., Mondays through Saturdays.

October 30: M. L. King Jr. is jailed in Birmingham on charges stemming from 1963 demonstrations. Soviet unmanned probes Cosmos 186 and 188 dock in orbit.

October 31: Community opponents of the proposed Yesler-Atlantic Urban Renewal Project fail to qualify a referendum for the city ballot. Ronald Reagan denies columnist Drew Pearson's allegation that a "homosexual ring" is operating out of the California governor's office.

November 1: Protesters challenge military and corporate recruiters on campuses in California, Iowa, Michigan, New York, and Oregon. Two men are charged in New York City for raping and killing a "hippie" couple during an LSD "orgy." Assistant professor of anthropology LaMont "Monty" West Jr. shocks ASUW audience by declaring that Jesus Christ was a "turned-on fellow" but a "masochist."

November 3: USSR and fraternal peoples hail the 50th anniversary of the glorious Bolshevik Revolution. Defense Secretary McNamara announces that the Soviets have been testing a "Fractional Orbital Bombardment System" which drops warheads from orbit rather than launching them ballistically. The Navy asks McNamara to cancel its version of the trouble-plagued TFX.

November 7: Seattle voters elect three CHECC (Choose an Effective City Coun-

cil) reformers to the Seattle City Council–Phyllis Lamphere and Tim Hill, along with State Representative Sam Smith, the first black to serve. County voters approve a slate of freeholders to write a new charter. All in all, it is the beginning of the end for the municipal Old Guard. Black candidates win election as mayors in Cleveland, Ohio (Carl Stokes), and Gary, Indiana (Richard Hatcher), and Kevin White is elected mayor of Boston on a pro-busing platform. Elsewhere, Selective Service director General Lewis Hershey threatens to revoke deferments of any students arrested in antiwar demonstrations. President Johnson signs the law creating the Corporation for Public Broadcasting.

November 8: Five hundred UW students protest against Dow Chemical recruiters.

November 9: U.S. lunar program gets back on track as NASA launches first Apollo capsule into space atop Saturn V, and lands Surveyor 6 on the moon.

November 12: The pastor of a Williamsburg, Virginia, Episcopal Church challenges a member of his congregation—President Johnson—to explain why the U.S. is in an "undeclared war" in Vietnam.

November 14: Five thousand demonstrators battle police while "welcoming" Secretary of State Dean Rusk to New York City.

November 15: After 190 missions, the X-15 rocket plane program suffers its first and only fatal crash. Senators Jackson and Magnuson announce that Fort Lawton is being studied as a possible antiballistic missile launching site.

November 16: Seattle is named as one of 63 "Model Cities" to qualify for new federal urban development and social service funds.

November 20: U.S. population tops 200 million. Bergen, Norway, joins Kobe, Japan, as a sister city of Seattle.

November 21: President Johnson signs the Air Quality Act of 1967. *Ramparts* editor Robert Scheer blasts U.S. "arrogance" during UW speech, and predicts rise of both the Far Left and Far Right as "Americans seek alternatives" to the status quo.

November 22: UN Security Council adopts Resolution 242 calling for Israeli withdrawal from "occupied territories." General Westmoreland declares that U.S. victory in a 20 day battle to take a hill (Dak To) in the Central Highlands signals "the beginning of a great defeat for the enemy." Blacks riot on Chicago's North Side. Great Britain devalues the pound, triggering an international "gold rush" and undermining the dollar.

November 23: Allen Ginsberg and several hundred friends "celebrate the end of the war" in a Greenwich Village demonstration.

November 27: Without any advance warning of a shake-up, President Johnson nominates Robert McNamara to head the World Bank. UW names Frank Byrdwell Jr. as its first "minority student counselor."

November 30: Minnesota Senator Eugene McCarthy announces he will run for president and "against the war." The Interstate Commerce Commission approves the long-sought merger of the Great Northern and Northern Pacific railroads, which ultimately creates the Burlington Northern line. The UW refuses to oust Professor Monty West over his religious opinions despite pressure from conservative clergy. Seattle Planning Commission approves construction of residential high-rise buildings in ten areas, which triggers a long battle with neighborhoods seeking to retain existing low densities.

December: Radical film-makers organize "Newsreel" in New York City.

December 3: Dr. Christian Bernard performs the first successful heart transplant in Capetown, South Africa (however, the patient dies 17 days later). Vietcong launch mortar and rocket attack against U.S. Army Headquarters at Long Ninh. Physicist Edward Teller stalks out of a TV interview at the UW with Don McGaffin.

December 5: Antiwar demonstration in New York City leads to the arrest of Allen Ginsberg and Dr. Spock, among 260 others. Congressional conferees approve $4 billion antipoverty budget for the next two years. First state survey of school racial mix reveals that nine Seattle schools have black majorities, although blacks make up only 10 percent of the total enrollment.

December 9: Lynda Bird Johnson weds Charles Robb in the White House. *P-I* editorializes against ABM base at Fort Lawton.

December 10: The first "commercial" atomic bomb is detonated under the New Mexico desert as part of an experiment in natural gas recovery.

December 11: The first Concorde SST rolls out at Toulouse, France. Illinois Sen. Charles Percy is briefly trapped by Vietcong fire during inspection tour. Official count puts South Vietnamese civilian casualties over 100,000 mark.

December 13: After a failed attempt to overthrow Greece's military junta, King Constantine flees the country. A self-described hit man attempts to extort $7,000 from Seattle restaurateur Ivar Haglund.

December 14: Army physician Captain Howard Levy is imprisoned for refusing to teach Special Forces personnel "how to kill." Alaska Sen. Ernest Gruening speaks at a Seattle rally against the war.

December 15: Floyd Turner is convicted of flag desecration in Superior Court (Turner appealed to the State Supreme Court, which reversed his conviction on September 3, 1970).

December 17: Scheduled ferry service between Seattle and Alaska resumes after a 13-year hiatus. Some 150 residents of Chicago's South Side ghetto crash an AMA conference on health care for the poor.

December 18: In a radio interview, retired Marine Corps Commandant Gen. David Shoup blasts the contention that Vietnam War entails vital U.S. interests as "pure, unadulterated poppycock"; he advocates negotiated withdrawal since the only way to win is to "commit genocide on that poor little country."

December 19: During a TV interview, President Johnson for the first time opens the door to NLF participation in peace talks. Bob Hope begins his first holiday show tour of Vietnam. Prodded by a long *P-I* investigation of jukebox and pinball extortion and tax evasion, the Seattle City Council votes not to renew the license of the city's largest operator. Mayor Braman names CAMP director Walter Hundley to head up Seattle's Model Cities Program.

December 31: U.S. forces in Vietnam now number 475,000. Bombing is extended to all of North Vietnam with few restrictions. Major riots occur in 75 U.S. cities during the year, killing 83 and injuring hundreds. Suicides in Seattle set a new record at 184 deaths, and homicides number 52, an increase of 20 over 1966 amid a generally rising crime rate. Also in 1967: SDS members at the UW found Draft Resistance–Seattle.

Zeitgeist: Israeli chemists synthesize tetrahydrocannabinol ("THC"), the active ingredient in marijuana. Major songs include The Doors' "Light My Fire," Jefferson Airplane's "Somebody to Love," Jimi Hendrix's "Purple Haze" (from the album, "Are You Experienced?"), and Scott McKenzie's "San Francisco (Be Sure to Wear Flowers in Your Hair)." The Who and Pink Floyd tour America, and Ginger Baker, Jack Bruce, and Eric Clapton organize Cream. Arthur Penn's *Bonnie and Clyde,* Mike Nichols' *The Graduate* (which makes stars of Simon & Garfunkel and Dustin Hoffman), Norman Jewison's *In the Heat of the Night,* and Phillippe de Broca's *King of Hearts* are released. The Green Bay Packers defeat the Kansas City Chiefs in the first Superbowl. Amana markets the first "radar range" microwave oven. The Farm Index reports that sales of cigarette (and joint) rolling paper reached 11.7 billion sheets, up from 10.3 billion in 1966. Seattle police report that juvenile drug busts in 1967 totaled 298, up from 52 in 1966; drinking busts dropped 20 percent, however. Adult drug busts tripled from 122 to 359 in the same period. More than 9,000 U.S. troops die in combat in Vietnam.

1968

January 1: Abbie Hoffman, Jerry Rubin, Paul Krassner, Dick Gregory, et al. announce creation of the Yippies (Youth International Party) and their plan to stage a "Festival of Life" during the Democratic National Convention in Chicago the following August.

January 3: UW announces that users of illegal drugs could be expelled.

January 5: Dr. Spock, William Sloan Coffin, and three others are indicted in Boston for counseling draft resisters. U.S. expresses "regret" for sinking Soviet ships while bombing Haiphong. Great Britain unveils new vertical take-off-and-landing (VTOL) fighter, the Harrier. Seattle School Superintendent Forbes Bottomly urges "leveling" with students about realities and myths of drug abuse.

January 7: First-class postage rises by a penny to seven cents. Open Door Clinic reports rise of "peace pill" (PCP) complications.

January 9: Sweden grants four AWOL U.S. sailors political asylum. First ad for a BMW ($2,658 FOB) appears in the *P-I*.

January 10: H. Rap Brown takes brief sanctuary in Cuban UN office to avoid arrest in New York. UW academic giants George Taylor and Giovanni Costigan cross swords over the war before an audience of 1,500.

January 11: Cambodia's Prince Sihanouk severs diplomatic ties with U.S. to protest "hot pursuit" of Vietcong into his territory. Retired Marine Gen. David Shoup announces that other former military officers have joined a new 1,600-member group opposing the war.

January 12: A Pennsylvania health official reports that six students went blind while staring at the sun under the influence of LSD; a week later an embarrassed Gov. Shafer reveals that it was all a hoax.

January 15: Jeannette Rankin, 87 years old and the first woman elected to Congress, leads 5,000 protesters organized by the YMCA, National Council of Jewish Women, and other mainstream groups in a march against the war in Washington, D.C.

January 17: President Johnson outlines $186 billion federal budget in his State of the Union address.

January 18: Police attack a crowd of 600 protesting Dean Rusk's appearance at San Francisco's Fairmont Hotel. Eartha Kitt denounces the war during a White House reception hosted by Lady Bird Johnson.

January 19: Pentagon announces that it will draft 72,000 more men in 1968 than the 230,000 drafted in 1967. President Johnson names Clark Clifford as his new Defense Secretary; he is confirmed January 30.

January 20: White House staff discover that a Mark Tobey painting was hung upside-down in the hall outside the Oval Office. Port of Seattle launches largest expansion in its history, at $87 million, to build container-handling facility.

January 21: A B-52 carrying H-bombs crashes in Greenland.

January 22: Dan Rowan and Dick Martin's "Laugh-In" turns the Sixties into schtick with the show's debut. The show dies May 14, 1973.

January 23: North Korean forces seize U.S. spy ship *Pueblo*. Mia Farrow, recently estranged from Frank Sinatra, departs U.S. for India to commune with Maharishi Mahesh Yogi.

January 25: Alexander Dubcek ascends to power in Czechoslovakia and launches the "Prague Spring" of liberalization.

January 26: Vietcong launch siege of Marine base at Khesanh.

January 29: Fidel Castro purges leadership of Cuban Communist Party. Vietcong shell Da Nang. CAPI activists march on Seattle City Hall demanding jobs for blacks.

January 31: Vietcong launches simultaneous attacks in Saigon and other South Vietnamese cities on the eve of the Tet lunar New Year holidays. Soon after, approval of Johnson's management of the war sinks to 26 percent in the polls. A Seattle City Council hearing concludes that there are no legal means to curb hippies in the U District. Frank Fidler succeeds Frank Hanawalt as principal of Garfield High as the latter takes over integration planning for the district.

February: San Francisco *Oracle* ceases publication.

February 1: The Beach Boys endorse Maharishi Mahesh's "Spiritual Regeneration Movement."

February 6: North Vietnamese deploy tanks for the first time in a successful assault on a Green Berets camp near Khesanh.

February 8: Police kill three and wound 33 as black students protest at a segregated bowling alley in Orangeburg, South Carolina. George Wallace formally announces his third-party bid for the presidency; a week later he taps former Georgia Gov. Marvin Griffin as his "interim" running-mate.

February 12: Jimi Hendrix makes his hometown superstar debut in a concert in the Arena.

February 13: King County voters leap part of the way with Forward Thrust, approving $334 million in bonds for the Kingdome, Youth Services Center, arterial improvements, new parks and recreation centers, the Seattle Neighborhood Improvement Program, Seattle fire stations, and Seattle sewer improvements. Bonds for rapid transit, community centers, county storm drainage system, and a Seattle maintenance facility garner majorities but fail to meet the 60 percent approval required for validation. Jim Ellis vows to resubmit the rapid transit program, which is the key to Forward Thrust's growth management strategy. National building trades unions meeting in Florida pledge to increase recruitment of blacks.

February 16: The mother of PFC Lewis Albanese accepts his posthumous Congressional Medal of Honor for giving his life while protecting comrades during a Vietnamese firefight on January 27. North Vietnam releases three captured U.S. pilots as peace gesture.

February 17: At an Oakland rally attended by 5,500 to mark Huey Newton's birthday, SNCC leader Stokely Carmichael accepts appointment as an officer of the Black Panther Party.

February 19: Presbyterian minister the Rev. Anthony Nugent rejects his clerical exemption and turns in his draft card to the Seattle Draft Board.

February 22: FAA announces that development of the SST will be delayed one year to save funds and allow Boeing to solve engineering problems. U.S. Sen. William Fulbright and others attack Administration "deceit" in portrayal of the Gulf of Tonkin incident. All four Beatles arrive at Maharishi Mahesh's ashram in India. Bobo the gorilla, a resident of the Woodland Park Zoo since 1953, dies at the age of 17; despite the best efforts of his companion Fifi, he left no heirs.

February 23: Marines recapture Hué. Pentagon announces draft goal of 48,000 in April.

February 25: Pro- and anti-immigrant demonstrators clash in London as Parliament debates restricting the historical right of Commonwealth citizens to move to Britain freely. San Francisco police battle crowds of hippies in the Haight. The U.S. Census Bureau confirms the "birth dearth" as new births dropped to an historic low of 17.9 per 1,000, or 3.5 million total, in 1967.

February 26: U.S. Command in Vietnam tightens censorship of press. North Vietnamese troops attack Laos. President Johnson proposes creation of Urban Mass Transit Administration (UMTA).

February 27: Having returned from a personal inspection tour, Walter Cronkite devotes his entire CBS evening newscast to the war, ending with a plea for negotiations and withdrawal. Seattle NAACP advocates closure of Horace Mann, Washington, and Garfield schools to spur integration in remaining schools.

February 28: Michigan Gov. George Romney withdraws from the race for the Republican nomination for president. Robert McNamara formally steps down as Secretary of Defense and is succeeded by Clark Clifford.

February 29: The summary report of the "Kerner Commission" on Civil Disorders faults excessive police force in ghettos. The full report is released on March 2.

March 1: John W. Garner steps down as HEW Secretary. Seven hundred UW students attend Vietnam teach-in organized by Cal Wilson.

March 4: Jeff Shero begins publishing *Rat* in New York City.

March 6: Army reports that pot smoking among combat troops in Vietnam doubled in 1967. Seattle City Council scales back R. H. Thomson Expressway from eight to six lanes.

March 8: Bill Graham opens the Fillmore East in New York City. Seattle police nab nine in U District marijuana sweep.

March 10: UW athletic director Jim Owens huddles with disgruntled black athletes led by Dave DuPree.

March 11: Federal Open Housing bill wins final passage. Polish students battle police in Warsaw. Workers begin demolition of historic Seattle Armory on Western Avenue.

March 12: Eugene McCarthy stuns President Johnson by garnering 42 percent of the vote in the New Hampshire primary.

March 13: Clouds of nerve gas drift outside the Army's Dugway Proving Grounds in Utah and poison 6,400 sheep in nearby Skull Valley.

March 16: Robert Kennedy announces candidacy for president. It would not be known for a year that on this same day Army troops commanded by Lt. William Calley were slaughtering civilians in the village of My Lai.

March 17: Protesters storm U.S. Embassy in London. U.S. and European central banks adopt two-tiered gold pricing to cool overheated markets as the British pound and the dollar continue to sink.

March 22: General Westmoreland is kicked upstairs as Army Chief of Staff; Gen. Creighton Abrams later takes over command of Vietnam forces. Yippie takeover of New York's Grand Central Station degenerates into a police riot. Adam

Clayton Powell returns to Harlem, ending his 18-month exile in the Bahamas to avoid imprisonment for contempt of court; he is "paroled" upon his return.

March 24: ACLU holds a "Pot Test" benefit at Eagles to raise funds for a challenge of state marijuana laws.

March 25: Registration begins for the first classes of the ASUW-sponsored Experimental College.

March 26: Enthusiastic crowds greet Robert Kennedy as he campaigns in Seattle. Senate Majority Leader Mike Mansfield openly opposes deployment of any additional U.S. troops to Vietnam.

March 27: Cosmonaut Yuri Gagarin, first man to orbit the earth, dies in a plane crash in the Soviet Union.

March 28: The Associated Press reports that U.S. and North Vietnamese officials have been conducting secret first face-to-face meetings for several weeks. A Memphis civil rights march led by M. L. King Jr. in sympathy with striking garbage workers degenerates into a riot. Spanish university students march to demand civil liberties from Generalissimo Francisco Franco's government.

March 29: UW Black Student Union members Aaron Dixon and Larry Gossett, local SNCC head Carl Miller, and high school student Trolice Flavors are arrested during a sit-in at Franklin High School.

March 31: President Johnson announces that he will not seek reelection. Australia announces that it will not increase its Vietnam deployment beyond the 9,000 troops already there. M. L. King Jr. warns that unless there is more aid for the poor and inner cities, new rioting could precipitate a "right-wing coup."

April 1: SNCC merges with the Black Panther Party during the Western Regional Black Youth Conference in San Francisco.

April 2: Eugene McCarthy and Richard Nixon sweep Wisconsin primaries.

April 3: Following a receptive communique from Hanoi, President Johnson announces that he will seek "direct contact" with North Vietnam.

April 4: James Earl Ray assassinates M. L. King Jr. in Memphis.

April 5: Riots shatter scores of cities: eight die in Chicago, four in Washington, D.C., and one each in Detroit, New York, Minneapolis, and Tallahassee. In Seattle, two arson fires are set and black teens pelt cars and buses with rocks at 22nd E. and E. Madison. (Ralph Abernathy is later named to succeed M. L. King Jr. as head of the Southern Christian Leadership Conference.) U.S. and South Vietnamese troops break 76-day siege of Marine base at Khesanh.

April 6: Riots spread and the death toll rises to 23. Oakland police raid Black Panthers' headquarters, killing Bobby Hutton and wounding three others, including Eldridge Cleaver.

April 7: Nine thousand mourners fill Memorial Stadium for a Seattle tribute to M. L. King Jr.

April 8: President Johnson and other dignitaries attend M. L. King Jr.'s funeral in Atlanta. Deaths from rioting rise to 33.

April 11: President Johnson signs federal open housing law. Thom Gunn is elected ASUW president.

April 12: A federal geologist warns that Mount St. Helens could erupt at any time.

April 13–14: During a visit in Seattle, Black Panther Party chair Bobby Seale appoints Aaron Dixon head of the party's new Seattle chapter.

April 14: Four thousand student protesters battle police in West Berlin.

April 17: National phone strike begins. A third of the Duke University student body strikes to protest discrimination in the hiring of nonacademic staff. The UW *Daily* exposes an earlier report that a Vietcong "recruiter" would visit campus as a hoax.

April 19: Seattle City Council approves a strong open housing ordinance with an emergency clause to take immediate effect. SDS and Draft Resistance launch a program of demonstrations to mark "Days of Resistance" through April 27.

April 20: Pierre Trudeau succeeds Lester Pearson as Prime Minister of Canada. Diane Prima reads in Seattle. Todd Gitlin addresses a two-day conference of "Northwest SDS—Draft Resistance" at the UW.

April 23: After administration rebuffs of student protests against Columbia University's expansion into the mostly black Morningside Park neighborhood, Mark Rudd leads a campus rebellion, seizing several buildings and one dean. Police storm in eight days later. Eugene McCarthy wins the Pennsylvania primary.

April 24: Some 80 Olympic Community College students stage sit-in at the Bremerton campus to protest the expulsion of student body president Frosty Adkins; they were arrested the next day after an all-night vigil.

April 25: Arthur Goldberg resigns as U.S. Ambassador to the UN. Chicago police raid YIP meeting and arrest 20.

April 26: National student strike against the war enlists as many as one million high school and college students. Some 2,000 boycott classes at the UW and 600-plus attend a rally in front of the Administration Building. (Larry Baker organized the event and delivered a list of seven demands to President Odegaard addressing minority recruitment and student rights.)

April 27: Sixty thousand rally against the war in New York's Central Park as part of a day of national demonstrations (a separate group clashes with police in Greenwich Village). Chicago police attack some 3,000 peace marchers. In Seattle, 2,000 citizens march peacefully against the war from the King County Court House to Seattle Center. Vice President Humphrey promises "the politics of joy" as he formally enters the presidential race.

April 28: Nearly 5,000 spectators flock to Larry Van Over's farm in Duvall to see (hear?) a piano drop from a helicopter.

April 29: *Hair* opens on Broadway. Washington State University archeologists announce the discovery of the 8,000-year-old "Marmes Man," the oldest human remains yet discovered in North America. T. A. Wilson succeeds 23-year Boeing president William Allen, who takes over as chairman of the board.

May 1: Police attack 700 occupiers and clear Columbia University buildings, triggering a full student strike. UW President Odegaard rejects "April Days" demands. King Olav V of Norway visits Seattle.

May 2: Clashes between French rightwingers and "Gauchistes" at the University of Nanterre quickly explode into a fullscale rebellion. The following day, University of Paris students led by Daniel Cohn-Bendit barricade the Sorbonne, and within a week 10 million French are out on a sympathy strike. U.S. phone workers' strike ends.

May 2–17: National Poor People's March, originally planned by M. L. King Jr., gathers in Washington, D.C., and demonstrators erect a "Resurrection City" near the Lincoln Memorial.

May 2: Black students occupy a building at Northwestern University to protest housing discrimination on the Evanston, Illinois, campus.

May 4: Betty Friedan leads a "drink-in" at the Men's Bar in New York's Biltmore Hotel but finds it closed.

May 6: E. J. Brisker, vice president of the UW BSU, presents five demands to improve recruitment and treatment of minority students.

May 7: Ten thousand students capture the heart of Paris and fly the red flag from the Arc de Triomphe. Soviets begin taking a hard line on Czech reforms when officials propose to reopen inquiry into the 1948 "suicide" of Prime Minister Masaryk. Robert Kennedy wins his first primary in Indiana. Alabama Gov. Lurleen Wallace (who succeeded husband George in 1964) dies.

May 10: Vietcong launch attacks against Saigon. Preliminary peace talks open in Paris.

May 13: In response to BSU demands, the UW agrees to intensify minority student recruiting.

May 14: Kennedy and Nixon win Nebraska primaries. Seattle's College Club welcomes its first black member.

May 15: German students clash with police in protests over new "emergency laws" curtailing public demonstrations. French Communist-led unions begin series of wildcat strikes in support of Gauchistes.

May 17: South Vietnamese premier Nguyen Van Loc resigns. SDS occupies a Morningside Heights tenement scheduled to be razed for a new Columbia University gym. UW BSU leader E. J. Brisker demands $50,000 in additional spending for minority programs. Father Daniel Berrigan, SJ, his brother, Father Philip Berrigan, and seven other Catholic protesters destroy draft records at Catonsville, Maryland.

May 18: Blacks riot in Salisbury, Maryland. Supporters of Seattle mystic Keith Rhinehart, founder of the Aquarian Foundation, protest his imprisonment on a 1965 conviction for sodomy.

May 20: Trial of Dr. Spock and three co-defendants for aiding draft evaders begins. UW BSU stages a four-hour sit-in at the Administration Building resulting in a UW commitment to double black enrollment, increase financial aid, and introduce Black Studies courses. Students begin a sit-in at San Francisco State College over the ROTC; a sit-in at the University of Hawaii began the day before over the dismissal of a popular professor (and ended May 30.)

May 21: French strikes idle 7 million. U.S. national debt reaches $1.6 trillion, or $8,000 per American then living.

May 22: Second police raid at Columbia University raises toll to 998 arrested and 200 injured. U.S. Marshals drag draft resister Robert Talmonson from his "sanctuary" in a Boston church. H. Rap Brown is sentenced to five years in prison on a federal firearms offense.

May 23: UW Faculty Senate endorses development of Black Studies curriculum. CAMP worker Kenno Carlos is arrested for flag desecration simply for explaining to high school students why some militants advocate flag burning (the charges are dismissed the following day).

May 24: Riots answer French President DeGaulle's attempts to suppress Parisian strikers and his call for a "mandate" in a national referendum.

May 26: Popular *P-I* columnist Douglass Welch ("The Squirrel Cage") dies at age 61 following surgery.

May 27: USS *Scorpion,* a nuclear-powered attack submarine, disappears with 99 crewmen in the Atlantic. U.S. Supreme Court upholds criminality of burning a draft card (only Justice Douglas dissented). Campaigning in Olympia, Republican presidential candidate Richard Nixon says Governor Evans is "definitely being considered" as his running mate.

May 28: Eugene McCarthy defeats Robert Kennedy in Oregon primary while Richard Nixon carries 71 percent of GOP vote.

May 29: Remnants of the Poor People's March demonstrate at the U.S. Supreme Court.

May 30: President DeGaulle dissolves the French Parliament, threatens to use troops in Paris, and refuses to resign. Muhammad Ali speaks at UW.

May 31: McCarthy and Kennedy debate on national television; later polling gives McCarthy the nod.

June 1: Sen. Walter Mondale and Pierre Salinger campaign respectively for Hubert Humphrey and Robert Kennedy at King County Democratic Convention, which repudiates Johnson's foreign policy. CBS airs the first episode of the British-made "The Prisoner," starring former "Secret Agent Man" Patrick McGoohan as a Kafkaesque captive on a dystopic isle (the series ended on September 11, 1969). Helen Keller dies at age 87.

June 3: Vietcong launch "Battle of Saigon." Valeria Solanis, founder and sole member of SCUM (Society to Cut Up Men), shoots and seriously wounds Andy Warhol, who had cast her in one of his films.

June 4: Sirhan Sirhan shoots Robert Kennedy as the senator celebrates a narrow victory in the California primary; Kennedy dies the following day. Saboteurs topple utility towers outside Oakland.

June 5: In the wake of Robert Kennedy's death, President Johnson forms Commission on the Causes and Prevention of Violence and dispatches Secret Service agents to guard all major candidates for president and vice president.

June 6: Dick Gregory, imprisoned in Olympia for participating in a Nisqually fish-in, begins a hunger strike.

June 8: James Earl Ray is captured in London.

June 11: Eldridge Cleaver is released after spending two months in an Oakland jail without a hearing on a parole violation.

June 13: Jerry Rubin is busted for pot in Greenwich Village. Allied Arts sponsors festival of underground films. Larry Gosset, Aaron Dixon, and Carl Miller are convicted of unlawful assembly in March 29 sit-in at Franklin High School.

June 14: Dr. Spock and co-defendants are convicted of violating federal law by counseling draft evaders. SDS National Convention in East Lansing, Michigan, endorses "small-c" communism. To the disappointment of many, the asteroid Icarus fails to hit the earth.

June 16: French police take control of the Sorbonne.

June 17: U.S. Supreme Court rules all forms of housing discrimination to be unconstitutional. KOL-FM inaugurates its "underground" format with host Robin Sherwood.

June 18: McCarthy wins plurality in New York primary.

June 19: Coretta Scott King addresses 40,000 Poor People's Campaign marchers at the Lincoln Memorial.

June 22: Hubert Humphrey tries to distance himself from President Johnson by advocating immediate cease-fire in Vietnam. State Republican Convention endorses income tax reform. Seven Spokane-based "Minutemen" are convicted of conspiring to rob Seattle banks to finance right-wing causes.

June 23: French voters give Gaullists a major victory, repudiating leftist students. Washington, D.C., police use tear gas to evict Poor People's Campaign marchers from their camp.

June 26: U.S. Marines announce that they will abandon Khesanh base as "too costly." U.S. returns Iwo Jima to Japan.

June 28: President Johnson signs bill imposing 10 percent surtax on income tax. Demonstrators and police clash in running street battles in Berkeley prompted by an attempt to "liberate" Telegraph Avenue in support of French students.

June 30: Soviet fighters force a U.S. troop transport carrying 266 bound for Vietnam to land in the Kurile Islands (they are released two days later following a U.S. apology for violating Soviet airspace). Lockheed's C-5 prototype finally gets into the air. National Guard is called into suppress Berkeley demonstrations led by the Young Socialist Alliance. Gaullists sweep French parliament elections.

July 1: U.S. combat deaths in Vietnam reach 9,557 for the first six months of 1968, more than died during all of 1967. Judge James Dore sentences Aaron Dixon, Larry Gossett, and Carl Miller to six months in jail for unlawful assembly during March's sit-in at Franklin High School, triggering riots in the Central Area. Number of blacks serving in the Seattle Fire Department rises to 16, up from one (future Chief Claude Harris) a year earlier.

July 2: Nelson Rockefeller campaigns in Seattle.

July 4: Dick Gregory is hospitalized on the 39th day of his hunger strike in an Olympia jail.

July 6: National Urban League director Whitney Young Jr. endorses "black power."

July 8: Seattle School District announces plan to convert Garfield into city's first "magnet school" to promote integration. Alex Foreman visits Seattle to help rejuvenate flagging efforts to organize a local Peace and Freedom Party.

July 10: Under intense Congressional pressure, the Pentagon scrubs development of a Navy version of the F-111 (building one plane for both the Air Force and Navy was the whole rationale for the original TFX contract). ACLU opens an office in the Central Area staffed by Tom Gayton and other volunteers.

July 12: Eugene McCarthy wins the cheers of Washington State Democratic Convention delegates in Tacoma, but Hubert Humphrey takes their votes, creating bitter divisions in the party.

July 13: New battles erupt between students and police in Paris.

July 15: Seattle is awarded $2.3 million in Emergency Employment Program funds to create jobs for 1,800. Soviets "postpone" withdrawal from Czechoslovakia following completion of Warsaw Pact "maneuvers."

July 16: Dick Gregory is released to finish his last 15 days of jail as a "trusty" under house arrest. San Francisco police battle with hippies in the Haight.

July 18: A report by the International Association of Police Chiefs severely criticizes the command structure of the Seattle Police Department.

July 20: Seattle Transit begins introducing new diesel buses in bright red livery.

July 21: Seattle City Council votes to put fluoridation to a public referendum.

July 23: Black nationalists duel with police in Cleveland, leaving seven dead and triggering a day of riots and four more deaths. City Center Joffrey Bailet and Crome Syrcus present Seattle debut of "Astarte," a "rock ballet."

July 26: Mexico City police attack a student rally on the anniversary of Fidel Castro's quixotic 1953 raid on Cuba's Moncado Barracks, killing three and arresting 200 (an unreported number die or are arrested over the next several days).

July 27: Leonard Nimoy, Star Trek's Mr. Spock, presides as Grand Marshal of the Seafair Parade.

July 28: Soviets warn Czech reformers that "time is running out." Nigerians crush last Biafran outpost as famine spreads.

July 29: Pope Paul IV reaffirms that artificial contraception is a sin for Catholics. Seven Seattle policemen and two civilians are wounded by gunfire and rocks during a Central Area riot prompted by a raid on the Black Panther Party office. Aaron Dixon is arrested for possession of a stolen typewriter; his attorney is William Dwyer.

July 31: South Center opens. Seattle police arrest 69 during Central Area melee. The Seattle–King County Bar Association protests the "mass arrests" and intercedes to win the freedom of most suspects.

August 1: Richard Nixon calls for U.S. to "phase out" of Vietnam on the eve of the Republican National Convention in Miami Beach. President Johnson signs bill authorizing $5.3 billion in low-income housing aid. UW Faculty Senate launches $200,000 fund drive to finance minority student tuitions.

August 4: Israeli planes strike inside Jordan.

August 5: Gov. Dan Evans delivers keynote speech at Republican National Convention.

August 7: Republicans nominate Richard Nixon on the first ballot. Washington State Stadium Commission unanimously endorses Seattle Center as best location for the Kingdome.

August 8: Republicans nominate Maryland Gov. Spiro T. Agnew for vice president. Two die during riots in nearby Liberty City. "Moderate" black leaders unanimously urge Mayor Braman to dismiss Seattle Police Chief Frank Ramon.

August 9: KING-TV runs footage of Seattle police beating protesters.

August 10: South Dakota Sen. George McGovern announces his candidacy for president. Clayton Van Lydegraf leads a radical coup to take over the local Peace and Freedom Party.

August 11: New Seattle Police Liaison Committee holds its first meeting in the Central Area.

August 13: Huge fire sweeps Todd Shipyard.

August 15: Sen. Eugene McCarthy campaigns in Seattle.

August 16: U.S. tests first missiles equipped with MIRV warheads. Riots erupt in Cincinnati after police kill a black youth. KIRO opens new "Broadcast House" designed by Fred Bassetti. Comedian Pat Paulsen "campaigns" for president in Seattle.

August 17: Georgia Gov. Lester Maddox declares his candidacy for the Democratic nomination for president. Riots break out in St. Petersburg, Florida. Electrical explosions black out much of downtown Seattle.

August 18: Vietcong launch attacks on 19 South Vietnamese cities and bases. Arabs riot in Jerusalem.

August 19: President Johnson rebuffs pleas to "slacken" the war. National Mobilization Committee files suit to force Chicago to grant parade permits during the upcoming Democratic National Convention. Seattle Model City Program outlines its master plan for the Central Area.

August 20: Warsaw Pact troops occupy Czechoslovakia to enforce the "Brezhnev Doctrine" of Soviet hegemony over Eastern Europe. *P-I* and KING TV record nocturnal visits by "pinball king" Ben Cichy to the home of King County Prosecutor Charles O. Carroll, prompting a state probe.

August 24: Illinois National Guardsmen enter Chicago with orders "to shoot to kill" in the event of any "disturbances." They are later joined by 6,000 regular Army troops.

August 25–30: Democratic National Convention nominates Hubert Humphrey for president and Maine Sen. Edmund Muskie for vice president. Chicago police repeatedly attack demonstra-

tors, organized by the Yippies and the Mobe. Meanwhile, in Ann Arbor, the Peace and Freedom Party nominates Eldridge Cleaver and Jerry Rubin for president and vice president.

August 29: Michael Leavy is convicted of failing to report for induction the previous May 21.

August 30: The Sky River Rock Festival and Lighter Than Air Fair, America's first true outdoor rock festival, opens a three-day run. Owners of the Seattle Pilots approve a city plan to fix up Sick's Stadium as a temporary home field until the Kingdome is finished.

August 31: Earthquake in Iran kills more than 20,000.

September 1: Soviet troops withdraw from Prague, but Soviet policy is clearly in force in the Czech government. A black and a white are murdered during racial clashes in Berea, Kentucky. The third National Conference on Black Power advocates creation of a black nation in the Southern U.S. UFW grape boycott begins its fourth year.

September 2: Berkeley declares a "civil disaster" in continuing street battles between protesters and police. Seattle Rainiers beat Spokane 4 to 1 in the final Pacific Coast League game in Sick's Stadium.

September 3: S. I. Hayakawa tells semanticists convention in San Francisco that television is the source of student unrest.

September 4: Some 150 off-duty policemen attack a group of Black Panthers in the hall of the Brooklyn criminal courts. Appearance of armed Black Panthers triggers several days of racial unrest at Rainier Beach High School. Police clash with protesters during a multiday "fish-in" on the Nisqually River.

September 5: America's first credit card–activated cash machine goes into service in Miami, Florida.

September 6: SNCC offices in Washington, D.C., are hit with gunfire (which is repeated over the next two nights). Robby Stern, Floyd Turner, Larry Sides, John Virgil, and Don Hauser are arrested during a "fish-in" at Olympia's Capital Lake (the "Fish-In Five" are acquitted in November). King County freeholders approve a new county charter for submittal to voters.

September 7: Feminists interrupt the Miss America Pageant in Atlantic City by unfurling a banner reading "Women's Liberation." Picketers also toss brassieres and other undergarments into a "Freedom Trash Can"; contrary to later reports, no one burns her bra. First local UFW Grape Boycott pickets target Seattle A&P supermarkets.

September 8: A California jury convicts Huey Newton of involuntary manslaughter in the October 28, 1967, shoot out with Oakland police. The first "Miss Black America" pageant is held in Atlantic City without protests.

September 10: Black students occupy University of Illinois building to protest inadequate housing. ASUW president Thom Gunn has his locks shorn to "come clean for Gene" McCarthy (albeit just in the nick of time).

September 11: Largest Seattle dope raid yet nets 24 suspects.

September 12: U.S. Supreme Court Justice William O. Douglas, while vacationing at his retreat in Goose Prairie, Washington, intercedes to prevent the first deployment of reservists to Vietnam on grounds that no war has been declared.

September 13: *New York Times* reports that Boeing is abandoning its original "swing-wing" design for the SST.

September 17: State Attorney General John O'Connell defeats Senate leader Martin Durkan in Democratic primary for governor. Black Republican Art Fletcher is nominated for lieutenant governor, and Slade Gorton wins Republican nod for attorney general. As the Republican nominee for land commissioner, Richard A. C. Greene promises to "go forth and commission the land" and takes his campaign to the beaches of Hawaii. Peace and Freedom Party holds its state convention at Seattle Center.

September 18: Someone sets fire to the UW's Clark Hall, housing the Navy ROTC program.

September 22: Soviets recover Zond 5 lunar probe which orbited the moon and returned to Earth. Washington Environmental Council attorney John Miller calls for state legal action to assure public access to privately owned beaches.

September 23: Vice Presidential candidate Agnew comes under fire for referring to a "Polack" and "fat Jap." Seattle School District distributes first textbooks dealing with the "role of racial minorities" in the U.S. Prompted by Black Panther tactics, the Seattle City Council passes a law prohibiting display of weapons for the purpose of intimidation.

September 24: Mexican troops battle students at the National University, killing 17 and arresting at least 1,000. Richard Nixon campaigns in Seattle. "Mod Squad" debuts on ABC (disbanded in 1970), and CBS starts the clock on "Sixty Minutes."

September 25: Seattle School District closes Washington Junior High because of racial tensions. "Here Come the Brides" debuts on ABC and ostensibly portrays the arrival of the Mercer Girls in frontier Seattle, where Perry Como croons, we have "the bluest skies you've ever seen," until 1970.

September 26: *Helix* begins publishing weekly with issue IV-8.

September 28: A peaceful march of 25,000 in Chicago commemorates the "Battle of Michigan Avenue" one month earlier.

September 27: Peace and Freedom Party protesters attempt to "arrest" Vice President Humphrey for "crimes against humanity" during a campaign speech in the Arena.

September 30: In a nationally televised speech from Salt Lake City, Vice President Humphrey pledges to halt U.S. bombing raids over North Vietnam and to escalate "de-Americanization" of the ground war in exchange for a sign of flexibility from Hanoi. Boeing rolls out the first 747 "Jumbo Jet" in Everett.

October 1: Seven thousand jam University Way for a "Love-U District Festival" sponsored by the ASUW and U District Chamber of Commerce and organized by the New American Community.

October 2: Senate probes into Abe Fortas's past compel President Johnson to withdraw his nomination as Chief Justice of the U.S. Supreme Court (Fortas resigns from the bench on May 14, 1969). President Johnson signs bill creating 504,000-acre North Cascades National Park.

October 3: Alabama Gov. George Wallace introduces Air Force General Curtis LeMay as his third-party running mate. The next day, LeMay refuses to rule out the use of nuclear weapons in Vietnam. A large bomb damages the Alameda County Court House where Huey Newton was tried.

October 4: The Shelter Half coffee house opens for dissident servicemen near Fort Lewis.

October 5: A Seattle police officer kills Black Panther Welton "Butch" Armstead during a bust for suspicion of car theft. A helicopter pilot discovers the wreckage of the airplane in which City Councilman Wing Luke perished with two others in 1965.

October 6: Two Seattle police patrol cars are hit by shotgun fire in the Central Area.

October 7: Seattle Black Panther Curtis Harris is convicted of threatening to kill a police officer during a September 18 confrontation in the courthouse.

October 8: Blacks riot in Washington, D.C., after police kill a black man.

October 9: South Vietnamese president Nguyen Van Thieu thwarts a military coup.

October 11: NASA launches first manned Apollo mission (7) into Earth orbit. Military coup deposes Panamanian president Arias after 11 days in office.

October 12: Summer Olympic Games open in Mexico City. A thousand service men and women march against the war in San Francisco. In Seattle, Gov. George Wallace campaigns while Gov. Ronald Reagan addresses Medal of Honor winners convention.

October 14: The "murder" of a fellow inmate prompts a mutiny by inmates in San Francisco's Presidio stockade (27 are later court-martialed on charges punishable by death).

October 16: During the Olympics awards ceremony, black medalists John Carlos and Tommie Smith raise their arms in a "black power" salute to protest racism. Resistance Union holds a teach-in at the UW.

October 18: Seattle Mayor Dorm Braman warns U District Rotary to brace itself for "guerrilla warfare." UW announces that it will cease managing the Applied Physics Laboratory on December 1.

October 19: UW professor Alex Gottfried and black activist Michael Ross lead an organizing convention for "The New Party" in Seattle.

October 20: Jacqueline Kennedy marries Aristotle Onassis. Boeing unveils design for a cheaper and simpler fixed-wing SST.

October 22: Berkeley students sit in at Sproul Hall to protest the UC's refusal to let Eldridge Cleaver teach (they are cleared out two days later). Greenwich Village Motherfuckers "liberate" Bill Graham's Fillmore East. Some 300,000 protesters mark International Antiwar Day in Japan. *Helix* photographer Roger Hudson is busted for selling *Helix* on the campus of Highline Community College south of Seattle.

October 24: Inspired by a campus speech by Jerry Rubin, 2,000 UW students "liberate" the Faculty Club.

October 25: Richard A. C. Greene's campaign holds a "Memorial Hi-U Pow Wow" at the Warren G. Harding Memorial in Woodland Park.

October 27: Bombs and sniper fire ravage several San Francisco police stations for two days. In London, an estimated 120,000 Brits march against the war in London.

October 29: Eugene McCarthy endorses Humphrey and announces that he will not run for reelection to the U.S. Senate or seek the 1972 nomination.

October 30: SDS leader Robby Stern calls for UW student strike on election day to protest lack of "alternatives."

October 31: U.S. halts all bombing runs north of the 17th parallel and agrees to NLF participation in the Paris peace talks, prompting a boycott by South Vietnam. Germany jails Daniel Cohn-Bendit.

November 1: Mark Rudd speaks at the UW and shows a Newsreel documentary of "The Columbia Revolt."

November 2: State Citizens' Committee on Crime calls for liberalization of laws against marijuana and abortion. Motion Picture Association of America unveils "voluntary" ratings.

November 4: Jordan's King Hussein crushes a Palestinian-led military coup attempt.

November 5: Richard Nixon and Spiro Agnew defeat Hubert Humphrey and Ed Muskie by only 510,000 popular votes but carry 32 states. George Wallace and Curtis LeMay win 13 percent of the vote and take five Southern states. Bedford-Stuyvesant voters make Shirley Chisholm the nation's first black woman to serve in the House of Representatives. Washington State voters sift through a long ballot including 14 initiatives, bond issues, and referenda to reject a ban on the export of raw logs (I-32) and the prohibition of racial discrimination in housing sales (R-35), while approving a labor-backed 12 percent lid on consumer credit interest (I-245) and breathalizer tests for drivers (I-242). Governor Evans and all incumbent officials win reelection, and Slade Gorton narrowly defeats John McCutcheon to become State Attorney General. King County voters approve the new charter and elect the state's first Chinese American Superior Court judge, Warren Chan. Seattle voters pass fluoridated water and flush the school levy down the drain.

November 6: Students at San Francisco State College strike to protest discrimination and dismissal of a Black Panther instructor. Mayor Braman reorganizes the top echelon of the police department.

November 7: Responding to a wave of robberies, the federal government orders all federally insured banks to install surveillance cameras. Black Panther member Sidney Miller is killed by a West Seattle grocery manager while allegedly shoplifting (the Panthers later name their free clinic in Miller's honor). Black Student Union members clash with administrators at Cleveland High School.

November 11: Former Marine Master Sgt. Donald Duncan speaks against the war at a Tacoma rally.

November 13: San Francisco State College closes after a day of police-student fighting.

November 14: U.S. Students mark "National Turn in Your Draft Card Day" on scores of campuses (150 demonstrate in Seattle). FBI Director J. Edgar Hoover tells a CBS reporter, "Justice is merely incidental to law and order." Italian students lead a nationwide general strike. The Tacoma Draft Counseling Center is torched.

November 16: President-elect Nixon names Patrick Buchanan as one of top two White House speech writers.

November 17: Enoch Powell renews his campaign for laws "to keep England white."

November 19: New York City teachers strike ends after giving 1.1 million children an unofficial seven-week vacation.

November 20: Zsa Zsa Gabor claims that she was beaten by Spanish police on Mallorca.

November 21: UW law professor Arval Morris urges legalization of doctor-assisted suicide for terminally ill patients.

November 23: Mounties arrest 114 during campus protests at Vancouver's Simon Fraser University.

November 26: Saigon agrees to rejoin Paris peace talks. Johnson Administration unveils program to provide free legal aid to the poor.

November 27: Eldridge Cleaver goes underground.

November 28: CAMP presents Seattle's first Black Film Festival.

November 29: John Lennon is convicted for possession of marijuana in London.

December 1: National Commission on Violence concludes that Chicago's response to Democratic Convention protests "can only be described as a police riot."

December 2: S. I. Hayakawa, new acting president of San Francisco State College, confronts protesters and wins right-wing kudos. President-elect Nixon names Henry Kissinger as his National Security Adviser. SDS leader Mark Rudd reports for induction ready to "organize" troops.

December 3: U.S. Sen. William Proxmire calls on President-elect Nixon to "junk" Boeing SST project. Elvis Presley's first television special in eight years launches his comeback. Central Association (now the Downtown Seattle Association) unveils plan for Westlake Park and closing Pine Street.

December 6: U.S. Sen. Henry Jackson declines to serve as Secretary of Defense; Nixon names Melvin Laird two days later.

December 7: On Pearl Harbor day, total American combat deaths in Vietnam pass 30,000.

December 10: Eldridge Cleaver surfaces in Algeria.

December 15: Liberal Mike Ryherd unseats Jeanette Williams as chair of the King County Democrats.

December 16: Spain revokes order expelling Jews imposed by Queen Isabella in 1492.

December 17: Federal Reserve Bank raises its discount rate a quarter point to 5.5 percent in effort to cool inflation, which is at its worst since 1950. Nine hundred "Citizens Against Freeways" crowd state hearing to protest planned Auburn-Bothell route.

December 18: Sen. Jackson announces that an ABM base will not be built at Fort Lawton after all.

December 19: Seattle jury acquits Black Panther Aaron Dixon of stealing a typewriter.

December 21-27: Apollo 8 circumnavigates the moon.

December 22: North Korea releases *Pueblo* crew.

December 29: Israeli jets blast Beirut airport in retaliation for increasing terrorist attacks.

December 30: Seattle experiences the big chill as temperatures drop to a record 10 degrees F.

December 31: Soviet SST, Tu-144, makes its maiden flight.

Zeitgeist: Carlos Castaneda's *The Teachings of Don Juan: A Yaqui Way of Knowledge,* Paul Ehrlich's *The Population Bomb,* Steward Brand's *The Whole Earth Catalog,* and Tom Wolfe's *The Electric Kool-Aid Acid Test* are published. Volkswagen sells nearly 570,000 new Bugs and vans, representing 57 percent of total U.S. import auto sales. ITT, Ling-Temco-Vought, and other companies trigger "merger mania" to assemble huge, diversified holding companies. Stanley Kubrick's *2001: A Space Odyssey,* Barry Shear's *Wild in the Streets,* Mel Brook's *The Producers,* the Beatles' animated *Yellow Submarine,* and Roman Polanski's *Rosemary's Baby* are released. The antiwar GI newspaper *FTA* (Fuck The Army) begins publication at Fort Knox. Members of the Yardbirds and the Byrds fly their separate ways, Cream evaporates, and the Band and Credence Clearwater Revival come together. The Beatles found Apple Records and release their biggest hit ever, "Hey, Jude," while Tiny Tim "Tiptoes Through the Tulips" on the "Tonight Show."

1969

January 3: Adam Clayton Powell returns to Congress.

January 4: Protestants attack a Catholic civil rights march from Belfast to Londonderry, Northern Ireland.

January 6: SDS National Council begins a five-day session in Ann Arbor which narrowly endorses promotion of a "youth movement" instead of Progressive Labor's program of "student-worker alliances."

January 8: University of Colorado study directed by Dr. Edward Condon shoots down existence of UFOs.

January 12: Some 5,000 antiracism marchers clash with London Bobbies during immigration protest.

January 15: President Johnson's final federal budget request totals $195 billion.

January 16: Responding to United Mexican-American Students, the UW stops selling grapes in its food concessions.

January 17: Black Panthers Jerome Huggins and Al Carter are shot dead by rivals during a meeting on the UCLA campus.

January 18: After nine weeks of bickering about the shape of the negotiating table, expanded peace talks begin in Paris. Police storm University of Tokyo to end occupation by students.

January 20: Richard Nixon is sworn (expletive deleted) in as 37th president of the U.S.

January 21: Trial of Clay Shaw, accused by Jim Garrison of conspiring in the assassination of President Kennedy, opens in New Orleans.

January 22: Naval Court of Inquiry announces that it will court martial USS *Pueblo* Captain Lloyd Bucher.

January 26: Someone murders Seattle civil rights leader Seattle Urban League director Edwin Pratt, 38, in front of his home (Seattle Police never make an arrest in the case). Offshore oil well accident begins spewing 235,000 gallons of crude along Santa Barbara's beaches.

January 27: Responding to Young Republicans, the UW resumes selling grapes at its food concessions.

January 29: Students occupy the administration building at the University of Chicago.

January 30: The Third World Liberation Front launches a minority student strike at Berkeley.

February: The first true women's liberation underground newspaper, *off our backs,* begins publication in Washington, D.C.

February 3: Seattle City Council approves creation of Department of Community Development, General Services Department, and Personnel Office in a major administrative reform.

February 7: Mayor Braman accepts appointment as Assistant Secretary of the U.S. Department of Transportation. Woodland Park Zoo opens new "Tropical House."

February 8: National Democratic Party names U.S. Sen. George McGovern to head a new Reform Commission.

February 9: Boeing 747 takes wing for the first time.

February 10: President Nixon asks Attorney General John Mitchell to research lowering voting age to 18.

February 11: County Commissioner John Spellman and former Gov. Albert Rosellini win nomination in the first primary election under the new King County Charter, along with finalists for seven of nine new County Council seats, and Seattle voters approve the school levy. Consortium of oil companies announces plan to build a $900 million pipeline from Alaska's North Slope to the Gulf of Alaska.

February 13: Police battle students at Duke University, University of Wisconsin, City College of New York, and Berkeley.

February 14: Peruvian patrol boats attack U.S. tuna fishing boats.

February 16: Seattle's Cirque Playhouse closes after 19 years.

February 17: San Francisco Mime Troupe returns to perform in Seattle after nearly a year's absence.

February 18: House Un-American Activities Committee changes its name to the House Committee on Internal Security, cleverly camouflaging itself from its Communist foes. San Jose authorities arrest the Rev. Kirby Hensley, founder of the Universal Life Church, for selling a mail-order Doctorate of Divinity without registering as "an institution of higher learning."

February 21: National Guard breaks up a strike at the UC Berkeley sponsored by the Third World Liberation Front.

February 23: President Nixon begins tour of Europe.

February 24: University of Pennsylvania students occupy Administration Building. UWSDS briefly occupies Loew Hall. Similar campus clashes took place at San Mateo State (January 7), San Fernando State and San Jose State (January 8), Howard University (January 30 and February 18), University of Massachusetts (February 13), and Rice University (February 24).

February 25: Washington State Commission on the Cause and Prevention of Civil Disorder, chaired by Secretary of State Lud Kramer, rips local police racism and brutality.

February 26: Minority students briefly occupy the president's office at Seattle Central Community College.

February 28: After deliberating for 56 minutes, a New Orleans jury acquits Clay Shaw of conspiring to assassinate President Kennedy. Black militants address the State Senate Ways and Means Committee as armed Panthers pose on the Capitol steps.

March 1: Hafez Assad takes control of Syria in coup.

March 2: Concorde SST makes its maiden flight. Soviet and Chinese soldiers clash along Manchurian border. Soviet and East German troops seal roads to West Berlin in a bid to frustrate the city's participation in West German elections. Seattle's largest arson fire to date destroys Pacific Trail factory.

March 3: Apollo 9 successfully tests docking between Command and Lunar Excursion Modules.

March 4: Some scientists engaged in military research at UW and other campuses strike or hold protest meetings.

March 6: SDS leads 9,000 in peaceful UW march against ROTC while the ASUW stages a forum which attracts another 1,500 students.

March 11: James Earl Ray pleads guilty to murdering M. L. King Jr. John Spellman is elected King County's first "Executive" and Republicans win majority on the new council.

March 12: The Beatles begin to unravel as Paul McCartney marries Linda Eastman (and survives rumors of his death later in the year). John Lennon marries Yoko Ono eight days later. Victor Steinbrueck leads a rally to protest urban renewal plan for Pike Place Market.

March 13: President Nixon unveils scaled-back Sentinel ABM system, now called "Safeguard." He appoints Art Fletcher Assistant Secretary of Labor.

March 14: Some 300 students disrupt a disciplinary hearing on five SDS members who participated in the February 24 Loew Hall demonstration. UW President Odegaard suspends eight more students.

March 17: Golda Meir succeeds Levi Eshkol (who died February 26) as Prime Minister of Israel.

March 18: U.S. begins secretly bombing Cambodia in violation of Congressional limits. Defense Secretary Melvin Laird coins the word "Vietnamization" to describe transfer of combat responsibility from the U.S. to its clients.

March 20: Attorney General Mitchell personally announces indictments against the "Chicago Eight" (later Seven), as well as indictments against eight Chicago policemen for brutality. Student strike at San Francisco State College ends; both sides claim victory. The trial of five Marines for their roles in the October 14 Presidio protest begins at Fort Lewis. State Supreme Court rules that gas tax funds may not be used for transit, not even for studies, and Seattle buses stop making change for fares.

March 22: Nine protesters, including five Catholic priests, pour blood on the carpets of the Dow Chemical offices in Washington, D.C. President Nixon directs that student protesters convicted of breaking any law be denied federal financial aid.

March 24: The state legislature repeals a 36-year-old law that had effectively banned the import of out-of-state wine.

Seattle City Council elects Floyd Miller as Acting Mayor.

March 25: Governor Evans signs state law allowing expansion of Seattle School Board from five to seven members.

March 27: Four Presidio defendants are convicted while charges are "withdrawn" against the fifth defendant due to his ill health. The National Council of SDS, meeting at the University of Texas in Austin, endorses Black Panther–sponsored principles calling for "liberation in the colonies, revolution in the mother country"; Progressive Labor proposals for "student-worker alliances" are shouted down, setting the stage for SDS's final split in June.

March 28: Dwight Eisenhower dies. Seattle-First National Bank dedicates its new 50-story headquarters at 1001 Fourth Avenue.

March 29: Community voters elect first 16 members of the advisory Central Area School Council.

April 1: U.S. troop deployment in Vietnam peaks at 543,400. Soldiers at South Carolina's Fort Jackson file suit to exercise the same civil rights as civilians. Federal District judge in Boston rules that draft law discriminates against nonreligious conscientious objectors. Black Arts West theater opens in the former Cirque Playhouse.

April 3: U.S. deaths in Vietnam since 1961 reach 33,641, exceeding by 12 the number of American troops killed in Korea. Nigeria begins peace talks with Biafran rebels. Federal indictments charge the Black Panthers with conspiring to plant bombs at major New York buildings and landmarks. Blacks riot in Chicago. An estimated 20,000 hippies swarm into Palm Springs.

April 4: A juror explains, "If it weren't for the First Amendment you guys wouldn't be here," as the "Oakland Seven" are acquitted. A massive earthquake does not happen and Western California does not sink into the Pacific, contrary to Edgar Cayce's famous prediction.

April 5: Antiwar marches in 50 cities attract an estimated 150,000 protesters. An artificial heart is implanted into a patient in Houston; it sustains him for 63 hours until a donor heart becomes available.

April 6: Protesters storm the Presidio in San Francisco.

April 8: The Seattle Pilots beat California 4 to 3 in their debut at Anaheim.

April 9: SDS-led protesters seize buildings at Harvard. A police raid the next day injures 37, provoking a student strike. UW SDS members disrupt a campus fashion show featuring Nancy Evans, wife of the governor.

April 11: Seattle Pilots shut out the Boston White Sox 7-0 in their first game in Sick's Stadium.

April 13: Five thousand people attend an "Easter egg hunt" and concert at Volunteer Park, which prompts Acting Mayor Miller to ban amplified music in parks.

April 14: Chinese Communist Party names Lin Piao as Mao's heir apparent. Six thousand Harvard students vote to extend class boycott. Seattle City Council appoints Don Wright to fill out Floyd Miller's term.

April 15: North Korean MIGs shoot down a U.S. reconnaissance plane over the Sea of Japan. Several thousand welfare recipients march in New York City to protest benefit cuts.

April 16: A federal judge in New York strikes down draft reclassification solely on the basis of participation in antiwar protests.

April 17: Sirhan Sirhan is convicted of murdering Robert Kennedy. Norman Mailer announces candidacy for mayor of New York City. Boeing wins contract to design Airborne Warning and Control System (AWACS). Harvard faculty asks for ban of ROTC.

April 18: Catholic civil rights activist Bernadette Devlin is elected to Parliament from Northern Ireland. Student occupations and other demonstrations continue at Stanford, Harvard, Yale, Cornell, University of Chicago, Queens College, and Princeton.

April 20: Berkeley residents take over a vacant UC-owned lot and begin building "People's Park." Anti-Defamation League criticizes SDS and other New Left groups for their support of Al Fatah Palestinian guerrillas led by Yasir Arafat.

April 22: Black and Puerto Rican students shut down New York City College for nearly two weeks. Robin Knox-Johnston completes first round-the-world voyage by a solo sailor.

April 23: Weyerhaeuser announces that it will cease sending recruiters to the UW.

April 24: An SDS attempt to shut down corporate recruiting at the UW's Loew Hall degenerates into farce when angry bees escape (accidentally?) from hives being trucked across campus.

April 25: UW Board of Regents announces that students will be allowed to attend and address its meetings for the first time. The Rev. Ralph Abernathy and 100 others are arrested while picketing a Charleston, South Carolina, hospital to support unionization. Black students occupy the faculty club at Colgate.

April 28: French President Charles DeGaulle resigns after losing a national vote-of-confidence referendum the day before. SDS helps to organize a "sick-in" with black workers to protest alleged racist policies at a Ford assembly plant in New Jersey. Students occupy buildings at Voorhees College, Memphis State University, Queens College, and St. Louis University, while Harvard students vote against resuming their strike. John Field, the UW's first full-time draft counselor, opens for business in the HUB; he is soon seeing 40 students a day. Dr. Spock speaks in Seattle.

April 29: Defense Secretary Laird says he is "willing to consider changes" to ROTC curricula to calm national campus turmoil. Radical Women and SDS scuffle with police while picketing in support of striking photo-finishers at Perfect Photo in Seattle.

April 30: State Attorney General Slade Gorton rules that card rooms, multi-coin pinball machines, and all other forms of gambling are illegal under the Washington constitution. Seattle police arrest 14 picketers marching in sympathy with striking photo-finishers.

May 1: In a Detroit speech, Attorney General Mitchell calls on college administrators and local governments to "crack down" on student dissent. Students vacate occupied buildings at Columbia and Stanford and a local judge convicts 169 for trespassing at Harvard.

May 3: David Brower loses a bitter power struggle within the Sierra Club and steps down as director. The UW Department of Architecture erects a temporary "environment" over Drumheller Fountain.

May 4: Several thousand citizens march in the Arboretum to oppose construction of the R. H. Thomson Expressway. More than 1,000 students march through Madison, Wisconsin, business district.

May 6: Seattle City Councilman Paul Alexander dies.

May 7: William Buckley sues Gore Vidal for libeling him as a "Crypto-Nazi" during joint commentaries on the Democratic National Convention on August 25, 1968. Student unrest hits Howard University, Dartmouth, Purdue, Indiana College, and CCNY.

May 8: State legislature approves a constitutional amendment for a single-rate income tax requiring voter approval.

May 10: Catholic Church purges the liturgical calendar of 40 saints, including St. Christopher; Santa Claus survives. As many as 3,000 students stage a "Zap-In" at Zap, North Dakota; local police are not amused and called in the National Guard.

May 13: President Nixon proposes establishing national lottery for the draft.

May 14: President Nixon proposes that the U.S. and North Vietnam withdraw their respective forces simultaneously. Abe Fortas resigns from the U.S. Supreme Court.

May 15: California State Police open fire on the defenders of Berkeley's People's Park, killing a bystander, James Rector, and blinding Alan Blanchard.

May 17: James Forman presents a bill for $60 million in reparations to Baptist leaders meeting in Seattle.

May 18: U.S. Apollo 10 lifts off for a dress rehearsal moon landing.

May 19: Supreme Court reverses Timothy Leary's 1966 conviction for failing to pay a federal tax on the marijuana found in his possession. Fresh riots break out in Newark. Seattle City Council appoints

Liem Tuai to fill out Paul Alexander's term; Tuai is the first Asian American to serve on the council since Wing Luke's death in 1965.

May 20: California National Guard helicopter gases thousands of students trapped during a demonstration on the Berkeley campus. On their twelfth charge, U.S. troops finally take "Hamburger Hill" from North Vietnamese defenders, with a loss of 55 U.S. lives and 400 Vietnamese. Don Phelps quits as Bellevue's only black school principal to protest racism. Under pressure from corporate clients, "maverick" state legislator Fran Holman and his brother William are expelled by their partners, the law firm of Holman, Perkins, Coie, Stone & Olson.

May 21: President Nixon nominates Warren Earl Burger to succeed Earl Warren as Chief Justice of the Supreme Court. Sirhan Sirhan is sentenced to death.

May 22: Black Student Union clashes with police at a demonstration demanding the resignation of one of Seattle Central Community College's five white trustees and the appointment of a black.

May 23: Eleven Quakers are arrested for "discommoding the steps of the [U.S.] Capitol" while reading the names of all U.S. servicemen killed thus far in Vietnam.

May 25: Thor Heyerdahl, of Kon Tiki fame, and crew set sail west from Morocco in a papyrus raft, the Ra, to prove that Egyptians could have populated South America. BSU leads a student strike at Seattle Community College. Trustee Carl Dakan resigns on May 27, but Governor Evans refuses to appoint anyone suggested by the BSU.

May 26: Dick Cavett debuts on ABC (the show ran until 1972, and failed to click in

two later revivals). Police arrest 34 demonstrators during clashes at SCC and Garfield.

May 27: Sixty or so black contractors form the Central Area Contractors Association, chaired by Tyree Scott, to press for a larger share of local construction business.

May 30: Twenty thousand rally in Berkeley in a peaceful protest of the suppression of People's Park.

June 1: Ralph Nader urges Congress to regulate rock concert sound levels (you always knew he was a square at heart). Prowar comments by Archbishop Connolly prompt four students to walk out of Seattle University commencement exercises.

June 3: U.S. House Internal Security Committee (son of HUAC) opens hearings on "threat" posed by SDS. President Nixon blasts the "self-righteous moral arrogance" of antiwar protesters but he praises the younger generation's "great cries" for honesty. Franklin High School Black Student Union stages a sit-in.

June 6: American League inspector declares Sick's Stadium "inadequate," threatening Seattle's Pilots franchise. The "Catonsville Nine" are convicted. Five, including the Berrigan brothers, go underground.

June 8: President Nixon announces withdrawal of 25,000 troops from Vietnam by August 31. Spain blockades road to Gibraltar in its dispute with Britain over ownership of "The Rock."

June 9: CORE director Roy Innis demands $6 billion from U.S. banks as "recoupment for the earnings of black folk." Construction of Evergreen State College begins near Olympia.

June 16: U.S. Supreme Court finds Congress' action unconstitutional in refusing to seat Adam Clayton Powell in 1967.

June 17: Seattle restaurant workers go on strike. Seattle City Council votes unanimously for urban renewal of the Pike Place Market.

June 18–22: SDS self-destructs during its national convention in Chicago, creating factions led by the "Weathermen" and Progressive Labor.

June 19: A suspected bomb is removed from the UW Haggett Hall dormitory; it turns out to be a gag.

June 20: White Rhodesians vote to sever all remaining ties with Great Britain and the Commonwealth in long dispute over racial policies. HEW awards $500,000 to the state to conduct a pilot program testing a "guaranteed annual income" as an alternative to traditional welfare.

June 22: Judy Garland, 47, dies in London.

June 23: Warren Burger succeeds Earl Warren as Chief Justice of the Supreme Court.

June 24: Blacks riot in Omaha, Nebraska.

June 27: Homosexuals fight back when New York police raid Greenwich Village's Stonewall Inn, and thereby launch the modern Gay Rights movement.

June 28: Seattle restaurant workers strike is settled as the first of 125,000 Shriners begin arriving in Seattle for their national convention.

June 29: Washington Plaza Hotel (the first tower of the current Westin) opens. At 3:30 a.m., a bomb with the force of a case of dynamite explodes in the UW Administration Building foyer.

June 30: With only Tim Hill dissenting, the Seattle City Council approves City Light's request to purchase Kiket Island at Deception Pass as a site for a future nuclear power plant.

July 3: President Nixon drops imposition of formal deadlines in ordering school desegregation. Former Rolling Stone Brian Jones drowns in his swimming pool. Stokely Carmichael resigns from the Black Panther Party.

July 5: UW Art School, Experimental College, and *Helix* co-sponsor the first Northwest Film Makers Festival at the UW.

July 7: Charles Evers, brother of Medgar, takes office as mayor of Fayette, Mississippi. He is the first black mayor since Reconstruction elected by a Mississippi town with both white and black voters. Dorian House opens in Seattle to offer counseling to homosexuals.

July 8: U.S. forces begin to withdraw from South Vietnam.

July 10: Five are arrested in protests during a Seattle parade of troops recently returned from Vietnam. Representatives of the Underground Press Syndicate convene in Ann Arbor, Michigan, for a three day conference.

July 11: U.S. First Court of Appeals overturns the convictions of Dr. Spock and three co-defendants on charges of abetting draft evasion. Soviets launch Luna 15 moon probe. NLF representatives participate in a "Voice of Women" conference in Vancouver, B.C.

July 13: Seventy-five young physicians and nurses seize the podium during the AMA national convention in New York to assail the "conservatism" of its leaders.

July 14: El Salvador attacks Honduras. Five firebombs set off at SCC do minor damage.

July 16: Apollo 11 lifts off for the moon.

July 17: National Association of Broadcasters agrees to eliminate all cigarette advertising on radio and television by September 1, 1973.

July 18: Thor Heyerdahl abandons his papyrus raft 600 miles short of his goal, Barbados. Black Panther conference in Oakland calls for "united front against fascism" and denounces the Weathermen.

July 19: Senator Edward Kennedy drives off a bridge on Chappaquiddick Island, and his passenger, Mary Jo Kopechne, drowns. His presidential hopes sink with her two days later when he is accused of leaving the scene of the accident. John Fairbanks arrives in Florida to become the first man to row a boat solo across the Atlantic. Ensemble Theater closes in Seattle.

July 20: Astronauts Neil Armstrong and Buz Aldrin land on the moon while Michael Collins orbits overhead in the Apollo 11 command module. President Nixon eases restrictions on U.S. citizens traveling to the People's Republic of China or purchasing Chinese goods.

July 22: Luna 15 lands on the moon. President Nixon heads west to begin round-the-world tour. Generalissimo Franco names Juan Carlos to succeed him and become Spain's first king since the Republic.

July 23: Governor Evans sketches first outlines of what will become the Washington Public Power Supply System (WPPSS) to build as many as 20 new nuclear reactors.

July 24: Governor Evans appoints Marvin Glass to SCC Board of Trustees.

July 25: In a speech reminiscent of Nixon's 1952 "Checkers" appeal, Senator Ted Kennedy asks for the nation's understanding in the wake of Chappaquiddick. Senator Fulbright calls ABM supporters in the Senate "stooges of the military," and later apologizes. Los Angeles police arrest Timothy Leary for contributing to the delinquency of a minor in connection with the drowning of a teenage girl at his California ranch. "Laugh-in" hosts Rowan and Martin kick off Seafair, which later features a "hippie float" built by the New American Community. Boyd Grafmyre stages a three-day "Seattle Pop Festival" at Gold Creek Park in Woodinville.

July 26: A New Jersey pier owned by United Fruit is destroyed by a large bomb on the sixteenth anniversary of Fidel Castro's raid on the Moncado Barracks.

July 27: Western Governors Conference meets in Seattle; Vice President Agnew visits the next day.

July 28: Mariner 6 transmits the first close-up views of the surface of Mars. Boeing reveals that it has let more than 12,000 workers go through attrition so far in 1969; its local payroll still numbers 87,600.

August 3: The Army arrests seven Green Berets and their commander on charges that they murdered a Vietnamese official they suspected of spying. CIA links are later exposed and the whole matter is abruptly dropped on September 29. Charlie Cecil Mink is arrested in Seattle for wearing a U.S. flag as a cape.

August 8: *L.A. Free Press* lists names of known narcotics agents, which later results in criminal indictments against the paper. President Nixon proposes "workfare" reforms for welfare system and revenue sharing with states and cities as part of his "New Federalism." Pacifist David Harris, husband of Joan Baez, begins three-year prison term for refusing induction.

August 9: Intruders brutally torture and murder actress Sharon Tate (wife of Roman Polanski), coffee heiress Abigail Folger, and three others in Polanski's Bel-Air home. Later in the day supermarket magnate Leno LaBianca and his wife are murdered in Los Angeles.

August 10: Apollo 11 astronauts emerge from three-week quarantine to check for moon bugs. At midnight, it becomes legal for women to sit at the bar in Washington state cocktail lounges and legal for either sex to transport drinks from the bar to a table. Seattle police fire tear gas during a battle with revelers at a concert on Alki Beach; a squad car is firebombed and six are arrested.

August 11: U District street people intervene in a drug bust, setting off a brief battle with police. Five are arrested, including "White Panther" Jim Emerson, and three officers are injured. Seattle City Council approves controversial "household tax" of $1 per month to subsidize transit system.

August 13: China charges that Russian troops have invaded its northern territory. Police and teens clash in U District.

August 14: After a week of deadly Catholic-Protestant clashes, British troops are deployed in Northern Ireland for the first time in 50 years. Riots flare again in U District.

August 15: Police detour traffic from U Way while volunteers spread out to "cool" any potential riots. Meanwhile, in upper New York State, the Woodstock Music and Art Fair transforms the tiny Catskills resort town of Bethel into a temporary city of 400,000.

August 16: "Negotiations" among U District merchants, residents, street people, and police begin. Police withdraw riot squad.

August 17: A large bomb causes serious damage to the Federal Office Building in Minneapolis–St. Paul.

August 18: President Nixon nominates Clement Haynsworth to succeed Abe Fortas on the Supreme Court. Seattle City Council president Myrtle Edwards dies.

August 19: Anti-Soviet Czechs battle police in Prague. Bobby Seale is arrested in San Francisco on murder charges stemming from the May 21 beating death of Panther Alex Rackley in New Haven, Connecticut.

August 20: Marine Midland Grace Trust Co. headquarters is bombed in Manhattan, injuring 13.

August 22: Eight Seattle Weathermen establish a collective. Michael Stillwell is charged with desecration for hanging a U.S. flag as a curtain in the window of his Capitol Hill apartment.

August 24: Members of the Alpha Company of 196th Light Infantry Brigade's 3rd Battalion, last among the 25,000 U.S. troops slated for withdrawal from Vietnam in one week, mutiny after a five-day battle and refuse orders to attack. The Army declines to discipline them.

August 27: Seattle School Board adopts new code prohibiting "disruptive behavior."

August 28: The Central Area Contractors Association, led by Tyree Scott, pickets county construction projects to protest underemployment of blacks in the building industry. One of the picketers, Hank

Roney, is later beaten by three white assailants.

August 30: Despite the best efforts of Thurston County Prosecutor Fred Gentry, the second Sky River Rock Festival opens in Tenino, south of Olympia.

Fall Season: Television tries to co-opt the sexual revolution with the debut of "Love, American Style" on September 29 (spent by 1974).

September 1: Military coup overthrows the Libyan monarchy. Controversial Episcopal Bishop James Pike disappears during a car trip with his wife in Jordan; he is found dead a week later.

September 2: Blacks riot in Fort Lauderdale, Florida, and Hartford, Connecticut.

September 3: Ho Chi Minh, aged 79, dies of natural causes in Hanoi.

September 4: Brazilian guerrillas kidnap U.S. Ambassador C. Burke Elbrick; he is exchanged for political prisoners two days later. Associated General Contractors agree to three of four Central Area Contractor Association's demands to expand construction hiring and subcontracting in Seattle.

September 7: Illinois Sen. Everett McKinley Dirksen, Republican Senate leader, dies.

September 8: U District clothier Ray Eckman is appointed to fill out Myrtle Edwards's term on the Seattle City Council.

September 10: Alaska begins auctioning off North Slope oil drilling leases.

September 16: President Nixon announces that 35,000 additional U.S. troops will leave Vietnam by December 15. Seattle voters reject blatant "law and order" candidates to nominate liberal Democrat Wes Uhlman and progressive Republican Mort Frayn for mayor.

September 18: U.S. House of Representatives approves constitutional amendment eliminating the Electoral College.

September 19: President Nixon cuts draft quota for last quarter of 1969 by 50,000 men. A bomb causes serious damage to the new Federal Office Building in New York City. The British Consul's office in the Norton Building is picketed in the first local protest inspired by events in Northern Ireland.

September 24: Trial of the Chicago Eight opens in Chicago, with William Kunstler and Leonard Weinglass leading the defense and Judge Julius Hoffman presiding. Central Area Contractors Association battle police while picketing construction sites at UW; President Odegaard orders a review of construction hiring practices.

September 25: A riot erupts in Chicago during federal hearings on building trades discrimination.

September 26: Julian Bond speaks in Seattle.

September 28: Social Democrat Willy Brandt leads his party to power in West German elections. UW reports fall enrollment at 32,600, an increase of 1,300 over 1968.

September 29: Catholic priest the Rev. James Groppi leads 2,000 welfare protesters in taking over the Wisconsin State Capitol in Madison.

September 30: Weatherwomen trash the Air Force ROTC portable on the UW campus.

October 1: *P-I* reporters Shelby Scates, Bill Sieverling, Don Carter, and Tom Read bring the long-simmering Seattle police pay-off scandal to a boil by reporting that gambling interests pressured City Council candidate Don Wright and offered

Assistant Chief Tony Gustin a $40,000 "salary" to monitor and frustrate enforcement. Congressional hearings reveal lucrative skimming and kickback scams in operation of Army clubs and PXs in Vietnam. As Canadian protesters close the Blaine border crossing, U.S. detonates nuclear warhead in underground ABM test on Amchitka Island in the Aleutians. Olaf Palme, a passionate critic of the Vietnam war, becomes head of ruling Social Democrats in Norway and prime minister-apparent.

October 2: A contingent of about 40 SDS activists trash UW ROTC quarters in Clark Hall and assault two officers.

October 4: TV personality Art Linkletter's daughter Diane commits suicide while on LSD.

October 5: Jacqueline Onassis decks a paparazzo in New York. Blacks riot in Las Vegas.

October 7: Atlanta elects Maynard Jackson as its first black mayor. Somebody blows up a statue of Chicago policeman Mathias Degan, who was killed by an alleged "anarchist bomb" during police suppression of a labor rally in Haymarket Square on May 4, 1886.

October 8: Weathermen rampage along Chicago's Gold Coast in the first engagement of the "Days of Rage National Action." Seattle Police Chief Ramon "retires" under pressure effective November 5, as reporting by Don McGaffin (then with KOMO) and others exposes huge illegal gambling network. Three thousand white construction workers rally downtown to protest requirements for more minority training and hiring imposed by local governments and the UW.

October 9: Mayor Miller orders total ban on gambling in Seattle; M. E. Cook be-

comes Acting Police Chief, aided by a "troika" of assistant chiefs, Eugene Corr, Tony Gustin, and Frank Moore. County Executive Spellman orders probe of County Sheriff Jack Porter for receiving a contribution from illegal bingo operator. Seattle University grad Major Patrick Brady becomes the first medic to earn the Congressional Medal of Honor for valor in Vietnam.

October 10: President Nixon "promotes" Lt. Gen. Lewis Hershey, head of the Selective Service System, to a figurehead job, effectively dismissing him (Hershey had supervised the drafting of 20 million men since 1940 but never saw combat himself). Acting Seattle Police Chief Cook resigns under pressure from his assistant chiefs.

October 11: Two hundred members of the Weather Underground battle Chicago police on the final Day of Rage. San Francisco's "Zodiac" killer murders a cab driver.

October 16: Plans are announced to construct a downtown Freeway Park over I-5. "Voice of Irate Construction Employees" (VOICE) organizes an Olympia rally of 3,000 white workers to protest minority hiring rules.

October 17: Defense Secretary Melvin Laird proposes international ban on biological weapons. FDA announces that cyclamate artificial sweeteners will be banned effective January 1, 1970. Frank Moore is named acting Seattle Police Chief.

October 18: North Korean troops ambush and kill four U.S. soldiers.

October 19: In a speech in New Orleans, Vice President Agnew rips antiwar protesters as an "effete corps of impudent snobs who characterize themselves as intellectuals." Antiwar protesters paralyze Tokyo.

October 21: Jack Kerouac dies at the age of 47.

October 22: In England, Paul McCartney denies that he's dead.

October 23: U.S. Ambassador Lodge walks out of Vietnam peace talks. Amid a fight between the Navy and UW over control of the Applied Physics Laboratory, the UW Faculty Senate adopts a resolution discouraging "classified" research on campus.

October 25: Palestinians trigger unrest in neutral Lebanon.

October 26: Nationwide strike against General Electric idles 140,000.

October 28: California bans the use of DDT pesticide effective January 1, 1970. Two thousand attend Youth Decency Rally in the Arena. Boeing wins NASA contract to build lunar rover "moon buggies" for Apollo Program.

October 29: Judge Hoffman orders Bobby Seale gagged and shackled for continuing to demand independent counsel. USAF announces retirement of B-58 Hustler supersonic strategic bombers.

October 30: Black women students seize the administration building at Vassar. Jim Owens suspends four black players from UW football squad for "lack of commitment." Seattle City Council votes to construct High Ross Dam despite environmental impact in U.S. and Canada.

October 31: Raphael Minichiello, a decorated Marine from Seattle facing court martial for a PX burglary, is captured in Rome after commandeering a TWA airliner on the West Coast and forcing it to fly 6,900 miles to Rome in the "longest" hijacking yet. *Time* magazine's cover story probes the issue of being homosexual in America.

November 1: National Commission on the Causes and Prevention of Violence paints a "bleak picture" of criminal law and penal policies. The remaining nine black UW football players refuse to travel Los Angeles for a game with UCLA, which crushes the Huskies 57 to 14.

November 2: President Nixon reveals several failed peace overtures to North Vietnam in a major address on the war. Diana Ross announces that she is leaving the Supremes.

November 4: President Nixon elevates Seattleite John Ehrlichman to be his assistant for domestic affairs. Wes Uhlman defeats Mort Frayn to become Seattle's youngest mayor at age 34; Wayne Larkin, Jeannette Williams, Liem Tuai, and George Cooley are elected to the Seattle City Council; and voters reject the transit household tax and school levy.

November 5: Judge Hoffman sentences Bobby Seale to four years in prison for contempt, thereby creating the Chicago Seven. Riot police in Cambridge, Massachusetts, attack 300 students protesting MIT's research on Multiple Independently Targeted Re-entry Vehicles (MIRVs), which would seriously tip the U.S.-Soviet strategic balance.

November 6: North Vietnamese regulars mark their deepest penetration in South Vietnam in an attack on a Mekong Delta base. Protesters blockade the MIT president's office. Police arrest 48 during a demonstration led by Michael Ross at Sea-Tac Airport to protest discrimination in construction employment.

November 7: San Francisco Mime Troupe performs in support of "liberating" the Raitt Hall "Commons" on the UW campus.

November 8: Protesters vandalize six draft boards in Boston.

November 9: UW reinstates three suspended black football players. Washington Secretary of State Lud Kramer takes a part-time job pumping gas to help pay off $10,000 in debts from his unsuccessful bid for Seattle mayor.

November 10: Bombs explode in the New York offices of General Motors, RCA, and Chase Manhattan Bank; a fourth bombing hits the New York Criminal Courts on November 12, and five Weathermen, including Jane Alpert, are arrested the following day.

November 11: Thousands march in several cities to show support for President Nixon on Veterans Day.

November 13: Vice President Agnew blasts the "tiny and closed fraternity of privileged men" controlling national media for criticism of the war and Nixon Administration.

November 14: Washington, D.C., police use tear gas to disperse several hundred antiwar protesters trying to march on the South Vietnamese Embassy. Eight protesters are arrested for trashing downtown storefronts while 3,500 march in Seattle against the war. Apollo 12 lifts off for the moon.

November 16: Seymour Hersh breaks the story of the 1968 My Lai massacre, under the command of Lt. William Calley, of 567 Vietnamese civilians.

November 17: Formal U.S.-Soviet Strategic Arms Limitation Treaty (SALT) negotiations commence in Helsinki, Finland.

November 18: Chuck Conrad and Alan Bean land on the moon while Seattle native Dick Gordon orbits overhead. U.S. House approves continued funding for Boeing SST, which is expected to employ 25,000 in the Seattle area. Janis Joplin is charged with using profanity during a Tampa, Florida, performance. Joseph P. Kennedy dies.

November 19: Congress passes law establishing draft lottery. The Democratic Party Reform Commission, chaired by U.S. Sen. George McGovern, votes to establish quotas to assure election of women and minority delegates.

November 20: Native Americans occupy Alcatraz Island. Vice President Agnew renews his attack on the "liberal media." Ambassador Lodge resigns as chief negotiator at the Paris peace talks. Forward Thrust unveils a new $1.1 billion rapid transit plan.

November 21: U.S. Senate fails to confirm the appointment of Clement Haynsworth to the Supreme Court. A new trial of Timothy Leary is ordered on 1966 charges that he failed to pay taxes on marijuana found on his person in Texas. Women's Commission, Radical Women, and Women's Liberation sponsor a lecture workshop at the UW.

November 24: President Nixon signs nuclear nonproliferation treaty.

November 25: ASUW president Steve Boyd and Student Mobilization Committee head Stephanie Coontz lead a "corporate meeting" of the student body. UW Committee on the Environmental Crisis sponsors an "Environmental Fair" at the HUB.

November 27: Seven hundred Army medics stationed in Pleiku fast on Thanksgiving Day to protest the war. Washington State reports that 3.8 percent of the Seattle workforce is unemployed, twice the 1968 figure.

November 28: *Chicago Sun-Times* publishes an article and photos showing a Vietcong prisoner who refused to talk being pushed out of an Army helicopter at high altitude.

November 29: U.S. combat casualties (killed and wounded) top 300,000.

December 1: Men born on September 14 "win" first draft lottery. The UW suspends SDS campus accreditation after 20 Weathermen trash ROTC offices in Savery Hall. Black Panthers open the Sidney Miller Free Medical Clinic at Spruce and 20th.

December 3: Charles Manson and three members of his "commune" are arrested for the Tate-LaBianca murders. KING-TV reporter Mike James hosts a special in which a woman describes an illegal abortion performed by Renton physician Dr. A. Frans Koome, an outspoken advocate of reproductive choice who immediately comes under criminal investigation.

December 4: Chicago police kill Black Panthers Fred Hampton and Mark Clark during an early morning raid of their apartment. Promoter Boyd Grafmyre's appeal in the *Helix* for Eagles' fans to refrain from smoking grass and other illegal activities in the auditorium sparks two nights of protests.

December 5: UW Faculty Senate votes to retain ROTC but with stricter limits on purely military courses. Black students briefly seize Harvard University's administration building and law professor Archibald Cox (later Watergate prosecutor) to press demands for reform. The "Eagles Liberation Front/Eagles Liberation Movement" (ELF/ELM) pickets the auditorium demanding lower ticket prices and fewer hassles.

December 6: Hell's Angels, hired for "security," stab a fan to death during the Rolling Stones' performance at the Altamont Music Festival. State Republicans vote to lower membership age to 18.

December 8: Washington Citizens for Abortion Reform announces that it will campaign for liberalization of state limits. Clergy and Laymen Concerned About Vietnam (CALCAV) announce that they will aid deserters in escaping to Canada; Dr. Edward Palmason, president of the Seattle School Board and a CALCAV member, is briefly entangled in the resulting controversy.

December 11: Harvard suspends 75 black students following renewed protests.

December 12: The U District Center holds an open house at 5525 University Way NE.

December 13: Draft Resisters–Seattle leaflet downtown stores urging shoppers to boycott Christmas in order to promote democratic socialism (it probably made sense at the time).

December 14: Under intense student pressure, the UW Philosophy Department extends John Chambless' contract (he was denied tenure and let go in Spring 1973).

December 15: President Nixon orders the withdrawal of 50,000 U.S. troops from Vietnam by April 15, 1970. Panamanian strongman General Omar Torrijos is deposed in a bloodless coup. Church of Latter-day Saints (Mormons) reaffirms its exclusion of blacks from the ministry. Dick Gregory leads a Seattle march for Central Contractors Association and minority employment. A bomb goes off that night at the Model City Program office in the Central Area. Pierce County votes to leave the Puget Sound Governmental Conference in a power struggle over land use planning.

December 17: Tiny Tim weds Victoria May Budinger on the Johnny Carson show. U.S. Air Force officially closes its "Project Blue Book" for investigating UFO sightings.

December 19: Mayor Uhlman names Cesar Chavez "First Citizen" during a Seattle visit to promote the United Farm Workers grape boycott.

December 22: Seattle City Council reject's Mayor Uhlman's proposal to raise parking meter rates and levy a tax on parking lots to subsidize public transit.

December 23: Hanoi releases names of 131 U.S. POWs held in North Vietnam.

December 25: Texan millionaire (later billionaire and independent presidential candidate) H. Ross Perot escorts a planeload of food and gifts for U.S. POWs to Vientienne, Laos, but North Vietnam refuses entry.

December 27: Weathermen condense in Flint, Michigan, for five-day "war council."

December 29: UW professor and land reform expert Dr. Roy Prosterman warns of impending disaster in South Vietnam due to the government's failure to improve rights and welfare of peasants. Two hundred "poor" picket Olympia demanding help.

December 30: President Nixon signs $9.1 billion tax cut despite mounting deficit.

December 31: U.S. forces reduce their deployment by 60,000 troops by the end of the year. Boeing employment declines to 80,000 during the year from a peak of 101,300. Seattle police investigations find 76 complaints of brutality and misconduct to be "valid" out of 300 filed during 1969. Sixty-nine bombings and an additional number of arson fires cause $3.5 million in property damage in Seattle during the year.

Zeitgeist: Major films of the year include Dennis Hopper's *Easy Rider,* Michelangelo Antonioni's *Zabriskie Point,* John Schlesinger's *Midnight Cowboy,* George Hill's *Butch Cassidy and the Sundance Kid,* Sam Peckinpah's *The Wild Bunch,* Costa-Gravas' *Z,* Arlo Guthrie's *Alice's Restaurant,* and the documentary of the 1967 Monterey Pops Festival. "Hot Fun in the Summertime," "Get Back," "Honky Tonk Woman," and "Lay Lady Lay" lead the charts, and the Jackson Five (when Michael was still black), the Fifth Dimension, Merle Haggard ("Okie from Muskogee"), Janis Joplin, Led Zepplin, and Santana record major hits. The Who produce *Tommy,* the first rock opera. The Beatles' last albums, "Abbey Road" and the "White Album," are released and their final days together are filmed for *Let It Be.* Noam Chomsky's *American Power and the New Mandarins* is published. Rural America tries to get the last laugh with the debut of "Hee Haw" on June 15 on CBS.

1970

January 1: President Nixon signs Environmental Protection Act, whose passage was largely engineered by Sen. Henry Jackson. Pentagon reports 1,403 desertions since July 1, 1966.

January 4: Inquest opens into death of Mary Jo Kopechne. United Mine Workers activist Joseph Yablonski, his wife, and daughter are found murdered in Pennsylvania (the killing is later traced to UMW president Tony Boyle).

January 6: A criminal probe begins into State Attorney General John O'Connell's "split" of a $2.3 million fee earned by San Francisco Mayor Joseph Alioto while representing state utilities in an antitrust action. White students boycott Mississippi's first integrated schools.

January 8: Fr. Kenneth Baker, SJ, succeeds Fr. Jack Fitterer, SJ, as president of Seattle University.

January 12: Biafran separatist movement collapses.

January 14: Federal grand jury opens investigation into links between illegal gambling and Seattle Police.

January 16: Mu'ammar Kadhafi takes control of Libya following a coup. George Jackson, John Clutchette, and Fleeta Drumgo are accused of killing a guard in California's Soledad Prison. Former King County Sheriff Tim McCullough is indicted by a grand jury for perjury in gambling scandal.

January 17: Jerry Rubin addresses an overflow crowd of 4,000 at the UW Student Union Building.

January 18: Weathermen Silas "Trim" Bissell and wife Judith are caught planting an incendiary bomb under the steps of a UW ROTC portable building.

January 19: President Nixon nominates Harrold Carswell to the U.S. Supreme Court, which rules that draft boards cannot reclassify protesters to punish them. Michael Lerner convenes the first organizing meeting of the new Seattle Liberation Front.

January 20: Despite increasing jitters over inflation and sinking Boeing employment, Seattle voters approve school levy on first try. Weathermen take over a peaceful antiwar demonstration at the UW and then storm Marine recruiters at Loew Hall.

January 21: Shelter Half coffee house and American Servicemen's Union conduct a "trial" of the U.S. Army in the HUB.

January 23: As the first shot in a long legal battle, the City of Seattle enjoins the owners of the Seattle Pilots from transferring the franchise to another city.

January 25: David Sucher, coordinator of the city-funded "Project Survival," announces plans for "Environmental Decency Day" on April 22.

January 26: Some 20,000 Filipinos riot in Manila to protest the Marcos regime.

January 27: U.S. Senate passes bill lowering penalties for personal possession and use of many drugs. American League rebuffs delegation of officials who offer to have local government buy the Seattle Pilots. White House unveils "operatic" new uniforms for guards.

January 29: Ninety-five day strike against General Electric ends.

January 30: Black Panthers sue federal government to halt harassment. State Senate passes liberalized abortion law subject to a referendum in the fall.

February 2: Seattle Mayor Uhlman proposes to shelve the R. H. Thomson Expressway and to cut I-90 from ten to eight lanes. Federal indictments name 12 Alameda County Sheriff's deputies for misconduct during the suppression of People's Park. Bertrand Russell dies.

February 6: Mayor Uhlman rejects an ATF request for police support in a planned raid on the Seattle Black Panthers. State Sen. Fred Dore's Seattle home is firebombed.

February 8: Congressional Democrats present the first televised "reply" to a presidential State of the Union address. Universal Life Church founder the Right Rev. Kirby Hensley presides over a *Helix* benefit at Eagles.

February 10: President Nixon outlines environmental goals, including donating much of Ft. Lawton to Seattle. Saul Alinsky speaks at the UW and calls Weathermen "militant loudmouths intent on confrontation for confrontation's sake."

February 11: A bomb explodes in the Berkeley Police Department parking lot, injuring two officers. American League agrees to leave the Pilots in Seattle. UW economics professor Dr. Henry Beuchel becomes an instant hero when he expels five members of the Seattle Liberation Front who attempted to disrupt his class.

February 13: UW names David Llorens to head first Black Studies degree program.

February 14: While the jury deliberates on the main charges, Judge Hoffman begins handing out contempt sentences to the Chicago Seven and their attorneys.

February 16: General Hershey officially retires as head of the Selective Service System. A bomb explosion at a San Francisco police precinct kills one officer and wounds five.

February 17: Seattle Liberation Front leads some 2,000 in an assault on the Fed-

eral Court House with tear gas, smoke bombs, rocks, and paint; 76 are arrested and 20 are injured. Capt. Jeffrey McDonald says that crazed hippies attacked him and slew his wife and two children at Ft. Bragg, North Carolina.

February 18: Federal jury acquits Chicago Seven of conspiracy but convicts five (all but Froines and Weiner) of crossing state lines with the intent to incite a riot. Secret inquest into death of Mary Jo Kopechne concludes with judge's report.

February 20: Only one of three bombs planted at the construction site of the new UW Architecture Building (Gould Hall) explodes.

February 21: Pentagon medics report "epidemic" of drug use among troops in Vietnam.

February 25: Maryland Sen. Charles Mathias charges that U.S. troops are fighting in Laos in violation of Congressional limits on the war. During a strike at the University of California at Santa Barbara, protesters burn down the Isla Vista branch of BankAmerica.

February 26: Police-gambling payoff investigators indict Frank Colacurccio and Charles Berger.

February 27: Governor Evans vetoes state benefit "bonus" for Vietnam Vets.

February 28: Press reports reveal a memorandum written by domestic affairs adviser Daniel Patrick Moynihan to President Nixon urging "benign neglect" in promoting civil rights and inner city development in order to permit past "progress" to be assimilated. After advancing for weeks, North Vietnamese and Pathet Lao troops close in on Vientienne. Jailers trim the locks of the Chicago Seven "Samsons" as they enter prison on contempt citations. Fort Lewis military police prevent 300 marchers led by the SLF and Friends of American Servicemen from entering the installation. Washington State Young Democrats elect Mike Lowry as their president. U.S. Sen. Henry Jackson and Mayor Uhlman meet with Native Americans over their claims to Fort Lawton land.

March 2: Texas sends Timothy Leary to jail for 10 years for possession of a "snuffbox" of grass. New Mobe Committee urges men to clog their draft boards with routine reports of their whereabouts as part of a "comply-in." Some 1,000 students jam a "hearing" convened to discipline *UW Daily* editor Bruce Olson.

March 3: A white mob attacks and overturns school buses carrying black children in Lamar, South Carolina. UW Department of Philosophy faculty votes not to extend the contract of visiting assistant professor and SLF leader Michael Lerner. Meanwhile, at the U District Post Office, Jan Tissot, Jon Van Veenendaal, Michael Reed, and Jeff Desmond, a police informer, set off a bomb which flattens one tire of a postal jeep.

March 4: U.S. Navy announces that it is surplusing Piers 90-91 and cutting back at Sandpoint. Washington Transit Advertising unveils "the Peoplebus," a Seattle Transit coach festooned with a fantasy scene painted by Splendid Sign Company artists Doug Fast and Gary Hallgren.

March 5: BSU and SLF members briefly occupy Thomson Hall to compel termination of all athletic and other arrangements with Brigham Young University.

March 6: A "bomb factory" in a Greenwich Village townhouse explodes, killing three leaders of the Weather Underground (Diana Oughton, Ted Gould, and Terry Robins). BYU turmoil spreads at the UW as roving gangs of demonstrators take over

six buildings in succession. The UW finally obtains a restraining order and allows city police on campus for the first time. Guatemalan guerrillas kidnap the U.S. ambassador; he is freed two days later.

March 8: UW announces that it will sever relations with BYU following completion of current athletic commitments. About 70 Native Americans and supporters, including Jane Fonda, briefly occupy Fort Lawton before being rounded up by MPs. Local feminists revive International Women's Day, originally established by American socialists in 1908 to honor and organize working women, with a conference at the UW.

March 9: Trial of H. Rap Brown opens in Maryland in connection with 1967 riots. A car bomb kills two associates of Brown; another bomb rips through the courthouse the next day and Brown disappears. UW acting president John Hogness addresses a campus rally of about 3,000 on the BYU issue and announces formation of a civil rights committee.

March 10: U.S. Army indicts Capt. Ernest Medina and four others for murder in connection with the My Lai massacre.

March 11: Major bombs go off in the Manhattan offices of the Secony Mobil Corporation, IBM, and Sylvania Electronics. A roving mass of about 1,000 led by the BSU and SLF invade nine UW buildings; scuffles injure 12. *P-I* reprints a Troy, Ohio, *Daily News* report that U.S. servicemen are being quarantined with an "incurable" form of venereal disease contracted in Vietnam.

March 12: A contingent of 200 Seattle police take positions on the UW campus, and BSU cancels further demonstrations while a bomb threat forces the evacuation of the Administration Building. Expo 70 opens in Osaka, Japan. President Nixon names Curtis Tarr to run Selective Service System.

March 13: Seattle attorney Alfred Schweppe wins an injunction to prevent the American League from moving the Pilots to Milwaukee. UW Faculty Senate endorses BSU position on BYU.

March 15: A U.S. freighter carrying munitions is hijacked to Cambodia. MPs arrest 77 protesters as they try again to occupy Fort Lawton. Spokane civil rights attorney Carl Maxey campaigns in Seattle for Senator Jackson's seat.

March 17: U.S. Army announces charges against 14 officers in connection with My Lai massacre.

March 18: With U.S. support, Lon Nol and Sisowath Sirik Matak overthrow Cambodia's Prince Sihanouk while he is visiting Moscow.

March 19: Some 250 delegates attend NOW's national convention in Des Plaines, Illinois; among their demands are passage of the Equal Rights Amendment and the replacement of the male editor of *Ladies Home Journal* with a woman. United Airlines acquires Seattle-based Western International Hotels, headed by Eddie Carlson.

March 20: Five-day national postal strike begins. An arson fire levels the Ozark Hotel, a flop house on Western Avenue, killing 20 and injuring 14 (the fire led to stringent new codes which had the inadvertent effect of closing thousands of low-income rooms and apartments in downtown Seattle).

March 25: President Nixon proposes dramatic expansion in Medicare/Aid eligibility. Called before a Senate subcommittee, Stokely Carmichael invokes the Fifth Amendment to refuse to testify about his

14 months of travel in the Third World. Governor Evans appoints the first black member of the UW Board of Regents, Seattle dentist Dr. Robert Flennaugh (at age 32, he is also the youngest Regent to date).

March 26: South Vietnamese President Thieu signs land reform act crafted in large part by UW agronomist Roy Prosterman. Air traffic controllers stage nationwide "sick-out."

March 27: President Nixon "authorizes" U.S. troops to cross into Cambodia during hot pursuits. Arsonists set $20,000 blaze in the UW's Parrington Hall. UW Regents hold first of several meetings with black students.

March 28: Anna Louise Strong, former Seattle School Board member and 1919 General Strike organizer, dies in Peking.

March 30: City Council votes to impose new 50-cent/month household tax to finance Seattle Transit. Bob Satiacum and U.S. Sen. Henry Jackson announce an understanding for development of a Native American cultural center at Fort Lawton.

March 31: Bankruptcy court approves sale of Pilots franchise to owners of the future Milwaukee Brewers.

April 2: Massachusetts Gov. Francis Sargent signs a state law allowing state residents to refuse to fight in "undeclared wars." Twelve Weathermen, including Bernadine Dohrn and Mark Rudd, are indicted in federal court in connection with the October 1969 Days of Rage. Native Americans launch a new assault on Fort Lawton.

April 3: Tom Hayden speaks at the UW.

April 4: Radio evangelist Carl McIntire's "March for Victory" in Washington, D.C., attracts about 8 percent of the predicted quarter million participants. Japanese leftists release an airliner which they had hijacked to North Korea five days earlier. Seattle City Councilmember Jeanette Williams proposes creation of a City Commission on the Status of Women.

April 5: Guatemalan kidnappers murder the West German ambassador after his government refuses to pay a ransom. Mayor Uhlman attends official opening of the University District Center.

April 7: Grand jury investigating Mary Jo Kopechne's death finds no basis for any indictments.

April 8: U.S. Senate rejects "mediocre" Judge Carswell's nomination to the Supreme Court 51 to 45. Addressing the Council of California Growers on student unrest, Gov. Ronald Reagan declares, "If it takes a bloodbath, let's get it over with. No more appeasement."

April 9: Florida Gov. Claude Kirk takes over personal management of the Manatee County schools and defies federal agents to enforce a desegregation order. The Rev. Daniel Berrigan goes underground to avoid imprisonment for destruction of draft records.

April 10: U.S. Navy announces that it will ship nerve gas from Okinawa to Oregon via Puget Sound. Paul McCartney makes it official that he has quit the Beatles.

April 12: Dave Wood, an aide to Mayor Uhlman, releases a staff paper discussing the possibility of a "third baby tax" to promote Zero Population Growth.

April 13: An explosion cripples the Apollo 13 mission as it nears the moon. Michigan Rep. Gerald Ford launches effort to impeach Supreme Court Justice William O. Douglas. Saboteurs dynamite a high-tension power pylon near Berkeley, disrupting electricity to the city and UC campus.

April 14: President Nixon nominates Harold Blackmun to the Supreme Court.

April 15: Police use tear gas to rout draft protesters in Berkeley and Eugene. SLF pickets IRS offices in solidarity with taxpayers.

April 16: Federal government indicts the "Seattle Eight," Mike Abeles, Jeff Dowd, Michael Justen, Joe Kelly, Michael Lerner, Roger Lippman, Charles Clark "Chip" Marshall III, and Susan Stern, for conspiracy to incite a riot at the February 17 "TDA" demonstration. The FBI arrests Abeles, Dowd, Kelly, Lerner, and Stern. ASUW elects "radical" Rick Silverman as new president. Apollo 13 jettisons its crippled rockets and uses the LEM engines to achieve the right reentry attitude for a safe landing.

April 17: Grand jury indicts Seattle Assistant Police Chief Cook for perjury in police payoff scandal.

April 18: Four thousand march peacefully against the war in downtown Seattle, escorted by police with daffodils tied to their night sticks. Seattle production of *Hair* opens at the Moore Theater.

April 19: National Moratorium Committee dissolves, having been superseded by the New Mobilization. Several Central Area properties are struck by bombs, including the home of State Rep. David Sprague.

April 20: President Nixon pledges to bring 150,000 U.S. troops back from Vietnam in 1971.

April 21: Communists and other progressive, peace-loving peoples celebrate 100th anniversary of the birth of Vladimir Illych Lenin. Yale students stage strike in sympathy with Bobby Seale and other Black Panthers arrested for murder of another Panther, Alex Rackley, in New Haven.

April 22: Environmentalists celebrate the first "Earth Day." U.S. sends ships to Trinidad to protect Americans during civil uprising. UW committee unveils draft "Student Bill of Rights."

April 24: Post Office reveals that bombs were mailed from Seattle to the White House and Selective Service System headquarters. Yale president Brewster Kingman declares that black revolutionaries could not receive a fair trial.

April 27: Seattle City Council passes ordinance making Pioneer Square the city's first "historic preservation district."

April 28: Protesters force cancellation of Honeywell, Inc., annual meeting in Minneapolis.

April 29: Arsonists set a fire in Seattle University's Xavier Hall.

April 30: U.S. forces launch "incursion" into Cambodia to disrupt North Vietnamese "headquarters" and supply routes. National Guard and state police fire tear gas and shotguns at protesters at Ohio State University in Columbus. Washington Natural Gas airs the possibility of building a pipeline for Alaskan gas to California via Washington. Municipal charges against 10 TDA protesters are dropped.

May 1: U.S. aircraft conduct their first bombing raids in North Vietnam since November 1968. Some 1,000 march in downtown Seattle and protesters trash the ROTC offices at the UW. Virtually every city and campus experiences some kind of protest, as President Nixon denounces "these bums, you know, blowing up campuses." State Republicans lose a suit to

impose delegate selection rules on the more conservative King County party.

May 2: Antiwar protesters burn the ROTC building at Ohio's Kent State University. Protesters and police clash at Yale, Stanford, and other campuses.

May 4: During antiwar protests at Kent State University, Ohio National Guardsmen open fire, killing four students (William Schroeder, Allison Krause, Jeffry Miller, and Sandra Scheuer) and injuring 15. The presidents of 37 U.S. universities telegram President Nixon urging withdrawal from Southeast Asia. ASUW and antiwar coalition calls for UW student strike. Seymour Hersch wins the Pulitzer Prize for uncovering the My Lai massacre.

May 5: More than 1,000 peaceful UW marchers pour onto the I-5 Freeway. Strikes and occupations occur at most major campuses. Interior Secretary Walter Hickel openly criticizes Nixon's war policies.

May 6: Some 10,000 marchers retake I-5 following a downtown rally, but this time police use tear gas to force them off. President Odegaard closes the UW and the city declares an official "day of reflection." President Nixon meets with six Kent State students and promises to investigate the shooting.

May 7: Police "vigilantes" beat protesters in the U District. President Nixon promises to "cool" antiprotest rhetoric and summons nation's governors to Washington for a "summit" on domestic unrest.

May 8: President Nixon speaks to the nation and says he and protesters have "same goals" of withdrawal and peace. Mayor Uhlman closes the I-5 Express Lanes to allow their use by some 15,000 marchers who rally in front of the Federal Court House in downtown Seattle. Acting

Police Chief Frank Moore condemns "vigilantes" who roamed the U District the previous night. New York construction workers ("hard hats") attack antiwar protesters during a demonstration on Wall Street (so much for a revolutionary student-worker alliance). Chicago authorities drop all charges against Black Panthers stemming from the December 6 police raid in which Fred Hampton and Mark Clark were killed.

May 9: Some 100,000 protesters assemble in Washington, D.C. A sleepless President Nixon pays a midnight visit to protesters encamped at the Lincoln Memorial. Some 600 Canadian protesters deface the Peace Arch at Blaine. King County Democrats endorse Carl Maxey over Senator Jackson and call for Nixon's impeachment. UAW president Walter Reuther dies in a plane crash.

May 11: Six black men are killed by Augusta, Georgia, police and National Guardsmen during riots provoked by the fatal beating of Charles Oatman in the Richmond County jail. Several thousand UW students at a campus rally "vote" to strike but not to close the campus. Six *UW Daily* staffers, including future *P-I* cartoonist Dave Horsey and "publisher" William Asbury, quit to protest Bruce Olson's editorial policies. "Radical" history teacher Sally Pangborn is dismissed from Garfield High School.

May 13: During Washington, D.C., hearings of the Commission on Obscenity and Pornography, Underground Press Syndicate staffer Thomas Forcade hits UW professor and Commissioner Otto Larsen in the face with a "cottage cheese pie."

May 14: Seattle Black Panther leader Elmer Dixon pleads his Fifth Amendment rights seventeen times during questioning by the House Internal Security Commit-

tee in Washington, D.C. The Rev. Ralph Abernathy condemns the Cambodia invasion during a Seattle speech. Police intercept a shipment of 168 pounds of peyote, worth $700,000, at Sea-Tac Airport.

May 15: Mississippi police fire into a Jackson State College dormitory, killing two students, James Green and Philip Gibbs. President Odegaard cancels UW classes as a memorial. Seattle police officer John Hannah kills Larry Ward during the attempted bombing of a Central Area realty.

May 17: About 100 members of People Against Nerve Gas (PANG) stage a "die-in" in downtown Seattle.

May 18: Protesters (mostly blacks) briefly occupy the office of Seattle University President Rev. Kenneth Baker, SJ, who later blasts "anarchists" for imposing "law of the jungle."

May 19: All four Forward Thrust bond issues (rapid transit, community centers, storm water, and health and safety facilities) fail, and Seattle voters reject building the Kingdome at Seattle Center. UW rejects student demands for campus referendum and clamps down on KUOW coverage of protests and strike activities.

May 21: Federal court rejects City of Seattle petition to halt planned nerve gas shipment. Six protesters are arrested after trashing the Seattle University Student Union cafeteria.

May 22: Protests halt inquest into shooting death of Larry Ward. Six of the Chicago Seven attend a rally for all of the Seattle Seven at the HUB.

May 23: President Nixon cancels nerve gas shipment through Puget Sound. Leftists clash with police in West Berlin. University Way is closed for the weekend to host the U District Street Fair, Seattle's first.

May 24: Weathermen issue underground "declaration of war" and threaten a major bombing.

May 25: UW faculty, staff, and students stage a "child-in" to press for a day care center.

May 27: Coroner's jury votes 3-2 that Larry Ward died by "criminal means." Seattle Police Department tries to strike a humorous note by adopting a porcine mascot and the slogan "Pride, Integrity, Guts."

May 28: Seven Seattle residents file a federal suit to prevent construction of Interstate 90 for failure to conform to new environmental laws. Police arrest 40 anti-Nixon protesters for "disrupting a religious service" during a Billy Graham crusade in Tennessee.

May 29: Help Eliminate Lawless Protesting (HELP) attracts 3,000 to a downtown rally defending Seattle Police. Contractors report sabotage of a UW building under construction.

June 1: Seattle City Council erases R. H. Thomson Expressway from official plans. Seattle area unemployment hits 10 percent, up from 4.5 percent at the beginning of the year.

June 2: University of Wisconsin researchers announce first synthesis of an artificial gene.

June 3: President Nixon pledges to withdraw 50,000 more troops by October 15. Seattle Police Tactical Squad commander Major Ray Carroll is demoted for "overreaction" during May riots.

June 4: Governor Evans calls for "calm" in reaction to campus disturbances, and explains that total "damages" at the UW

equal the cost of one season's clean-up at Husky Stadium.

June 5: Boeing unveils mock-up of the SST but loses contract bid for the B-1 supersonic bomber to North American. "Students for Responsible Expression" win a restraining order against ASUW support for the campus strike. UW students vote to reject proposal for eight-day break preceding national elections.

June 9: Harry Blackmun takes his seat on the Supreme Court.

June 10: President Nixon names George Schultz as the first director of the new Office of Management and Budget. Bill Thompson, a six-year veteran of Korea and Vietnam, is court-martialed for refusing to return to Vietnam. Three hundred Seattle taxis drive through downtown Seattle to protest the murder of a driver on June 1.

June 12: Commandos seize 60 Western hostages in Jordan to force concessions from King Hussein.

June 15: U.S. Supreme Court rules that conscientious objectors need not base their moral beliefs on religion.

June 16: Vice President Agnew verbally attacks the only student member of a new commission on student unrest. Newark voters elect the city's first black mayor, Kenneth Gibson.

June 17: U.S. House gives final passage to bill lowering the voting age in all elections to 18 effective January 1, 1971. Although national unemployment is at its lowest in 15 years (4.5 percent), rising inflation prompts President Nixon to ask for voluntary wage and price restraints. Court of Military Review voids Presidio mutiny convictions.

June 18: Edward Heath leads his Tories to victory over Labor in Great Britain. Governor Evans advocates new study of third floating bridge.

June 19: Having previously failed to fire lecturer Angela Davis for being a Communist, UCLA Regents dismiss her for giving "extreme" speeches off campus. Black Panthers rally at Lincoln Memorial, where David Hilliard calls for a new constitution.

June 20: Vice President Agnew says that Democratic war critics have "a psychological addiction to an American defeat."

June 21: Pennsylvania Central Railroad, the nation's largest, files for bankruptcy. The Rev. Jesse Jackson speaks at Garfield High School.

June 22: President Nixon signs 18-year-old-vote law but asks for a ruling to confirm its constitutionality. Superior Court rules the Larry Ward inquest verdict to be void because it was not unanimous.

June 23: On the 11th day of protests against a new U.S.-Japan defense treaty, more than three quarters of a million Japanese take to the streets in numerous cities. An era ends when Charles Rangel defeats Adam Clayton Powell Jr. to win the Democratic Congressional nomination from Harlem. Perjury trial of former Seattle Police Assistant Chief M.E. Cook opens with six witnesses who testify to paying off police.

June 24: In a largely symbolic act, the U.S. Senate Foreign Relations Committee votes to repeal the Gulf of Tonkin Resolution.

June 25: American Medical Association votes to permit members to offer abortions for social and economic reasons, not just in cases of danger to the mother.

June 26: New riots erupt in Northern Ireland after British courts jail Bernadette Devlin, Member of Parliament, for fomenting unrest.

June 29: Seattle Police Major David Jessup testifies that he went "under cover" and shared payoffs with three assistant chiefs of police. Michael Lerner drops a libel suit against the *P-I* for a profile of the SLF. Andrew Young joins a black-led boycott of the Unitarian General Assembly meeting in Seattle.

June 30: Last U.S. combat units reportedly leave Cambodia. Mayor Uhlman reveals that unknown messengers delivered a total of $1,500 in cash to his office in an apparent attempt to implicate him in the police payoff scandal. Assistant Chief Fuller testifies that City Councilman Charles Carroll received $300 a month in payoffs; Carroll later denies.

July 1: New York voters approve nation's most lenient abortion law. President Nixon names David Bruce as U.S. negotiator for the Paris peace talks.

July 2: Defying a court injunction, thousands mass at the Flying M Ranch in Eatonville for the Buffalo Party Convention and Pig Roast, a thinly disguised rock festival; a fan dies the next day when he is washed over a waterfall.

July 3: A bomb shatters windows in the University Federal Bank branch on NE 45th St.

July 5: Riots erupt in Asbury Park, New Jersey. The final day of the Atlanta International Pops Festival draws an estimated 500,000.

July 6: Mayor Uhlman names Oakland Police Chief Charles R. Gain to serve as "interim" chief of the Seattle Police. Gain draws immediate criticism from Black

Panthers (his hometown nemeses) and the SLF.

July 8: U.S. House gives final approval to Newspaper Preservation Act allowing "joint operating agreements" between "competing" metropolitan newspapers. Boeing wins contract to build and test two AWACS prototypes.

July 9: Federal jury convicts Assistant Chief Cook of perjury in denying knowledge of payoffs to a grand jury. ASUW president Rick Silverman warns that UW is preparing to take editorial control of the *Daily.*

July 11: Democratic "doves" dominate state convention to pass a liberal platform. Police break up a legal "block party" near Ravenna Park.

July 13: FBI declares the Black Panther Party to be America's "most dangerous" of "extremist organizations." U.S. Sen. Edward Brooke is assaulted during a march in New Bedford, Massachusetts, scene of five days of interracial rioting.

July 23: After years of skirmishes, Egyptian President Nasser accepts U.S. plan for cease fire with Israel. A federal grand jury indicts 13 members of the Weather Underground for conspiracy to bomb government buildings. Erik Lacitis launches the *New Times Journal,* which folds after five issues.

July 24: A contingent of 40 blacks "occupies" New York's Ellis Island. Washington Secretary of State Lud Kramer repeals voter eligibility rule barring non-English speakers.

July 25: In continuing dispute of delegate selection, the State GOP Convention refuses to seat the King County delegation.

July 26: Despite assistance from "Venceremos Brigades" of American vol-

unteers, Cuba fails to meet its goal of harvesting 10 million tons of sugar cane.

July 29: César Chavez's grape boycott yields contracts with most California growers.

August 1: An MIT study warns that a proposed fleet of 500 SSTs could create global air pollution comparable to major volcanic eruptions.

August 2: A 747 is hijacked to Cuba for the first time. Seattle-born actress Frances Farmer dies in Indianapolis.

August 4: Mayor Uhlman names former Oakland Police Chief Edward Toothman to succeed Chief Gain as interim Seattle Police Chief.

August 5: Robert Kennedy Jr. and Robert Sargent Shriver III are charged with possession of marijuana in Hyannisport.

August 7: A judge and three would-be kidnappers die in a shoot-out with police in San Rafael, California, in an attempt to spring James Haley during his trial for killing a prison guard (the "rescue" was spearheaded by Jonathan Jackson, brother of George Jackson, who was also charged with killing a guard at Soledad Prison the previous January). The kidnappers' guns are traced to UCLA lecturer Angela Davis, who disappeares (she was captured on October 13, tried as an accessory, and acquitted in 1972).

August 10: U.S. House passes the Equal Rights Amendment (ERA) by 350 to 15.

August 11: FBI captures "Catonsville Nine" fugitive, Fr. Daniel Berrigan, SJ. César Chavez begins a hunger strike to protest Teamsters' tactics in trying to break the UFW.

August 12: President Nixon signs bill replacing the Post Office Department with a quasi-corporate U.S. Postal Service.

August 16: Former HEW Secretary John Gardner announces formation of national "Common Cause" to press for government reforms.

August 18: After months of delay fighting local officials and environmentalists, the Army finally sinks a boatload of nerve gas off the coast of Florida. Chief Toothman fires Maj. David Jessup for "unofficer-like conduct" (Jessup was chiefly responsible for blowing the whistle on Seattle Police payoffs).

August 20: Ford unveils the Pinto. About 100 persons picket the Opera House appearance of the Russian Moiseyev Ballet to protest treatment of Jews in the Soviet Union.

August 24: A bomb levels the University of Wisconsin's math building, site of alleged military research, killing a graduate student.

August 26: Mayor Uhlman declares "Woman's Day" on the 50th anniversary of the ratification of the 19th Amendment.

August 28: SLF-sponsored Third Sky River Rock Festival begins an 11-day run on a farm on the Washougal River, 20 miles east of Vancouver.

August 29: Three die in East Los Angeles when a peace march degenerates into a riot.

August 31: Philadelphia police raid Black Panthers' office. New Haven jury convicts Panther Lonnie McLucas of conspiracy in murder of Alex Rackley.

Fall Season: "The Mary Tyler Moore Show" debuts on September 19, followed by the debut of "The Odd Couple" on September 24.

September 1: "End the War" amendment in the U.S. Senate fails on a vote of 39 to 55. Seattle Police Department's highest ranking black officer, Lt. Milton Price, "retires" and complains about "tokenism" in minority recruitment.

September 3: George Tielsch arrives from Garden Grove, California, to become the new permanent Seattle Police Chief. Black construction workers advocate Tyree Scott begins jail sentence on charges stemming from the 1968 Sea-Tac protests.

September 4: Federal government releases funds to begin construction of Fred Bassetti's controversial and long-delayed new Federal Office Building.

September 6: Palestinian terrorists blow up a 747 in Cairo (passengers and crew were released first) in the first of four hijackings of Western passenger planes during the month. Seattle's first "bed race" is held in Ballard.

September 9: Blue Streak inaugurates Seattle's first express park-and-ride transit service between Northgate and downtown.

September 10: Vice President Agnew says he won't stand for "pusillanimous pussyfooting." Eugene McCarthy campaigns for Carl Maxey in Seattle.

September 13: Weather Underground helps spring Timothy Leary from prison at the California Men's Colony West near San Luis Obispo.

September 15: Chris Bayley defeats incumbent King County Prosecutor Charles O. Carroll in the Republican Primary; King County Democrat Ed Heavey tops black activist attorney Lem Howell for the Democratic nod. Senator Jackson crushes Carl Maxey, and Congressman Tom Pelly survives a challenge from Joel Pritchard. A new weekly underground paper, *Sabot,* appears in Seattle (it folds after 13 issues on December 11, 1970).

September 17: Palestinians, supported by Syrian troops, battle Jordanian forces in a virtual civil war which ends in victory for King Hussein on September 26.

September 18: Jimi Hendrix, age 27, dies of an overdose in London.

September 21: ASUW president Rick Silverman tells Vice President Agnew that he is a "political joke" during a TV debate moderated by David Frost. Portions of the new North Seattle Community College campus open for classes.

September 26: The National Commission on Campus Unrest calls for President Nixon to heal breach between youth culture and mainstream society or risk "civil war."

September 28: Egyptian President Nasser dies; Anwar Sadat succeeds him on October 14. Some 33,000 students clog the UW for fall quarter.

October 2: An explosion equivalent to two dozen sticks of dynamite rocks a building at the University of Oregon. Jimi Hendrix is buried in Renton.

October 4: Janis Joplin, age 27, dies of an overdose in Hollywood.

October 5: Quebec separatists kidnap a British consular officer (his body is found on October 17).

October 6: Bolivia plunges into civil war. Some 200 cyclists stage a downtown "bike-in" to protest automobiles.

October 7: President Nixon proposes a "standstill" ceasefire in Vietnam and release of all POWs.

October 8: Two bombs cause $150,000 in damage to ROTC classrooms in the UW's Clark Hall; "Quarter Moon Tribe" claims responsibility. Bombings also strike San Rafael and Santa Barbara.

October 10: Washington Environmental Council launches signature drive for Initiative 43 establishing a State Shorelines Protection Act.

October 10—12: Multiple bombs explode in Rochester, New York City, and Orlando.

October 14: A bomb guts Harvard's Center for International Affairs; a women's collective called "Proud Eagle Tribe" says it planted the bomb to protest the arrest of Angela Davis the day before. Seattle School Board's first hearing on a desegregation plan which would mandate busing some 2,000 students draws a hostile crowd in West Seattle.

October 16: An Ohio jury clears National Guardsmen of blame in the Kent State killings. Canada rounds up 250 Quebeçois. Boeing shuts down operations in its original "Red Barn" factory.

October 19: On the federal government's motion, Judge Hoffman dismisses all "Chicago Eight" conspiracy charges against Bobby Seale.

October 20: Dr. Timothy Leary emerges from the underground in Algeria. ASUW Women's Commission details sex discrimination on campus.

October 24: President Nixon denounces his own Presidential Commission on Obscenity and Pornography as "morally bankrupt" (the panel had advocated repeal of all forms of censorship).

October 29: Antiwar protesters pelt President Nixon's motorcade with rocks and eggs in San Jose.

October 31: The Army declares 900 acres of Fort Lawton to be surplus, clearing the way for city acquisition. Two thousand march against the war from Seattle Center to downtown.

November 2: The Rev. Louis Gaffney, SJ, succeeds the embattled Reverend Baker, SJ, as president of Seattle University.

November 3: Avowed Marxist Salvador Allende Gossens takes office as president of Chile. State and local voters sort through a crowded ballot to reelect U.S. Sen. Henry Jackson and all Congressional incumbents; liberalize abortion (HJR 20); reject a flat-rate income tax (HJR 42), a ban on disposable containers (I-256), and a 19-year-old vote (HJR 6); elect Republican Chris Bayley as King County Prosecutor in a squeaker over Ed Heavey; and place Seattle Transit under the mayor's direct control. Massachusetts voters make the Rev. Robert Drinan, SJ, the first Catholic (and Jesuit) priest elected to Congress.

November 5: A Pentagon review blames President Johnson for botching the war in Vietnam. The Union of the Unemployed rallies 200 at Boeing Plant 2.

November 6: Judge George Boldt opens pretrial hearings on the conspiracy charges against the "Seattle Seven" (the eighth defendant, Michael Justesten, went underground).

November 9: Charles DeGaulle dies.

November 10: Frank Ruano, who led the drive to block construction of the Kingdome at Seattle Center, launches a campaign to recall County Executive John Spellman.

November 11: Seattle School Board adopts mandatory busing scheme to desegregate selected middle and high schools.

November 16: State Land Commissioner Bert Cole bans oil drilling in Puget Sound. ASUW Women's Commission files sex discrimination charges against the UW.

November 17: Trial of Lt. Calley for My Lai massacre begins at Ft. Benning, Georgia. Soviet Union's Luna 17 probe deploys a remote-controlled robot tractor to explore the moon's surface.

November 19: Hafez-al-Assad takes control of Syria following a coup.

November 20: A court martial acquits Staff Sgt. David Mitchell, the first soldier to be tried in connection with the My Lai massacre.

November 21: U.S. planes bomb Haiphong and other North Vietnamese targets.

November 23: U.S. commandos blast their way into a Hanoi prison but find no U.S. POWs. Seattle Seven trial opens in Tacoma.

November 24: Seattle Seven defendants stage a walk-out to protest prosecution's exclusion of younger people from the jury. Architect George Bartholick unveils plan to expand Woodland Park Zoo by lidding Aurora Avenue.

November 25: President Nixon fires Interior Secretary Walter Hickel, who had broken with the administration on Vietnam and environmental issues. Novelist Yukio Mishima commits hari-kari after Japanese troops fail to heed his call for a nationalist coup. Seattle Seven trial is disrupted anew over jury selection. Only 200 show up for a UW rally protesting the war.

November 26: A Bolivian attempts to stab Pope Paul VI during a visit to Manila.

November 27: FBI Director J. Edgar Hoover tells a Senate hearing that Frs. Daniel and Philip Berrigan (now in prison) had planned to kidnap Henry Kissinger.

November 28: The Black Panther-sponsored Revolutionary People's Constitutional Convention assembles in Washington, D.C.

November 30: A large bomb damages the U.S. embassy in Phnom Penh, Cambodia. The Italian Parliament defies the Vatican to legalize divorce. A U.S. House committee investigating Supreme Court Justice William O. Douglas concludes that there are no grounds for his impeachment.

December: *Seattle* Magazine publishes its final issue.

December 1: Five thousand protest South Vietnamese Vice President Ky's visit to San Francisco.

December 2: U.S. Senate confirms William Ruckelshaus as the first director of the new Environmental Protection Agency.

December 3: Quebeçois separatists free British Trade Commissioner James Cross after holding him for 59 days. U.S. Senate defeats new appropriation for Boeing SST, effectively killing the project. State Supreme Court reverses Floyd Turner's conviction for flag desecration on the grounds that the prosecution had failed to prove "evil intent."

December 4: César Chavez is jailed (for the first time) in Salinas, California, for defying a court ban against the UFW's lettuce boycott. House Internal Security Committee releases testimony by an unnamed "informant" accusing Seattle Black Panthers of several local bank robberies and bombings. Conservative Republican Ken Rogstad announces he will step down as head of the King County GOP (he is succeeded by Dennis Dunn).

December 10: Judge Boldt declares a mistrial and cites six of the Seattle Seven for contempt (Susan Stern was out ill).

December 14: Riots in Poland topple Vladyslaw Gomulka, but Communists maintain power through combination of repression and concession. President Nixon appoints former Democrat John Connally as Treasury Secretary. A brawl during a hearing on the original six contempt citations results in new contempt citations for all Seattle Seven defendants, who are sent to prison without bail.

December 16: A former Army intelligence officer tells a Senate hearing that the Army conducted illegal surveillance of U.S. civilians and public officials.

December 17: Black picketers halt construction at the UW.

December 21: U.S. Supreme Court rules that Congress has the power to lower the voting age to 18 only for federal offices without a constitutional amendment (Amendment XXVI lowered the voting age for all elections in 1971). Eddie Carlson is named president of United Airlines. Mayor Uhlman appoints Al Petty Superintendent of Buildings, making him the first black to head a city department.

December 23: Bolivia releases Regis Debray, French comrade of Che Guevara, and author of the influential *Revolution in the Revolution*.

December 30: After years of consumer complaints and unpaid taxes, the State of Washington shuts down car dealer Ralph Williams.

December 31: Congress repeals the Tonkin Gulf Resolution and adopts the Cooper-Church Amendment restructuring U.S. actions in Cambodia. The Sixties end officially. Long estranged by personal and stylistic conflicts, the Beatles officially dissolve their partnership. U.S. forces in Vietnam drop to 280,000 troops. U.S. Census reports that Seattle population declined nearly 5 percent during the 1960s from 557,087 to 530,831; King County as a whole gained 198,000 to reach 1.13 million.

Zeitgeist: The digestion of the Sixties begins with publication of Theodore Roszak's *The Making of a Counter Culture,* Charles Reich's *The Greening of America,* Alvin Toffler's *Future Shock,* Kate Millet's *Sexual Politics,* Erich Segal's *Love Story,* and Richard Bach's *Jonathan Livingston Seagull.* Conflicting military myths battle it out on screen with release of Franklin Schaffner's *Patton* and Robert Altman's *M*A*S*H;* Arthur Penn's *Little Big Man* ambushes Custer anew; and Bob Rafelson's *Five Easy Pieces* confirms Jack Nicholson's stardom. Architectural visionary Paolo Soleri begins building "Arcosanti" near Phoenix. Simon & Garfunkel dominate the Grammys with "Bridge Over Troubled Waters" and the Carpenters are voted best new group. Crosby, Stills and Nash add Neil Young to the roster. Documentaries of Woodstock and Altamont (*Gimme Shelter*) are released while the opening of *Jesus Christ, Superstar* and several hit singles with spiritual themes portend that rock is getting religion.

1971

January 1: Governor Evans begins closing state mental health institutions as part of reforms intended to protect civil rights and encourage "community-based treatment."

January 7: Federal courts enjoin most uses of DDT nine years after publication of *Silent Spring.*

January 8: Ninth Court of Appeals orders that the Seattle Seven be freed on bail.

January 9: Eldridge Cleaver confines Timothy Leary in Algiers under a "revolutionary bust." Wreckers begin razing the Burke Building and Rivoli Theater for the new Federal Office Building.

January 12: Nixon signs repeal of the Tonkin Gulf Resolution and agrees to narrower limits within which to conduct the war. Federal government indicts the Rev. Philip Berrigan and five others for conspiring to kidnap Henry Kissinger. Surgeon General recommends banning smoking in public areas. Georgia's new governor, Jimmy Carter, calls for an end to racism in his inaugural address. Norman Lear's "All in the Family" debuts on CBS and runs until September 1983.

January 15: Egypt dedicates the Aswan Dam on the Nile.

January 18: Sen. George McGovern announces that he is running for the Democratic presidential nomination in 1972. Seattle "In-City Living Task Force" proposes development of high-rise housing for 50,000 residents in the Denny Regrade. Trial of Eatonville rock festival organizers on contempt of court begins in Tacoma.

January 19: Indian fishing rights advocate Hank Adams is shot in Tacoma.

January 22: President Nixon proposes a "New American Revolution" through revenue sharing and federal reforms to empower local governments. UW Human Rights Commission advocates the firing of coach Jim Owens and athletic director Joe Kearney. ASUW elects "moderate" Ralph Anderson as its new president.

January 25: Idi Amin leads a coup to depose Ugandan president Milton Obote. Charles Manson and three female devotees are convicted in the Tate-LaBianca murders. U.S. Supreme Court rules that employers may not discriminate in hiring women simply because they have young children. City ethics board clears Councilmen Ted Best and Charley Carroll of wrong doing in accepting gambler donations.

January 26: Seattle unveils plan for downtown Waterfront Park and Aquarium (two days later, city consultants advocate putting the aquarium at Golden Gardens despite neighborhood opposition). Henry Moore's "Vertebrae—1968" is dedicated at the new Seattle-First National Bank Building.

January 30: Apollo 14 lifts off for the moon. Rioting erupts anew during an antiwar march in East Los Angeles.

February 1: Justice Court Judge Janice Niemi dismisses pornography charges against a First Avenue book store (two days later, Chief Tielsch announces that he is disbanding the city's "smut squad").

February 4: Protesters splatter doors and halls of the Olympic Hotel during a conference of defense contractors.

February 7: U.S. artillery and aircraft support a massive South Vietnamese incursion into Laos. Women gain the vote in Switzerland.

February 8: Jordanian army clashes with Palestinians. National Guard quells four days of riots in Wilmington, North Carolina.

February 9: A major earthquake jolts Los Angeles, killing 45 in the collapse of a veterans hospital, injuring more than 1,000, and causing $1 billion in damage. Protest led by the Oriental Student Union (OSU) briefly closes Seattle Central Community College. Federal sting reaps more than 1,000 pounds of pot at a U District drive-in.

February 10: Seattle Police arrest nine during a clash with about 100 UW marchers led by the "International People's Movement" to protest the invasion of Laos; an earlier rally at the HUB drew 1,500.

February 15: Black Panthers and Black Muslims battle in downtown Atlanta.

February 19: Democratic National Committee approves delegate selection reforms to ensure "diversity."

February 20: Minority employment advocates, building trades unions, and contractors agree to a federally brokered "Seattle Plan" to create 110 new minority trainee positions in local construction projects.

February 21: More than 3,000 U.S. and Canadian citizens demonstrate at Blaine against oil tanker traffic between Alaska and Washington State.

February 25: Chapin Scott Paterson, an Army draftee on the way to basic training at Fort Lewis, hijacks a Seattle-bound jet from San Francisco to Vancouver, B.C.

February 27: Bernie Whitebear, head of United Indians of All Tribes, outlines plan for cultural center as part of a compromise for public use of Fort Lawton.

March 1: The Weathermen detonate a bomb in a U.S. Capitol rest room. Leslie Bacon is later taken into custody as a material witness and sent to Seattle to testify before a federal grand jury (she refused and was jailed on May 12).

March 2: Oriental Student Union (OSU) protesters briefly occupy Seattle Central Community College.

March 7: Pentagon unveils new ad campaign with theme, "Today's Army wants to join you."

March 8: U.S. Supreme Court requires conscientious objectors to oppose all war, not just the one in Vietnam. Court martial of Capt. Ernest Medina, commander of the company responsible for the My Lai massacre, begins. Members of the "Citizens Commission to Investigate the FBI" burgles the FBI office in Media, Pennsylvania, and later publishes files revealing the existence of an illegal Counter Intelligence Program (COINTELPRO) to monitor and harass the civil rights and antiwar movements and the underground press.

March 21: Seattle Policeman Robert Ellmore shoots and kills Leslie Allen Black, a black, following a high-speed auto chase in the Central Area. An inquest finds the shooting "unjustified" on April 16.

March 23: Congress sends Amendment XXVI to the U.S. Constitution, which lowers the age of full citizenship to 18, to the states for ratification. Former Washington State Attorney General John O'Connell and San Francisco Mayor Joseph Alioto are indicted for conspiracy to bribe government officials during 1962 antitrust litigation against electrical equipment manufacturers.

March 24: Last-gasp effort to revive the SST fails in Congress and Boeing lays off 7,000 workers.

March 25: KRAB-FM wins a landmark FCC ruling rebuffing a two-year investigation of the station for obscene programming.

March 26: UFW and Teamsters settle their jurisdictional dispute over migrant lettuce pickers.

March 29: Court martial convicts Lieutenant Calley of premeditated murder of 22 civilians at My Lai and sentences him to life in prison. President Nixon intervenes on April 1 to "personally review" the case and orders Calley freed from the stockade.

April 2: Assistant Police Chief Eugene Corr resigns after being demoted by Chief Tielsch for talking with corruption probers without the chief's knowledge.

April 5: Seattle City Council approves construction of aquarium at Golden Gardens.

April 6: Three radicals win election to Berkeley City Council.

April 7: President Nixon announces that he will withdraw 100,000 more troops from Vietnam by December 1.

April 10: U.S. Ping-Pong team begins unprecedented tour of the People's Republic of China.

April 12: Civil war erupts in Ceylon (Sri Lanka). Indictments are announced in Chicago describing a bizarre conspiracy to murder Mayor Daley and the Rev. Jesse Jackson, head of "Operation Breadbasket." New grand jury renews probe of Seattle police corruption.

April 15: State Supreme Court derails Harley Hoppe's "Overtaxed, Inc." campaign to repeal King County Charter. The

U District Center and ASUW sponsor an 11-day "Community Conference."

April 16: Local realtors Bob McDonald and Jim Youngren post a billboard message on Aurora at NE 167th reading, "Will the *last person* leaving Seattle *turn out the lights.*"

April 17: Seattle Peace Action Coalition leads 2,500 in an antiwar march from downtown to Seattle Center.

April 18: "Earth Station 7," housing Environmental Works and Country Doctor Clinic, opens in a former fire station on Seattle's Capitol Hill.

April 19: Lon Nol and his cabinet resign in Cambodia. Several hundred Vietnam Veterans Against the War demonstrate in Washington, D.C., and then camp on Capitol Hill.

April 20: U.S. Supreme Court upholds constitutionality of mandatory busing to redress school segregation. Students march from Garfield High School to the Municipal Building and picket the City Council to protest recent police shootings of blacks.

April 22: Haitian "President for Life" Papa Doc Duvalier dies and is succeeded by his son, "Baby Doc."

April 23: Vietnam veterans fling their military medals on the steps of the Capitol. King County Prosecutor Chris Bayley charges Seattle policeman Robert Ellmore with manslaughter in the killing of Leslie Black on March 21.

April 24: A quarter million march in Washington, D.C., during one of the largest demonstrations in American history. A simultaneous demonstration in San Francisco marshals 150,000-plus.

April 26: Oil tanker spill at Port Angeles causes major environmental damage.

May 1: Amtrak begins operating the nation's passenger rail system. Jim Deagle, Judy Williams, Dave Sucher, and friends publish the first issue of *The Seattle Sound News,* which folds the following August.

May 2: Federal police clear an encampment of 30,000 antiwar protesters in Washington, D.C. Jane Fonda and Donald Sutherland address a "GI Antiwar Rally" of 1,000 in Tacoma.

May 3: Erich Honecker succeeds Walter Ulbricht as leader of East Germany. Washington, D.C., police arrest Abbie Hoffman, Rennie Davis, and 7,000 other protesters for tying up traffic. They are herded into Robert F. Kennedy Stadium. Seattle City Council votes to establish Seattle Arts Commission (succeeding the advisory Municipal Arts Commission founded in 1955). People's Coalition for Peace and Justice pickets the entrance to The Highlands, an exclusive residential compound in north Seattle. Queen Elizabeth II visits Vancouver, B.C.

May 5: Fifteen hundred protesters briefly blockade the U.S. Capitol before being arrested. A Coalition for Peace and Justice march by 2,000 in downtown Seattle degenerates into a trashing binge for which 18 are arrested.

May 7: Another round of downtown Seattle trashing results in 45 additional arrests.

May 9: Two Buddhists immolate themselves in Hué.

May 13: A New York jury acquits 13 Black Panthers of an alleged conspiracy to bomb schools, police stations, and other public facilities. U.S. Senate appoints first female pages.

May 14: Swiss government expels Timothy Leary and his wife Rosemary.

May 15: First-class stamp rises to 8 cents.

May 18: Auto mechanics begin long and violent strike against local dealerships.

May 19: Last-gasp attempt to revive the SST dies in the U.S. Senate. Leslie Bacon is jailed for contempt for refusing to answer questions during grand jury probe of March 1 U.S. Capitol bombing.

May 20: Governor Evans vetoes broad gambling bill but allows bingo and raffles.

May 23: White House adviser reveals that the armed forces discharges 20,000 drug addicts each year.

May 25: A hung jury leads New Haven to dismiss charges against Bobby Seale and Ericka Huggins in connection with the murder of Panther Alex Rackley. Panther leaders George Sam Jr. and Warren Kimbro had previously pled guilty to second degree murder. Seattle voters elect the first members to 10 citizens councils to advise the School Board.

May 26: Juan Corona is arrested in Yuba City, California, for killing 20 migrant workers in the worst serial murder to date.

May 31: Sixty members of Vietnam Veterans Against the War march in Seattle's Memorial Day parade.

June: First "Last Whole Earth Catalog" is published and 400,000 copies are printed before year's end (Stewart Brand published the original Catalog in March 1969).

June 1: President Nixon declares drugs "Public Enemy No. 1." Grand jury indicts three former Seattle policemen for perjury and graft. Seattle City Council gives final approval for stronger Seattle Arts Commission.

June 4: Activists attempt to "arrest" Selective Service chief Curtis Tarr in his Washington, D.C., office. Mayor Uhlman

testifies before the police payoffs grand jury.

June 7: Soyuz 11 links up with Salute to establish first orbiting space station.

June 10: Army court martial convicts Sgt. William Higdon of corruption in managing servicemen's clubs in Vietnam.

June 12: Mexican police and "Falcons" death squads kill 43 student protesters.

June 13: The *New York Times* begins publishing excerpts from "The Pentagon Papers," secret strategic analyses of the Vietnam War, provided by Daniel Ellsberg. Nixon Administration seeks to suppress publication, but the Supreme Court rules against "prior constraint" on June 30.

June 14: Friends of the Market launch initiative drive to expand Pike Place Market historic district and forestall urban renewal. U.S. Navy retires bell-bottom pants from official uniforms.

June 15: Vernon Jordan named new head of the Urban League.

June 17: UW hires avowed Marxist professor Phil Meranto; it later discovers that he had been arrested in protests at the University of Illinois, threatens to fire him, makes him a campus cause célèbre, and ends up keeping him.

June 22: By a vote of 57 to 42, the U.S. Senate adopts a resolution advocating the complete withdrawal of U.S. troops by the spring of 1972 (Congress had previously rejected the McGovern-Hatfield Amendment requiring withdrawal by December 31, 1971).

June 26: U.S. Justice Department issues arrest warrant for Daniel Ellsberg.

June 28: U.S. Supreme Court remands some 30 death sentences, including that of Richard Speck, to the lower courts for reconsideration.

June 29: After completing 24 days aboard the Salute space station, three Soyuz 11 cosmonauts die when their capsule depressurizes upon reentry.

June 30: The voting age is lowered to 18 with ratification of Amendment XXVI to the Constitution. City Councilman Ted Best resigns; Ken Rogers is appointed to fill his seat (he fails to survive the September 21 primary election).

July 1: Longshoremen's strike idles Seattle and other West Coast ports (until October 8).

July 3: Jim Morrison, aged 27, dies of a heart attack. Buffalo Party stages a small rock festival in North Bend.

July 5: Bill Graham closes the Fillmore in San Francisco.

July 7: ASUW scraps the "Tyee" yearbook for lack of interest.

July 9: Henry Kissinger arrives in Peking for secret talks with Chou En-lai.

July 15: President Nixon announces that he will visit the People's Republic of China within a year.

July 20: Jeff Desmond tells the *P-I* that he was acting as a government informer and provocateur in abetting the March 3, 1970, U District Post Office bombing.

July 27: Grand jury indicts 32 former police officers and local officials, including former prosecutor Charles O. Carroll, former police chief Frank Ramon, former King County Sheriff Jack Porter, and sitting Seattle City Council President Charles M. Carroll, for conspiracy to abet illegal gambling and police payoffs; nine more indictments follow the next day.

July 30: Apollo 15 lands on the moon with a Boeing-built "Lunar Rover." During their three days on the moon, astronauts name a crater in honor of the science fic-

tion saga *Dune,* written by Seattle *P-I* reporter Frank Herbert.

August 1: George Harrison hosts a benefit concert for Bangladesh in New York's Madison Square Garden, the first of many such fundraisers.

August 2: Secretary of State William Rogers announces that the U.S. will support PRC admission to the UN.

August 3: Neighbors in Need, Radical Women, and Service Employees Local 8 lead 200 in a Seattle march demanding the release of federal food surpluses to feed the hungry.

August 9: President Nixon signs emergency unemployment act to aid Seattle and other depressed local economies.

August 10: Citizens Against Mandatory Busing (CAMB) obtains an injunction against Seattle School District desegregation plan (the injunction is lifted in time for opening day on September 1).

August 13: Festival-71, the precursor of Bumbershoot, opens at Seattle Center.

August 15: President Nixon announces "New Economic Policy" (shades of Lenin) to attack 6.6 percent inflation and 5.8 percent unemployment by freezing prices, rents, and wages for 90 days; blocking gold sales; and raising tariffs. The Dow Jones Average posts a 33 point gain the next day to close at 888.93, while most unions vow to defy the restraints.

August 19: The Washington State ACLU's office staff goes on strike in Seattle to protest "demeaning" conditions.

August 20: The Army reduces Lieutenant Calley's sentence from life to 20 years.

August 21: San Quentin guards kill "Soledad Brother" George Jackson and five inmates during an attempted escape. Jackson's attorney, Stephen Bingham, is later charged in absentia (he went underground) with smuggling weapons to Jackson.

August 22: FBI arrests 20 activists in Camden, New Jersey, and five in Buffalo, New York, for attempting to steal and destroy draft records.

August 24: A Cook County grand jury indicts Assistant State's Attorney Edward Hanrahan and 13 police officers with obstructing justice during the investigation of the killing of Black Panthers Fred Hampton and Mark Clark in December 1969.

August 26: NOW leads 6,000 in a New York City march demanding "51 percent of everything."

August 29: South Vietnamese vote in elections widely regarded as rigged in favor of President Thieu.

September 3: Satsop Riverfair and Tin Cup Races, the last and largest of the state's rock festivals, welcomes 45,000 to Grays Harbor County; one of the organizers, Gary Friedman, is later identified as a state drug investigator.

September 8: The Kennedy Center for the Performing Arts opens in Washington, D.C.

September 9: Inmates of New York's Attica Prison riot and take 38 guards hostage. The prisoners kill one guard and wound three during the stand-off. Chinese Defense Minister Lin Pao, Mao's heir apparent, dies in plane crash while fleeing the collapse of his attempted coup against his not-quite-ready-to-retire predecessor.

September 11: Nikita Khrushchev dies.

September 12: Some 1,000 hike along railroad tracks around Lake Union to promote "Burke-Gilman Trail."

September 13: New York State Police kill nine hostages and 33 prisoners during "rescue" raid at Attica Prison. King County approves subsidy to keep failing suburban "Metropolitan Transit" bus company alive.

September 14: Trial begins on Marco DeFunis' charge that the UW Law School denied him admission due to preferential enrollment policies for minorities.

September 17: U.S. Supreme Court Associate Justice Hugo Black announces that he will retire (he dies one week later).

September 21: Liberal Democrat Mike Ryherd and Republican "Tax Rebel" Harley Hoppe win nominations for King County Assessor in the primary election as the county tests "punchcard voting" in Bellevue and Mercer Island. Seattle voters pit James Kimbrough against Bruce Chapman and John Miller against Junius Rochester for open City Council seats vacated by Ted Best and Charley Carroll. Two anti-busing candidates win nominations for Seattle School Board.

September 22: Captain Medina is acquitted of My Lai charges. American Indian Movement (AIM) activists attempt to "arrest" the deputy director of the Bureau of Indian Affairs in Washington, D.C., for "stifling" reforms. Marco DeFunis wins his Superior Court suit against the UW, which appeals.

September 28: President Nixon signs long-delayed bill extending draft for two more years.

September 29: State grand jury indicts three sitting members of the Liquor Control Board and its former chairman for graft and grand larceny.

September 30: Sen. Mike Mansfield's budget rider requiring U.S. withdrawal from Vietnam within six months passes the U.S. Senate by 57 to 38. Longshoremen's strike spreads to East and Gulf coasts.

October 4: Citizens protest proposed closing of Public Health Hospital on Beacon Hill. Evergreen State College opens.

October 7: President Nixon announces creation of permanent wage and price control boards as part of "Phase 2" of his economic policies. *Newsday* implicates Nixon confidant Bebe Rebozo in corrupt New York land development. The *Los Angeles Times* exposes Nixon's personal gardener as an illegal alien.

October 8: Court order suspends West Coast Longshoremen's strike on its 100th day.

October 10: The reconstructed London Bridge is dedicated in Lake Havasu City, Arizona.

October 13: *P-I* reports that the Seattle Police tried to block airing of PBS "Dream Machine" program reporting police complicity in local bombings. "Youth Against War and Fascism" protesters battle with police and supporters of "Soviet Jewry Freedom Bus" in downtown Seattle.

October 14: Shah of Iran throws lavish party to celebrate 2,500th anniversary of the founding of the Persian Empire.

October 16: Black Panther and former SNCC head H. Rap Brown is shot and captured during an attempted hold-up in New York City.

October 20: West German Socialist Chancellor Willy Brandt is awarded the Nobel Peace Prize for his "Ost Politik"; Pablo Neruda receives the Nobel for literature the next day. New AEC head James Schlesinger says nuclear agency will now promote "public interest." Black and white students fight at Lincoln High School,

prompting new human relations programs.

October 21: President Nixon nominates William Rehnquist and Lewis Powell to succeed Hugo Black and John Harlan on the U.S. Supreme Court, while Attorney General Mitchell denies the American Bar Association prior review of the nominations.

October 22: Superior Court Judge W. R. Cole voids grand jury indictments against Seattle and King County police and officials as unconstitutional under new grand jury law which took effect May 11. President Nixon names federal Judge George Boldt to chair new federal Pay Board. Soviet Premier Kosygin visits Vancouver, B.C.

October 25: UN General Assembly seats the People's Republic of China and ousts Taiwan's Republic of China delegates.

October 26: Protest by students and parents at Franklin High School earns commitment by School District to add Asian American instructors.

October 29: Seattle Model City Program begins expansion into Ballard/North Greenwood, Southwest Seattle, and Southeast Seattle.

October 30: In a stunning rebuff of President Nixon's policy, the U.S. Senate rejects his foreign aid bill.

October 31: The IRA launches a new wave of terror to force Britain to abandon Northern Ireland, with bombings of London's Post Office Tower and Westminster Barracks.

November 2: The polls are opened for the first time to voters between the ages of 18 and 21. Seattle voters endorse the Friends of the Market initiative by 76,369 to 53,264; reject creation of an appointed

Finance Department to replace the elected Comptroller and Treasurer; establish campaign finance reporting for municipal candidates; and elect "progressive Republicans" John Miller and Bruce Chapman to the City Council. Anti-busing candidate Delwin Chafe defeats School Board president Palmason. Harley Hoppe edges past Mike Ryherd to become King County Assessor. Governor Evans appoints the state's new Women's Commission.

November 3: Federal Pay Board imposes 5 percent cap on wage raises.

November 4: Eugene McCarthy campaigns for president in Seattle; Governor Reagan arrives the next day and raises $100,000 for state Republicans.

November 6: AEC detonates an underground nuclear explosion at Amchitka.

November 11: Federal Price Board sets a 2.5 percent cap on annual price increases for new products. President Nixon announces that Earl Butz (later undone by his ethnic humor) will succeed Clifford Hardin as Agriculture Secretary. Ten thousand watch and listen at the UW Hec Edmundson Pavilion as Professor Giovanni Costigan and William Buckley spar over the issues of the day; most observers credit Costigan with a TKO.

November 12: President Nixon announces that 45,000 troops will leave Vietnam by February 1, 1972. The Rev. Louis Gaffney, SJ, is named permanent president of Seattle University.

November 13: Mariner 9 enters orbit around Mars, but a planet-wide dust storm frustrates initial photographic survey.

November 14: City of Seattle and United Indians of All Tribes announce agreement on sharing surplus Fort Lawton land.

November 15: Rival supporters of Eldridge Cleaver and Huey Newton clash in a Los Angeles courtroom. State Court of Appeals voids the state's flag desecration law in the case of Harold Spence, arrested in Seattle on May 10, 1970, for tapping a peace symbol to the U.S. flag.

November 16: U.S. Court of Appeals halts all land assembly and pre-construction activity on I-90 until an environmental impact statement is prepared. Prosecutor Chris Bayley's home is torched.

November 17: Grand jury launches probe of "phone freaks" (proto-hackers), who bypass telephone billing computers to place free long-distance calls.

November 18: Sen. Henry Jackson officially declares his candidacy for president. The UW Experimental College introduces the nation's first course of instruction in Chinese acupuncture.

November 19: U.S. Ninth Circuit Court of Appeals voids Judge Boldt's contempt citations against the Seattle Seven as not sufficiently "specific."

November 20: U.S. House Black Caucus calls for a national convention of black political leaders.

November 22: U.S. Supreme Court strikes down an Idaho law giving men hiring preference over women through the application of "unrelated criteria." King County adopts punchcard voting for all future elections.

November 24: A passenger going by the name of D. B. Cooper hijacks a Northwest Airlines 727 and forces it to land at Sea-Tac, where he collects $20,000 and four parachutes and releases 37 passengers before ordering the plane's crew to fly to Reno. He vanishes enroute and is presumed to have parachuted from the aft door. (Fragments of the ransom money were found 25 years later in Oregon, but "Cooper's" fate remains a mystery.) Seattle City Council endorses "compromise" for 10-lane I-90 Freeway.

November 27: In the first of many similar confrontations, a father demands custody of his young son from the mother, who has joined a "Children of God" commune in Burlington, Washington.

November 28: First White House Conference on the Aging opens. SuperSonics owner Sam Schulman offers to help finance expanding the Coliseum to 20,000 seats.

November 30: King County Council gives final approval to begin building the Kingdome. Seattle petition drive is launched to halt construction of Forward Thrust aquarium at Golden Gardens. Peggy Maze, director of Neighbors in Need, endorses federal proposal to expand food stamps and distribute surplus food in Seattle.

December 1: U.S. Treasury Secretary John Connally proposes 10 percent devaluation of the dollar. Mariner 9 transmits first photos of the Martian moon Phobos. I. F. Stone publishes the final edition of the *Weekly* he began nineteen years earlier.

December 3: Indian and Pakistani forces clash in full-scale war; on December 5, East Pakistan declares its independence as the new nation of Bangladesh. Soviet probe soft-lands on Mars but is quickly disabled by a dust storm.

December 6: Seattle nightclub operator and alleged racketeer Frank Colacurcio is convicted in Spokane of conspiring to promote illegal gambling. Nobelist Linus Pauling defends his controversial advocacy of massive doses of Vitamin C during a Seattle visit.

December 7: Ohio drops all charges against protesters in the Kent State disturbances.

December 8: University District Development Council unveils plan for U Way pedestrian mall.

December 9: President Nixon vetoes first comprehensive federal day-care bill.

December 11: The third trial of Huey Newton ends with a hung jury; he is released four days later after serving two years in jail.

December 13: U.S. abstention allows passage of new UN resolution urging Israeli withdrawal from "occupied lands."

December 15: East Pakistan forces surrender to India and Bangladesh rebels; an orgy of assassinations and vengeance killings begins.

December 18: International "Group of 10" monetary accord devalues the U.S. dollar by 8.57 percent in effort to boost exports. The Rev. Jesse Jackson, recently suspended as director of the SCLC's Operation Breadbasket, announces that he will organize an independent "Operation PUSH" (People United to Save Humanity).

December 20: Zulfika Ali Bhutto becomes president of Pakistan in the wake of its Bangladesh defeat. First surplus food arrives in Seattle for distribution through 34 area food banks. Testimony of psychologist Jennifer James and other experts persuades the King County Council not to stiffen penalties against prostitutes. Mayor Uhlman endorses downtown aquarium.

December 23: President Nixon commutes Jimmy Hoffa's sentence for jury tampering and fraud. He also signs law establishing the National Cancer Institute and launching $1.6 billion "war" on the disease, advocated by Senator Magnuson and Seattle physician William Hutchinson.

December 26: U.S. aircraft commence five days of massive "Christmas Day" bombing in North Vietnam as part of Kissinger's strategy to convince Hanoi that it should sue for peace because Nixon is a "madman." Two dozen Vietnam Veterans Against the War "liberate" the Statue of Liberty and fly an inverted U.S. flag from her crown. The Rev. Dean Leffler delivers his retirement sermon as dean of St. Mark's Episcopal Cathedral.

December 28: New York Mayor John Lindsay, a converted Democrat, announces that he will seek his new party's nomination for president. President Nixon signs welfare reform bill. Eighty-eight Vietnam Veterans Against the War are arrested during a White House protest.

December 30: Federal grand jury issues conspiracy indictments against Pentagon Papers–purloiners Daniel Ellsberg and Anthony Russo. President Nixon signs bill extending unemployment benefits for 13 additional weeks. Seattle Chamber of Commerce endorses flat-rate state income tax. Indian activist Hank Adams announces that he will lead a delegation to Hanoi.

December 31: U.S. forces in Vietnam shrink to 140,000 troops. Boeing employment in the Puget Sound area shrinks to 38,000, while 90,000 are unemployed statewide. Crime in Seattle posts the most dramatic decline in the nation, falling more than 13 percent. Fourteen thousand newly legal abortions are performed in Washington during 1970. National health care expenditures hit $75 billion in 1970, an increase of $31 per American at twice the average rate of inflation.

Zeitgeist: Dee Brown's *Bury My Heart at Wounded Knee* and Tom Robbins' *Another Roadside Attraction* are published. Stanley Kubrick's *A Clockwork Orange* and Woody Allen's *Bananas* are released, along with Bernardo Bertolucci's *The Conformist,* Peter Bogdanovich's *The Last Picture Show,* Robert Altman's *McCabe and Mrs. Miller,* and Jan Troell's *The Emigrants.* Tobacco ads are eliminated on TV and radio. Simon & Garfunkel split the song sheets, Alice Cooper introduces "Shock Rock," a precursor of heavy metal, and an increasingly eclectic group of performers reach the charts, including the Allman Brothers Band; John Denver; Earth, Wind & Fire; Roberta Flack; Michael Jackson (solo); Olivia Newton-John; the Osmonds; Helen Reddy; Carly Simon; and Rod Stewart.

1972

January: Preview issue of *Ms* magazine sells 300,000 copies in eight days. The first regular issue appears in July.

January 1: Austrian diplomat Kurt Waldheim succeeds U Thant as Secretary General of the United Nations.

January 4: Maine Sen. Edmund Muskie and Alabama Gov. George Wallace declare their candidacies for president. Federal government warns UW that it is engaging in sex discrimination in hiring.

January 5: President Nixon signs bill launching development of the Space Transportation System, or "Space Shuttle."

January 6: United Parcel Service (which was founded by James Casey in Pioneer Square in 1907) gives Seattle $100,000 to refurbish Pioneer Place and its pergola.

January 7: Time bombs are found in safe deposit boxes in seven U.S. banks with notes demanding freedom for all "political prisoners." Howard Hughes debunks Clifford Irving's putative "autobiography" of him in a telephone press conference. Seattle Police deploy first unarmed "Community Service Officers."

January 8: Aeromechanics announce they will sue to overturn federal Pay Board denial of negotiated wage increases for Boeing workers.

January 10: Four die in gun battle between police and Black Muslims in Baton Rouge, Louisiana.

January 11: George McGovern campaigns in Seattle.

January 12: State House votes to open all committee meetings to the public and press for the first time.

January 17: Harry Bridges leads his West Coast longshoremen off the job again and endorses a possible ILWU merger with the Teamsters.

January 18: Tim Manring and allies launch campaign opposing proposed Bay Freeway in February 8 referendum.

January 22: Seattle Community College faculty vote to strike over wages.

January 25: President Nixon unveils his "secret" eight-point peace plan for Vietnam. Congresswoman Shirley Chisholm announces candidacy for president.

January 26: The Rev. Daniel Berrigan, SJ, wins parole.

January 27: G. Gordon Liddy reviews a $1 million program of espionage and dirty tricks against Democrats with Attorney General John Mitchell, later head of the Committee to Re-Elect the President (CREEP). Maurice Stans steps down as Commerce Secretary to chair CREEP fundraising.

January 30: On "Bloody Sunday," British troops kill 13 Catholics during a civil rights march in Londonderry, Northern Ireland.

January 31: Hanoi unveils its "secret" peace plan. Liem Tuai triumphs in a long power struggle to win election as president of the Seattle City Council.

February 1: Boeing rolls out its first AWACS (a modified 707) at Renton. Judge Gaines, presiding over the Alioto-O'Connell fee splitting trial, dies.

February 2: Irish mob torches British Embassy in Dublin.

February 3: Disgruntled Seattle police and firemen picket City Hall over wages. Courts enjoin SCC faculty from striking.

February 4: Boeing advertises for bids to dismantle and haul away its SST mock-up.

February 7: President Nixon signs first Federal Campaign Financing Act to limit spending and contributions. Seattle City Council mandates unit pricing in local grocery stores. Comedienne Phyllis Diller shows off her new facelift.

February 8: Seattle voters kill the Bay Freeway from I-5 to Seattle Center, reprogram R. H. Thomson Expressway bonds, and approve a school levy by just 19 votes. U.S. Attorney Stan Pitkin announces that Seattle will be a "target city" in a new federal antidrug campaign.

February 10: State Senate completes passage of an equal rights amendment for submittal to state voters.

February 11: *P-I* report reveals that King County Board of Equalization members gave themselves $400,000 in property tax breaks. ASUW elects Ann Johnson as its first woman president since World War II. Washingtonians bilked by Glenn Turner's "Dare to Be Great" success seminars begin receiving refunds in excess of $300,000 thanks to a state consumer protection law suit.

February 12: U.S. Commission on Marijuana and Drug Abuse unanimously endorses elimination of criminal penalties for possession and use of pot.

February 17: After nine years of appeals, publisher Ralph Ginzburg finally begins a three year federal sentence for obscenity stemming from his *Eros* magazine (he is paroled after eight months). Kathleen Armstrong, accused in the University of Wisconsin bombing, is captured in Canada.

February 18: California Supreme Court rules capital punishment unconstitutional.

February 20: President Nixon arrives in Peking for an eight-day visit. West Coast longshoremen return to work after approving new contract.

February 21: President Nixon confers with Mao Tse-tung. Trial of Fr. Philip Berrigan and six other activists for conspiring to kidnap Henry Kissinger and sabotage federal buildings begins in Harrisburg, Pennsylvania, hence the "Harrisburg Seven."

February 22: Pat Nixon reveals that China will donate two pandas to the Washington, D.C., zoo. Metro launches round of community meetings on draft plan for all-bus transit system. U.S. Immigration Service begins deportation proceedings against Babak Zahraie, an Iranian student at the UW and foe of the Shah, as a "subversive."

February 23: Angela Davis freed on bail after 16 months in jail.

February 24: The Rev. Daniel Berrigan, SJ, is released from prison due to ill health.

February 25: Seattle City Council rejects appointment of Richard Ford, Port of Seattle counsel, to succeed John Nelson as City Light Superintendent.

February 26: Senator Muskie calls conservative New Hampshire publisher William Loeb "a gutless coward." Following the failure of the state legislature to adopt a redistricting plan, federal court names UW geography professor Richard Morrill to draw up new congressional and legislative districts for Washington State. Seattle Schools unveil expanded desegregation plan for elementary and middle schools.

February 29: Columnist Jack Anderson soars to the top of Nixon's Enemies List when he publishes a memo by ITT lobbyist Dita Beard describing how her corporation agreed to help fund the

Republican convention in exchange for a favorable antitrust ruling.

March 2: U.S. launches Pioneer 10 towards Jupiter; the probe will become the first manmade object to leave the solar system, and it bears a greeting to any alien civilizations which might encounter it.

March 5: During a Sonics game under the Coliseum's leaking roof, Spencer Haywood slips in a puddle of rainwater on the court.

March 7: Edmund Muskie wins the New Hampshire primary with 48 percent to George McGovern's 36 percent.

March 8: ASUW launches first trial run of "U-Trans" express buses.

March 9: Three hundred members of the American Indian Movement (AIM) ransack a trading post at Wounded Knee, South Dakota, on the Pine Ridge Reservation where Gen. George Custer's 7th U.S. Cavalry massacred a peaceful band of Sioux in December 1890. Clifford Irving, his wife, and an associate are indicted for fraud in the Howard Hughes' "autobiography" caper.

March 10: California Republican Congressman Paul McCloskey, a leading critic of the war, drops his challenge to the renomination of Richard Nixon.

March 13: Seattle City Council debates legalizing "private prostitution" without solicitation, e.g., "call girls."

March 14: George Wallace wins the Florida Democratic primary.

March 15: Howard Hughes takes residence at the Bayshore Inn in Vancouver, B.C. Thom Gunn runs *The Seattle Flag* up the pole.

March 16: President Nixon denounces court-ordered busing as having "gone too far" and proposes $2.5 billion in federal school aid to achieve "equal educational opportunity."

March 18: Four police officers are wounded before killing a sniper firing randomly from the Bush Hotel in the International District. A congressional study conducted by economists Lester Thurow and Robert E. G. Lucas reports that the income gap between the nation's richest 20 percent and poorest fifth has doubled in the past 20 years. A special federal panel advocates hospitalizing heroin addicts instead of jailing them.

March 19: President Nixon outlines programs to promote "black capitalism."

March 21: State Rep. Jim McDermott, M.D., the first Democrat elected to represent the heretofore staunchly Republican 43rd District, announces his candidacy for governor.

March 22: U.S. Senate sends the Equal Rights Amendment to the states for ratification. National Commission on Marijuana and Drug Abuse urges legalization of personal use of pot. U.S. Supreme Court strikes down Massachusetts law banning sale of contraceptives to unmarried individuals. The historic Cascade Hotel at First and Yesler collapses during renovation.

March 25: Some 30,000 march in Washington, D.C., to protest welfare cuts.

March 26: Jury acquits San Francisco Mayor Alioto, former Washington Attorney General O'Connell, and all other defendants of bribery and corruption charges. ITT lobbyist Dita Beard is hospitalized.

March 27: Deployment of U.S. troops in Vietnam falls below 100,000. Surviving two "Soledad Brothers," John Clutchette and Fleeta Drumgo, are acquitted of charges of killing a prison guard in 1970.

Draft state redistricting plan shocks most officials.

March 28: In a bargain with the government not to reopen original conspiracy charges, the Seattle Seven accept sentencing for contempt.

March 29: Leslie Bacon is indicted for perjury during grand jury testimony on the U.S. Capitol bombing. Seattle School Board president Dr. Robert Tidwell resigns in frustration over busing plan "bickering."

March 30: Regular North Vietnamese troops surge across the DMZ in record numbers. Great Britain imposes direct rule over Northern Ireland.

April 2: Sen. Henry Jackson denies a *New York Times* report that Boeing directly financed some of his campaign advertising in Wisconsin. Lenny Wilkens announces that he will step down as Sonics' coach but return to the court as a player.

April 4: George McGovern wins the Wisconsin primary. Adam Clayton Powell dies. Popular *P-I* columnist Jack Jarvis dies. Mayor Uhlman appoints architect Art Skolnik to direct Pioneer Square Historic District. "Walkin' Will" Knedlick announces that he will campaign for lieutenant governor on foot. A fierce wind storm in southwest Washington kills six and injures 200.

April 5: Prosecution of the Harrisburg Seven ends in a mistrial, but Fr. Philip Berrigan and Sister Elizabeth McAlister are convicted of smuggling letters in and out of prison (and later sentenced to two years). Fr. Berrigan returns to prison to complete a six-year sentence as part of the Catonsville Nine. State Superior Court clears topless dancing in Seattle.

April 6: State Supreme Court overturns Superior Court injunction against mandatory busing in Seattle.

April 10: Seattle City Council reaffirms development of High Ross Dam and votes to take over direct municipal operation of animal control programs from the Humane Society. Senator William Proxmire reveals his "hair plug" implants.

April 13: U.S. Senate passes bill limiting presidential "war powers."

April 14: U.S. Senator Sam J. Ervin Jr. orders presidential aides to testify regarding ITT–White House links.

April 15: U.S. aircraft resume full-scale bombing of Hanoi and Haiphong, prompting demonstrations in most major U.S. cities and a wave of campus confrontations. Mayor Uhlman outlines a plan for "Little City Halls" at a conference on citizen participation sponsored by the Central Seattle Community Council Federation.

April 16: Apollo 16 lifts off for the moon. A pair of Chinese giant pandas, Ling-Ling and Hsing-Hsing, arrive in Washington, D.C.

April 20: A rally of 2,000 UW students votes to strike and to support a Vietnamese student, Nguyen Thai Binh, resisting possible deportation for antiwar activity (Binh is killed on July 2 while attempting to hijack an airliner to Hanoi). National Guard occupies the University of Maryland campus and 4,000 rally at the University of Wisconsin.

April 21: Some 1,000 UW students demand that the Regents endorse a resolution opposing the war in Vietnam; they decline. Protesters try to close El Camino Real near Stanford University and pelt General Westmoreland with tomatoes in El Paso. Panel of federal judges approves controversial redistricting plan for the state. Governor Evans dedicates Evergreen State College.

April 22: Some 50,000 march in New York City and 30,000 march in San Francisco against the war. KING-TV and a coalition of community groups launch "People Power," a series of citizen-feedback forums.

April 23: Charlie Smith, a former black slave and the oldest living American, celebrates his 130th birthday.

April 24: Kenneth McDonald, one of Seattle's leading civil liberties attorneys, is literally thrown out on his ass from a Boeing stockholders' annual meeting on the order of Chairman Allen; McDonald, a shareholder, had sought approval of a probe into Boeing's alleged support for Senator Jackson's campaign.

April 27: After losing the Massachusetts and Pennsylvania primaries, Senator Muskie scuttles his presidential campaign. Marxist philosopher Herbert Marcuse speaks at the UW.

April 30: Some 1,000 rally on Mercer Island to protest Soviet mistreatment of Jews.

May 1: North Vietnamese troops capture Quang Tri and other cities just south of the DMZ.

May 2: J. Edgar Hoover dies; President Nixon names L. Patrick Gray III acting FBI director the next day. Washington Sen. Henry Jackson abandons his bid for the Democratic nomination for president after placing fourth in the Ohio primary. Two Kitsap County men are indicted for attempting to sell a bogus D. B. Cooper interview.

May 6: A large bomb damages the Seattle University ROTC building and nearby Jesuit residence in Loyola Hall.

May 8: U.S. begins mining North Vietnamese ports, despite risk of damaging Soviet and Chinese vessels. Seattle City Council gives preliminary approval for high-level West Seattle bridge.

May 9: Some 2,000 antiwar protesters march from the UW to the Federal Court House, where they make camp.

May 10: *The Seattle Flag* publishes a credible (but spurious) interview with "D. B. Cooper."

May 11: Federal Appeals Court overturns contempt citations against Chicago Seven and their attorneys. Department of the Interior approves construction of an oil pipeline from the North Slope to Valdez, Alaska. Campus police scuffle with about 80 protesters at the UW.

May 12: Police clash with 3,000 protesters in San Francisco; a small bomb explodes in the UW's Loew Hall.

May 15: Arthur Bremer shoots and paralyzes Alabama Gov. George Wallace during a presidential campaign appearance in Laurel, Maryland; Wallace wins the Michigan and Maryland primaries the following day. The U.S. returns Okinawa and nearby islands, captured during World War II, to Japan.

May 16: A new trial of Alioto and O'Connell begins in federal court.

May 17: Sylvia Jane Brown, a Barnard College student from Bellevue, is jailed for refusing to testify on political activities before a federal grand jury in Seattle; she is freed after serving nine days of an 18-month sentence.

May 18: Weathermen claim credit for a bomb which explodes in a Pentagon rest room. An extortionist demands $200,000 to reveal the location of bombs he claims are aboard the *Queen Elizabeth II;* British bomb experts parachute onto the ship and find no explosives. Boeing unveils a design concept for a 12-engine flying oil tanker (what a great idea!).

May 19: Four major dairies are fined for fixing prices in sales to state school districts.

May 21: Laszlo Toth attacks Michelangelo's *Pietà* with a hammer in the Vatican. More than 170 protesters are arrested in Washington, D.C., as 7,000 rally against the war.

May 23: U.S. reveals use of laser-guided "smart bombs" in Vietnam. Hitchhiking becomes legal in Washington state. U.S. Army turns 391 acres of Fort Lawton over to the City of Seattle. George McGovern wins Oregon and Rhode Island primaries.

May 26: President Nixon and Soviet leaders agree on outline for first Strategic Arms Limitation Treaty (SALT-I) during Moscow summit.

May 27: First Northwest Folklife Festival begins at Seattle Center.

May 28: "White House Plumbers" enter Democratic National Committee offices undetected to plant bugs and photograph documents. *P-I* reveals secret ties between the White House and Teamster leaders Hoffa and Beck. Hubert Humphrey and George McGovern debate in Los Angeles.

May 30: Japanese terrorists in the employ of the PLO slaughter 28 in Tel Aviv's Airport.

May 31: President Nixon arrives in Warsaw after visiting the Shah of Iran. Department of Commerce rejects industry pleas to delay imposition of inflammability standards on children's sleepware on

July 29; Senator Magnuson credits Children's Orthopedic Hospital physician Abe Bergman, MD, for leading the fight for passage of his 1967 legislation and for the White House's rare display of spine in the face of corporate pressure.

June 1: Black construction workers halt I-90 project in protest over minority hiring; pickets spread to other sites.

June 3: Sally Priesland, first American woman rabbi, is ordained in Reform Judaism.

June 4: San Jose jury acquits Angela Davis.

June 6: George McGovern consolidates his lead for the Democratic nomination by winning primaries in California, New Jersey, New Mexico, and South Dakota.

June 7: Black construction workers "rampage" through Seattle Central Community College rehab project.

June 8: South Vietnamese bombers accidentally drop napalm on civilians fleeing Trang Bang; an AP photograph of running children, including a nine-year-old girl, Phan Thi Kim Phuc, who had stripped off her burning clothes, becomes one of the enduring images of the war. U.S. Senate confirms Richard Kleindienst to succeed John Mitchell as Attorney General.

June 9: Sen. Martin Durkan announces that he will run for governor.

June 12: Seattle City Council confirms Gordon Vickery as new City Light Superintendent.

June 17: Five men are arrested during a break-in at Democratic Party offices in the Watergate complex in Washington, D.C. Additional arrests follow.

June 18: EPA Director William Ruckleshaus announces that DDT will be banned from virtually all uses effective December 31.

June 19: Mayor Uhlman and City Council members Phyllis Lamphere, Jeanette Williams, and John Miller propose creation of "Seattle 2000 Commission" to involve citizens in planning the city's long-range future. Former Governor Rosellini announces he will run for his old job. Federal charges against Alioto et al. are dismissed.

June 20: McGovern takes the New York primary; it's all over. Democratic National Committee files $1 million suit against CREEP for the Watergate break-in. President Nixon names General Creighton Abrams to succeed General Westmoreland as Army Chief of Staff.

June 28: George McGovern abandons his plan for a $1000-a-year guaranteed income. Betty Fletcher is elected as the first woman president of the Seattle–King County Bar Association.

June 29: President Nixon announces that U.S. will return to Paris for peace talks. U.S. Supreme Court rules death penalty to be "cruel and unusual" as currently administered, and denies journalists the right to protect confidential sources from grand jury inquiries.

June 30: Democratic National Convention credentials committee disqualifies Mayor Daley and 58 other "uncommitted" Illinois delegates.

July 1: Under public pressure from his wife Martha (and other forces), John Mitchell resigns as head of CREEP.

July 3: Seattle City Council finally puts the aquarium downtown.

July 4: Japanese Liberal Democrats elect Kakuei Tanaka as the new prime minister.

July 5: Boeing wins federal export license to sell airliners to the People's Republic of China.

July 6: Seattle–King County Drug Commission task force urges decriminalizing marijuana for personal use.

July 7: Sponsors of Initiative 262 to liberalize state liquor sales claim that petitions with over 100,000 signatures have been stolen.

July 10–13: Democratic National Convention at Miami Beach nominates South Dakota Sen. George McGovern and Missouri Sen. Thomas Eagleton. It is the first convention conducted under rules (written in large part by McGovern) assuring participation by women and minorities and limiting the influence of elected officials and political professionals.

July 10: Trial of Daniel Ellsberg opens.

July 11: President Nixon appoints Dixy Lee Ray to the Atomic Energy Commission.

July 13: Larry O'Brien steps down as head of the chair of the Democratic National Committee to chair McGovern's campaign; he is succeeded by Jean Westwood. Federal judge empowers Tyree Scott's United Construction Workers Association to monitor minority hiring. Location shooting for *The Night Stalker* with Darren McGavin begins in Pioneer Square.

July 17: Teamsters endorse Richard Nixon's reelection.

July 18: Egyptian president Anwar Sadat expels all Soviet military advisers.

July 19: AFL-CIO head George Meany declines to endorse either Nixon or McGovern, and releases individual unions to pick and choose.

July 20: Metro Council votes to submit all-bus transit plan to voters. Seattle Human Rights Commission votes to investigate employment discrimination against "long hairs."

July 23: Selective Service System drops requirement for conscientious objectors to perform alternative service.

July 26: North American Rockwell wins contract to build Space Shuttle.

July 28: Jane Fonda visits Hanoi.

July 31: McGovern tosses Eagleton overboard following revelations of his running mate's previous psychiatric treatment; former Peace Corps director R. Sargent Shriver takes Eagleton's place on a sinking ship on August 8.

August 1: *Washington Post* publishes first of many articles by reporters Bob Woodward and Carl Bernstein linking the White House to the Watergate burglary and other "dirty tricks."

August 2: U.S. Senate votes to cut off Vietnam war funding within four months if Hanoi releases POWs.

August 3: U.S. Senate ratifies SALT I. Paul Goodman, author of *Growing Up Absurd,* dies.

August 8: U.S. Navy announces that it will begin giving women sea duty for the first time.

August 10: U.S. House rejects Vietnam cut-off legislation.

August 13: Former Attorney General Ramsey Clark returns from two-week visit to Hanoi. This trip and later disclosure that former Kennedy Press Secretary Pierre Salinger had consulted with the North Vietnamese in Paris embroils McGovern in charges of undermining American negotiators.

August 17: U.S. House votes to ban "crosstown busing" for school desegregation. Mayor Uhlman appoints Jack Richards new fire chief. Trial of Tyree Scott for trespassing at SCCC during black construction workers' protest ends with a hung jury.

August 18: Sierra Club obtains federal injunction against logging on 34 million acres of National Forests. FBI agents shoot and capture a would-be skyjacker at Sea-Tac.

August 20: Antiwar demonstrators scuffle with Republican delegates and members of the American Nazi Party on the eve of the GOP National Convention in Miami Beach. "Zippies" stage a marijuana smoke-in.

August 21: Gov. Evans visits the 3,000-plus antiwar protesters encamped in Miami's Flamingo Park but declines to share a joint.

August 22: As Miami police round up 212 protesters, President Nixon brushes off challenges from governors Rockefeller and Reagan to win renomination for president.

August 23: Miami police arrest 679 protesters as thousands tie up traffic ground the GOP convention. Seattle Supersonics trade Lenny Wilkens to Cleveland.

August 26: A critic of the Warren Commission claims that the president's brain is missing (the Kennedy family apparently withheld JFK's preserved brain from the National Archives).

August 27: Socialist David Barrett (a Seattle University graduate) leads his New Democrats to victory in British Columbia's provincial elections.

August 28: President Nixon pledges to end the draft by July 1973. State Shorelines Management Board rejects I-90 Environmental Impact Statement as inadequate. Seattle City Council rejects liberalizing prostitution laws and approves new Office of Executive Policy.

Fall Season: "M*A*S*H" brings an acerbic and fundamentally pacifist perspective to war with its debut on September 17. It isn't demobilized until 1983, and ranks as the ninth most popular show in television history.

September 1: Bobby Fischer becomes America's first world chess champion when he defeats Boris Spaasky in Iceland.

September 2: Fifty-eight Munich police officers are injured during a battle with leftist demonstrators in the "Olympic Village" compound. North Cascades highway opens. Tricia Nixon hands Fort Lawton deed over to City of Seattle.

September 4: U.S. swimmer Mark Spitz wins his seventh gold medal in the Munich Olympics. George McGovern campaigns in Seattle.

September 5: Black September guerrillas kill two Israeli athletes and capture nine in their compound at the Munich Olympics. While trying to escape that night, five terrorists and all of their hostages die in a shootout with German police.

September 6: Mandatory busing begins smoothly in Seattle.

September 7: Citizens Against Mandatory Busing deliver recall petitions against two School Board members too late for the November 1972 election.

September 9: Boeing announces new "7X7" project (which leads to development of the 757 and 767).

September 10: Boeing announces sale of ten 707s to China.

September 11: Democrats charge that Watergate burglars were paid agents of President Nixon's reelection campaign funded through Maurice Stans; GOP and White House deny the charge.

September 12: Sargent Shriver campaigns in Seattle.

September 14: U.S. Senate approves U.S.-Soviet "freeze" of offensive nuclear arsenals.

September 15: Israel launches massive retaliatory raid to root out PLO guerrillas in southern Lebanon. Federal grand jury indicts G. Gordon Liddy, E. Howard Hunt, and the original burglars for conspiracy in the Watergate break-in. UW President Charles Odegaard announces that he will retire in September 1973.

September 17: North Vietnam releases three U.S. pilots.

September 18: Dr. Spock campaigns in Seattle as the presidential candidate of the new People's Party.

September 19: Former Gov. Albert Rosellini wins a rematch with Gov. Dan Evans by defeating Martin Durkan, Jim McDermott, and Perry Woodall in the Democratic primary. Joel Pritchard wins the GOP nomination to fight Democratic attorney John Hemplemann for the right to succeed Tom Pelly as Congressman from the First District, while J. J. "Tiny" Freeman, friend of the drinking man, wins the GOP nomination to challenge Congressman Brock Adams in the Seventh. King County voters finally put Metro in the transit driver's seat (after four previous electoral rejections beginning in 1958). Seattle voters reject COMET initiative to restore trolleys and turn Seattle Transit over to City Light.

September 23: President Marcos declares martial law in the Philippines.

October 2: McGovern calls the Nixon Administration "the most morally corrupt in history." Eight days after Norwegians voted no, Denmark voters endorse joining the expanded Common Market. Malcolm Stamper becomes president of Boeing as T. A. Wilson takes over board chairmanship from William Allen on his retirement.

October 4: U.S. Senate gives final approval to $24.6 billion Clean Water Act; it overrides Nixon's veto two weeks later and denies him authority to "impound" or "rescind" appropriated funds. "Dare to Be Great" promoter Glenn Turner is jailed for contempt in Florida.

October 3: U.S. Supreme Court Justice Douglas blocks Air Force discharge of Capt. Susan Struck for being pregnant. CAMB files recall petitions to oust two more Seattle School Board members.

October 6: Indian activists Russell Means and Hank Adams lead a caravan from Seattle headed for a rally in Washington, D.C. Five robbers hijack a Greyhound bus enroute from Seattle to Vancouver, B.C.

October 9: A Tennessee official reveals that he was approached by GOP aide Donald Segretti to help conduct political espionage and "sabotage" against Democrats during the presidential primaries.

October 11: Roberto Maestes leads Chicano activists in occupying the abandoned Beacon Hill School, which they propose to convert into El Centro de la Raza.

October 12: McGovern campaigns in Seattle again.

October 13: Majority of Seattle City Council endorses leasing Beacon Hill School for Chicano center.

October 14: Seattle is one of 40 U.S. ports opened to Soviet shipping under a new agreement.

October 16: U.S. House Majority Leader Hale Boggs dies in a plane crash in Alaska. Seattle City council gives preliminary approval to reducing marijuana penalties.

October 19: President Nixon vows to ignore appropriations and to block federal spending where he chooses.

October 20: President Nixon signs Revenue Sharing bill to return $30 billion in federal taxes to state and local governments over the next five years. Senator Magnuson complains that GOP "tricks" are "like a novel—a Fu Manchu novel."

October 21: North Vietnam Premier Pham Van Dong says he will release U.S. POWs in exchange for a cease-fire.

October 22: *Time* and *Newsweek* report agreement on a Vietnam peace settlement. Navy charges 25 black seamen but no whites in connection with interracial fighting aboard the aircraft carrier *Kitty Hawk* on October 12.

October 23: Jackie Robinson, first black allowed to play major league baseball, dies.

October 24: U.S. halts bombing north of the 20th parallel.

October 31: Hanoi's deadline for new peace agreement comes and goes without action due to South Vietnamese resistance.

November 1: Ezra Pound dies in his adopted Italy.

November 2: Native American protesters occupy Bureau of Indian Affairs office in Washington, D.C. Asian American protesters sling mud (literally) during Kingdome ground-breaking ceremony near the International District.

November 7: President Nixon crushes McGovern by carrying 60.7 percent of the popular vote and every state except Massachusetts and the District of Columbia. Washington voters elect Gov. Dan Evans to a third term but strengthen Democrats in the Legislature while reelecting incumbent state officers. They also face the longest list of ballot issues in state history. They approve:

Initiative 276 to establish campaign reporting and the Public Disclosure Commission (and the weaker reforms of Referenda 24 and 25);

Initiative 43-B establishing the State Shorelines Management Act (while rejecting the more restrictive 43 version);

Initiative 40-B "model litter control act (while rejecting the stricter 40 version mandating returnable bottles);

five of six "Washington Futures" bond issue referenda (Referendum 30 transportation bonds failed);

House Joint Resolution 21 to allow merged county-municipal governments;

HJR 47 to eliminate the turn-out minimum for validating school levies;

HJR 61 establishing equal rights under the State Constitution for men and women;

Senate Joint Resolution 1 and Initiative 44 to cut property taxes;

SJR 2 to repeal the State Constitution's ban of lotteries;

SJR 38 to allow home rule county officials to set their own salaries; and

SJR 52 liberalizing old Constitutional debt limits.

Voters reject:

Initiative 258 to legalize dog racing ("See Spot Run, See Spot Die");

Initiative 261 to scrap the state Liquor Control Board; and

HJR 1 to mandate periodic review of tax exempt institutions.

Seattle voters dynamite a $40 million bond issue to repair bridges, narrowly elect Joel Pritchard to Congress, and reelect Brock Adams despite Tiny Freeman's "hefty" challenge.

November 12: Angry Chicanos storm the Seattle City Council when it rejects the lease for El Centro de la Raza. Dr. Richard Fuller announces that he will retire as head of the Seattle Art Museum, which he founded and built 40 years earlier.

November 14: Dow Jones average tops 1000 mark for the first time. Private Billy Smith is acquitted of "fragging" two officers in Vietnam. Filipino leader Bob Santos heads a multiracial march demanding more federal housing aid in Seattle.

November 16: Baton Rouge, Louisiana, sheriffs kill two black students during demonstrations at Southern University. President Nixon sacks the Rev. Theodore Hesburgh, president of Notre Dame University, as chairman of the U.S. Human Rights Commission.

November 17: Juan Peron returns to Argentina after a 17-year exile in Spain.

November 19: Seattle 2000 Commission convenes its first meeting at the Seattle Center with some 500 attendees. August Mardesich deposes R. R. Bob Greive, Democratic leader of the State Senate for the previous 16 years.

November 20: Henry Kissinger huddles with Le Duc Tho in Paris to work out final peace agreement. Seattle City Council approves new Office of Women's Rights.

November 21: Appeals Court reverses convictions against five of the Chicago Seven because of Judge Hoffman's prejudicial conduct of the original trial. City Light Chief Vickery suspends 16 workers for taking "extended coffee breaks" (as observed by private detectives in City Light's employ).

November 27: Nordstrom opens its remodeled downtown Seattle store.

November 29: Fr. Philip Berrigan wins parole; he leaves prison on December 20.

December 4: Reproductive rights activist Dr. Frans Koome is fined $500 and given a year's probation for performing an abortion on a 16-year-old patient in Renton.

December 7: Apollo 17 lifts off for NASA's final mission to the moon.

December 8: E. Howard Hunt's wife Dorothy dies in a plane crash; her purse contains $10,000 in cash, alleged to be a CREEP payoff for her husband's silence. Acting FBI Director L. Patrick Gray later burns all files pertaining to Hunt.

December 9: Robert Strauss succeeds Jean Westwood as chair of the Democratic National Committee. U.S. District Court lifts injunction on logging in national forests. President Nixon names Seattle-born aide Egil Krogh Jr. Undersecretary of the Department of Transportation, and names Patrick Moynihan ambassador to India.

December 10: Roberto Maestes weds Estella Ortega in the Chicano-occupied Beacon Hill School which will become El Centro de la Raza.

December 11: Astronauts Eugene Cernan and Harrison Schmitt become the last men to walk on the moon, while Ronald Evans orbits overhead in the Apollo 17

command module. Seattle City Council approves creation of the Department of Human Resources, headed by Ed Singler.

December 12: White House concedes existence of "Plumbers" unit originally formed to "plug leaks" in the White House and gather damaging information on Daniel Ellsberg.

December 16: King County Democrats elect liberal Marcus Kunian as their new chair.

December 18: U.S. resumes bombing Hanoi and Haiphong.

December 20: President Nixon threatens to cut off aid unless South Vietnam accepts peace accord. UN Ambassador George Bush is named to succeed Sen. Robert Dole as chair of the Republican National Committee effective January 15, 1973.

December 22: A group of 90 antiwar protesters march to present the Seattle City Council with a petition asking for a hearing on Seattle's "involvement" with the war.

December 23: About 350 antiwar protesters march through stores in the downtown Seattle shopping district.

December 26: Harry Truman dies. Seattle City Council approves El Centro lease and improvements. Study rates conditions in half of state prisons "inhuman."

December 29: ACLU files suit to block dismissal of Seattle gay rights leader John Singer by the U.S. Equal Employment Opportunity Commission. *Life* magazine suspends publication after 36 years.

December 30: U.S. stops bombing North Vietnam when Hanoi signals that it will return to Paris for peace talks on January 8.

Zeitgeist: Stanley Kubrick's *A Clockwork Orange,* Francis Ford Coppola's *The God-*

father, John Boorman's *Deliverance,* Lina Wertmuller's *The Seduction of Mimi,* and Luis Bunuel's *The Discreet Charm of the Bourgeoisie* are released, and Robert Redford wins in *The Candidate.* America, David Bowie, the Doobie Brothers, the Eagles, Bette Midler, Seals & Croft, Paul Simon (solo), Tanya Tucker, and ZZ Top score hits. The 1950s slide back into vogue with the opening of *Grease* on Broadway.

Winding Down from the Sixties: 1973–1994

1973

January 8: U.S. planes bomb U.S. base at Da Nang.

January 11: Howard Hunt pleads guilty in Watergate conspiracy trial before Judge John Sirica. President Nixon ends wage-price controls.

January 22: In *Roe v. Wade,* U.S. Supreme Court severely limits the right of states to restrict abortions.

January 23: Lyndon Johnson dies.

January 27: U.S., Republic of Vietnam, Democratic Republic of Vietnam, and National Liberation Front sign peace accords. Defense Secretary Melvin Laird announces the end of the military draft and organization of all-volunteer armed services.

February 12: North Vietnam releases 142 U.S. prisoners of war.

February 21: Pathet Lao and Laotian government sign cease-fire.

February 27: Members of the American Indian Movement (AIM) seize buildings and 11 hostages at Wounded Knee, South Dakota. On March 11, negotiations are interrupted by gunfire, in which an FBI agent and an Indian are shot, and the siege continues until May 8.

March 8: The Grateful Dead's Ron "Pig Pen" McKernan, almost 27, dies of liver failure.

March 29: Last U.S. support troops leave Vietnam. H. Rap Brown is convicted of armed robbery.

April 1: "Last" of 590 U.S. prisoners of war released by North Vietnam.

April 30: White House aides John Ehrlichman, H. R. Haldeman, and John

Dean, and Attorney General Richard Kleindienst resign amid charges of Watergate cover-up. President Nixon addresses the nation.

May 11: Charges against Daniel Ellsberg are dismissed due to White House misconduct in bugging his phone and raiding his psychiatrist's office.

May 14: NASA launches Skylab (actually an adapted third stage of a Saturn V). Three astronauts later rendezvous with the "space station" and spend 28 days onboard.

May 17: North Carolina Sen. Sam Ervin and Tennessee Sen. Howard Baker open Senate Select Committee hearings on Watergate.

May 18: Justice Department names Archibald Cox Special Watergate Prosecutor.

May 19: Government Accounting Office estimates that CREEP paid $460,000 in illegal contributions to silence Watergate burglars.

May 20: Seventeen are acquitted in trial of the Camden 28 for destruction of draft files.

May 29: Los Angeles voters elect the city's first black mayor, Tom Bradley.

June 8: During a convention in Boulder, Colorado, the Underground Press Syndicate votes to change its name to "Alternative Press Syndicate."

June 13: President Nixon freezes retail food prices.

June 20: Juan Peron returns to Brazil after a 20-year exile in Spain.

June 25: John Dean spills the beans to Senate Watergate hearing chaired by Sen. Sam Ervin Jr.

June 27: Appeals Court overturns all but one charge against Father Berrigan and Sister McAlister.

June 29: President Nixon tells nation it has a "serious energy problem."

July 16: White House aide Alexander Butterfield reveals existence of White House taping system. U.S. Senate begins inquiry into illegal U.S. bombing missions over Cambodia in 1969 and 1970.

July 23: President Nixon "stonewalls" Senate demand for his White House tapes. He ultimately releases partial transcripts ("expletive deleted") on November 26.

July 28: Six hundred thousand fans gather for a rock concert at a race course in Watkins Glen, New York. A skydiver dies during a descent into the crowd.

August 14: U.S. bombing of Cambodia halts.

August 22: President Nixon names Henry Kissinger Secretary of State, succeeding William P. Rogers.

August 31: A Florida jury acquits the "Gainesville Eight" (seven members of the Vietnam Veterans Against the War and a supporter) of attempting to disrupt the 1972 Republican National Convention.

September 4: The Justice Department indicts John Ehrlichman and three "Plumbers" (Egil Krogh Jr., David R. Young, and G. Gordon Liddy) for the Ellsberg break-in.

September 11: Military junta murders Chilean President Salvador Allende and establishes dictatorship which continues until 1989.

October 6: Israeli forces repulse Egyptian and Syrian attacks on Yom Kippur; fighting with heavy casualties on all sides continues until October 24.

October 10: Vice President Spiro Agnew pleads "nolo contendere" to corruption charges stemming from his Maryland governorship, and resigns. Michigan Congressman Gerald R. Ford is confirmed as his successor two days later and takes the oath of office on December 6.

October 19: The Organization of Petroleum Exporting Countries (OPEC) imposes an embargo on all oil exports to the U.S. in retaliation for its support for Israel during the "Yom Kippur War." The embargo, which triggered long gas lines, energy shortages, and hyperinflation, is lifted six months later.

October 20: President Nixon orders Attorney General Elliot Richardson to fire Archibald Cox as Watergate Special Prosecutor. Richardson resigns and Nixon fires Deputy Attorney General William Ruckleshaus when he also refuses to dismiss Cox. Solicitor General Richard Bork finally carries out the order. Leon Jaworski is ultimately named as the new Watergate prosecutor on November 1.

November 8: President Nixon addresses the nation on the "energy emergency." He later proposes conservation and development initiatives to achieve "energy independence."

November 7: Congress overrides President Nixon's veto of the "War Powers Act," which restricts a president's military prerogatives without Congressional authority.

November 16: President Nixon signs bill authorizing construction of the Trans-Alaska Pipeline.

November 17: While at Disney World, President Nixon declares, "People have got to know whether or not their president is a crook—well, I'm not a crook."

November 21: A "gap" of 18.5 minutes in duration is discovered in a key White House recording of a June 20, 1972, conversation between President Nixon and Haldeman. Presidential secretary Rose Mary Woods takes the rap.

December 4: In a new trial on contempt citations, four charges against members of the Chicago Seven and attorneys are upheld, but the judge waives any additional penalty. President Nixon names William Simon as nation's first "energy czar."

December 15: Italian kidnappers release J. Paul Getty's grandson after five months in exchange for $2.8 million. The kidnappers had previously sent police Getty's severed ear to prove their authenticity.

Zeitgeist: Pablo Picasso dies on April 8. First major histories of the Vietnam War, David Halberstam's *The Best and the Brightest* and Frances Fitzgerald's *Fire in the Lake* are published. George Roy Hill's *The Sting*, George Lucas' *American Graffiti*, and Bernardo Bertolucci's *Last Tango in Paris* are released. Universal Price Code (those little black bands on every label) are adopted to computerize retail inventories and check-out lines. Roberta Flack and Stevie Wonder dominate the Grammys.

1974

January: Fighting resumes in South Vietnam.

February 4: Publishing heiress Patricia Hearst is kidnapped by the "Symbionese Liberation Army" in San Francisco. The SLA demands that Randolph A. Hearst, president of the *San Francisco Examiner* and son of William Randolph Hearst, organize and fund a program to feed the poor in Oakland. (The program is coordinated by Washington State Secretary of State Lud Kramer and Neighbors in Need founder Peggy Maze with $2 million, but it is marred by poor quality and fights. The program rans out of funds on March 26. SLA members are later convicted of the murder of the superintendent of Oakland's public schools in November 1973.)

March 1: Seven former White House aides are indicted for the Watergate cover-up, including Haldeman, Ehrlichman, and Mitchell.

March 18: OPEC officially ends oil embargo, but fuel prices remain at record highs.

March 29: A federal grand jury indicts eight National Guardsmen for "violating civil rights" in firing on Kent State protesters.

April 15: Patty Hearst participates in an SLA bank robbery. She had professed her membership in the SLA in a tape released April 3.

April 29: President Nixon releases transcripts of most Watergate tapes.

May 9: U.S. House Judiciary Committee opens hearings on the impeachment of President Nixon.

May 16: San Francisco authorities indict four Black Muslims for the 12 "Zebra Killings" which had terrorized the city over the previous five months.

June 30: Selective Service law expires and the draft ends.

July 12: John Ehrlichman and three "plumbers" are convicted for organizing break-in at the office of Daniel Ellsberg's psychiatrist.

July 24: U.S. Supreme Court orders President Nixon to surrender tapes.

July 25: Reversing previous opinions, the U.S. Supreme Court bans the use of mandatory busing between inner-city and suburban school districts in order to address school desegregation.

July 29: Mama Cass, three years past her 27th birthday, dies of a ham sandwich.

July 30: U.S. House Judiciary Committee adopts last of three Articles of Impeachment against President Nixon.

July 31: Alec Fisken and Dick Clever launch *The Seattle Sun.* It lasts a decade, and its original entertainment section, *The Rocket,* survives as an independent tabloid.

August 5: President Nixon releases "smoking gun" tapes showing he authorized the FBI to obstruct the investigation of the Watergate break-in.

August 9: Richard Nixon resigns as president, and Gerald Ford is sworn in as the 39th President of the United States. Ford later taps Nelson Rockefeller to serve as his Vice President.

August 20: U.S. House votes 412 to 3 to accept the report of the Judiciary Committee, including impeachment articles.

September 8: President Ford grants Nixon an unconditional pardon for all federal crimes he "committed or may have committed."

September 16: Federal judge dismisses all charges against AIM leaders Russell Means and Dennis Banks stemming from the occupation of Wounded Knee.

October 20: Muhammad Ali regains the world heavyweight title (which had been voided in 1967) by knocking out George Foreman.

November 8: Lieutenant Calley is paroled after serving little more than three years.

November 14: Jane Alpert emerges from the underground and surrenders to face charges involving the 1969 bombings in New York.

November 20: Federal prosecutors file antitrust charges ultimately leading to the break-up of the AT&T telephone monopoly.

December 2: After decades of debate, the House of Representative enacts a sweeping set of reforms to reduce the power of seniority and key committees. Ways and Means chairman (and amateur swimmer) Wilbur Means resigns on December 30.

December 12: Georgia Gov. James Earl "Jimmy" Carter announces his candidacy for the Democratic nomination for president.

December 21: *New York Times* publishes details of systematic illegal domestic surveillance conducted by the CIA during the "Vietnam era."

Zeitgeist: Mel Brook's *Blazing Saddles*, Roman Polanski's *Chinatown, Monty Python and the Holy Grail,* and Francis Ford Coppola's *The Godfather, Part II* are released. Stevie Wonder and Olivia Newton-John dominate the Grammys, while Abba, the Average White Band, Jimmy Buffet, Billy Joel, Elton John, Kiss, Barry Manilow, and Dolly Parton make the big time. Jefferson Airplane goes to warp as Jefferson Starship.

1975

January 1: Former Attorney General John Mitchell, John Ehrlichman, and H.R. Haldeman are convicted of obstructing justice during the Watergate investigation.

February 6: Sen. Henry Jackson announces candidacy for president.

March 29: U.S. begins evacuating South Vietnamese civilians from Da Nang as North Vietnamese troops march toward Saigon.

April 17: Cambodian capital of Phnom Penh falls to Khmer Rouge forces.

April 21: North Vietnamese overrun Saigon's last defensive outpost.

April 25: South Vietnamese President Thieu flees Saigon.

April 29: Last U.S. helicopter lifts off from the roof of the U.S. Embassy in Saigon as North Vietnamese troops take over the city.

May 12: Cambodian forces seize merchant ship *Mayaguez;* 38 Americans die during "rescue" operation two days later.

May 27: Alaska Supreme Court votes unanimously to permit personal possession and use of marijuana.

June 10: A special commission headed by Vice President Rockefeller details CIA abuses, including "CHAOS" program which illegally monitored 300,000 members of the antiwar movement, and secret tests of LSD on unwitting individuals.

July 17: Apollo and Soyuz capsules dock in orbit.

August 27: Federal jury acquits Kent State National Guardsmen.

September 5: Lynette Alice "Squeaky" Fromme, a follower of Charley Manson, attempts to assassinate President Ford in Sacramento.

September 18: San Francisco police "rescue" Patricia Hearst while killing her captors. She is convicted of armed robbery on March 20, 1976.

September 22: Sara Jane Moore, an "activist," attempts to assassinate President Ford in San Francisco.

October 9: Dissident Soviet physicist and human rights activist Andrei Sakharov wins the Nobel Prize for Peace.

October 11: George Carlin hosts the debut of NBC's "Saturday Night Live."

October 30: In response to President Ford's pledge to veto any legislation "bailing out" New York City from its financial woes, *Daily News* prints headline: "Ford to City: Drop Dead."

November 12: Supreme Court Justice William O. Douglas retires after 36 years on the bench.

November 17: Eldridge Cleaver ends his seven-year exile and is arrested in the U.S.

Zeitgeist: Steven Spielberg's *Jaws* devours the box office while Milos Forman's *One Flew Over the Cuckoo's Nest* runs away with Oscars for best actor (Nicholson), actress (Louise Fletcher), and picture. Bruce Springsteen releases "Born to Run" and lands on the cover of both *Time* and *Newsweek*.

1976

January 8: Chou En-lai dies.

January 19: Jimmy Carter wins Iowa caucuses.

January 24: George Wallace defeats Carter in Mississippi caucuses.

January 30: U.S. Supreme Court strikes down federal campaign spending limits while upholding public financing and contribution limits.

March 20: Patricia Hearst is convicted of bank robbery.

March 31: David Brewster launches *The Weekly* (now *Seattle Weekly*).

April 27: After winning in New York on April 6, Senator Jackson loses the Pennsylvania primary to Carter, which effectively ends his candidacy (officially on May 1.)

July 4: U.S. celebrates the bicentennial of the Declaration of Independence.

November 2: Jimmy Carter defeats President Ford by comfortable margin of 1.7 million popular votes and 57 electoral votes.

Zeitgeist: Johnnie Taylor's "Disco Lady" is awarded the first "Platinum" for a single exceeding sales of 2 million (the 1960s have definitely ended for music). Paddy Chayevsky's *Network* wins Oscars for Peter Finch and Faye Dunaway, but Sylvester Stallone's *Rocky* takes the title for best pic.

1977

January 21: President Carter initiates pardons for nearly 10,000 draft evaders.

1979

November 3: Five members of the Communist Workers Party are gunned down when their anti-Klan rally in Greensboro, N.C., is attacked by KKK and Nazi Party thugs. Two juries acquit the murderers, but a civil suit results in a $351,000 judgment against the City of Greensboro on June 8, 1985.

1980

November 4: Former California Gov. Ronald Reagan garners 51 percent of the popular vote and all but five states and D.C. to defeat President Carter and independent John Anderson.

1982

November 11: Vietnam Veterans Memorial is dedicated in Washington, D.C.

1983

October 25: U.S. forces invade Caribbean island of Grenada to "rescue" American medical students during comic-opera revolution. "Vietnam syndrome" reportedly kicked.

1989

April 12: Abbie Hoffman dies in an apparent suicide.

1990

January: U.S. forces invade Panama and later capture Manuel Noriega for trial as a drug dealer. "Vietnam syndrome" reportedly kicked.

June: Cold War ends with the fall of the Berlin Wall.

August: Failed coup against Mikhail Gorbachev effectively liquidates the Soviet Union.

1991

February: U.S.-led forces invade Iraq. "Vietnam syndrome" reportedly kicked.

1992

November 3: Arkansas Gov. Bill Clinton, a 46-year-old member of the Baby Boom and an alleged draft-evader, free love practitioner, and pot-smoker, defeats President George Bush and independent H. Ross Perot.

1994

February 3: President Clinton lifts trade embargo against Vietnam.

February 7: A Mississippi jury finally convicts Medgar Evers's killer.

November 28: Jerry Rubin is struck and killed by a car while jaywalking.

1995

July 11: President Clinton grants U.S. diplomatic recognition to the Democratic Republic of Vietnam.

August 9: Grateful Dead founder Jerry Garcia dies at age 53.

Appendix A
Helix Index

I-1

I-2

Vol-Num. (Ordinal) Date: Cover art and artist where known

I-1   (1) 3/23/67: Multiple mastheads including Ray Collins' "Peeping Fred Lives"

I-2   (2) 4/13/67: Jacques Moitoret's masthead, Id Bust, UDM, etc.

I-3   (3) 4/27/67: Maryl Clemmens' Chief Seattle Flower Potlatch poster

I-3.5   (4) 5/4/67: Gary Eagle's OCS Light Show Poster with Egyptian

I-4   (5) 5/16/67: Walt Crowley's Peace/War Diptych

I-5   (6) 6/2/67: G. Eagle's 6/11 Be-In Poster with Indian

I-6   (7) 6/23/67: "U.S. Invaded" Parody

I-7   (8) 7/7/67: William Ward's figures with torch (Crowley's "Needle" on back)

I-8   (9) 7/28/67: Cartoon of U District scenes (McKinistry?)

I-9   (10) 8/16/67: Crowley's robot with tombstone

I-10   (11) 9/1/67: Ward drawing of Dylan with grass

II-1   (12) 9/15/67: Crowley's "Yakima's Bitter Harvest" *(New volumes started every 10 issues or so)*

I-3.5

I-4

I-5

II-2   (13) 9/29/67: Crowley's Vitruvian Man/ Open Door Clinic

II-3   (14) 10/20/67: Crowley's Apocalypse (and draft induction)/G. Eagle's flower child with fireworks (flopped double cover)

II-4   (15) 11/2/67: Crowley's "Super Cop"/ Paul Dorpat's "Oversex" mezzotint (double cover)

II-5   (16) 11/16/67: Napoleon postcards and cartoons (metro-page format)

II-6   (17) 12/1/67: Moitoret's 3-color process butterfly nymph

II-7   (18) 12/11/67: Ward's Meher Baba/ Interesting Particulars (double cover)

II-8   (19) 1/4/68: R. Allen Jensen's "Zeus"/ "Helix Calendar" (double cover)

II-9   (20) 1/18/68: Moitoret's art deco idyll "20 cents the Copy"

II-10 (21) 2/1/68: Tortured figure (W. Blake) and headlines

III-1 (22) 2/15/68: Dorpat's hippie chicks

III-2 (23) 2/29/68: Ward's Che Guevara

III-3 (24) 3/14/68: "Skip" montage of Tao signs and Escher

III-4 (25) 3/28/68: Crowley's brain-tree

III-5 (26) 4/11/68: Crowley "Media Mash/ Piano Drop" poster

III-6 (27) 4/25/68: Dorpat's Country Joe poster

III-7 (28) 5/9/68: Paul Heald's discs on wavy lines

III-8 (29) 5/24/68: Crowley's "Nation That Controls Magnetism"

III-9 (30) 6/6/68: "Ugly Baby" Cover

III-10 (31) 6/20/68: Moitoret's moon, stars, and Helix "balloon"

IV-1   (32) 7/3/68: Crowley's eagle/tv/fist/ bodies

I-9

I-10

II-4

III-12 (33) 7/18/68: Moitoret's flowers with toy airplane *(Misnumbered, actually IV-2)*

IV-3 (34) 8/1/68: Mona Lisa, clock, and Beatles

IV-4 (35) 8/15/68: Crowley's "Progress" (Sky River Rock Festival poster on reverse)

IV-5 (36) Special Edition: Crowley's Sky River Rock Festival poster *(Not dated or numbered)*

II-6 (37) 8/29/68: Green "Sky River Rock" *(first Omega-84; Misnumbered, actually IV-6)*

IV-7 (38) 9/12/68: Dorpat's "Christ Is Coming"

IV-8 (39) 9/26/68: Larry Heald's "Shazam Society" pyramids etc. on yellow paper *(Subsequent issues published more or less weekly)*

IV-9 (40) 10/3/68: Crowley's "Community Not Chaos" poster

IV-10 (41) 10/10/68: Zac Reisner's cartoon of Seattle building interiors

V-1 (42) 10/17/68: G. Washington dollar portrait

V-2 (43) 10/24/68: Mayor Dorm Braman "Conspiracy"

V-3 (44) 10/31/68: Cannon "Ballot"

V-4 (45) 11/7/68: Nixon "Bird" and tv images

V-5 (46) 11/14/68: Red and green nudes

V-6 (47) 11/21/68: Greenish-yellow montage with hands and birds

V-7 (48) 11/27/68: LBJ and Nixon, Safeco sign, etc.

V-8 (49) 12/5/68: Dark blue stress diagram of interlocking gears

V-9 (50) 12/12/68: Cartoon of stoned kid "Hey, man I feel goofy"

V-10 (51) 12/19/68: Eye floating in red clouds

VI-1 (52) 12/26/68: Madonna with Afro by Mary Ida Hendrickson

II-4

First Omega-84 (II-6)

III-8

VI-2   (53) 1/9/69: Crowley's "Utopia"

VI-3   (54) 1/16/69: Double image of woman with drapery

VI-4   (55) 1/23/69: Ward's floating figure with mystical signs

VI-5   (56) 1/30/69: Alan Lande's checkerboard box

V1-6   (57) 2/6/69: Reprint of Seattle Union Record cover (50th anniversary of Seattle General Strike)

VI-7   (58) 2/13/69: Rorschach image of woman

VI-8   (59) 2/20/69: Larry Heald's pyramids etc.

VI-9   (60) 2/27/69: Crowley's "Electric Guitar Player" Helix benefit

VI-10   (61) 3/6/69: Sky River Rock mud puddle scene (last Omega-84)

VII-1   (62) 3/13/69: Compressed photo of UW anti-ROTC demo (on yellow paper)

VII-2   (63) 3/20/69: Second Anniversary: montage of past covers

VII-3   (64) 3/26/69: Paul Temple's "Prison" photo

VII-4   (65) 4/3/69: Bevis' cartoon of hot dog and hamburger

VII-5   (66) 4/10/69: Dorpat's "Pledge Your Allegiance" with topless women

VII-6   (67) 4/17/69: Hans-George Reich cartoon of man blowing up city

VII-7   (68) 4/24/69: Striated pattern in yellow and red

VII-8   (69) 5/1/69: Crowley's "May Day" icon

VII-9   (70) 5/8/69: "Market Faces" photo

VII-10   (71) 5/15/69: Crowley/Lande "Problem or Solution" diptych

VIII-1   (72) 5/22/69: Medieval cartoon

III-10

IV-4 (Back)

IV-8

VIII-2 (73) 5/29/69: Crowley's "Foliate" People's Park poster

VIII-3 (74) 6/5/69: Women with penis photo collage

VIII-4 (75) 6/12/69: "Communal Cover" montage of clippings

VIII-5 (76) 6/19/69: Ward's "We Are All One" folding cover

VIII-6 (77) 6/26/69: Dorpat's "Wharton T. Funk" photo collage

VIII-7 (78) 7/3/69: Warren G. Harding Memorial Bandstand poster

VIII-8 (79) 7/10/69: Steve Shaefer's drawing of Arab riding insect

VIII-9 (80) 7/17/69: "Mutations Speaks/Virgin Moon"

VIII-10 (81) 7/24/69: Crowley's "Last Rising of a Virgin Moon"

IX-1 (82) 7/31/69: Lande and Ward's geese and heart in red circle

IX-2 (83) 8/7/69: Blue fireworks explosion

IX-3 (84) 8/14/69: "Police Riot—Pigs Declare War on Youth"

IX-4 (85) 8/21/69: "Back to Normal?" montage of Lande's riot photos

IX-5 (86) 8/28/69: Lande's "Sky River Lives!"

IX-6 (87) 9/4/69: Lande's black and red photo of Sky River stage

IX-7 (88) 9/11/69: Falcon-headed Egyptian god Horus

IX-8 (89) 9/18/69: Lande's face in purple and black

IX-9 (90) 9/25/69: Lande's "Welcome Students" photo of UW excavation

IX-10 (91) 10/2/69: Ward's drawing of woman and unicorn

X-1 (92) 10/9/69: Photo of wrecked cars with trees

VI-9

IX-3

X-10

X-2   (93) 10/16/69: Naked man and women: "What Is This Man Doing?"

X-3   (94) 10/23/69: Milo Johnstone's gabled house (price rises to $.25)

X-4   (95) 10/30/69: Dark blue skull (two sections)

X-5   (96) 11/6/69: Crowley's cartoon of Edsel being crushed

X-6   (97) 11/13/69: Lande's montage of drawings of revolutionaries

X-7   (98) 11/20/69: Photos from 11/14 Mobilization (yellow and blue)

X-8   (99) 11/27/69: Crowley's turkey as Great Seal

X-9   (100) 12/4/69: Ray Collins' Santa giving finger

X-10   (101) 12/11/69: Lande's "Hampton Assassinated!"

X-11   (102) 12/18/69: Crowley's Karl Marx as Santa (*Last issue in 1969. Volume XI began in 1970 and was maintained for balance of publication.*)

XI-1   (103) 1/2/70: Drawing of Janus-headed woman

XI-2   (104) 1/8/70: Nude female torsos in purple frame

XI-3   (105) 1/15/70: Face with crystal ball and skull

XI-4   (106) 1/22/70: "Helix Benefit" photo with hippies and car in field

XI-5   (107) 1/29/70: Crowley's freeway landscape of "drained and filled" Lake Washington

XI-6   (108) 2/5/70: Dorpat's "Do What's Right" Universal Life benefit

XI-7   (109) 2/12/70: Crowley's "Conspiracy" black powder bomb

XI-8   (110) 2/19/70: Lande/Crowley's "Who Is the Real Conspiracy?"

XI-9   (111) 2/26/70: Temple's photo of
alley with blood; "Wes Uhlman
Interview; Shanghaied"

XI-10 (112) 3/5/70: Temple's "Memo to
Seattle—Watch Your Step"

XI-11 (113) 3/12/70: Lande's photo of
Jane Fonda under E. Cleaver
poster

XI-12 (114) 3/19/70: Crowley's
Caterpillar/Butterfly (*3rd an-niversary*)

XI-13 (115) 3/26/70: Drawing of
Medusa in gray and green

XI-14 (116) 4/2/70: Drawing of Allen
Ginsberg, "New Poem"

XI-15 (117) 4/9/70: Victory goddess in
blue concentric field

XI-16 (118) 4/16/70: Crowley's
spaceman with exploding planet

X-9

XI-17 (119) 4/23/70: Lande's
"Conspiracy Comes Home"
photo

XI-18 (120) 4/30/70: French king in red
frame

XI-19 (121) 5/7/70: Lande's panoramic
photo of Freeway march

XI-20 (122) 5/14/70: Roger Hudson's
photo of Mayor Wes Uhlman and
Federal Marshal

XI-21 (123) 5/21/70: "Struck/Death
Penalty"

XI-22 (124) 5/28/70: Cartoon charac-
ters on descending graph

XI-23 (125) 6/11/70: Larry Heald's
drawing of Helix door "Closed" (*Last
issue)*

XI-23

Appendix B

Major Musical Events in Seattle in the Sixties

Note: Listings reflect advertised performers; some actual performances might vary. Due to erratic advertising and press notices, most but not all Eagles concerts are listed through mid-1970.

1964

August 21: The Beatles perform in the Coliseum.

1965

April 24: Bob Dylan and Joan Baez perform in the Arena.

May 24: Pete Seeger performs in the Opera House.

December 2: Rolling Stones, Ian Whitcomb, Paul Revere and the Raiders, and the Liverpool Five perform in the Coliseum.

1966

March 25: Bob Dylan performs in the Arena.

July 20: Rolling Stones return to the Coliseum.

August 25: The Beatles return to the Coliseum.

November 5: KRAB-FM presents the area's first light show in Kirkland's Center for the Seven Lively Arts.

November 16: Seattle Folklore Society presents its first concert, featuring Mance Lipscomb and Fred McDowell.

November 23: ASUW stages a "Little Silly Dance" ("LSD") with the Daily Flash and a light show at the Hub.

December 3: Milo Johnstone and the UW Parnassus Club present "The Public Works" in the Frye Hotel; this was Seattle's first true light show–dance, featuring lights by the Union Light Co. and music by the West Coast Natural Gas.

1967

January 14: Free University of Seattle stages the first light show and dance at Eagles Auditorium.

March 19: Six thousand attend Seattle's first "Trips Festival" at Eagles. The event was staged by Trips Lansing and managed by Sid Clark. It included a "Family Entertainment" staged by Tom Robbins and the Shazzam Society, and music by the Seeds, Daily Flash, and Emergency Exit.

March 31: ASUW sponsors performances by Country Joe and the Fish and the Daily Flash at the HUB.

April 8: Country Joe and the Fish perform at Eagles.

April 23: Free U stages light show "demonstration" at Hec Edmonson Pavilion. City Councilman Charley Carroll attends and sees no evil.

May 7: Overall Cooperative Structure (OCS) holds concert/light show at Eagles to benefit the Free U.

May 21: OCS presents the Magic Fern and the Chrome Syrcus with lights by Union Light Company at Eagles.

June 9: Country Joe and the Fish perform with the P. H. Phactor Jug Band at Eagles (the Fish performed with the Blues Interchange and the Magic Fern on June 11).

June 16: The Monterey Pop Festival makes stars of Jimi Hendrix, Janis Joplin, and a host of others.

June 25: P. H. Phactor and the Magic Fern perform at Eagles following a be-in at Cowen Park.

July 14: OCS presents the Grateful Dead in their first Seattle concert, with Magic Fern and the Daily Flash at Eagles.

July 16: The Grateful Dead perform at a Golden Gardens be-in with the Magic Fern and Family Tree.

July 23: The Doors open at Eagles.

August 20: "Underground Rock Festival" at Eagles features Magic Fern, Time Machine, Crome Syrcus, Clockwork Orange, Good Karma Lawn Service, Willowdale Handcar Jug Band, United Flight Service, Chime of Freedom, and Prism.

August 25: The Monkees perform in the Coliseum

September 8 & 9: Grateful Dead perform at Eagles.

September 15: Magic Fern and Clockwork Orange perform at Eagles.

September 16: Peanut Butter Conspiracy performs with Time Machine at Eagles.

September 22: Youngbloods perform with John Handy at Eagles.

September 30: Buffy St. Marie performs in the Opera House.

November 10: The Doors return to Eagles.

November 17–18: West Coast Natural Gas and Tripsichord Music Box open the new "San Francisco Sound" concert hall in the former Encore Ballroom at 13th and Pike. Country Joe and the Fish perform with United Empire Loyalists and Fat Jack at Eagles.

1968

January 27: The Grateful Dead and Quicksilver Messenger Service perform at Eagles.

February 2: Charles Lloyd performs at Eagles with lights by Retina Circus.

February 3: Judy Collins performs in the Arena.

February 9: The Fugs (Ed Sanders, Tuli Kupferberg, and Ken Weaver) perform at Eagles.

February 12: Jimi Hendrix makes his hometown debut in a concert in the Arena.

March 9: Paul Butterfield Blues Band appears with Fat Jack at Eagles.

March 24: ACLU holds a "Pot Test" benefit at Eagles to raise funds for a challenge of state marijuana laws.

April 5: Blue Cheer and Fat Jack perform at Eagles.

April 21: Helix and KRAB stage a "Media Mash" at Eagles with Country Joe and the Fish, Magic Fern, Time Machine, Uncle Henry, Indian Puddin' & Pipe, Canterbury Tales, Blues Feedback, Great Excelsior Jazz Band, and Murray Roman.

April 28: Country Joe and the Fish perform at the "Piano Drop" in Duvall.

May 29: Cream (Eric Clapton, Jack Bruce, and Ginger Baker) perform at Eagles.

June 7: Chamber Brothers perform at Eagles.

June 15: Pat O'Day produces another Teen Spectacular at Seattle Center.

June 16: Ravi Shankar performs in the Arena.

June 21: Iron Butterfly performs at Eagles.

June 28: Butterfield Blues Band performs at Eagles.

July 5: Blue Cheer performs at Eagles.

July 12: The Doors perform in the Arena.

July 19: Vanilla Fudge performs at Eagles.

July 26: Steppenwolf performs at Eagles.

July 28: "Magic Theatre" cruise aboard the Virginia V features music by Juggernaut. John Handy Quintet performs in the first of several Sunday "Jazz in the Parks" programs co-sponsored by Rainier Beer and the Seattle Jazz Society.

August 2: Moby Grape performs at Eagles.

August 9: Pink Floyd performs at Eagles.

August 24: Mothers of Invention perform in the Arena.

August 30: The Sky River Rock Festival and Lighter Than Air Fair, America's first true outdoor rock festival, opens a three-day run in a pasture near Sultan, Washington. Some 50 bands signed up to play, but no one remembers who all showed up. We know that Big Mama Thornton was there, and James Cotton, and Country Joe and the Fish, and Richard Pryor, Dino Valenti, Byron Pope, It's A Beautiful Day, Peanut Butter Conspiracy, Alice Stuart Thomas, the Youngbloods, Santana, New Lost City Ramblers, and local groups such as Juggernaut and Easy Chair. The Grateful Dead arrived unscheduled on the last day.

September 6: Jimi Hendrix performs in the Arena, with the Soft Machine, Vanilla Fudge, and Eire Apparent.

October 1: "Love-U District Festival" on University Way NE, sponsored by the ASUW and U District Chamber of Commerce and organized by the New American Community, features Youngbloods, Frumious Bandersnatch, Santana, Country Weather, Juggernaut, Mother Tucker's Yellow Duck, Congress of Wonders, Alice Stewart, Cliff Wagner & the Second Coming, Floating Bridge, Caliope, and "the lovely Diane and her dance of death."

October 4: Donovan performs in the Arena.

October 6: Byron Pope Ensemble, Floating Bridge, Juggernaut, and International Brick perform at an Eagles benefit for Draft Resistance–Seattle.

October 23: Gordon Lightfoot performs in the Opera House.

October 25: Canned Heat warms Eagles.

November 17: Grateful Dead perform at Eagles benefit for Indian fishing rights.

November 29: Big Brother and the Holding Company, starring Janis Joplin, and the Chicago Transit Authority perform in the Arena.

December 8: The Crazy World of Arthur Brown stages "A Night in Hell" at the Arena.

1969

January 25: The Steve Miller Band performs at Eagles.

February 7: Three Dog Night and Steppenwolf perform in the UW's Hec Edmundson Pavilion.

February 8: The Association performs in the Arena.

February 15: Charles Lloyd and the James Cotton Blues Band perform at Eagles.

February 21: Iron Butterfly and the Collectors perform in the Seattle Center Exhibition Hall.

February 28: Muddy Waters and Otis Spann perform at Eagles.

March 7: MC-5 performs at Eagles.

March 9: Youngbloods, Floating Bridge, Juggernaut, and Popcorn perform at Helix's second anniversary benefit at Eagles

March 22: Ten Years After and the Don Ellis Orchestra perform at Eagles.

March 28: Creedence Clearwater Revival performs in the Exhibition Hall.

April 19: The Guess Who perform in the Arena.

May 3: The ASUW sponsors "Spring Flush" rock marathon in Hec Edmundson Pavilion with Santana, It's a Beautiful Day, Peanut Butter Conspiracy, Country Weather, Spring, Alice Stuart Thomas, Gazebo, and Juggernaut.

May 12: A rock concert is held at the former Aqua Follies theater on Green Lake.

May 16: Taj Mahal performs at Eagles.

May 23: Jimi Hendrix performs in the Coliseum.

May 25: Helix and the New American Community sponsor a "model" concert and be-in at Volunteer Park to demonstrate that music and park neighbors can co-exist.

May 30: Helen Parker stages a "Sunrise to Sunset" rock festival in Duvall.

June 6: Big Mama Thornton performs at Eagles.

June 21: Joe Cocker performs at Eagles.

June 26: Steve Miller performs at Eagles.

July 4: Helen Parker stages another mini-rock festival in Duvall.

July 11: Paul Revere and the Raiders headline three-day "Teen Spectacular" at Seattle Center.

July 12: Creedence Clearwater Revival performs in the Arena.

July 25: Boyd Grafmyre stages a three-day "Seattle Pop Festival" at Gold Creek Park in Woodinville with this line-up: Chuck Berry, Black Snake, Tim Buckley, the Byrds, Chicago Transit Authority, Albert Collins, Crome Syrcus, Bo Diddley, the Doors, Floating Bridge, the Flock, Flying Burrito Brothers, Guess Who, It's a Beautiful Day, Led Zepplin, Charles Lloyd, Lonnie Mack, Lee Michaels, Rockin Fu, Murray Roman, Santana, Spirit, Ten Years After, Ike & Tina Turner, Vanilla Fudge, and the Youngbloods—for $6 a day or $15 for all three

July 28: Diana Ross and the Supremes, and Stevie Wonder perform in the Opera House.

August 2: Jethro Tull and Black Snake perform at Eagles.

August 8: Eric Clapton and Steve Winwood's new "supergroup," Blind Faith, performs in the Coliseum.

August 14: John Mayall performs at Eagles.

August 20: The Grateful Dead, New Riders of the Purple Sage, and Sanpaku perform at the Greenlake Aquatheater.

August 30: Second Sky River Rock Festival attracts 25,000 to a pasture near Tenino to hear Anonymous Artists of America, Black Snake, Blue Bird, Cleanliness & Godliness Skiffle Band, Collectors, Congress of Wonders, James Cotton, Country Weather, Country Joe and the Fish, Crome Syrcus, Crow, Dovetail, Floating

Bridge, Flying Burrito Brothers, Frumonious Bandersnatch, Grapefruit, Guitar Shorty, Buddy Guy, Dan Hicks and His Hot Licks, Dr. Humbead's New Tranquility String Band, Juggernaut, Kaleidoscope, Los Flamencos de Santa Lucia, Fred McDowell, Steve Miller, New Lost City Ramblers, Pacific Gas & Electric, Peter, Terry Reid, Mike Russo, Sons of Champlin, Mark Spoelstra, Alice Stuart, Yellowstone, Youngbloods, and Elyse Weinberg.

September 12: Sly and the Family Stone perform with Juggernaut in the Arena.

September 19: It's a Beautiful Day and Tyrannosaurus perform at Eagles.

September 27: Iron Butterfly and Blues Image perform in the Arena.

September 28: Tim Buckley performs in the Opera House.

October 3: Delaney, Bonnie and Friends perform at Eagles.

October 11: Eagles Auditorium is the scene of a near riot as 2,500 fans try to see Chicago Transit Authority. Jefferson Airplane performs in the Arena.

October 15: Ike and Tina Turner perform at the Showcase, 2212 Fourth Avenue.

October 25: Jerry Lee Lewis performs in the Opera House.

October 31: Donovan performs in the Arena.

November 7: Country Joe and the Fish perform at Eagles

November 8: Moody Blues perform in the Arena.

November 14: Taj Mahal and Crome Syrcus perform at Eagles.

November 16: Ray Charles performs in the Arena; Mason Williams and Jennifer perform in the Opera House.

November 21: An Off-Broadway "rock musical" called "Your Own Thing" is performed in the Opera House.

November 26: The Steve Miller Band performs at Eagles.

November 27: Lightnin' Hopkins performs at the Medicine Show Tavern, 1119 Pike.

December 14: Peter, Paul & Mary perform in the Arena to benefit the ACLU.

1970

January 9: Sly and the Family Stone perform in the Arena.

January 23: Three Dog Night and Hoyt Axton perform in the Arena.

January 27: BB King performs with Floating Bridge and Golden Earring at Eagles.

January 30: It's a Beautiful Day performs at Eagles.

February 13: Cold Blood and Bigfoot perform at Eagles.

February 20: John Mayall performs at Eagles.

February 27: Michael Bloomfield and friends perform at Eagles.

February 28: Canned Heat performs at Eagles.

March 13: Chicago performs at Eagles.

March 27: Albert Collins and Redbone, "the first all-American Indian rock group," perform at Eagles to benefit United Indians of All Tribes.

April 4: Paul Butterfield Band, the Byrds, and Blue Mountain Eagle perform at Eagles.

April 11: The James Cotton Blues Band, Purple Haze, and Sweet Rolle perform at Eagles.

April 19: Joe Cocker & the Grease Band perform in the Arena.

May 2: Blood, Sweat and Tears performs at the HEC Edmundson Pavilion, while Creedence Clearwater Revival performs in the Coliseum,

May 8: Ike and Tina Turner perform in the Arena. Mountain, People, and Black on White Affair perform at Eagles.

May 15: Small Faces and Ambergris perform at Eagles.

May 16: Strawberry Mountain Fair rock festival opens near Vancouver, BC.

June 5: Doors perform in the Coliseum.

June 17: Crosby, Stills, Nash and Young perform in the Coliseum.

July 2: Defying a court injunction, thousands mass at the Flying M Ranch in Eatonville for the Buffalo Party Convention and Pig Roast, a thinly disguised rock festival; a fan dies the next day when he is washed over a waterfall.

July 5: Youngbloods perform at Sick's Stadium.

August 28: Third Sky River Rock Festival begins an 11-day run on a farm on the Washougal River, 20 miles east of Vancouver. The event is staged by the "Hydra Collective" of the SLF, not the New American Community, and it attracts a peak of 12,000 attendees.

September 18: Jimi Hendrix dies.

November 12: Elvis Presley performs in the Coliseum.

1971

January 22: Rock and roll marathon at Eagles honors memory of Jimi Hendrix.

September 3: Satsop Riverfair and Tin Cup Races, the last and largest of the state's rock festivals, welcomes 45,000 to Grays Harbor County; one of the organizers, Gary Friedman, is later identified as a state drug investigator.

Bibliography
and Sources

Bennett, Lerone, Jr. *Before the Mayflower.* New York: Penguin Books, 1984.

Boller, Paul F., Jr. *Presidential Campaigns.* New York: Oxford University Press, 1984.

Brooks, Tim. *The Complete Directory to Prime Time Network TV Shows.* New York: Ballantine Books, 1988.

Buhle, Mari Jo, et al. *Encyclopedia of the American Left.* New York: Garland Publishing, 1990.

The Daily, University of Washington, selected issues, 1965–72.

Davis, Flora. *Moving the Mountain: The Women's Movement in America since 1960.* New York: Touchstone Books (Simon & Schuster), 1991.

Fairclough, Adam. *To Redeem the Soul of America: The Southern Christian Leadership Conference and Martin Luther King, Jr.* Athens: University of Georgia Press, 1987.

Gitlin, Todd. *The Sixties: Years of Hope, Days of Rage.* New York: Bantam Books, 1993.

Halberstam, David. *The Best and the Brightest.* New York: Random House, 1969.

———. *The Fifties.* New York: Ballantine/Fawcett Columbine, 1993.

Helix, all issues, March 1967–June 1970.

Honig, Doug, and Laura Brenner. *On Freedom's Frontier: The First Fifty Years of the American Civil Liberties Union in Washington.* Seattle: ACLU-W, 1987.

Hornsby, Alton, Jr. *Milestones in 20th-Century African-American History.* Detroit: Visible Ink, 1993.

Johnstone, Milo. *The Magic Decade.* Seattle: M. Johnstone, 1994.

Jones, Landon Y. *Great Expectations, America & the Baby Boom Generation.* New York: Coward, McCann & Geoghegan, 1980.

Karnow, Stanley. *Vietnam: A History.* New York: Penguin Books, 1984.

Lewison, Mark. *The Beatles Day by Day: A Chronology 1962–1989.* New York: Harmony Books, 1990.

McNeil, Alex. *Total Television.* New York: Penguin Books, 1991.

Milam, Lorenzo. *The Myrkin Papers.* Bellevue, WA: Duck Press, 1969.

Mills, Howard A. "The Seattle *Helix:* An Underground Looks at the Times." M.A. thesis, University of Montana, Missoula, 1970.

The New York Times, selected issues, 1960–72.

Nite, Norman N. *Rock On Almanac.* New York: Harper Perennial, 1992.

Outlook, selected issues, 1967–72.

Pearson, Hugh. *The Shadow of the Panther: Huey Newton and the Price of Black Power in America.* Reading, MA: Addison-Wesley, 1994.

Peck, Abe. *Uncovering the Sixties: The Life & Times of the Underground Press.* New York: Pantheon Books, 1985.

Perry, Charles. *Haight Ashbury: A History.* New York: Random House/Rolling Stone Press, 1984.

Perry, Paul. *On the Bus: The Complete Guide to the Legendary Trip of Ken Kesey and the Merry Pranksters and the Birth of the Counterculture.* New York: Thunder's Mouth Press, 1990.

Rorabaugh, W. J. *Berkeley at War: The 1960s.* New York: Oxford University Press, 1989.

Sale, Kirkpatrick. *SDS.* New York: Random House/Vintage, 1974.

Seattle Magazine, all issues, 1964–70.

Seattle Post-Intelligencer, all issues, 1960–72.

The Seattle Times, selected issues, 1960–72.

Stern, Susan. *With the Weathermen: A Personal Journal of a Revolutionary Woman.* Garden City, NY: Doubleday & Company, 1975.

Taylor, Quintard. *The Forging of a Black Community: Seattle's Central District from 1870 through the Civil Rights Era.* Seattle: University of Washington Press, 1994.

Trager, James. *The People's Chronology.* New York: Holt, Rinehart and Winston, 1979.

University Herald, selected issues, 1965–72.

Viorst, Milton. *Fire in the Street: America in the 1960s.* New York: Simon & Schuster, 1979.

Wachsberger, Ken, ed. *Voices from the Underground: Insider Histories of the Underground Press.* Tempe, AZ: Mica Press, 1993.

Ward, Ed, et al. *Rock of Ages: The Rolling Stone History of Rock & Roll.* New York: Summit Books (Rolling Stone Press), 1986.

Wells, Tom. *The War Within: America's Battle over Vietnam.* Berkeley: University of California Press, 1994.

The World Almanac. New York: Newspaper Enterprise Association, 1959 et seq.

Zinn, Howard. *A People's History of the United States.* New York: Harper Perennial, 1980.

Index

This index covers the main narrative, pages 3–190